VOICES OF THE MARTYRS

KINGSTONE
COMICS

VOICES OF THE MARTYRS

THE WITNESSES

WRITERS:

BEN AVERY, ART AYRIS

EDITOR:

KELLY J. AYRIS

LETTERS:

ZACH MATHENY

PRODUCTION DESIGN:

NATE BUTLER, ZACH MATHENY, KEN RANEY

Published by Kingstone Comics
www.Kingstone.co
Copyright © 2016

Printed in USA

KINGSTONE
COMICS

The Witnesses

1. STEPHEN
Pencils: Edgar Bercasio
Inks: Edgar Bercasio
Colors: Mark McNabb

69. JUDE
Pencils: Sergio Cariello
Inks: Sergio Cariello
Colors: Fabricio Guerra

17. JOHN MARK
Pencils: Danny Bulanadi
Inks: Danny Bulanadi
Colors: Ben Prenevost

75. MARY
Pencils: Richard Bonk
Inks: Chris Ivy
Colors: Emily Kanalz

31. BARNABAS
Pencils: Danny Bulanadi
Inks: Danny Bulanadi
Colors: Emily Kanalz

97. PERPETUA
Pencils: Jeff Slemons
Inks: Jeff Slemons
Colors: Joel Chua

47. LUKE
Pencils: Geof Isherwood
Inks: Geof Isherwood
Colors: Fabricio Guerra

123. POLYCARP
Pencils: Kyle Hotz
Inks: Jason Moore
Colors: Mark McNabb

63. JAMES
Pencils: Danny Bulanadi
Inks: Danny Bulanadi
Colors: Ben Prenevost

145. JUSTIN MARTYR
Pencils: Richard Bonk
Inks: Chris Ivy
Colors: Emily Kanalz

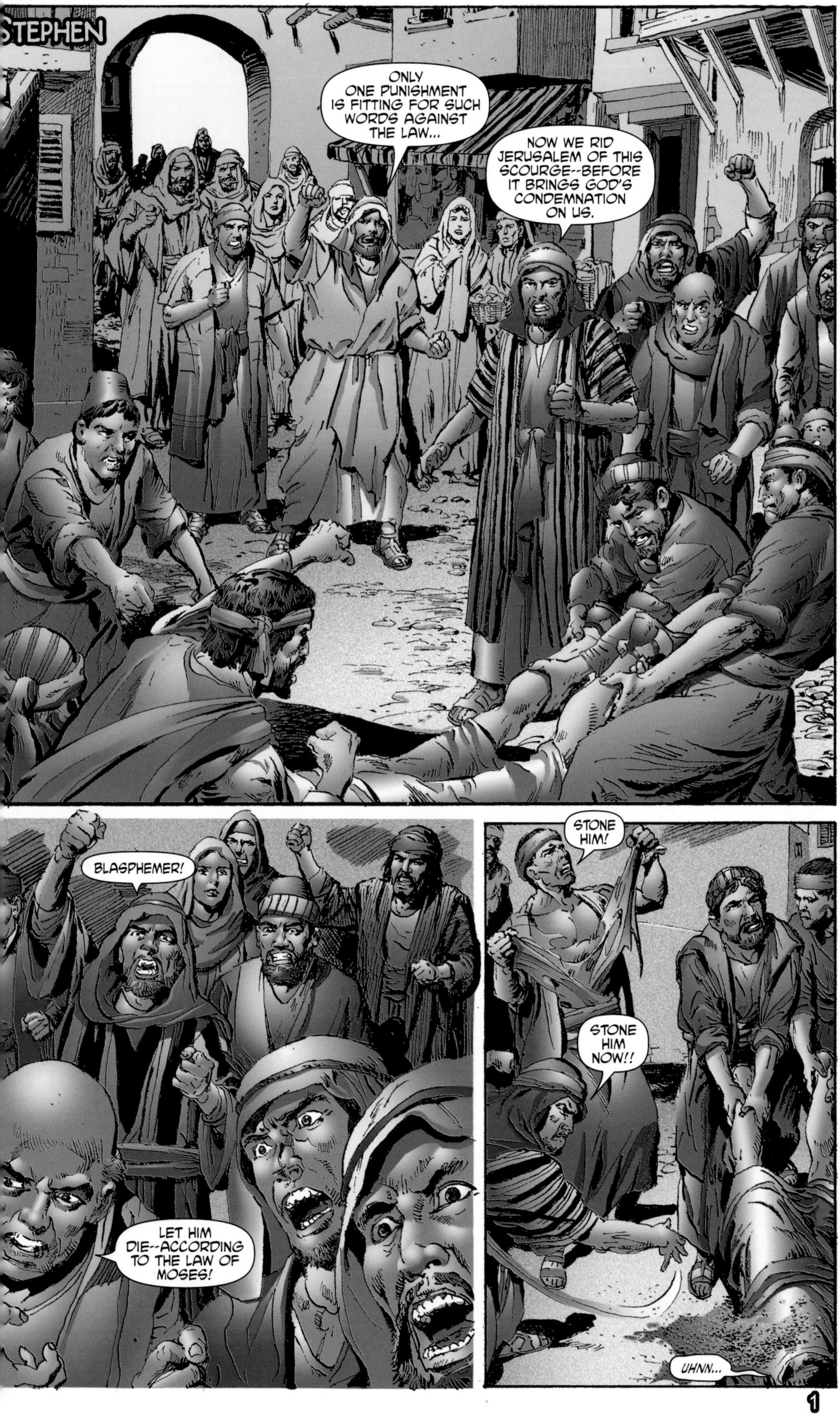
STEPHEN
ONLY ONE PUNISHMENT IS FITTING FOR SUCH WORDS AGAINST THE LAW...
NOW WE RID JERUSALEM OF THIS SCOURGE--BEFORE IT BRINGS GOD'S CONDEMNATION ON US.
BLASPHEMER!
LET HIM DIE--ACCORDING TO THE LAW OF MOSES!
STONE HIM!
STONE HIM NOW!!
UHNN...

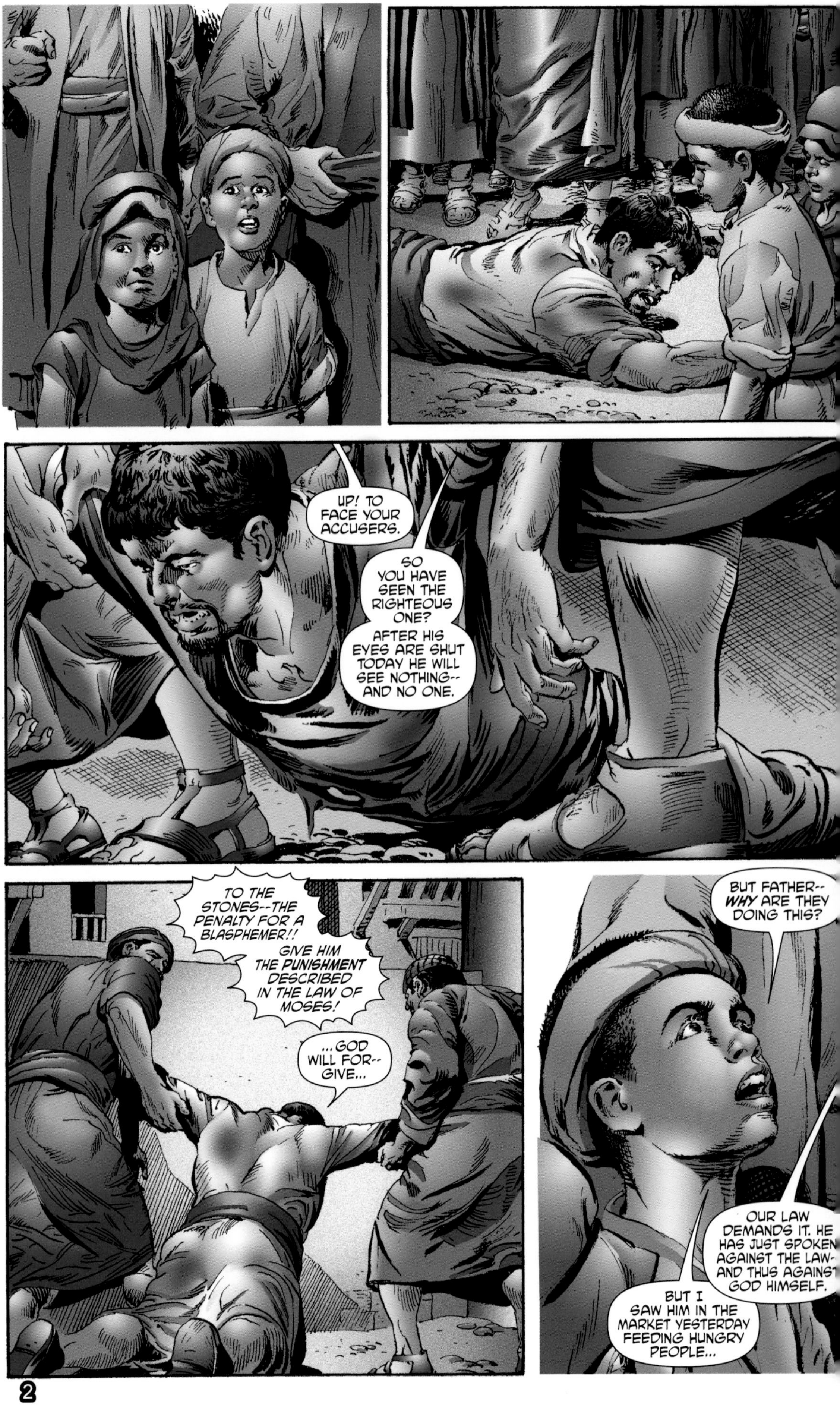
UP! TO FACE YOUR ACCUSERS.
SO YOU HAVE SEEN THE RIGHTEOUS ONE?
AFTER HIS EYES ARE SHUT TODAY HE WILL SEE NOTHING-- AND NO ONE.
TO THE STONES--THE PENALTY FOR A BLASPHEMER!!
GIVE HIM THE PUNISHMENT DESCRIBED IN THE LAW OF MOSES!
...GOD WILL FOR-GIVE...
BUT FATHER-- WHY ARE THEY DOING THIS?
OUR LAW DEMANDS IT. HE HAS JUST SPOKEN AGAINST THE LAW-AND THUS AGAINST GOD HIMSELF.
BUT I SAW HIM IN THE MARKET YESTERDAY FEEDING HUNGRY PEOPLE...

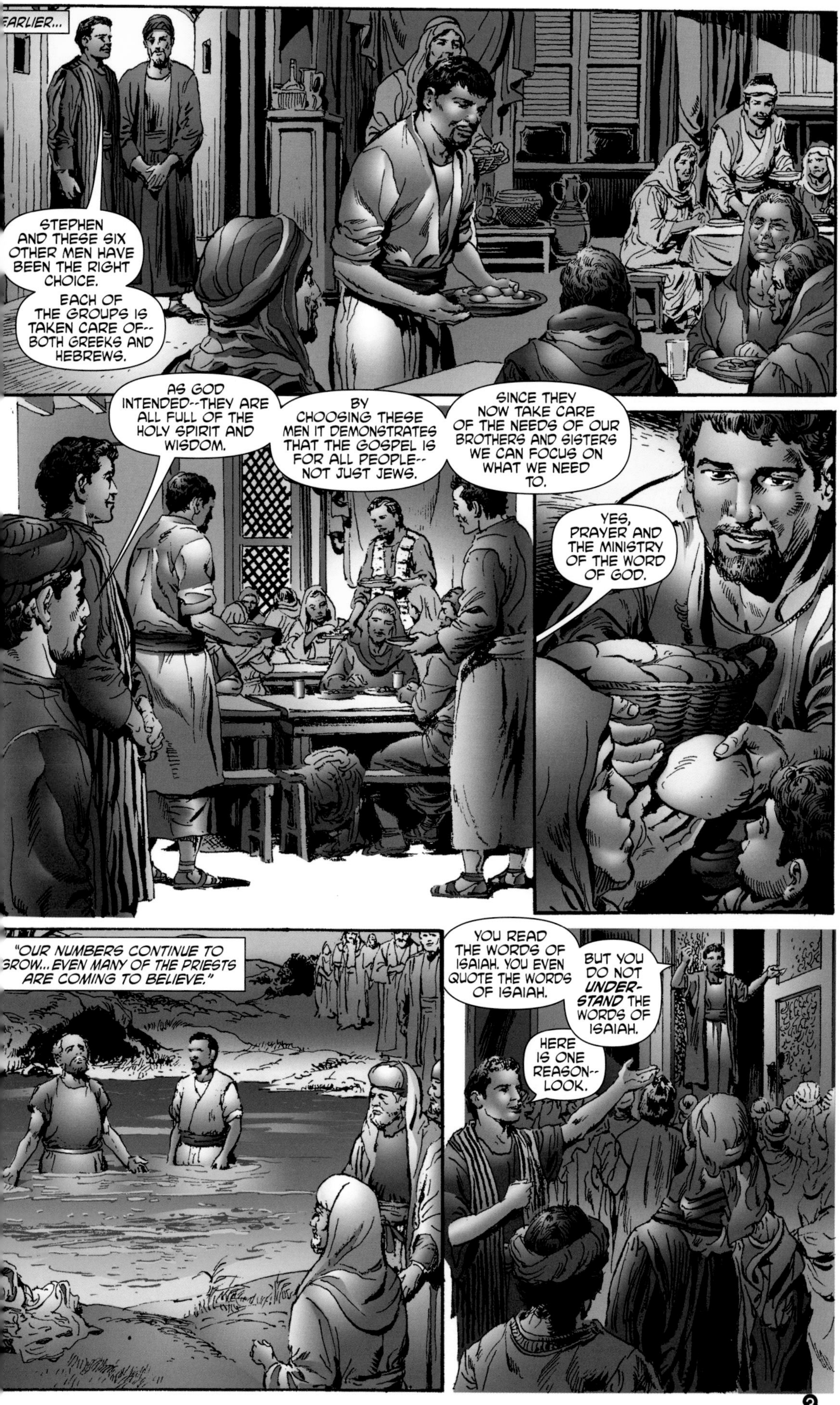
EARLIER...
STEPHEN AND THESE SIX OTHER MEN HAVE BEEN THE RIGHT CHOICE.
EACH OF THE GROUPS IS TAKEN CARE OF-- BOTH GREEKS AND HEBREWS.
AS GOD INTENDED--THEY ARE ALL FULL OF THE HOLY SPIRIT AND WISDOM.
BY CHOOSING THESE MEN IT DEMONSTRATES THAT THE GOSPEL IS FOR ALL PEOPLE-- NOT JUST JEWS.
SINCE THEY NOW TAKE CARE OF THE NEEDS OF OUR BROTHERS AND SISTERS WE CAN FOCUS ON WHAT WE NEED TO.
YES, PRAYER AND THE MINISTRY OF THE WORD OF GOD.
"OUR NUMBERS CONTINUE TO GROW... EVEN MANY OF THE PRIESTS ARE COMING TO BELIEVE."
YOU READ THE WORDS OF ISAIAH. YOU EVEN QUOTE THE WORDS OF ISAIAH.
BUT YOU DO NOT *UNDERSTAND* THE WORDS OF ISAIAH.
HERE IS ONE REASON-- LOOK.

AS ISAIAH PROPHESIED--HE WAS LED LIKE A LAMB TO THE SLAUGHTER. JUST AS A SHEEP BEFORE ITS SHEARERS IS SILENT, SO HE--JESUS--DID NOT OPEN HIS MOUTH.

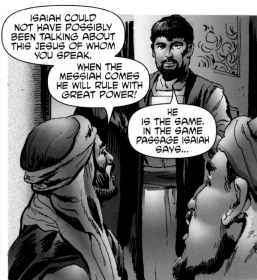

ISAIAH COULD NOT HAVE POSSIBLY BEEN TALKING ABOUT THIS JESUS OF WHOM YOU SPEAK.

WHEN THE MESSIAH COMES HE WILL RULE WITH GREAT POWER!

HE IS THE SAME. IN THE SAME PASSAGE ISAIAH SAYS...

...HE WAS ASSIGNED A GRAVE WITH THE WICKED, AND WITH THE RICH IN HIS DEATH.

A MAN OF WEALTH GAVE HIS BURIAL PLACE TO JESUS-- THOUGH DEATH COULD NOT CONTAIN HIM!

WHAT ARE YOU DOING?!

THIS MAN IS TO APPEAR BEFORE THE SANHEDRIN.

WHAT RIGHT DO YOU HAVE TO TAKE HIM FROM US?

FOR PREACHING REBELLION.

BEN NATHEN-- COME WITH ME!

WHAT'S THE RUSH?

ANOTHER CHRIST FOLLOWER IS BEING BROUGHT TO TRIAL.

FOR WHAT?

BLASPHEMY, OF COURSE.

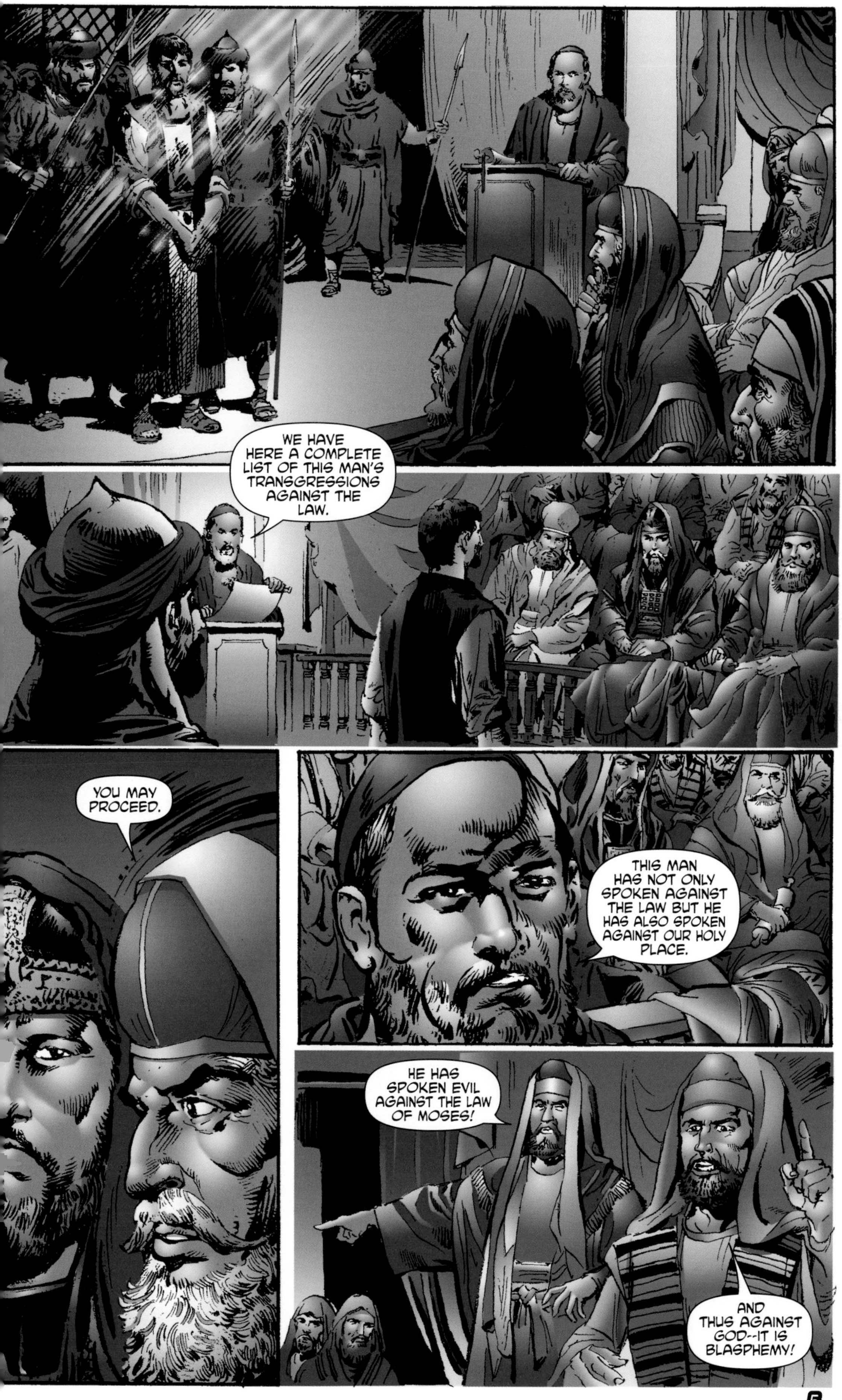
WE HAVE HERE A COMPLETE LIST OF THIS MAN'S TRANSGRESSIONS AGAINST THE LAW.
YOU MAY PROCEED.
THIS MAN HAS NOT ONLY SPOKEN AGAINST THE LAW BUT HE HAS ALSO SPOKEN AGAINST OUR HOLY PLACE.
HE HAS SPOKEN EVIL AGAINST THE LAW OF MOSES!
AND THUS AGAINST GOD--IT IS BLASPHEMY!

ARE THERE ANY WITNESSES?

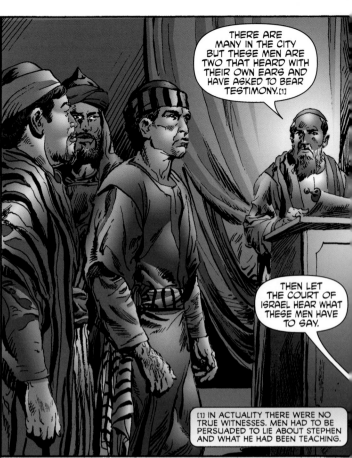

THERE ARE MANY IN THE CITY BUT THESE MEN ARE TWO THAT HEARD WITH THEIR OWN EARS AND HAVE ASKED TO BEAR TESTIMONY.[1]

THEN LET THE COURT OF ISRAEL HEAR WHAT THESE MEN HAVE TO SAY.

[1] IN ACTUALITY THERE WERE NO TRUE WITNESSES. MEN HAD TO BE PERSUADED TO LIE ABOUT STEPHEN AND WHAT HE HAD BEEN TEACHING.

THAT MAN. WE HAVE HEARD HIM SPEAK EVIL AGAINST OUR PEOPLE.

HE SAID THAT THE DEAD MAN JESUS WOULD DESTROY THIS VERY PLACE WHERE WE STAND AND CHANGE ALL OF OUR CUSTOMS GIVEN TO US BY OUR FATHER MOSES.

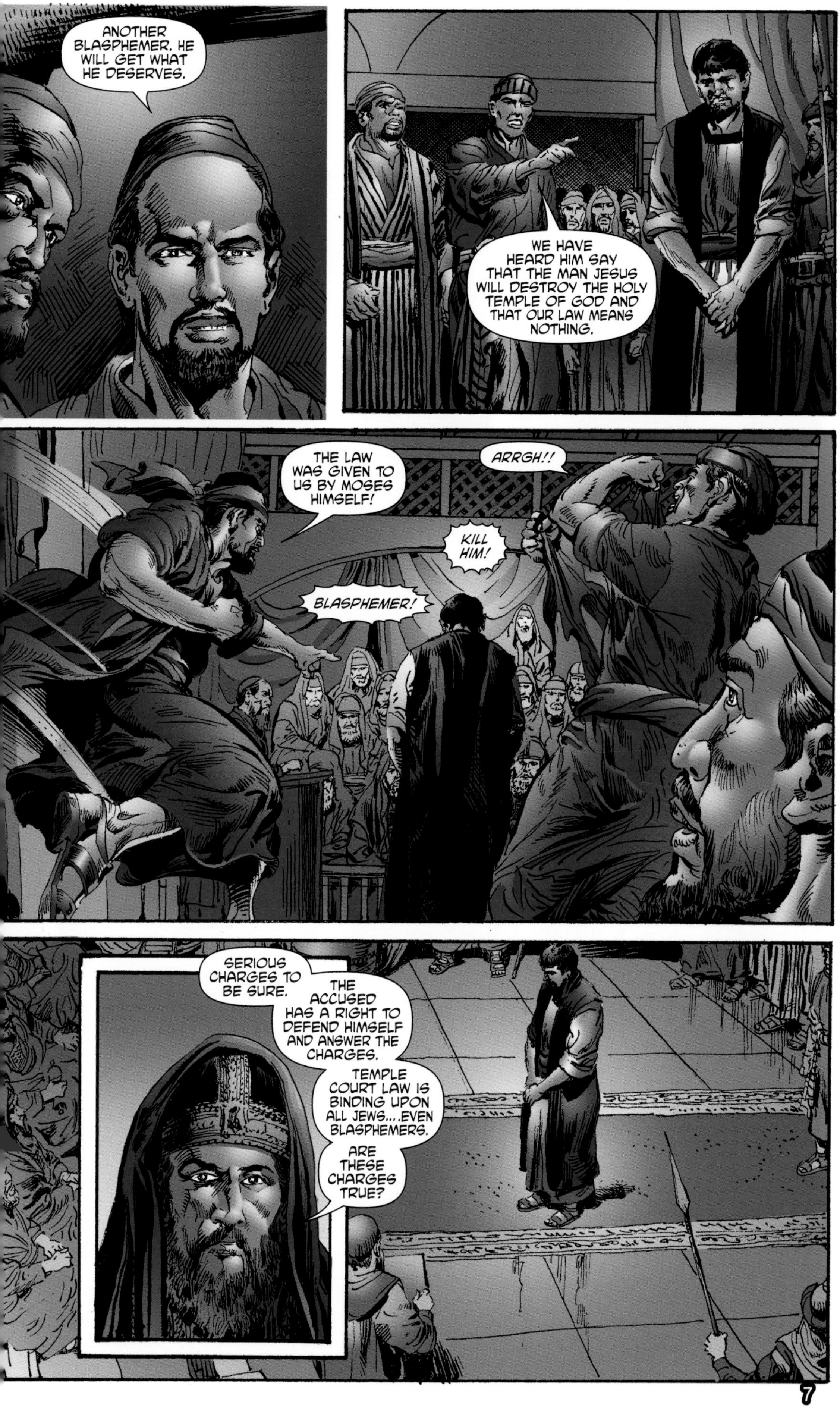
ANOTHER BLASPHEMER. HE WILL GET WHAT HE DESERVES.
WE HAVE HEARD HIM SAY THAT THE MAN JESUS WILL DESTROY THE HOLY TEMPLE OF GOD AND THAT OUR LAW MEANS NOTHING.
THE LAW WAS GIVEN TO US BY MOSES HIMSELF!
ARRGH!!
KILL HIM!
BLASPHEMER!
SERIOUS CHARGES TO BE SURE.
THE ACCUSED HAS A RIGHT TO DEFEND HIMSELF AND ANSWER THE CHARGES.
TEMPLE COURT LAW IS BINDING UPON ALL JEWS....EVEN BLASPHEMERS.
ARE THESE CHARGES TRUE?

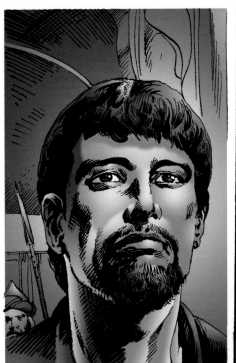

HIS FACE....HIS FACE IS LIKE THAT OF AN ANGEL.

I SEE IT.

MY FATHERS AND MY BROTHERS--LISTEN TO ME!

WE EACH HERE TODAY KNOW THAT THE GOD OF GLORY APPEARED TO OUR FATHER ABRAHAM AND TOLD HIM TO GO TO THIS LAND WHICH HE TOLD HIM ABOUT.

HE PROMISED ABRAHAM THAT HIS DESCENDANTS WOULD POSSESS THIS LAND AND HE GAVE OUR FOREFATHER THE COVENANT OF CIRCUMCISION.

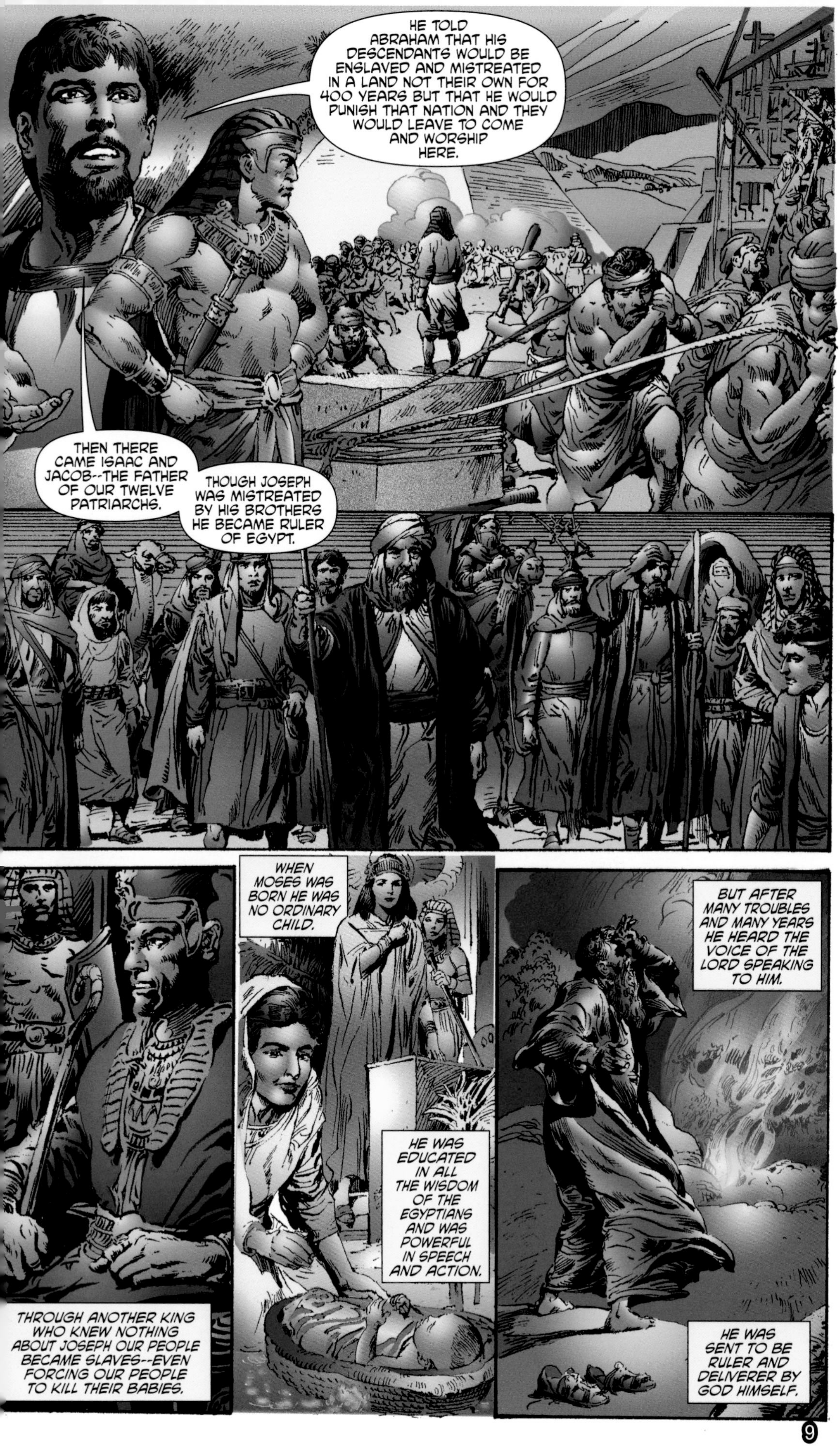
HE TOLD ABRAHAM THAT HIS DESCENDANTS WOULD BE ENSLAVED AND MISTREATED IN A LAND NOT THEIR OWN FOR 400 YEARS BUT THAT HE WOULD PUNISH THAT NATION AND THEY WOULD LEAVE TO COME AND WORSHIP HERE.
THEN THERE CAME ISAAC AND JACOB--THE FATHER OF OUR TWELVE PATRIARCHS.
THOUGH JOSEPH WAS MISTREATED BY HIS BROTHERS HE BECAME RULER OF EGYPT.
THROUGH ANOTHER KING WHO KNEW NOTHING ABOUT JOSEPH OUR PEOPLE BECAME SLAVES--EVEN FORCING OUR PEOPLE TO KILL THEIR BABIES.
WHEN MOSES WAS BORN HE WAS NO ORDINARY CHILD.
HE WAS EDUCATED IN ALL THE WISDOM OF THE EGYPTIANS AND WAS POWERFUL IN SPEECH AND ACTION.
BUT AFTER MANY TROUBLES AND MANY YEARS HE HEARD THE VOICE OF THE LORD SPEAKING TO HIM.
HE WAS SENT TO BE RULER AND DELIVERER BY GOD HIMSELF.

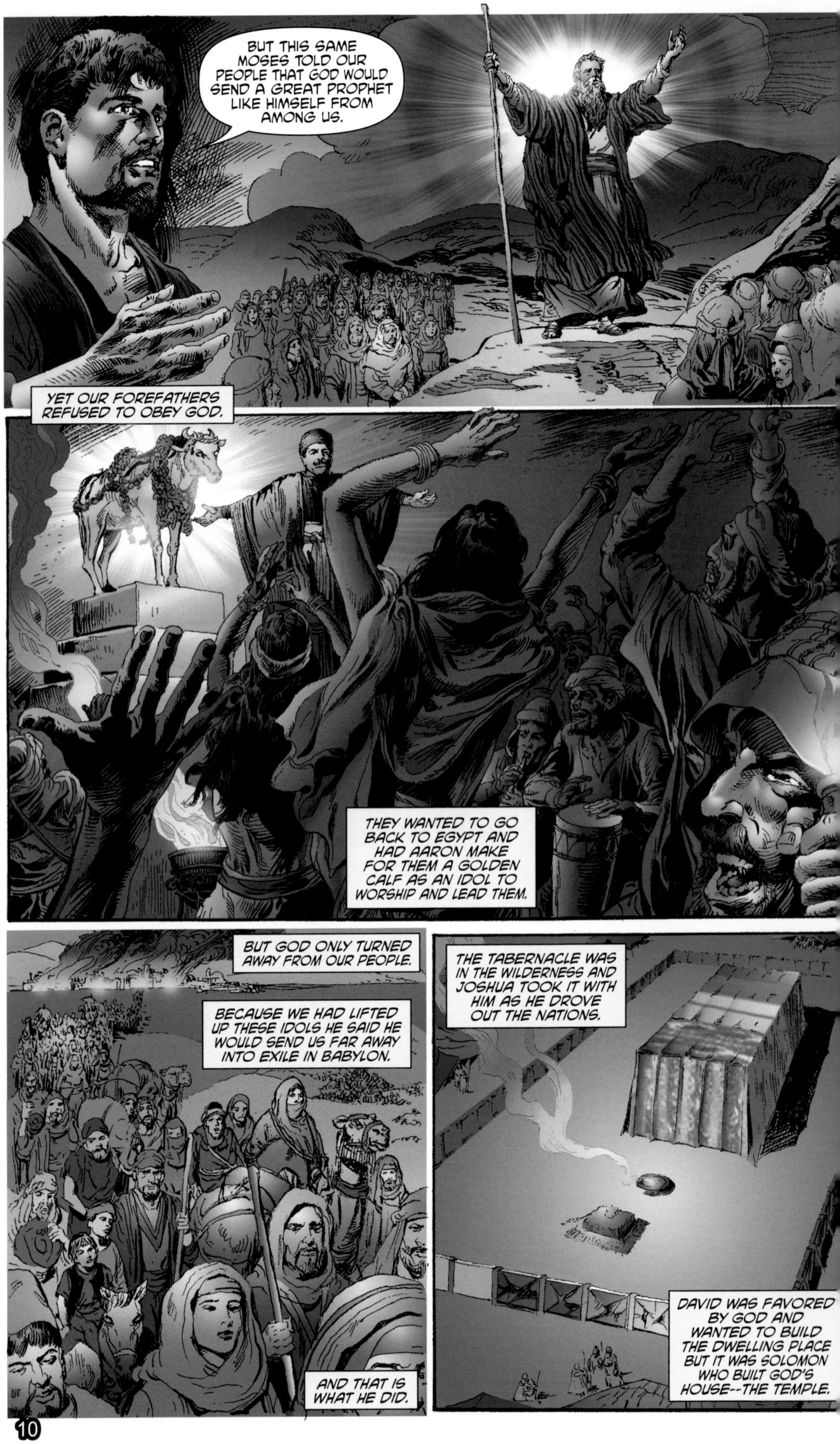
BUT THIS SAME MOSES TOLD OUR PEOPLE THAT GOD WOULD SEND A GREAT PROPHET LIKE HIMSELF FROM AMONG US.
YET OUR FOREFATHERS REFUSED TO OBEY GOD.
THEY WANTED TO GO BACK TO EGYPT AND HAD AARON MAKE FOR THEM A GOLDEN CALF AS AN IDOL TO WORSHIP AND LEAD THEM.
BUT GOD ONLY TURNED AWAY FROM OUR PEOPLE.
BECAUSE WE HAD LIFTED UP THESE IDOLS HE SAID HE WOULD SEND US FAR AWAY INTO EXILE IN BABYLON.
AND THAT IS WHAT HE DID.
THE TABERNACLE WAS IN THE WILDERNESS AND JOSHUA TOOK IT WITH HIM AS HE DROVE OUT THE NATIONS.
DAVID WAS FAVORED BY GOD AND WANTED TO BUILD THE DWELLING PLACE BUT IT WAS SOLOMON WHO BUILT GOD'S HOUSE--THE TEMPLE.

DON'T YOU UNDERSTAND?! THE MOST HIGH GOD DOES NOT LIVE IN HOUSES BUILT BY MAN.

SPEAKING THROUGH THE PROPHETS HE TOLD US THAT HEAVEN WAS HIS THRONE AND EARTH HIS FOOT-STOOL.

WHAT KIND OF HOUSE CAN WE BUILD SINCE HE CREATED ALL THINGS?

YOU ARE A STIFF-NECKED PEOPLE!

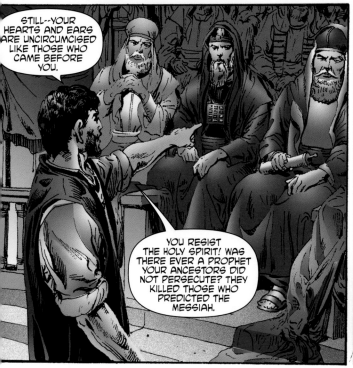

STILL--YOUR HEARTS AND EARS ARE UNCIRCUMCISED LIKE THOSE WHO CAME BEFORE YOU.

YOU RESIST THE HOLY SPIRIT! WAS THERE EVER A PROPHET YOUR ANCESTORS DID NOT PERSECUTE? THEY KILLED THOSE WHO PREDICTED THE MESSIAH.

AND NOW YOU HAVE BETRAYED AND MURDERED HIM.

EVEN THOUGH YOU RECEIVED A LAW THAT WAS GIVEN BY ANGELS YOU HAVE NOT OBEYED IT.

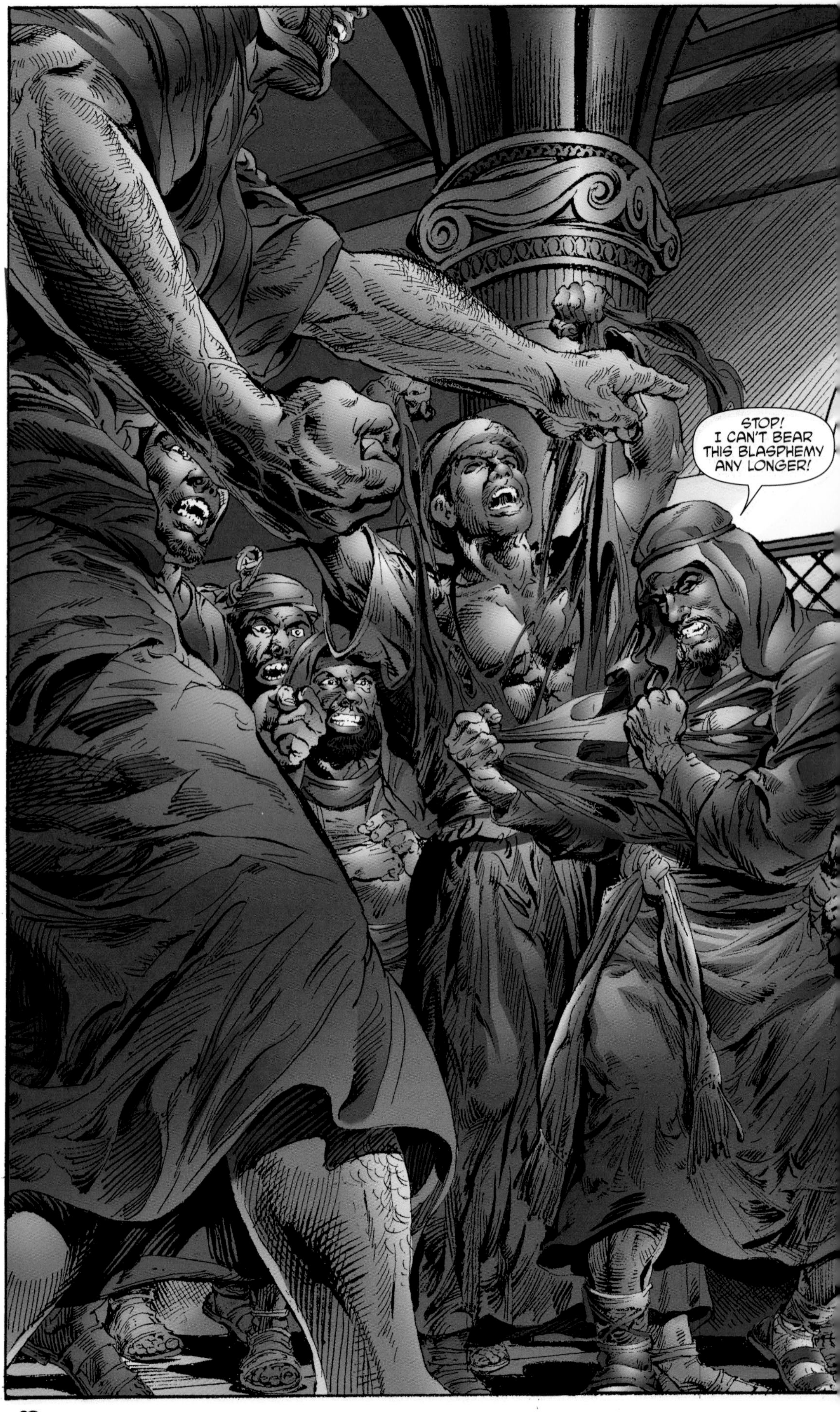
STOP! I CAN'T BEAR THIS BLASPHEMY ANY LONGER!

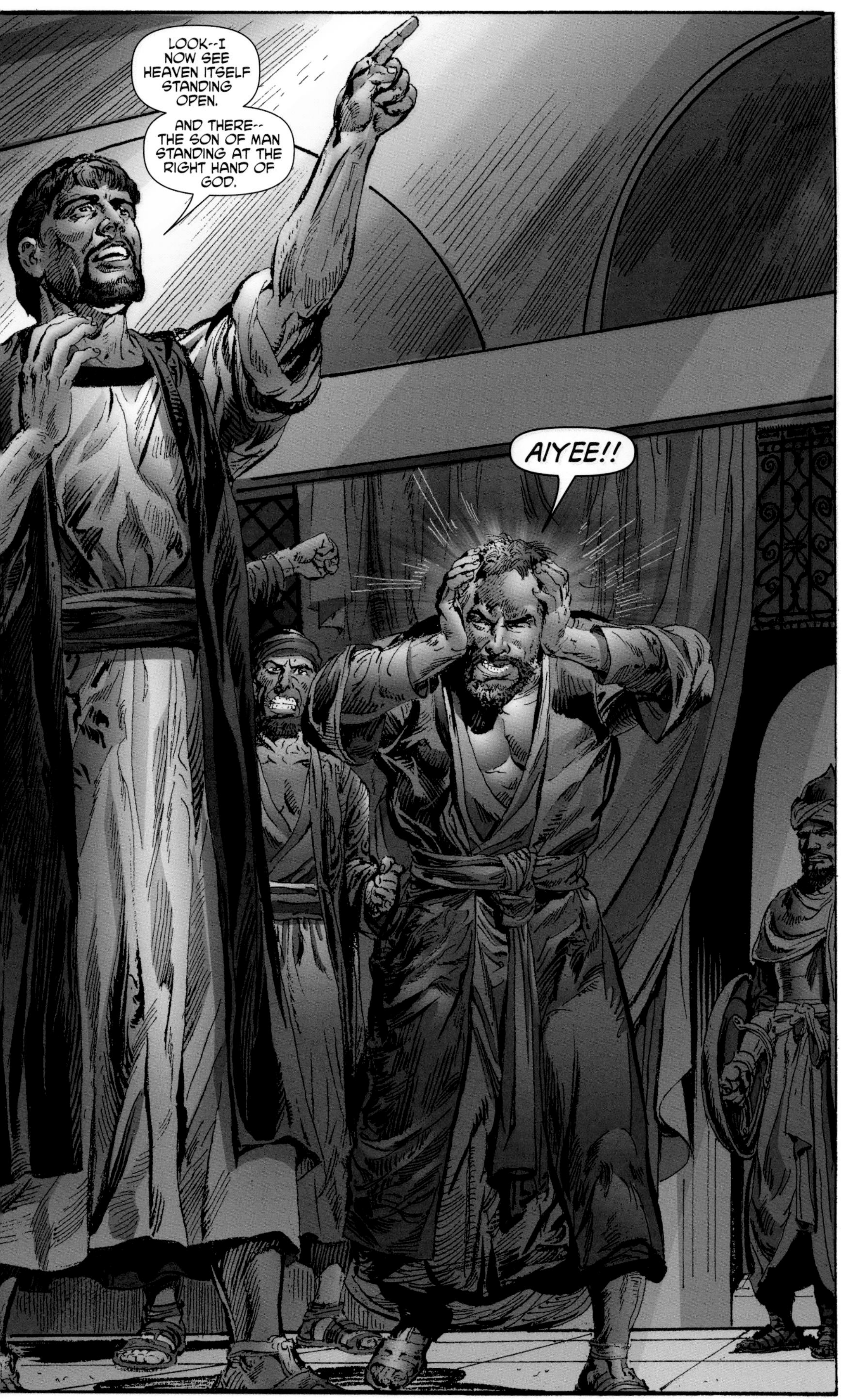
LOOK--I NOW SEE HEAVEN ITSELF STANDING OPEN.
AND THERE-- THE SON OF MAN STANDING AT THE RIGHT HAND OF GOD.
AIYEE!!

STONES OF GOD'S JUDGMENT.

STONES OF GOD'S PLEASURE...

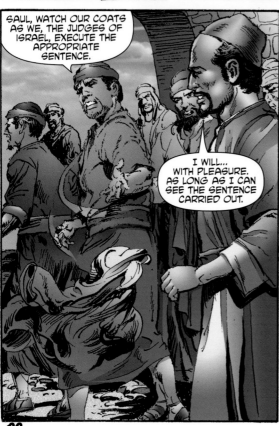

SAUL, WATCH OUR COATS AS WE, THE JUDGES OF ISRAEL, EXECUTE THE APPROPRIATE SENTENCE.

I WILL... WITH PLEASURE. AS LONG AS I CAN SEE THE SENTENCE CARRIED OUT.

THE SANHEDRIN HAS SPOKEN. HE MUST DIE. THE PRICE OF BLASPHEMY!

WHO WILL BE THE FIRST TO LAY HIS HAND AGAINST HIM?!

I WILL!

14

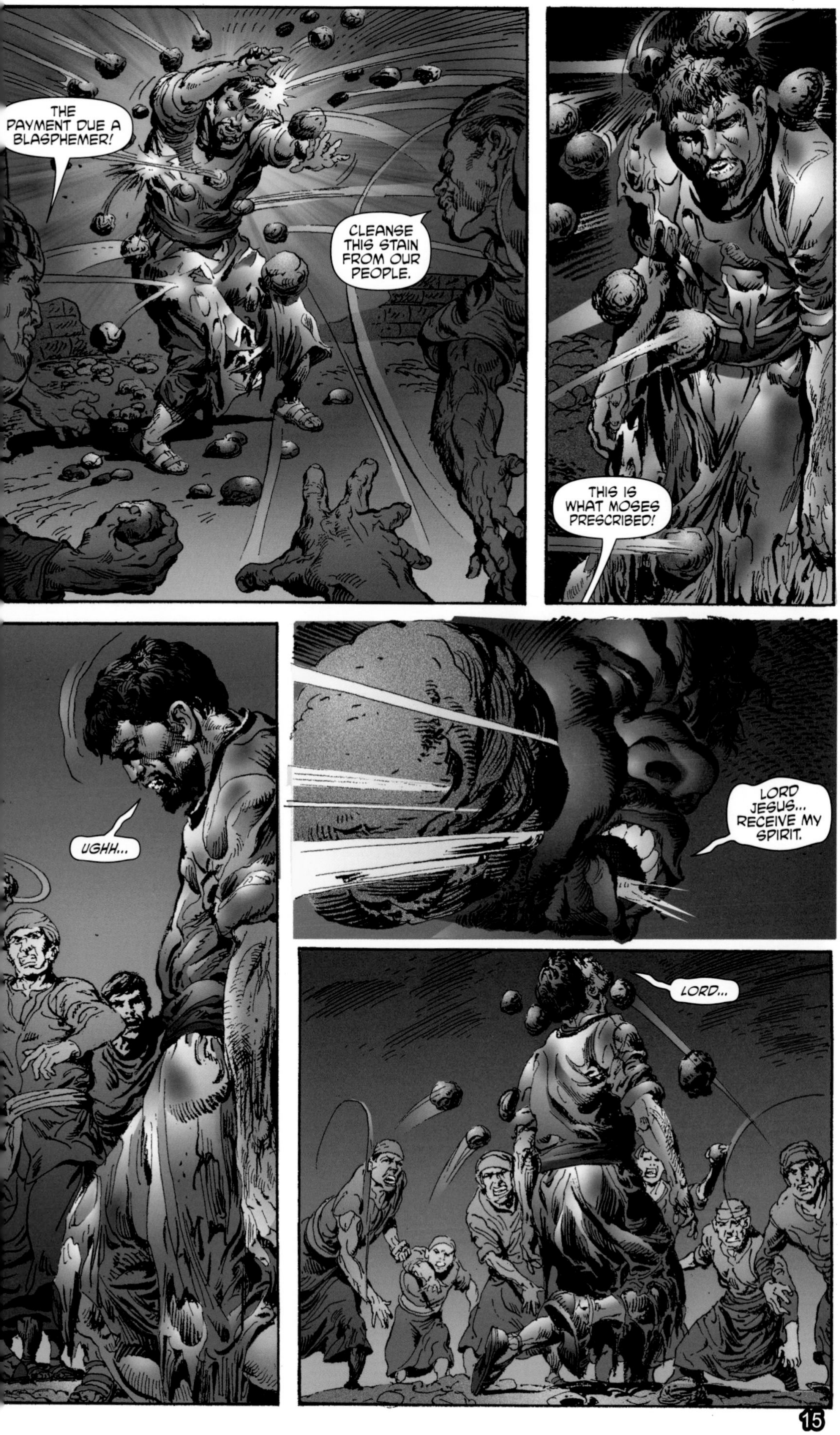
THE PAYMENT DUE A BLASPHEMER!
CLEANSE THIS STAIN FROM OUR PEOPLE.
THIS IS WHAT MOSES PRESCRIBED!
UGHH...
LORD JESUS... RECEIVE MY SPIRIT.
LORD...

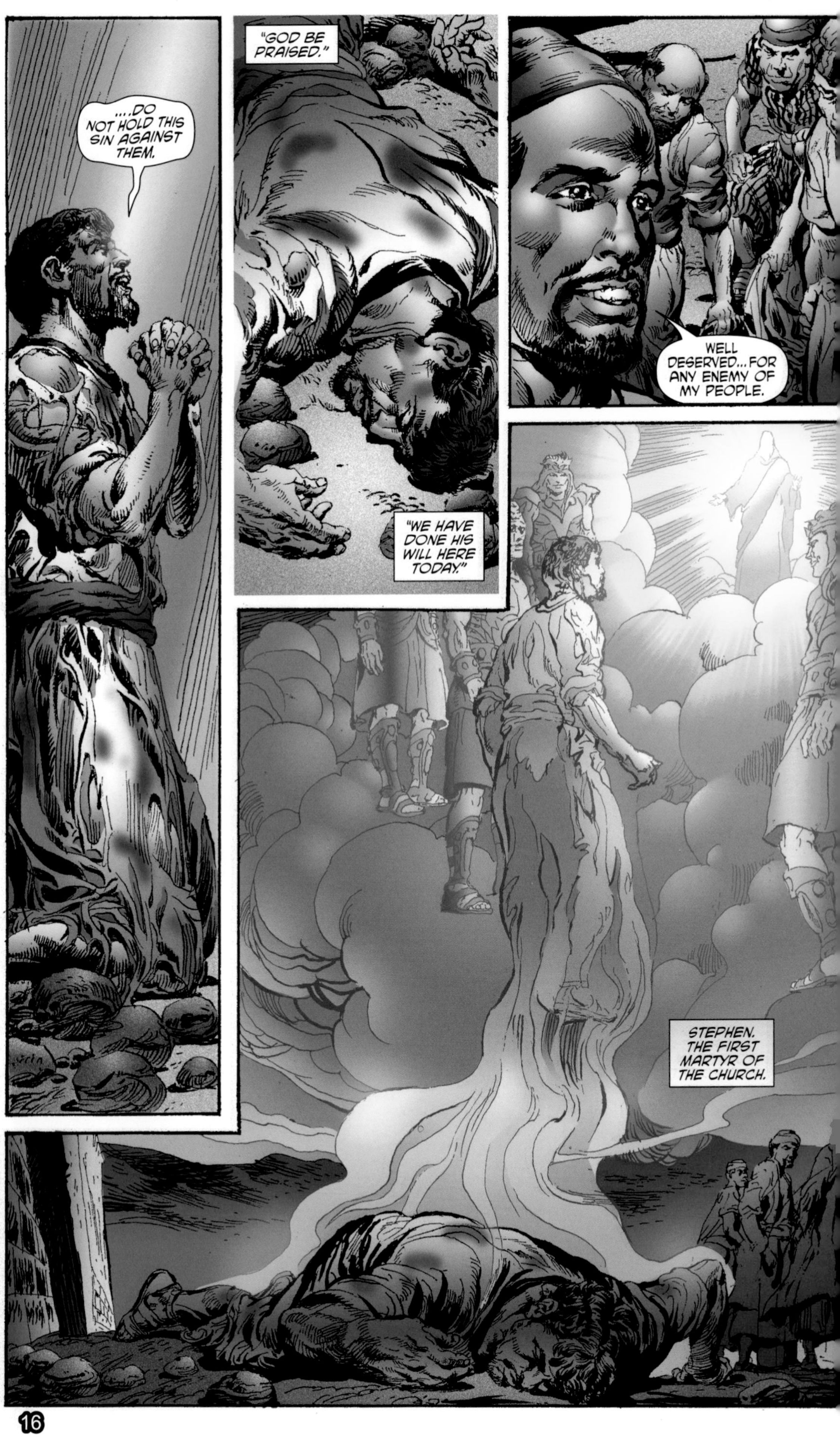
...DO NOT HOLD THIS SIN AGAINST THEM.
"GOD BE PRAISED."
"WE HAVE DONE HIS WILL HERE TODAY."
WELL DESERVED...FOR ANY ENEMY OF MY PEOPLE.
STEPHEN. THE FIRST MARTYR OF THE CHURCH.

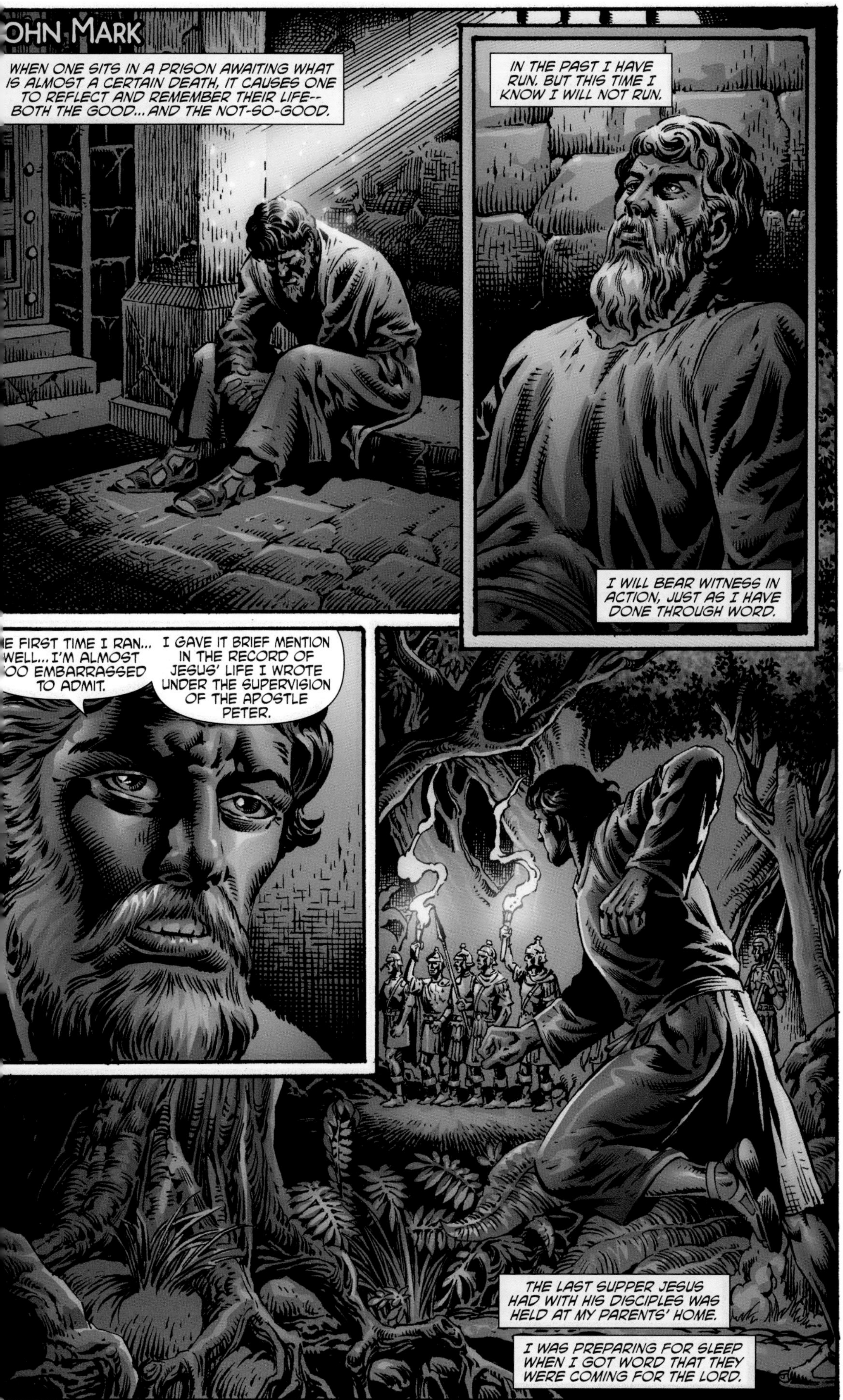
OHN MARK
WHEN ONE SITS IN A PRISON AWAITING WHAT IS ALMOST A CERTAIN DEATH, IT CAUSES ONE TO REFLECT AND REMEMBER THEIR LIFE-- BOTH THE GOOD... AND THE NOT-SO-GOOD.
IN THE PAST I HAVE RUN. BUT THIS TIME I KNOW I WILL NOT RUN.
I WILL BEAR WITNESS IN ACTION, JUST AS I HAVE DONE THROUGH WORD.
E FIRST TIME I RAN... WELL... I'M ALMOST OO EMBARRASSED TO ADMIT.
I GAVE IT BRIEF MENTION IN THE RECORD OF JESUS' LIFE I WROTE UNDER THE SUPERVISION OF THE APOSTLE PETER.
THE LAST SUPPER JESUS HAD WITH HIS DISCIPLES WAS HELD AT MY PARENTS' HOME.
I WAS PREPARING FOR SLEEP WHEN I GOT WORD THAT THEY WERE COMING FOR THE LORD.

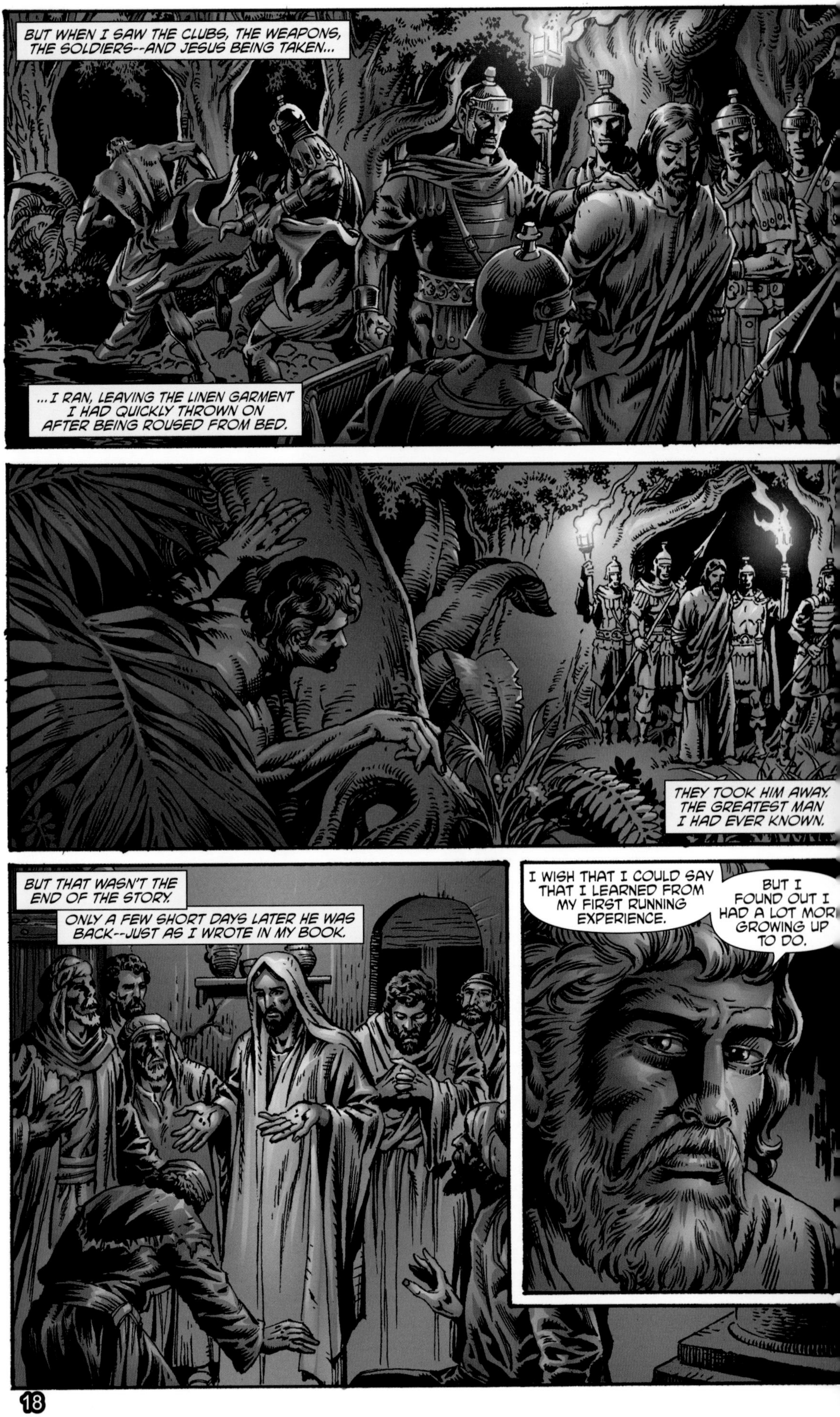
BUT WHEN I SAW THE CLUBS, THE WEAPONS, THE SOLDIERS--AND JESUS BEING TAKEN...
...I RAN, LEAVING THE LINEN GARMENT I HAD QUICKLY THROWN ON AFTER BEING ROUSED FROM BED.
THEY TOOK HIM AWAY. THE GREATEST MAN I HAD EVER KNOWN.
BUT THAT WASN'T THE END OF THE STORY.
ONLY A FEW SHORT DAYS LATER HE WAS BACK--JUST AS I WROTE IN MY BOOK.
I WISH THAT I COULD SAY THAT I LEARNED FROM MY FIRST RUNNING EXPERIENCE.
BUT I FOUND OUT I HAD A LOT MOR GROWING UP TO DO.

ON MY SECOND RUN I ABANDONED TWO GREAT MEN--NOT TO MENTION THE LORD'S PLAN FOR ME.

IT WAS NOT THAT I DID NOT HAVE THE PROPER UPBRINGING--I HAD THE BEST.

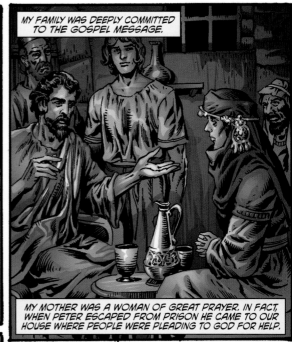

MY FAMILY WAS DEEPLY COMMITTED TO THE GOSPEL MESSAGE.

MY MOTHER WAS A WOMAN OF GREAT PRAYER. IN FACT, WHEN PETER ESCAPED FROM PRISON HE CAME TO OUR HOUSE WHERE PEOPLE WERE PLEADING TO GOD FOR HELP.

MY COUSIN WAS THE ONE AND ONLY BARNABAS.

LIKE HIS NAME HE WAS A GREAT ENCOURAGER-- AND A PARTNER WITH THE APOSTLE PAUL HIMSELF.

I NOT ONLY MET THE APOSTLE PAUL--

I ACTUALLY TRAVELED WITH THEM AS ONE OF THEIR CO-WORKERS.

THAT IS WHEN MY RUNNING *REALLY* CAUSED SOME SERIOUS TROUBLE.

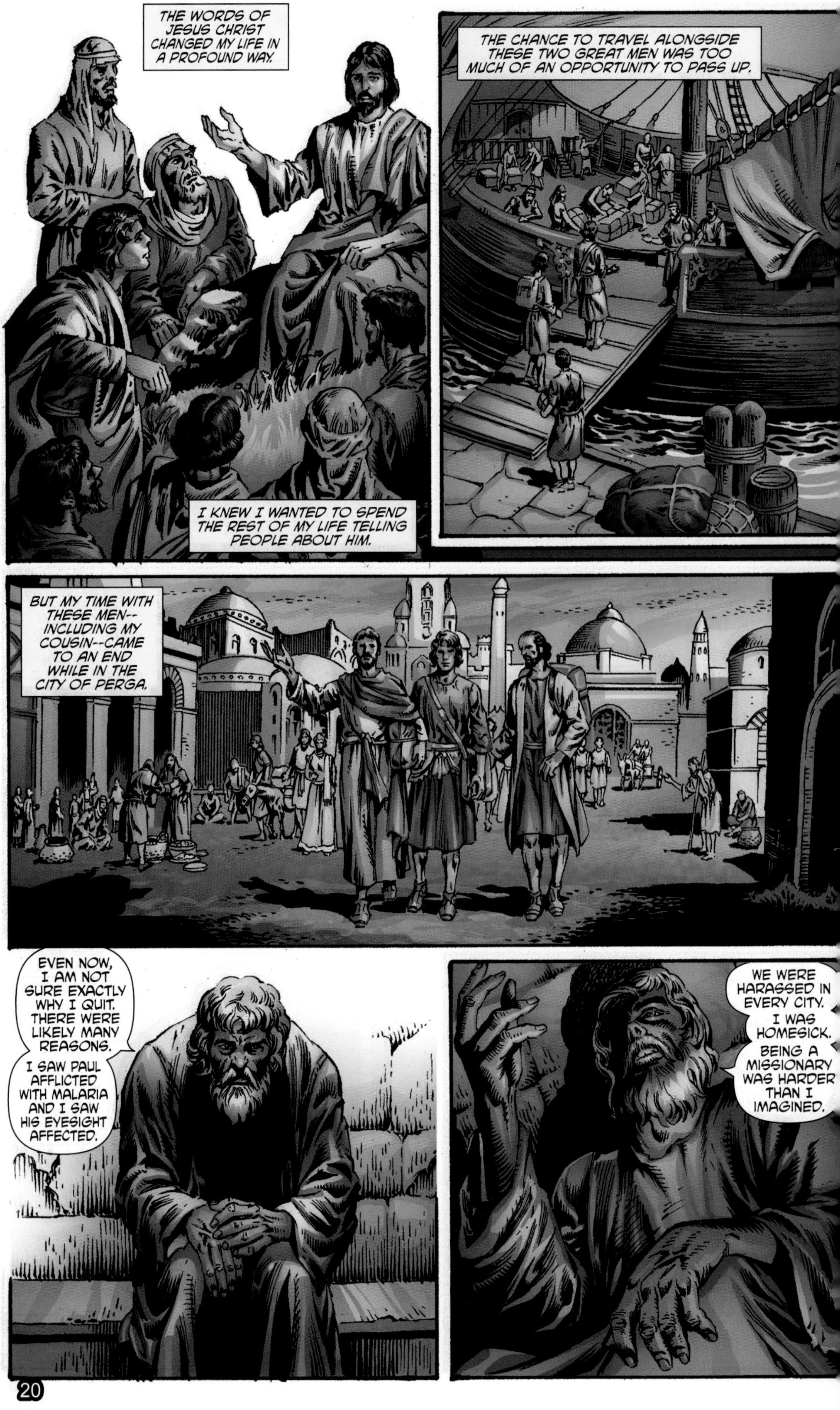
THE WORDS OF JESUS CHRIST CHANGED MY LIFE IN A PROFOUND WAY.
I KNEW I WANTED TO SPEND THE REST OF MY LIFE TELLING PEOPLE ABOUT HIM.
THE CHANCE TO TRAVEL ALONGSIDE THESE TWO GREAT MEN WAS TOO MUCH OF AN OPPORTUNITY TO PASS UP.
BUT MY TIME WITH THESE MEN--INCLUDING MY COUSIN--CAME TO AN END WHILE IN THE CITY OF PERGA.
EVEN NOW, I AM NOT SURE EXACTLY WHY I QUIT. THERE WERE LIKELY MANY REASONS.
I SAW PAUL AFFLICTED WITH MALARIA AND I SAW HIS EYESIGHT AFFECTED.
WE WERE HARASSED IN EVERY CITY.
I WAS HOMESICK.
BEING A MISSIONARY WAS HARDER THAN I IMAGINED.

AND SO I SIMPLY LEFT THEM--TO THE CONSTERNATION OF MY COUSIN BARNABAS.

AND TO THE *GREAT* IRRITATION OF PAUL.

I HADN'T QUIT FOLLOWING CHRIST BUT I WASN'T READY FOR THAT LIFE--YET.

IN ANTIOCH--THE CITY WHERE WE WERE FIRST CALLED CHRISTIANS, I FINALLY FELT I WAS READY TO REJOIN THE MISSIONARY FORCE.

I WAS READY. BUT THE APOSTLE WAS NOT...

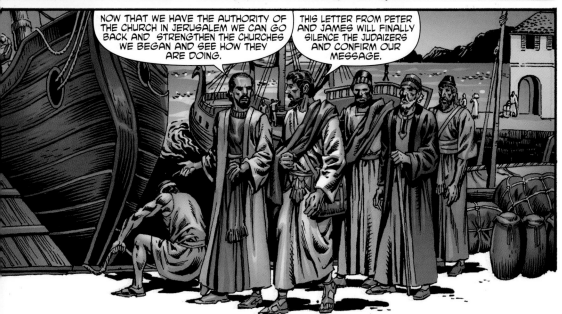

NOW THAT WE HAVE THE AUTHORITY OF THE CHURCH IN JERUSALEM WE CAN GO BACK AND STRENGTHEN THE CHURCHES WE BEGAN AND SEE HOW THEY ARE DOING.

THIS LETTER FROM PETER AND JAMES WILL FINALLY SILENCE THE JUDAIZERS AND CONFIRM OUR MESSAGE.

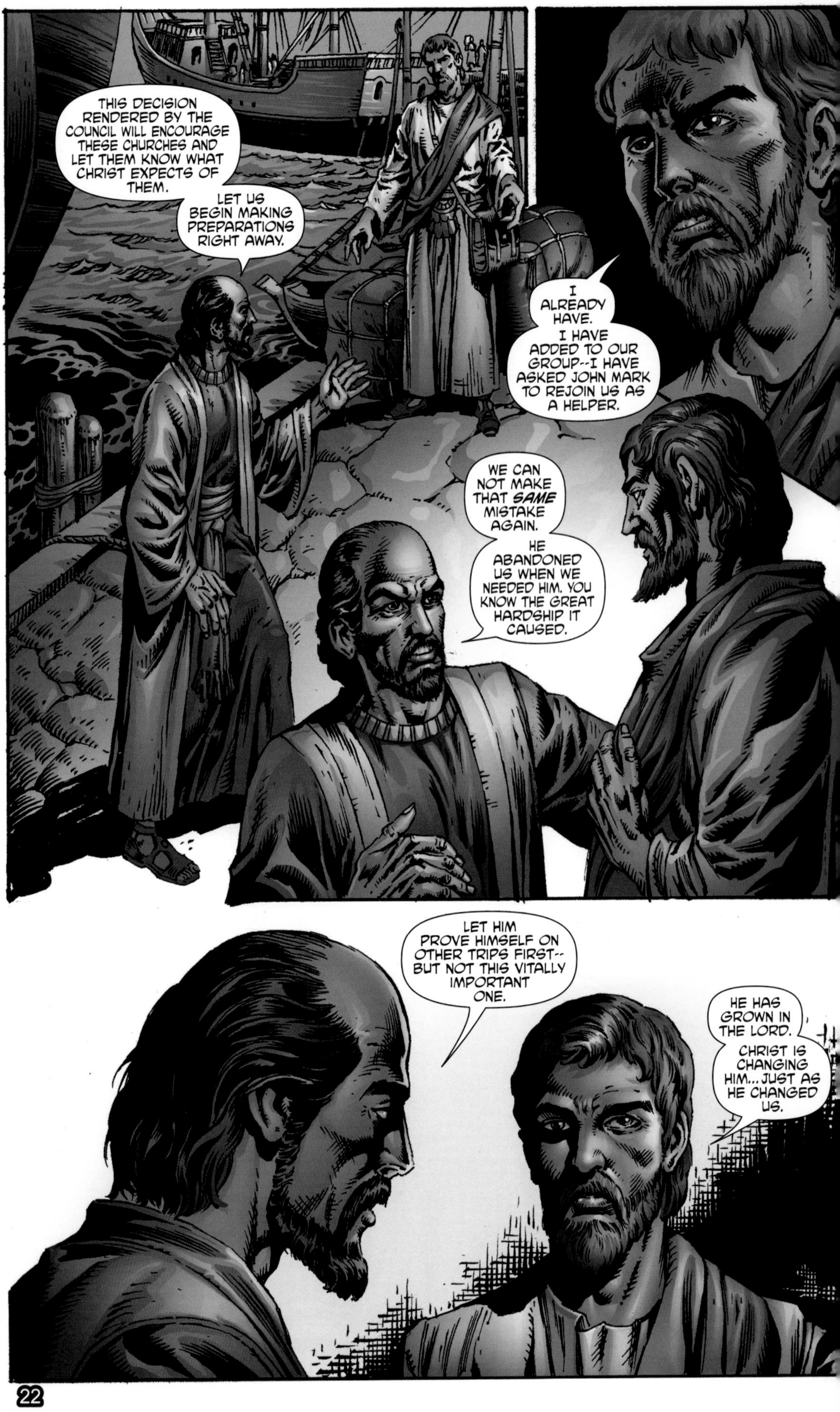
THIS DECISION RENDERED BY THE COUNCIL WILL ENCOURAGE THESE CHURCHES AND LET THEM KNOW WHAT CHRIST EXPECTS OF THEM.
LET US BEGIN MAKING PREPARATIONS RIGHT AWAY.
I ALREADY HAVE.
I HAVE ADDED TO OUR GROUP--I HAVE ASKED JOHN MARK TO REJOIN US AS A HELPER.
WE CAN NOT MAKE THAT SAME MISTAKE AGAIN.
HE ABANDONED US WHEN WE NEEDED HIM. YOU KNOW THE GREAT HARDSHIP IT CAUSED.
LET HIM PROVE HIMSELF ON OTHER TRIPS FIRST-- BUT NOT THIS VITALLY IMPORTANT ONE.
HE HAS GROWN IN THE LORD.
CHRIST IS CHANGING HIM... JUST AS HE CHANGED US.

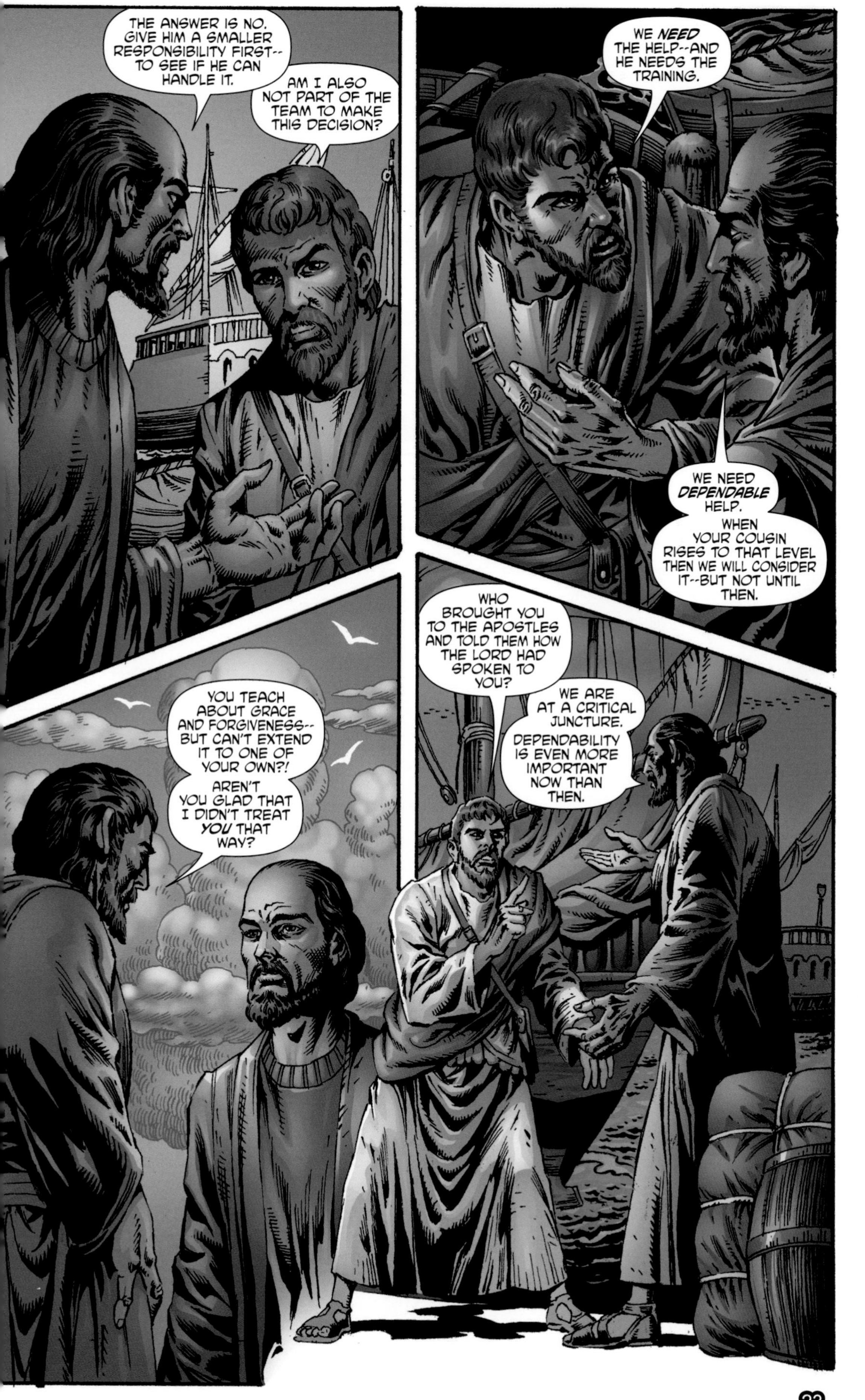
THE ANSWER IS NO. GIVE HIM A SMALLER RESPONSIBILITY FIRST-- TO SEE IF HE CAN HANDLE IT.
AM I ALSO NOT PART OF THE TEAM TO MAKE THIS DECISION?
WE *NEED* THE HELP--AND HE NEEDS THE TRAINING.
WE NEED *DEPENDABLE* HELP.
WHEN YOUR COUSIN RISES TO THAT LEVEL THEN WE WILL CONSIDER IT--BUT NOT UNTIL THEN.
YOU TEACH ABOUT GRACE AND FORGIVENESS-- BUT CAN'T EXTEND IT TO ONE OF YOUR OWN?!
AREN'T YOU GLAD THAT I DIDN'T TREAT *YOU* THAT WAY?
WHO BROUGHT YOU TO THE APOSTLES AND TOLD THEM HOW THE LORD HAD SPOKEN TO YOU?
WE ARE AT A CRITICAL JUNCTURE.
DEPENDABILITY IS EVEN MORE IMPORTANT NOW THAN THEN.

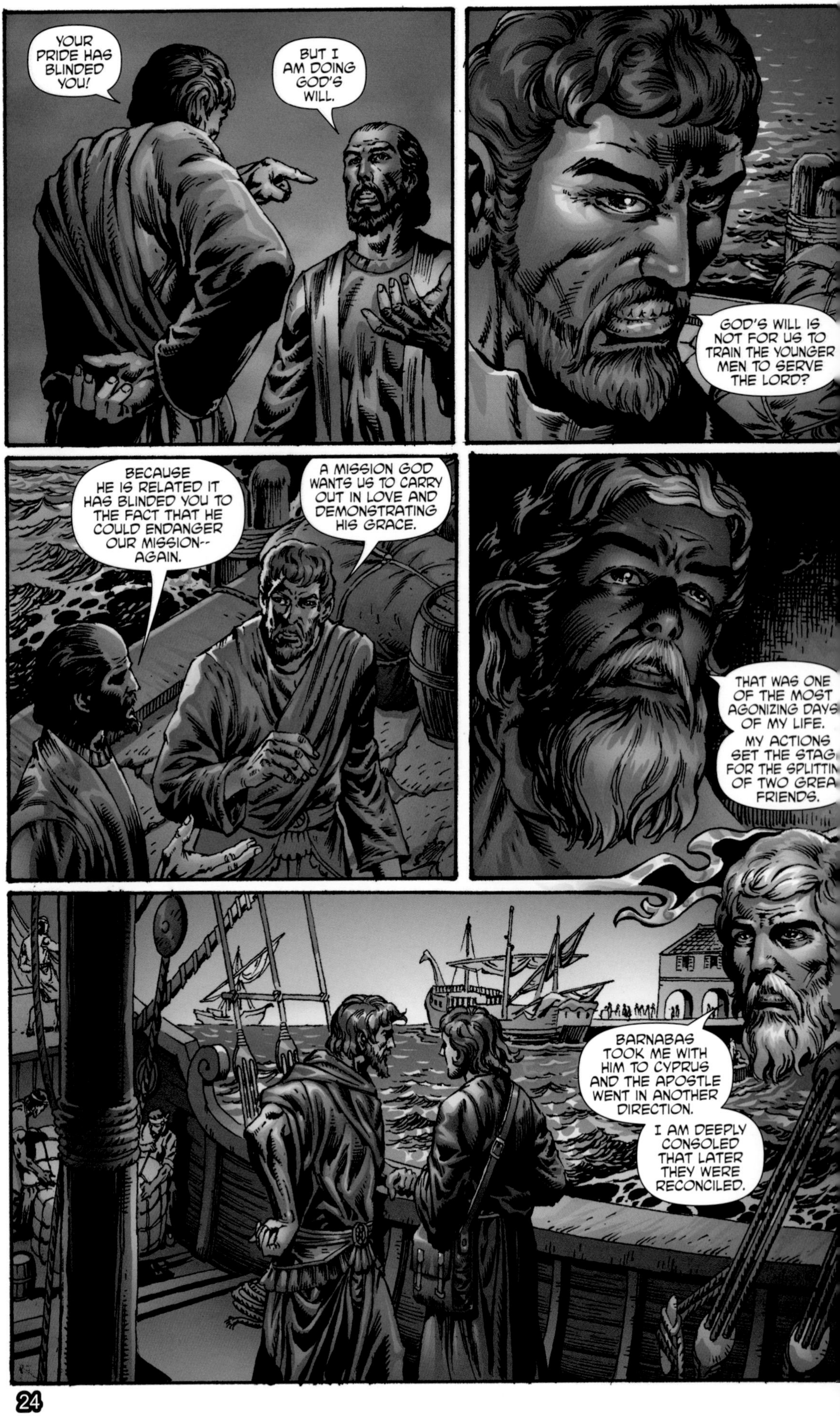
YOUR PRIDE HAS BLINDED YOU!
BUT I AM DOING GOD'S WILL.
GOD'S WILL IS NOT FOR US TO TRAIN THE YOUNGER MEN TO SERVE THE LORD?
BECAUSE HE IS RELATED IT HAS BLINDED YOU TO THE FACT THAT HE COULD ENDANGER OUR MISSION-- AGAIN.
A MISSION GOD WANTS US TO CARRY OUT IN LOVE AND DEMONSTRATING HIS GRACE.
THAT WAS ONE OF THE MOST AGONIZING DAYS OF MY LIFE.
MY ACTIONS SET THE STAG FOR THE SPLITTIN OF TWO GREA FRIENDS.
BARNABAS TOOK ME WITH HIM TO CYPRUS AND THE APOSTLE WENT IN ANOTHER DIRECTION.
I AM DEEPLY CONSOLED THAT LATER THEY WERE RECONCILED.

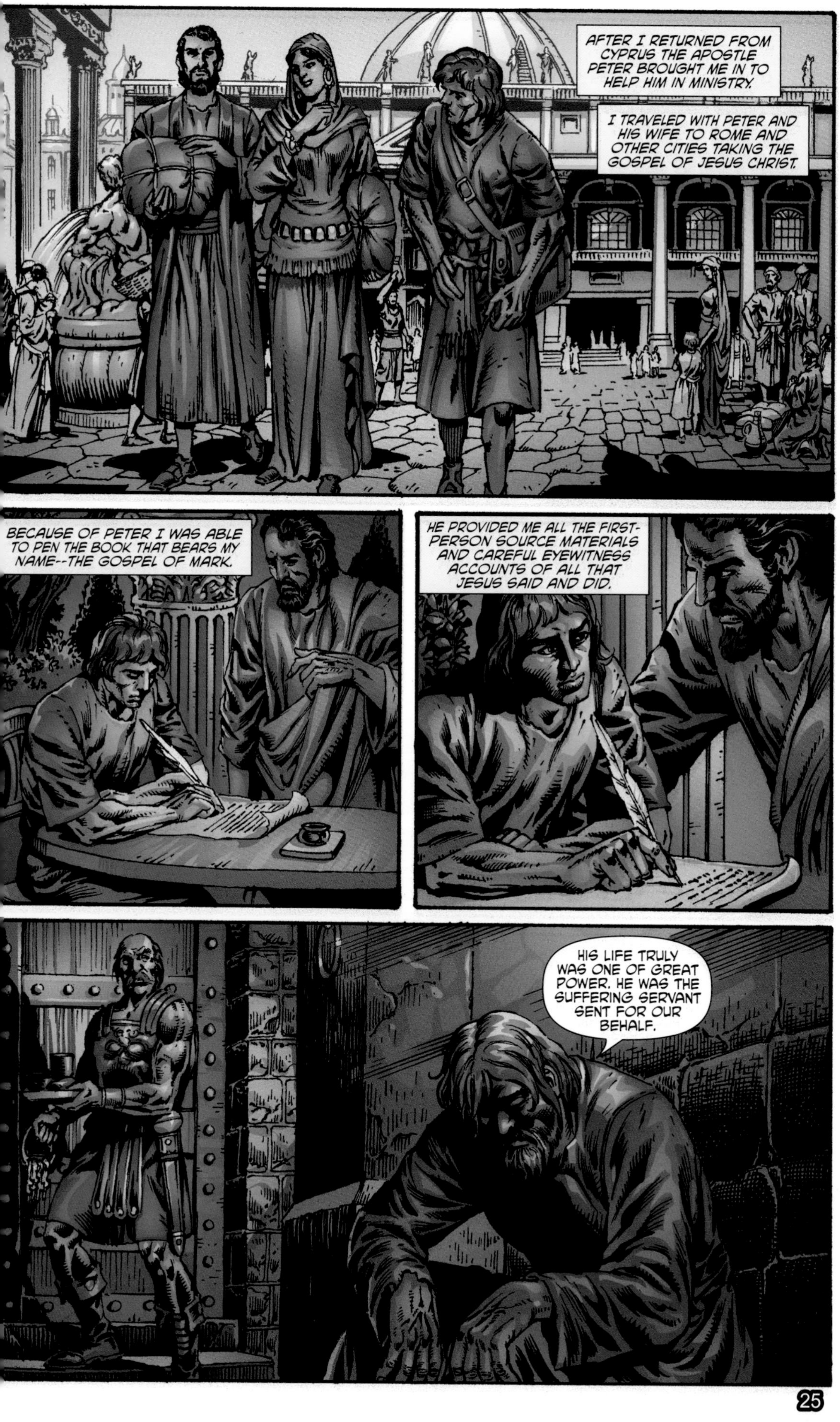
AFTER I RETURNED FROM CYPRUS THE APOSTLE PETER BROUGHT ME IN TO HELP HIM IN MINISTRY.
I TRAVELED WITH PETER AND HIS WIFE TO ROME AND OTHER CITIES TAKING THE GOSPEL OF JESUS CHRIST.
BECAUSE OF PETER I WAS ABLE TO PEN THE BOOK THAT BEARS MY NAME--THE GOSPEL OF MARK.
HE PROVIDED ME ALL THE FIRST-PERSON SOURCE MATERIALS AND CAREFUL EYEWITNESS ACCOUNTS OF ALL THAT JESUS SAID AND DID.
HIS LIFE TRULY WAS ONE OF GREAT POWER. HE WAS THE SUFFERING SERVANT SENT FOR OUR BEHALF.

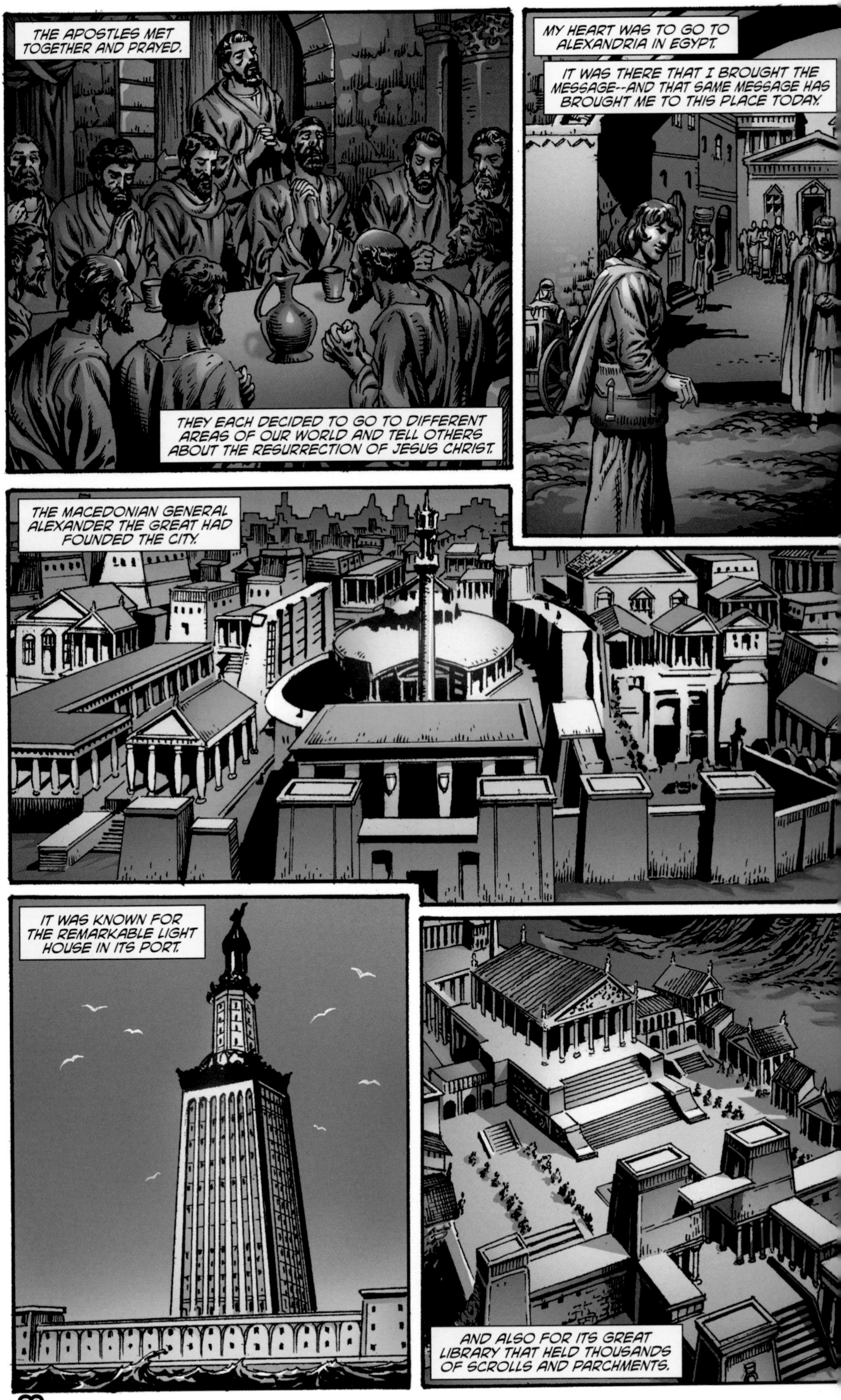
THE APOSTLES MET TOGETHER AND PRAYED.
THEY EACH DECIDED TO GO TO DIFFERENT AREAS OF OUR WORLD AND TELL OTHERS ABOUT THE RESURRECTION OF JESUS CHRIST.
MY HEART WAS TO GO TO ALEXANDRIA IN EGYPT.
IT WAS THERE THAT I BROUGHT THE MESSAGE--AND THAT SAME MESSAGE HAS BROUGHT ME TO THIS PLACE TODAY.
THE MACEDONIAN GENERAL ALEXANDER THE GREAT HAD FOUNDED THE CITY.
IT WAS KNOWN FOR THE REMARKABLE LIGHT HOUSE IN ITS PORT.
AND ALSO FOR ITS GREAT LIBRARY THAT HELD THOUSANDS OF SCROLLS AND PARCHMENTS.

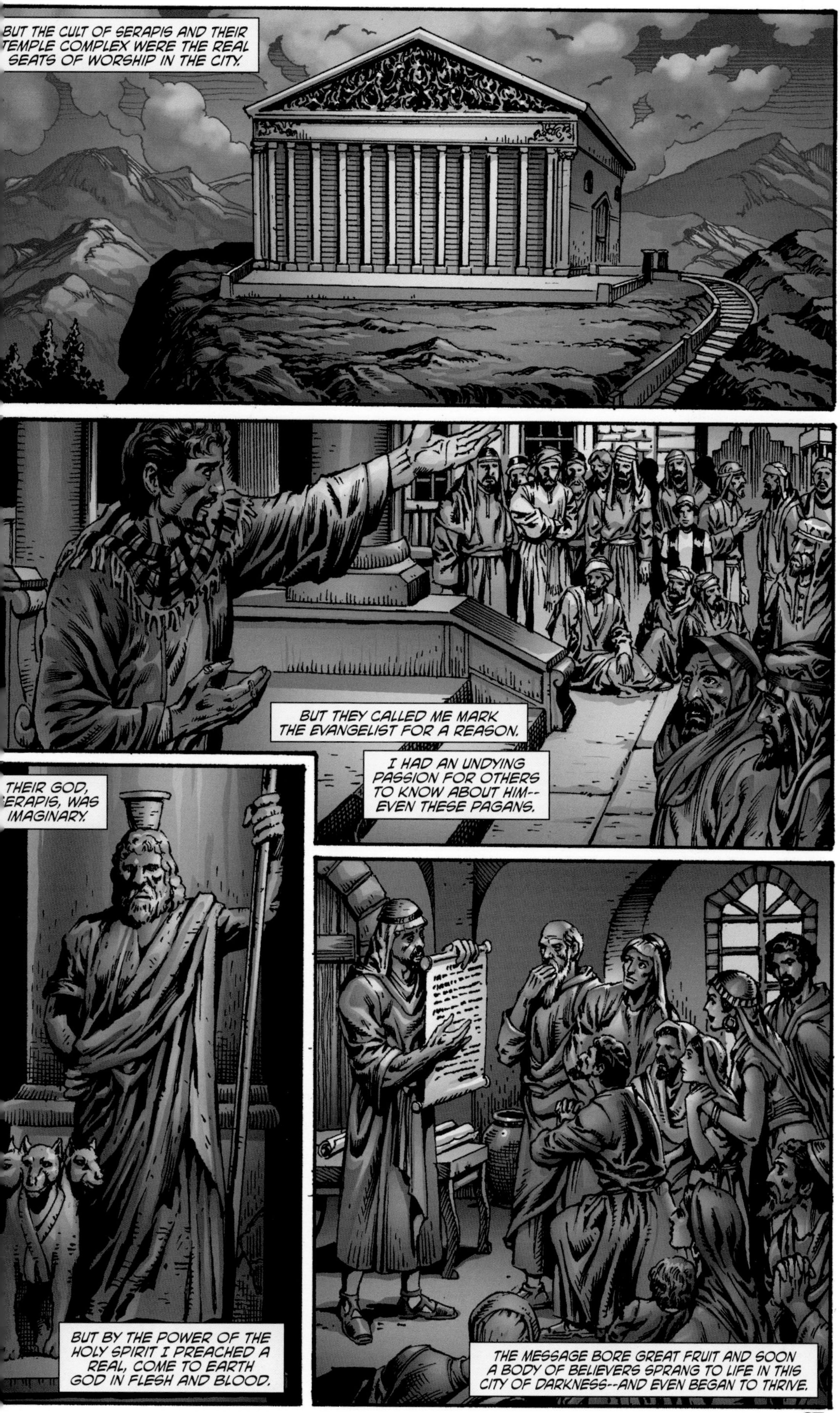
BUT THE CULT OF SERAPIS AND THEIR TEMPLE COMPLEX WERE THE REAL SEATS OF WORSHIP IN THE CITY.
BUT THEY CALLED ME MARK THE EVANGELIST FOR A REASON.
I HAD AN UNDYING PASSION FOR OTHERS TO KNOW ABOUT HIM-- EVEN THESE PAGANS.
THEIR GOD, SERAPIS, WAS IMAGINARY.
BUT BY THE POWER OF THE HOLY SPIRIT I PREACHED A REAL, COME TO EARTH GOD IN FLESH AND BLOOD.
THE MESSAGE BORE GREAT FRUIT AND SOON A BODY OF BELIEVERS SPRANG TO LIFE IN THIS CITY OF DARKNESS--AND EVEN BEGAN TO THRIVE.

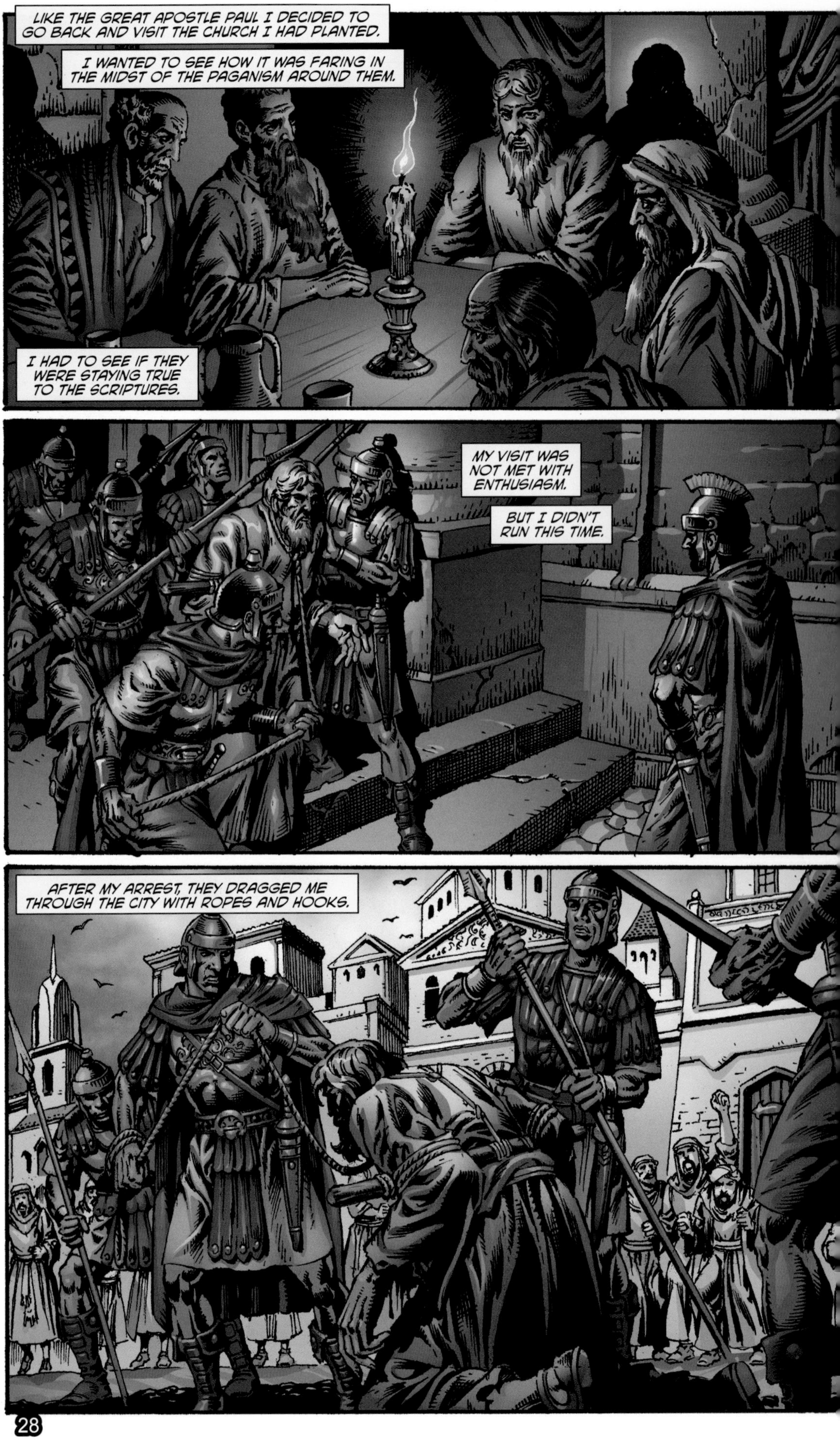
LIKE THE GREAT APOSTLE PAUL I DECIDED TO GO BACK AND VISIT THE CHURCH I HAD PLANTED.
I WANTED TO SEE HOW IT WAS FARING IN THE MIDST OF THE PAGANISM AROUND THEM.
I HAD TO SEE IF THEY WERE STAYING TRUE TO THE SCRIPTURES.
MY VISIT WAS NOT MET WITH ENTHUSIASM.
BUT I DIDN'T RUN THIS TIME.
AFTER MY ARREST, THEY DRAGGED ME THROUGH THE CITY WITH ROPES AND HOOKS.

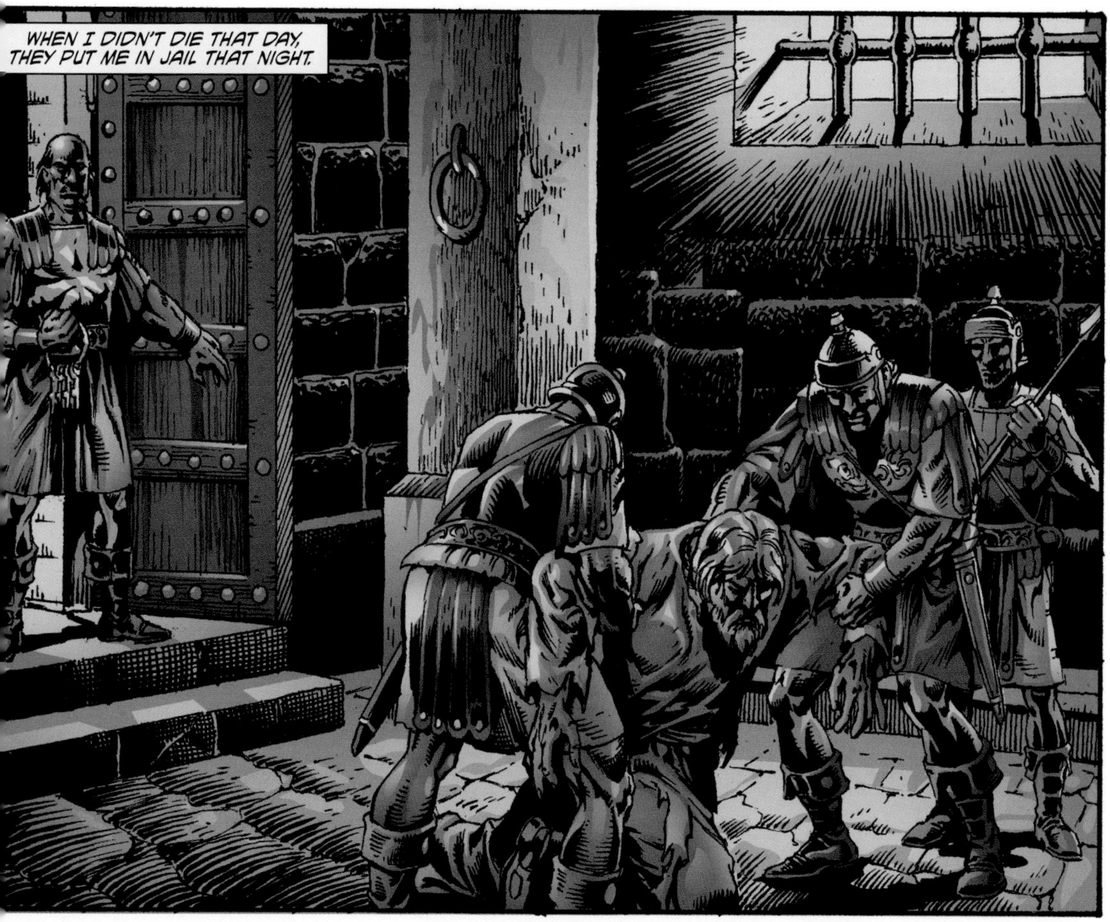
WHEN I DIDN'T DIE THAT DAY, THEY PUT ME IN JAIL THAT NIGHT.

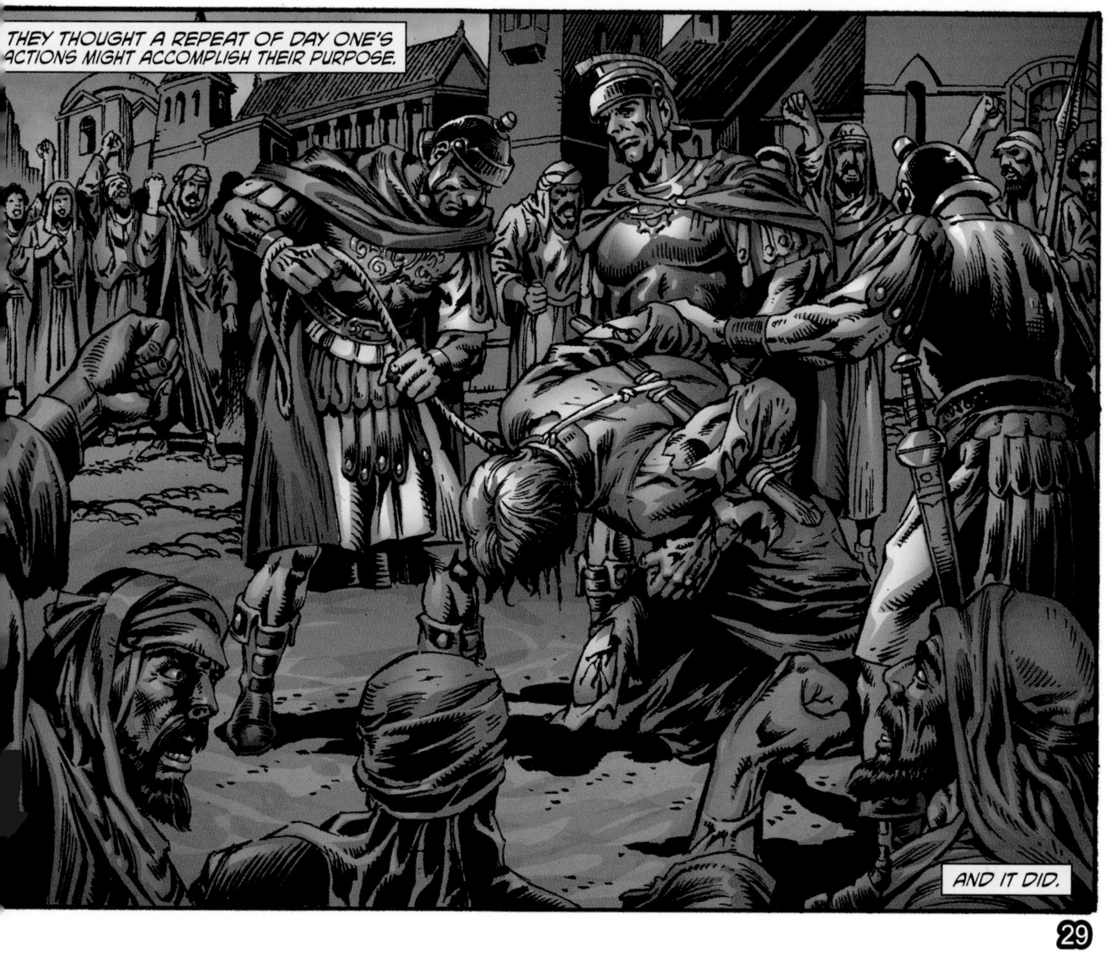
THEY THOUGHT A REPEAT OF DAY ONE'S ACTIONS MIGHT ACCOMPLISH THEIR PURPOSE.
AND IT DID.

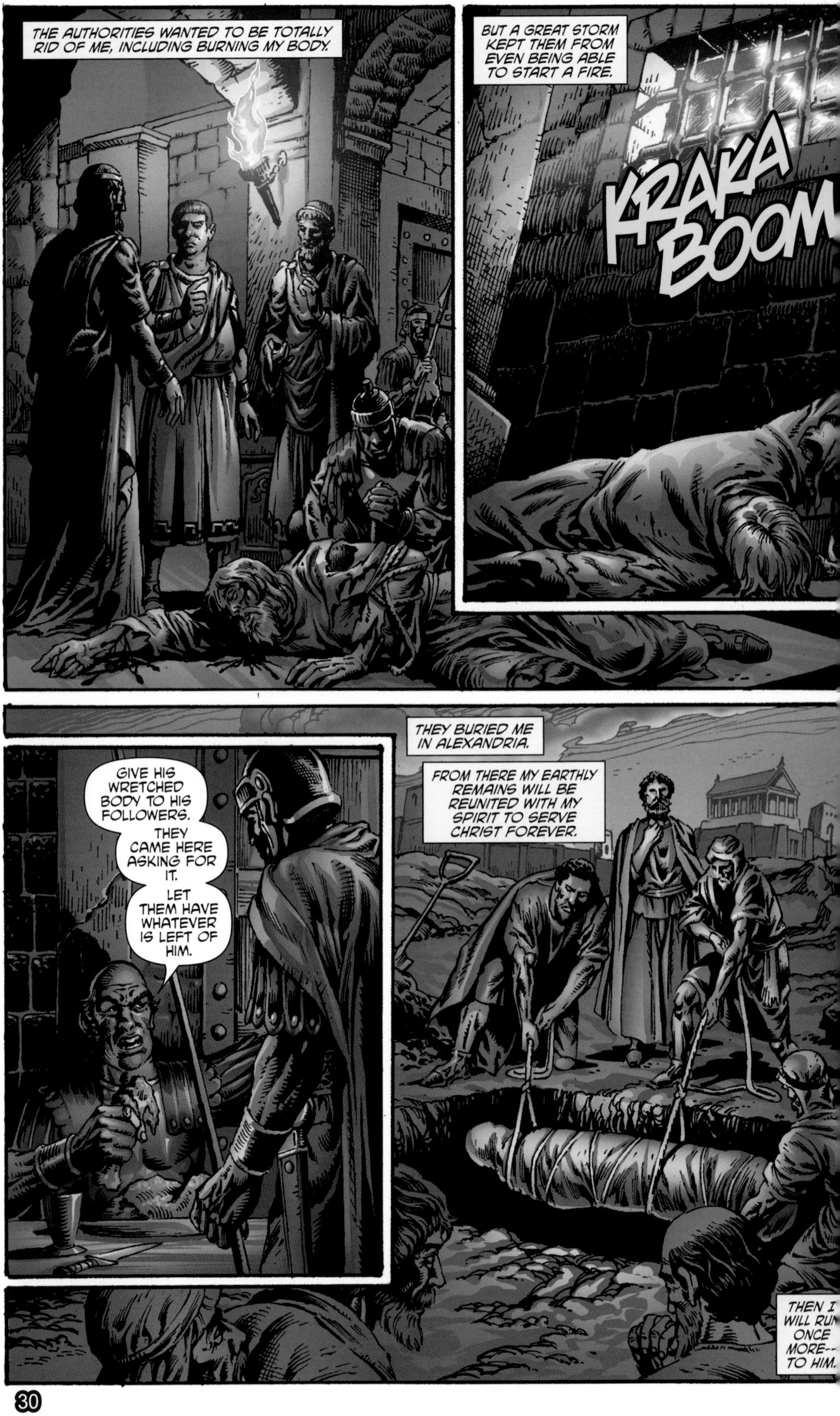
THE AUTHORITIES WANTED TO BE TOTALLY RID OF ME, INCLUDING BURNING MY BODY.
BUT A GREAT STORM KEPT THEM FROM EVEN BEING ABLE TO START A FIRE.
KRAKA BOOM
GIVE HIS WRETCHED BODY TO HIS FOLLOWERS.
THEY CAME HERE ASKING FOR IT.
LET THEM HAVE WHATEVER IS LEFT OF HIM.
THEY BURIED ME IN ALEXANDRIA.
FROM THERE MY EARTHLY REMAINS WILL BE REUNITED WITH MY SPIRIT TO SERVE CHRIST FOREVER.
THEN I WILL RUN ONCE MORE-- TO HIM.

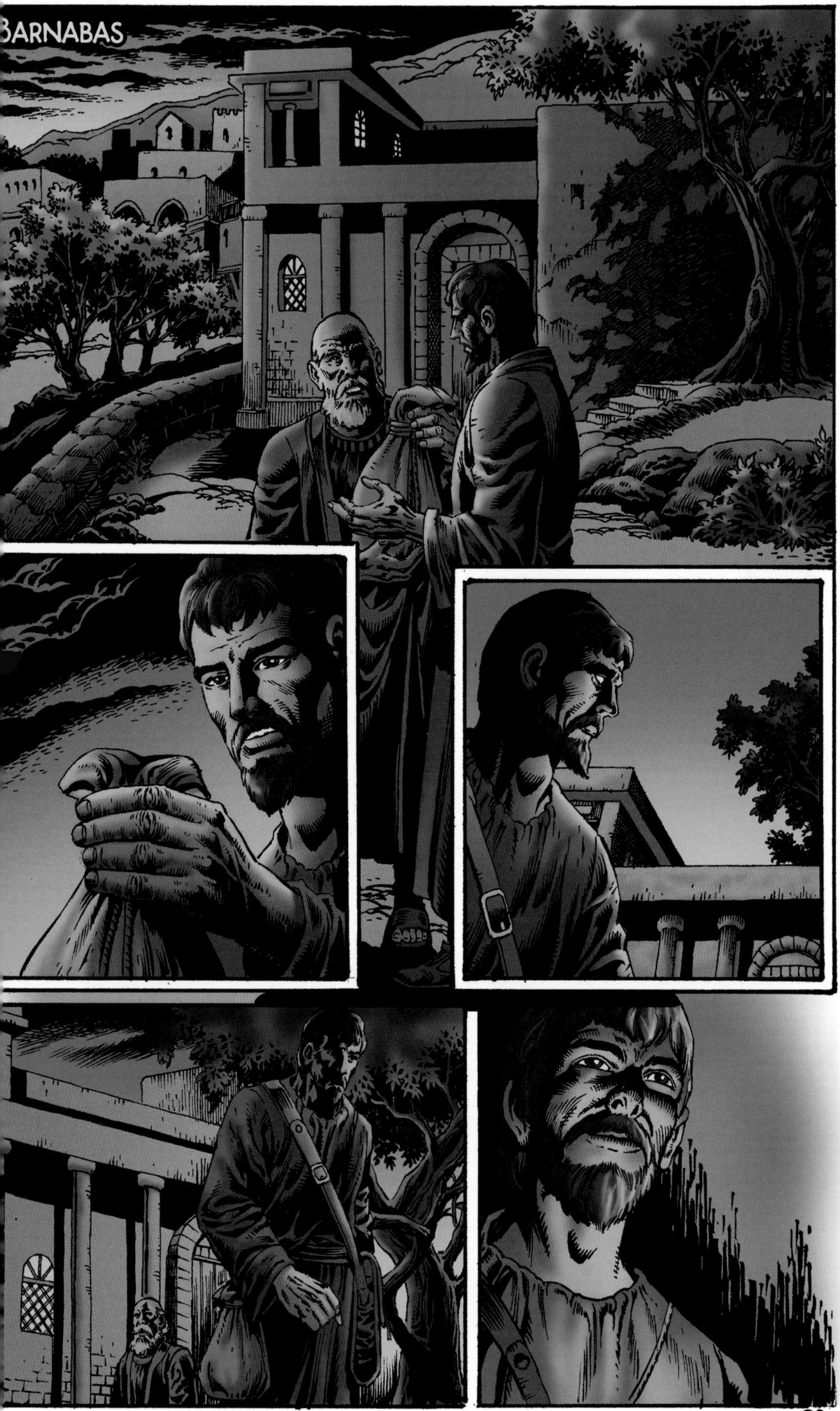

JERUSALEM. A FEW MONTHS AFTER CHRIST'S DEATH, RESURRECTION, AND ASCENSION.

HELLO, RACHEL. MIRIAM.

AH! BARNABAS! WELCOME BACK!

THANK YOU, DEAR SISTER!

BARNABAS!

I TRUST YOUR TRAVELS WENT WELL, "JOSEPH..."

THEY DID, "SIMON!"

I'D FORGOTTEN THAT BOTH OF YOU GO BY NAMES NOW THAT WEREN'T YOUR GIVEN NAMES!

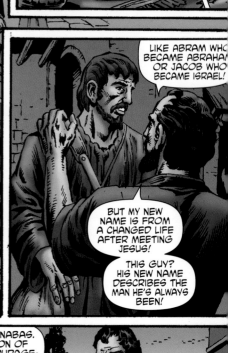

LIKE ABRAM WHO BECAME ABRAHAM! OR JACOB WHO BECAME ISRAEL!

BUT MY NEW NAME IS FROM A CHANGED LIFE AFTER MEETING JESUS!

THIS GUY? HIS NEW NAME DESCRIBES THE MAN HE'S ALWAYS BEEN!

THANK YOU, PETER. NOW, I HAVE SOME BUSINESS WITH YOU!

BARNABAS, WHAT IS THIS?

I SAW PEOPLE HERE IN NEED.

I SOLD THE FIELD I OWN.

USE THE MONEY AS NEEDED TO HELP THEM.

BARNABAS. "SON OF ENCOURAGEMENT." WE GAVE YOU THE RIGHT NAME.

BUT YOUR FIELD?

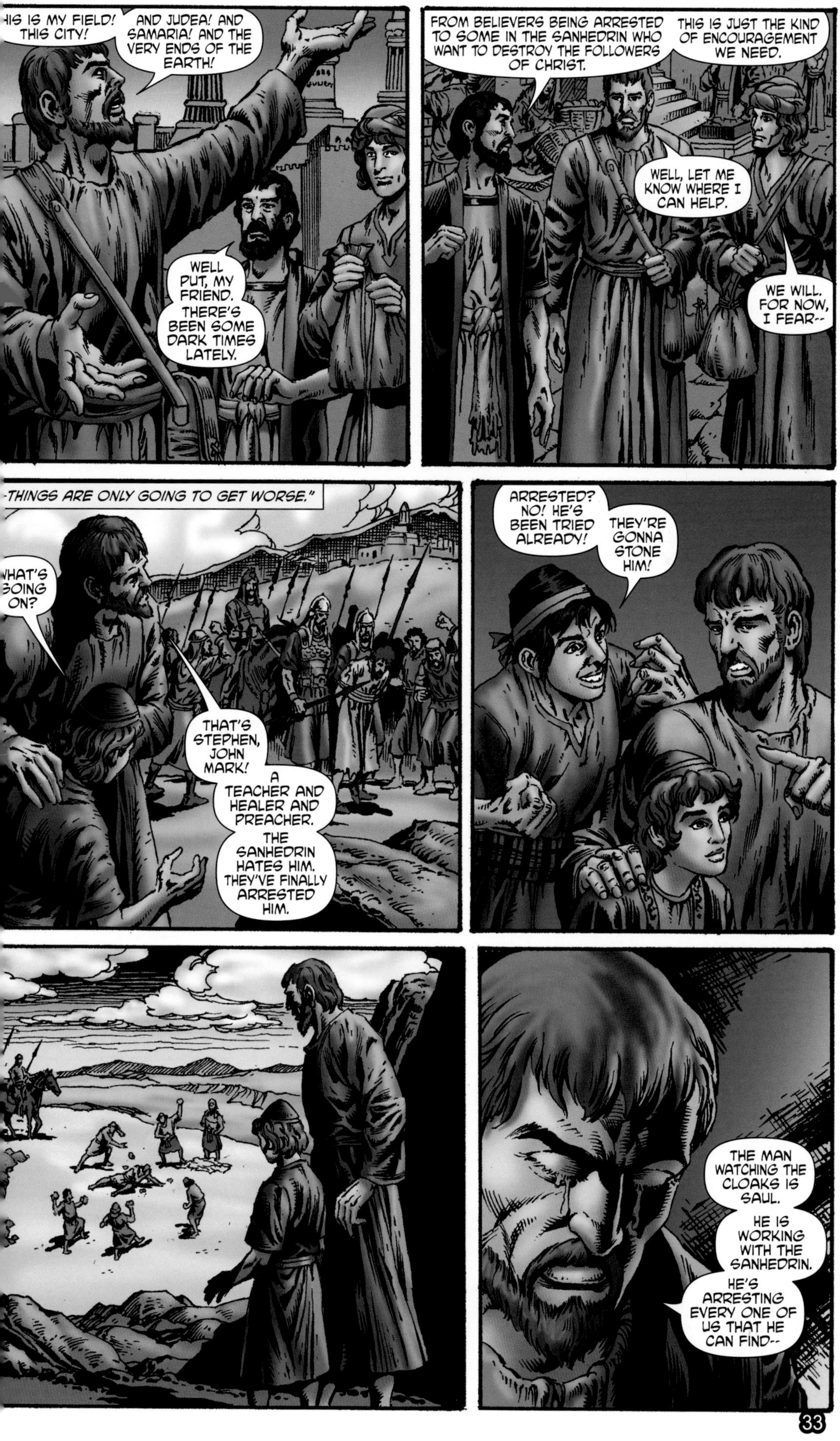
HIS IS MY FIELD! THIS CITY!
AND JUDEA! AND SAMARIA! AND THE VERY ENDS OF THE EARTH!
WELL PUT, MY FRIEND. THERE'S BEEN SOME DARK TIMES LATELY.
FROM BELIEVERS BEING ARRESTED TO SOME IN THE SANHEDRIN WHO WANT TO DESTROY THE FOLLOWERS OF CHRIST.
THIS IS JUST THE KIND OF ENCOURAGEMENT WE NEED.
WELL, LET ME KNOW WHERE I CAN HELP.
WE WILL. FOR NOW, I FEAR--
-THINGS ARE ONLY GOING TO GET WORSE."
HAT'S OING ON?
THAT'S STEPHEN, JOHN MARK!
A TEACHER AND HEALER AND PREACHER.
THE SANHEDRIN HATES HIM. THEY'VE FINALLY ARRESTED HIM.
ARRESTED? NO! HE'S BEEN TRIED ALREADY!
THEY'RE GONNA STONE HIM!
THE MAN WATCHING THE CLOAKS IS SAUL.
HE IS WORKING WITH THE SANHEDRIN.
HE'S ARRESTING EVERY ONE OF US THAT HE CAN FIND--

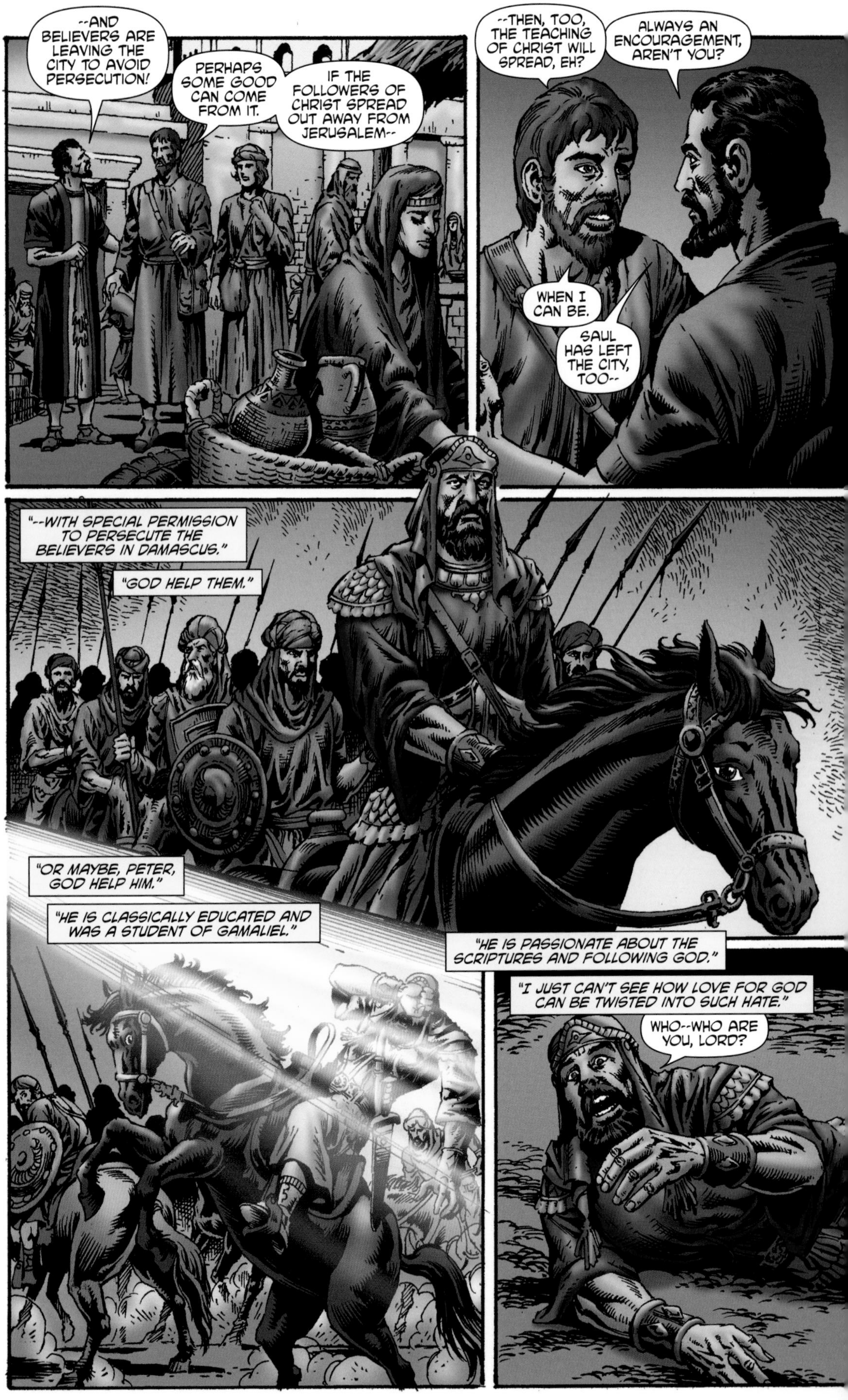
--AND BELIEVERS ARE LEAVING THE CITY TO AVOID PERSECUTION!
PERHAPS SOME GOOD CAN COME FROM IT.
IF THE FOLLOWERS OF CHRIST SPREAD OUT AWAY FROM JERUSALEM--
--THEN, TOO, THE TEACHING OF CHRIST WILL SPREAD, EH?
ALWAYS AN ENCOURAGEMENT, AREN'T YOU?
WHEN I CAN BE.
SAUL HAS LEFT THE CITY, TOO--
"--WITH SPECIAL PERMISSION TO PERSECUTE THE BELIEVERS IN DAMASCUS."
"GOD HELP THEM."
"OR MAYBE, PETER, GOD HELP HIM."
"HE IS CLASSICALLY EDUCATED AND WAS A STUDENT OF GAMALIEL."
"HE IS PASSIONATE ABOUT THE SCRIPTURES AND FOLLOWING GOD."
"I JUST CAN'T SEE HOW LOVE FOR GOD CAN BE TWISTED INTO SUCH HATE."
WHO--WHO ARE YOU, LORD?

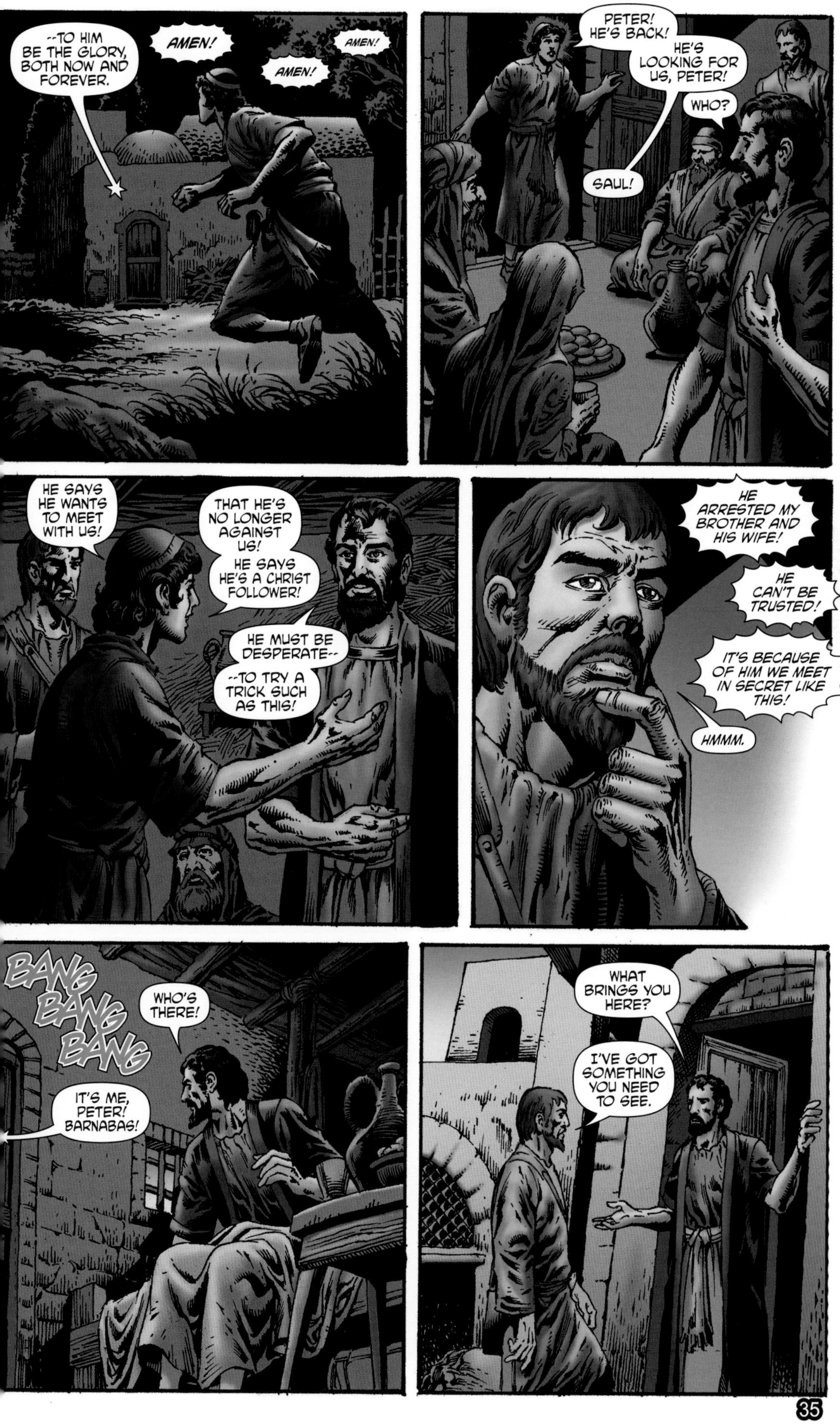
--TO HIM BE THE GLORY, BOTH NOW AND FOREVER.
AMEN!
AMEN!
AMEN!
PETER! HE'S BACK!
HE'S LOOKING FOR US, PETER!
WHO?
SAUL!
HE SAYS HE WANTS TO MEET WITH US!
THAT HE'S NO LONGER AGAINST US!
HE SAYS HE'S A CHRIST FOLLOWER!
HE MUST BE DESPERATE--
--TO TRY A TRICK SUCH AS THIS!
HE ARRESTED MY BROTHER AND HIS WIFE!
HE CAN'T BE TRUSTED!
IT'S BECAUSE OF HIM WE MEET IN SECRET LIKE THIS!
HMMM.
BANG BANG BANG
WHO'S THERE!
IT'S ME, PETER! BARNABAS!
WHAT BRINGS YOU HERE?
I'VE GOT SOMETHING YOU NEED TO SEE.

WHAT? BARNABAS! HAVE YOU LOST YOUR MIND BRINGING HIM HERE!?!

I LISTENED TO HIM, PETER. YOU SHOULD, TOO.

HE HAS SEEN JESUS. OUR LORD SCOLDED HIM FOR PERSECUTING US.

HE WAS BLINDED AND WENT INTO DAMASCUS.

ANANIAS, ONE OF THE CHRISTIANS SAUL WOULD HAVE PERSECUTED, HAD A VISION--

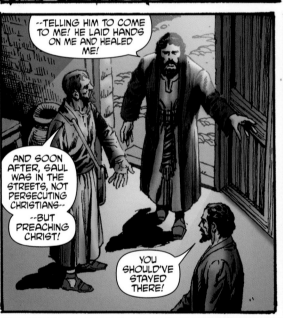

--TELLING HIM TO COME TO ME! HE LAID HANDS ON ME AND HEALED ME!

AND SOON AFTER, SAUL WAS IN THE STREETS, NOT PERSECUTING CHRISTIANS--

--BUT PREACHING CHRIST!

YOU SHOULD'VE STAYED THERE!

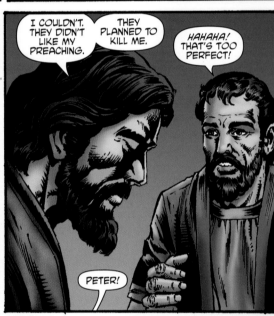

I COULDN'T. THEY DIDN'T LIKE MY PREACHING. THEY PLANNED TO KILL ME.

HAHAHA! THAT'S TOO PERFECT!

PETER!

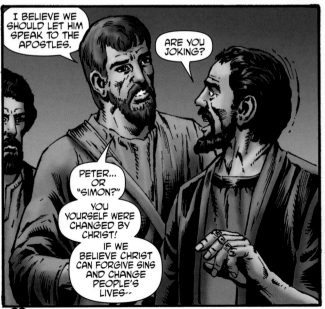

I BELIEVE WE SHOULD LET HIM SPEAK TO THE APOSTLES.

ARE YOU JOKING?

PETER... OR "SIMON?" YOU YOURSELF WERE CHANGED BY CHRIST! IF WE BELIEVE CHRIST CAN FORGIVE SINS AND CHANGE PEOPLE'S LIVES--

--THEN WE MUST BELIEVE THAT APPLIES EVEN TO ONE SUCH AS HIM! LET HIM COME BEFORE THE APOSTLES.

I DON'T KNOW...

--AND I PREACHED WHAT I KNEW OF CHRIST IN DAMASCUS.

UNTIL THEY CHASED ME OUT.

THE THINGS YOU HAVE DONE TO US... HOW DO WE KNOW THIS ISN'T A TRICK?

YOU HAVE TORN FAMILIES APART AND IMPRISONED INNOCENT PEOPLE!

ENOUGH!

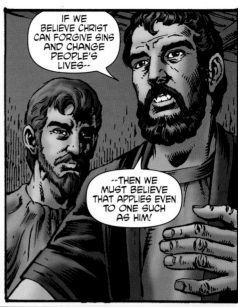

IF WE BELIEVE CHRIST CAN FORGIVE SINS AND CHANGE PEOPLE'S LIVES--

--THEN WE MUST BELIEVE THAT APPLIES EVEN TO ONE SUCH AS HIM!

THE APOSTLES LET SAUL PREACH...

...IN CHRIST, THERE IS NO JEW OR GREEK! WE ARE ALL ONE...

BUT SAUL'S FERVENT PREACHING MADE ENEMIES IN JERUSALEM.

HE WAS SENT TO SERVE IN TARSUS, WHERE HE HAD FAMILY.

SOME TIME LATER.

BARNABAS, THE APOSTLES HAVE A MISSION FOR YOU.

A MISSION?

YES. I'D PREFER YOU STAY HERE, BUT YOU ARE NEEDED--

"--IN THE CITY OF ANTIOCH."

"THERE IS A GROUP OF GREEK JEWS-- HELLENISTS--WHO HAVE TURNED TO CHRIST."

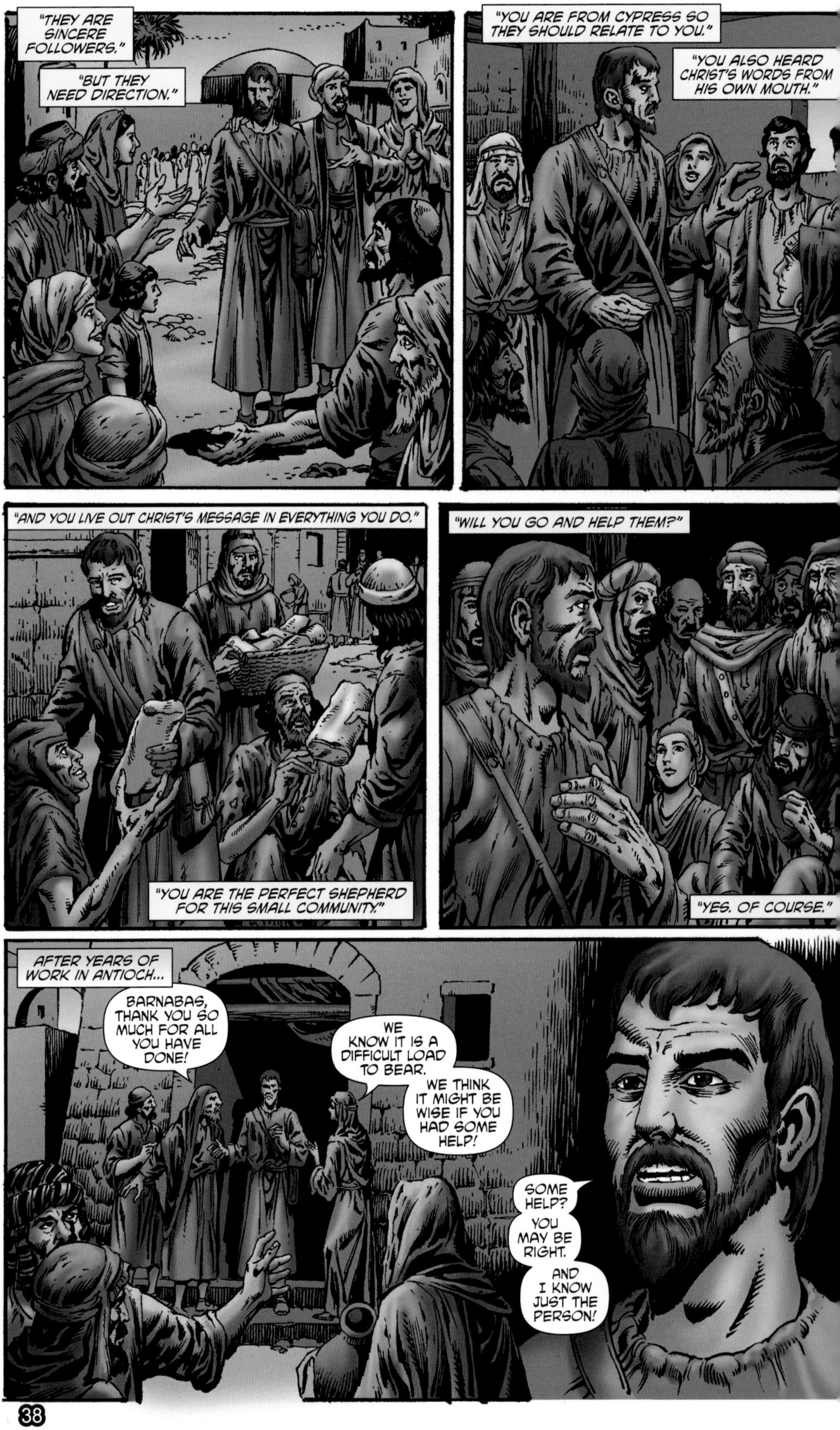
"THEY ARE SINCERE FOLLOWERS."
"BUT THEY NEED DIRECTION."
"YOU ARE FROM CYPRESS SO THEY SHOULD RELATE TO YOU."
"YOU ALSO HEARD CHRIST'S WORDS FROM HIS OWN MOUTH."
"AND YOU LIVE OUT CHRIST'S MESSAGE IN EVERYTHING YOU DO."
"YOU ARE THE PERFECT SHEPHERD FOR THIS SMALL COMMUNITY."
"WILL YOU GO AND HELP THEM?"
"YES. OF COURSE."
AFTER YEARS OF WORK IN ANTIOCH...
BARNABAS, THANK YOU SO MUCH FOR ALL YOU HAVE DONE!
WE KNOW IT IS A DIFFICULT LOAD TO BEAR.
WE THINK IT MIGHT BE WISE IF YOU HAD SOME HELP!
SOME HELP?
YOU MAY BE RIGHT.
AND I KNOW JUST THE PERSON!

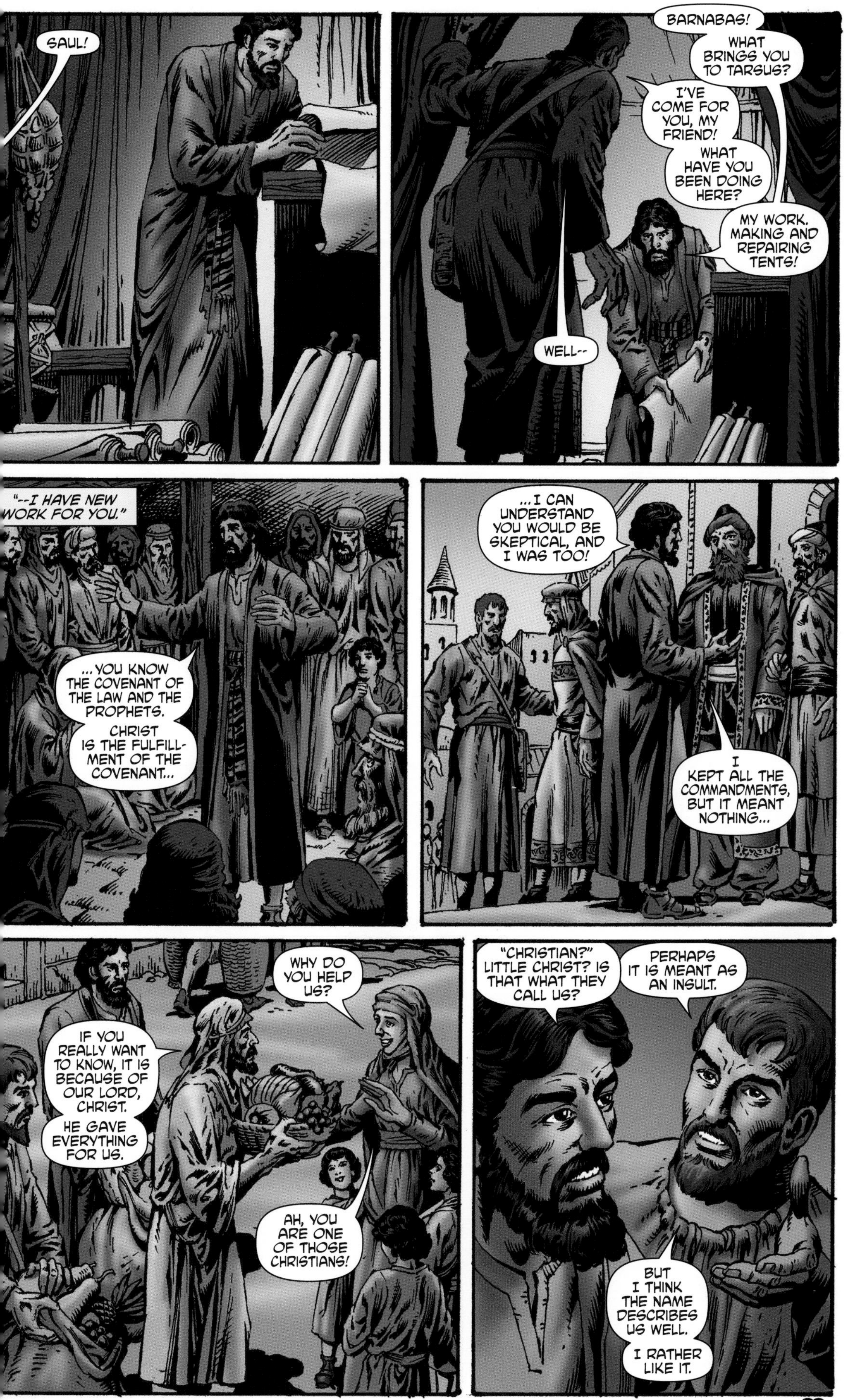
SAUL!
BARNABAS!
WHAT BRINGS YOU TO TARSUS?
I'VE COME FOR YOU, MY FRIEND!
WHAT HAVE YOU BEEN DOING HERE?
MY WORK. MAKING AND REPAIRING TENTS!
WELL--
"--I HAVE NEW WORK FOR YOU."
...YOU KNOW THE COVENANT OF THE LAW AND THE PROPHETS.
CHRIST IS THE FULFILLMENT OF THE COVENANT...
...I CAN UNDERSTAND YOU WOULD BE SKEPTICAL, AND I WAS TOO!
I KEPT ALL THE COMMANDMENTS, BUT IT MEANT NOTHING...
WHY DO YOU HELP US?
IF YOU REALLY WANT TO KNOW, IT IS BECAUSE OF OUR LORD, CHRIST.
HE GAVE EVERYTHING FOR US.
AH, YOU ARE ONE OF THOSE CHRISTIANS!
"CHRISTIAN?" LITTLE CHRIST? IS THAT WHAT THEY CALL US?
PERHAPS IT IS MEANT AS AN INSULT.
BUT I THINK THE NAME DESCRIBES US WELL.
I RATHER LIKE IT.

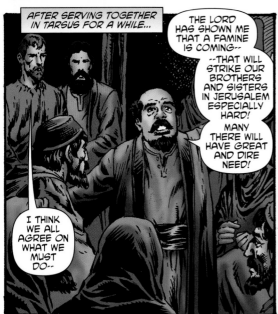

AFTER SERVING TOGETHER IN TARSUS FOR A WHILE...

THE LORD HAS SHOWN ME THAT A FAMINE IS COMING--

--THAT WILL STRIKE OUR BROTHERS AND SISTERS IN JERUSALEM ESPECIALLY HARD! MANY THERE WILL HAVE GREAT AND DIRE NEED!

I THINK WE ALL AGREE ON WHAT WE MUST DO--

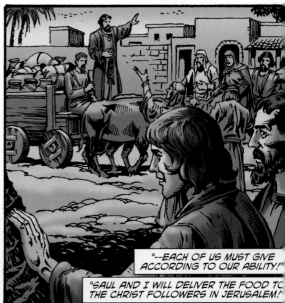

"--EACH OF US MUST GIVE ACCORDING TO OUR ABILITY!"

"SAUL AND I WILL DELIVER THE FOOD TO THE CHRIST FOLLOWERS IN JERUSALEM!"

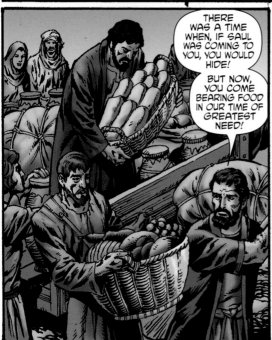

THERE WAS A TIME WHEN, IF SAUL WAS COMING TO YOU, YOU WOULD HIDE!

BUT NOW, YOU COME BEARING FOOD IN OUR TIME OF GREATEST NEED!

RETURNING HOME, BARNABAS' COUSIN, JOHN MARK, CAME WITH THEM TO JOIN THEIR WORK IN ANTIOCH.

BUT THAT WORK DID NOT LAST MUCH LONGER...

WE HAVE HEARD THE LORD SPEAK CLEARLY.

HIS HOLY SPIRIT HAS TOLD US TO SET THESE MEN APART FOR GOD'S WORK.

THE WORK HE HAS CALLED THEM TO.

AND SO, WE MOVE FARTHER AWAY FROM JERUSALEM WITH JESUS' MESSAGE.

YES. WE'RE GOING TO BE AROUND GREEKS AND ROMANS AND HELLENIST JEWS MORE AND MORE.

I'VE BEEN THINKING ABOUT A NAME CHANGE.

I'D LIKE TO BE CALLED PAUL, A NAME FROM MY FAMILY'S GREEK BACKGROUND.

CHANGING YOUR NAME TO REFLECT YOUR MISSION? A GREAT THOUGHT!

THEY TRAVELED AROUND, PREACHING THE WORD OF GOD IN SYNAGOGUES--

...ADAM BROUGHT DEATH INTO THIS WORLD--

--AND CHRIST CAME TO BRING LIFE...

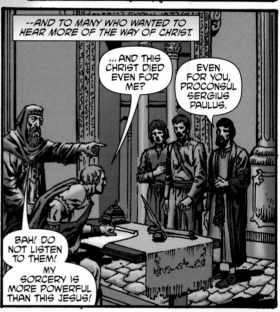

--AND TO MANY WHO WANTED TO HEAR MORE OF THE WAY OF CHRIST.

...AND THIS CHRIST DIED EVEN FOR ME?

EVEN FOR YOU, PROCONSUL SERGIUS PAULUS.

BAH! DO NOT LISTEN TO THEM! MY SORCERY IS MORE POWERFUL THAN THIS JESUS!

YOU, SORCERER, ARE A CHILD OF THE DEVIL!

YOUR "POWERS" ARE TRICKS AND LIES!

THE HAND OF THE TRUE LORD IS AGAINST YOU!

YOU TRY TO BLIND OTHERS FROM THE TRUTH--

--SO NOW, FOR A TIME, YOU WILL BE BLINDED FROM ALL LIGHT!

WHAT... WHAT... HELP ME! PLEASE!

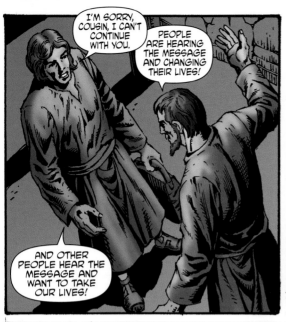

I'M SORRY, COUSIN, I CAN'T CONTINUE WITH YOU.

PEOPLE ARE HEARING THE MESSAGE AND CHANGING THEIR LIVES!

AND OTHER PEOPLE HEAR THE MESSAGE AND WANT TO TAKE OUR LIVES!

DON'T LET FEAR DRIVE YOU AWAY!

YOU ARE A GREAT HEL TO US!

EVERY-WHERE WE GO IT SEEM WE MAKE ENEMIES! IT'S TOO DANGEROU I'M GOING HOME...

IT'S GOOD HE SHOWS US HIS TRUE CHARACTER NOW.

BECAUSE HE'S RIGHT.

EVERYWHERE WE GO PEOPLE ACCEPT THE MESSAGE--

"--AND OTHER PEOPLE HATE IT AND PLOT AGAINST US."

I HAVE HEARD YOU SPEAK OF THE CHRIST AND MY SOUL IS STIRRED.

I SEE YOU HAVE FAITH TO BE HEALED.

I DO.

WELL, THEN, STAND UP!

I... I... LOOK AT ME!

IT'S THE GODS!

THE GODS HAVE COME TO US DISGUISED AS HUMANS!

THE STRONG SILENT ONE MUST BE ZEUS! THE TALKATIVE ON! IS HERMES, HI! MESSENGER!

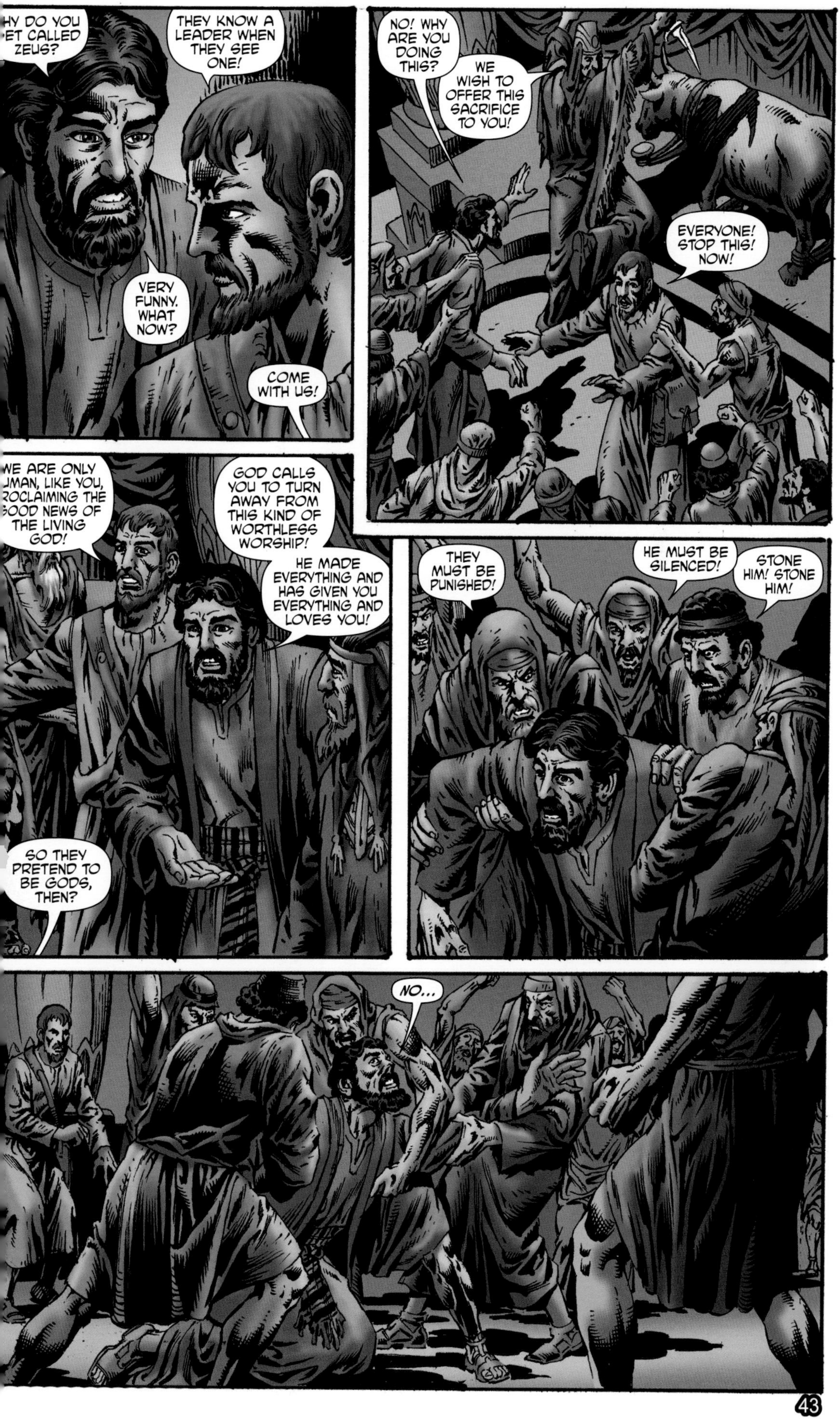
HY DO YOU
ET CALLED ZEUS?
THEY KNOW A LEADER WHEN THEY SEE ONE!
VERY FUNNY. WHAT NOW?
COME WITH US!
NO! WHY ARE YOU DOING THIS?
WE WISH TO OFFER THIS SACRIFICE TO YOU!
EVERYONE! STOP THIS! NOW!
WE ARE ONLY
UMAN, LIKE YOU,
ROCLAIMING THE
GOOD NEWS OF THE LIVING GOD!
GOD CALLS YOU TO TURN AWAY FROM THIS KIND OF WORTHLESS WORSHIP!
HE MADE EVERYTHING AND HAS GIVEN YOU EVERYTHING AND LOVES YOU!
SO THEY PRETEND TO BE GODS, THEN?
THEY MUST BE PUNISHED!
HE MUST BE SILENCED!
STONE HIM! STONE HIM!
NO...

"PAUL! PLEASE ANSWER ME--"

--CAN YOU SPEAK? THEY LEFT YOU FOR DEAD!

I'M... ALIVE... BUT I THINK IT'S TIME TO MOVE ON FROM HERE...

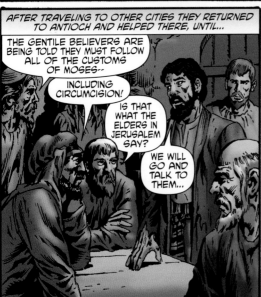

AFTER TRAVELING TO OTHER CITIES THEY RETURNED TO ANTIOCH AND HELPED THERE, UNTIL...

THE GENTILE BELIEVERS ARE BEING TOLD THEY MUST FOLLOW ALL OF THE CUSTOMS OF MOSES--

INCLUDING CIRCUMCISION!

IS THAT WHAT THE ELDERS IN JERUSALEM SAY?

WE WILL GO AND TALK TO THEM...

JERUSALEM.

--THE GENTILES ARE HEARING CHRIST'S MESSAGE AND FOLLOWING IT!

BUT CHRIST'S MESSAGE DID NOT REQUIRE CIRCUMCISION!

DON'T PUT A WALL IN THEIR WAY THAT OUR LORD DID NOT INTEND!

BUT ARE WE JUST ABANDONING THE LAW OF MOSES, THEN?

THAT'S NOT WHAT PAUL IS SAYING.

GOD HAS GIVEN HIS HOLY SPIRIT TO THE GENTILES.

NOT BECAUSE OF CIRCUMCISION, BUT BECAUSE OF FAITH!

I AGREE! WE SHOULD NOT MAKE IT DIFFICULT!

WE SHOULD WRITE A LETTER WITH GUIDELINES TO THE GENTILES...

THIS IS GOING TO TAKE A WHILE.

THAT'S GOOD. IT MEANS THEY ARE TRULY THINKING ABOUT IT.

44

AFTER MUCH DISCUSSION AND DEBATE.

TAKE THIS TO THE PEOPLE IN ANTIOCH.

IT CONFIRMS WE WILL NOT REQUIRE CIRCUMCISION OF GENTILES.

AND IT ASKS GENTILES TO FOLLOW MORAL GUIDELINES.

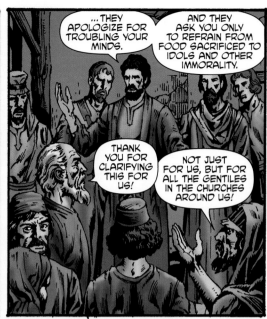

...THEY APOLOGIZE FOR TROUBLING YOUR MINDS.

AND THEY ASK YOU ONLY TO REFRAIN FROM FOOD SACRIFICED TO IDOLS AND OTHER IMMORALITY.

THANK YOU FOR CLARIFYING THIS FOR US!

NOT JUST FOR US, BUT FOR ALL THE GENTILES IN THE CHURCHES AROUND US!

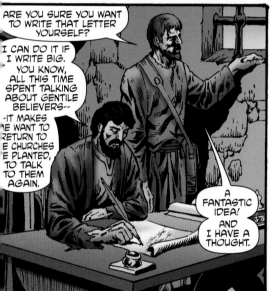

ARE YOU SURE YOU WANT TO WRITE THAT LETTER YOURSELF?

I CAN DO IT IF I WRITE BIG. YOU KNOW, ALL THIS TIME SPENT TALKING ABOUT GENTILE BELIEVERS--

--IT MAKES ME WANT TO RETURN TO THE CHURCHES WE PLANTED, TO TALK TO THEM AGAIN.

A FANTASTIC IDEA! AND I HAVE A THOUGHT.

I WOULD LIKE TO HAVE JOHN MARK JOIN US AGAIN.

WHAT? NO!

HE'S A DIFFERENT MAN NOW! WE SHOULD GIVE HIM A SECOND CHANCE!

HE DESERTED US ONCE! WHAT IF HE DOES IT AGAIN? THOSE JOURNEYS ARE TOO DANGEROUS AND IMPORTANT TO RISK THAT!

PAUL... YOU OF ALL PEOPLE UNDERSTAND WHAT IT MEANS TO CHANGE! TO BECOME SOMEONE NEW! TO RECEIVE A SECOND CHANCE!

45

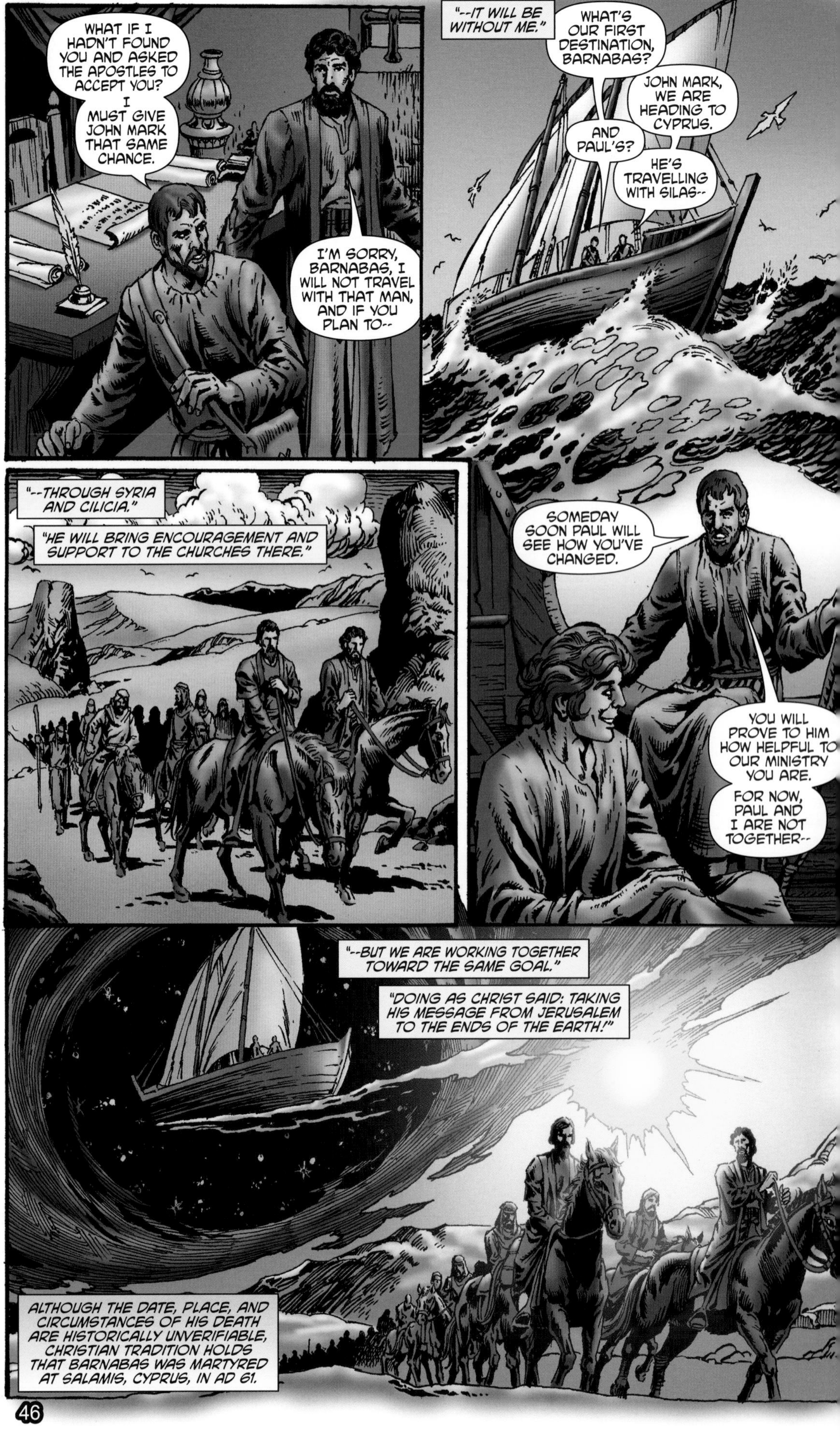

WHAT IF I HADN'T FOUND YOU AND ASKED THE APOSTLES TO ACCEPT YOU?
I MUST GIVE JOHN MARK THAT SAME CHANCE.
I'M SORRY, BARNABAS, I WILL NOT TRAVEL WITH THAT MAN, AND IF YOU PLAN TO--
"--IT WILL BE WITHOUT ME."
WHAT'S OUR FIRST DESTINATION, BARNABAS?
JOHN MARK, WE ARE HEADING TO CYPRUS.
AND PAUL'S?
HE'S TRAVELLING WITH SILAS--
"--THROUGH SYRIA AND CILICIA."
"HE WILL BRING ENCOURAGEMENT AND SUPPORT TO THE CHURCHES THERE."
SOMEDAY SOON PAUL WILL SEE HOW YOU'VE CHANGED.
YOU WILL PROVE TO HIM HOW HELPFUL TO OUR MINISTRY YOU ARE.
FOR NOW, PAUL AND I ARE NOT TOGETHER--
"--BUT WE ARE WORKING TOGETHER TOWARD THE SAME GOAL."
"DOING AS CHRIST SAID: TAKING HIS MESSAGE FROM JERUSALEM TO THE ENDS OF THE EARTH!"
ALTHOUGH THE DATE, PLACE, AND CIRCUMSTANCES OF HIS DEATH ARE HISTORICALLY UNVERIFIABLE, CHRISTIAN TRADITION HOLDS THAT BARNABAS WAS MARTYRED AT SALAMIS, CYPRUS, IN AD 61.

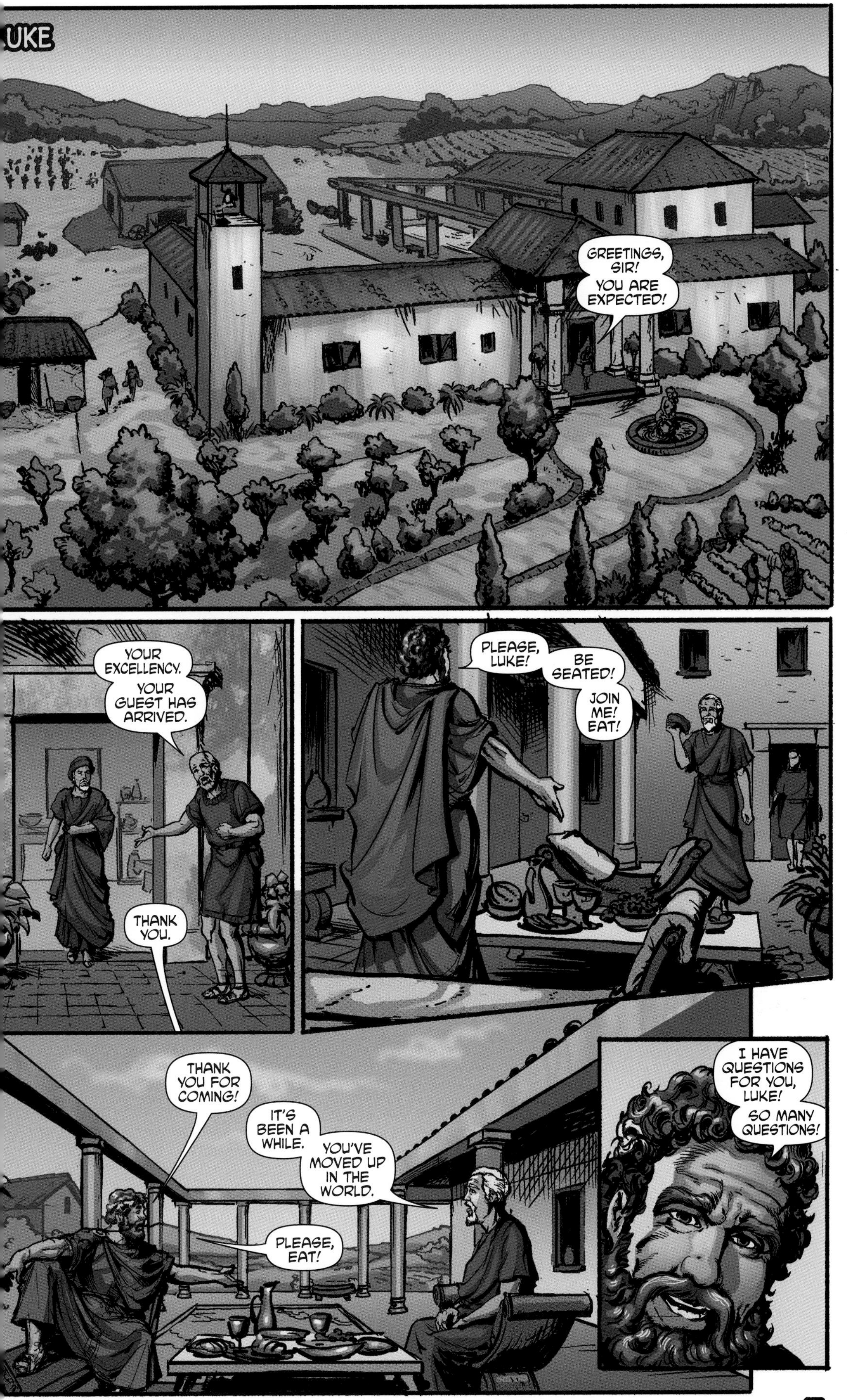
GREETINGS, SIR!
YOU ARE EXPECTED!
YOUR EXCELLENCY.
YOUR GUEST HAS ARRIVED.
THANK YOU.
PLEASE, LUKE!
BE SEATED!
JOIN ME! EAT!
THANK YOU FOR COMING!
IT'S BEEN A WHILE.
YOU'VE MOVED UP IN THE WORLD.
PLEASE, EAT!
I HAVE QUESTIONS FOR YOU, LUKE!
SO MANY QUESTIONS!

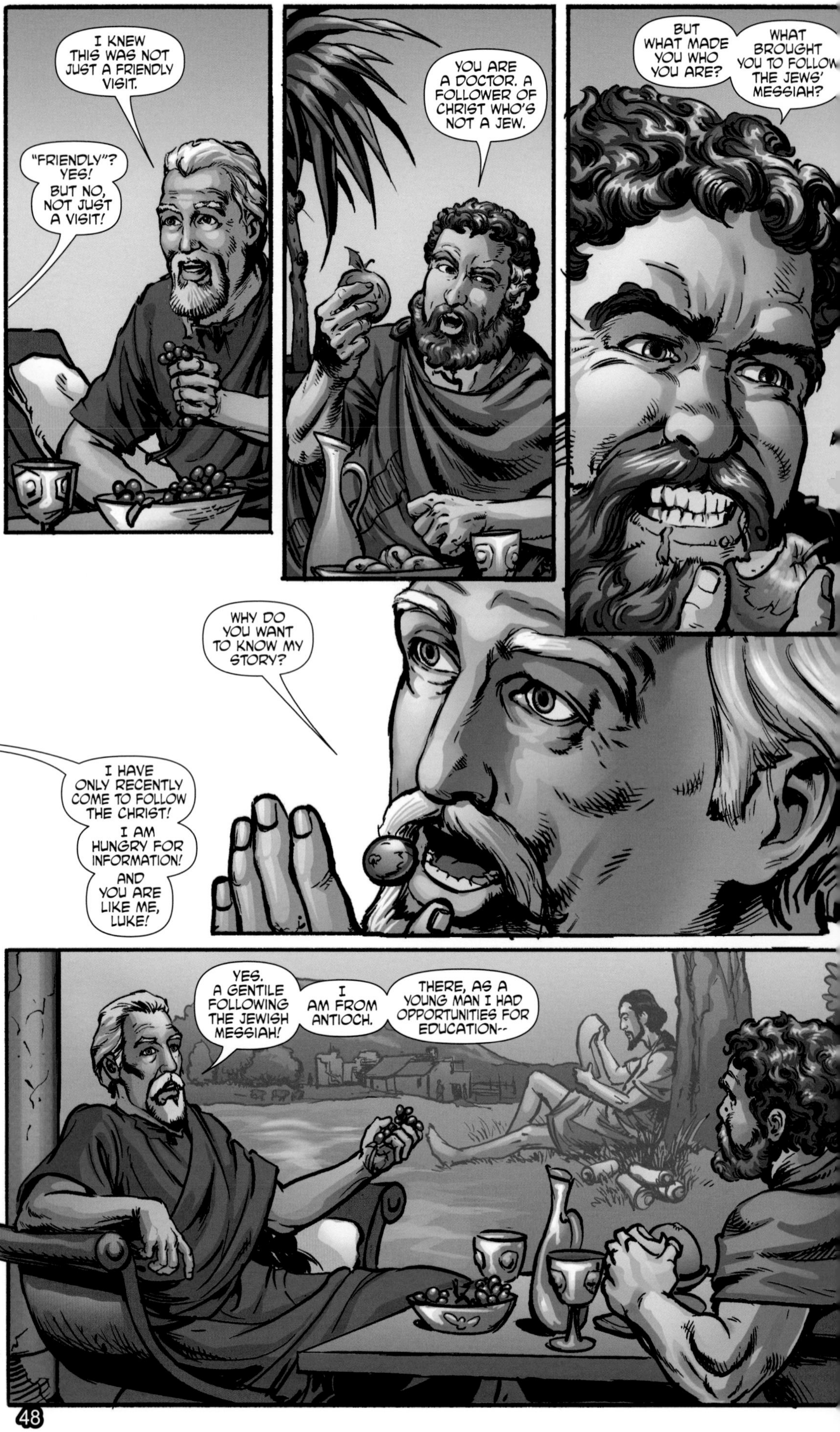
I KNEW THIS WAS NOT JUST A FRIENDLY VISIT.
"FRIENDLY"? YES!
BUT NO, NOT JUST A VISIT!
YOU ARE A DOCTOR. A FOLLOWER OF CHRIST WHO'S NOT A JEW.
BUT WHAT MADE YOU WHO YOU ARE?
WHAT BROUGHT YOU TO FOLLOW THE JEWS' MESSIAH?
WHY DO YOU WANT TO KNOW MY STORY?
I HAVE ONLY RECENTLY COME TO FOLLOW THE CHRIST!
I AM HUNGRY FOR INFORMATION!
AND YOU ARE LIKE ME, LUKE!
YES. A GENTILE FOLLOWING THE JEWISH MESSIAH!
I AM FROM ANTIOCH.
THERE, AS A YOUNG MAN I HAD OPPORTUNITIES FOR EDUCATION--

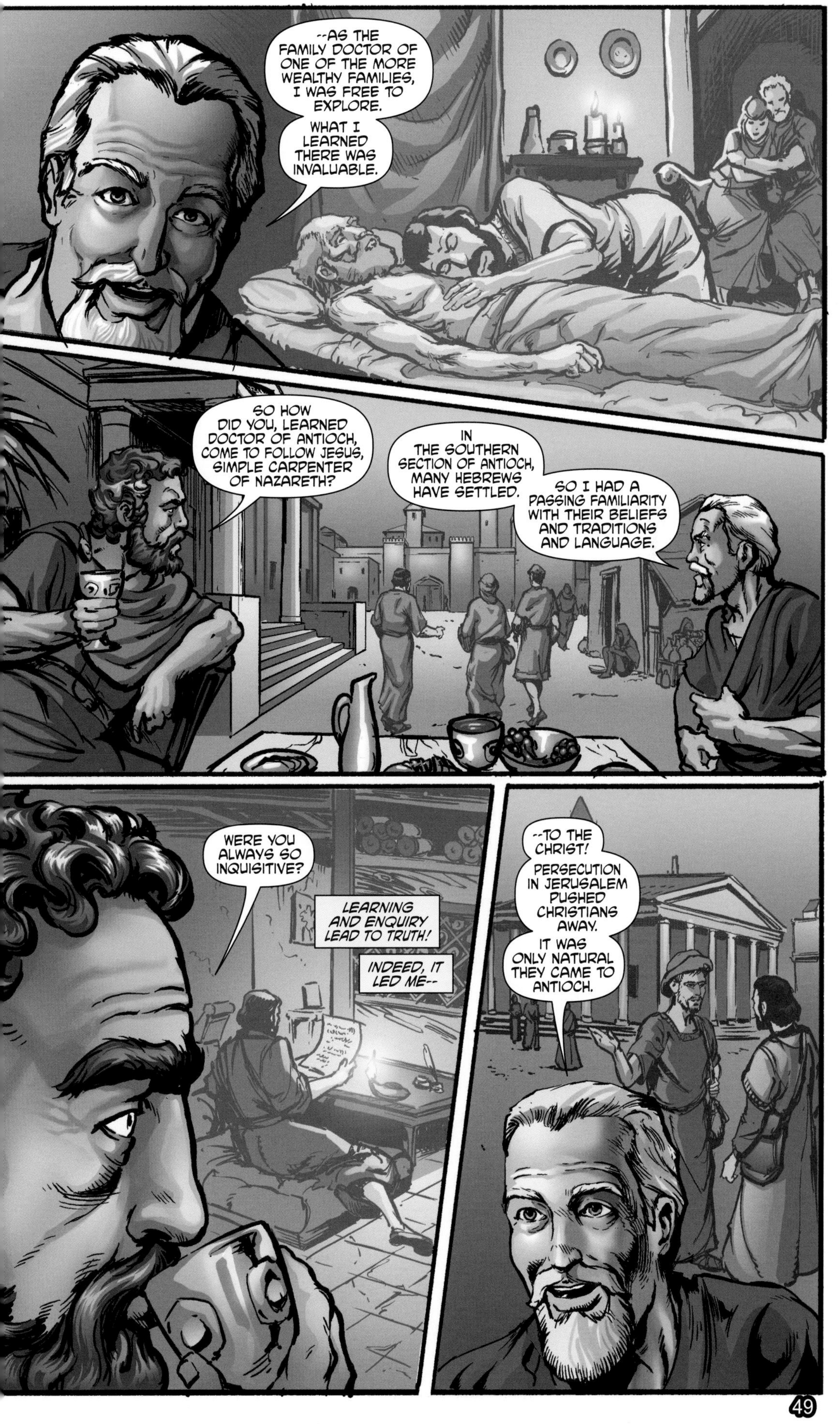
--AS THE FAMILY DOCTOR OF ONE OF THE MORE WEALTHY FAMILIES, I WAS FREE TO EXPLORE.
WHAT I LEARNED THERE WAS INVALUABLE.
SO HOW DID YOU, LEARNED DOCTOR OF ANTIOCH, COME TO FOLLOW JESUS, SIMPLE CARPENTER OF NAZARETH?
IN THE SOUTHERN SECTION OF ANTIOCH, MANY HEBREWS HAVE SETTLED.
SO I HAD A PASSING FAMILIARITY WITH THEIR BELIEFS AND TRADITIONS AND LANGUAGE.
WERE YOU ALWAYS SO INQUISITIVE?
LEARNING AND ENQUIRY LEAD TO TRUTH!
INDEED, IT LED ME--
--TO THE CHRIST!
PERSECUTION IN JERUSALEM PUSHED CHRISTIANS AWAY.
IT WAS ONLY NATURAL THEY CAME TO ANTIOCH.

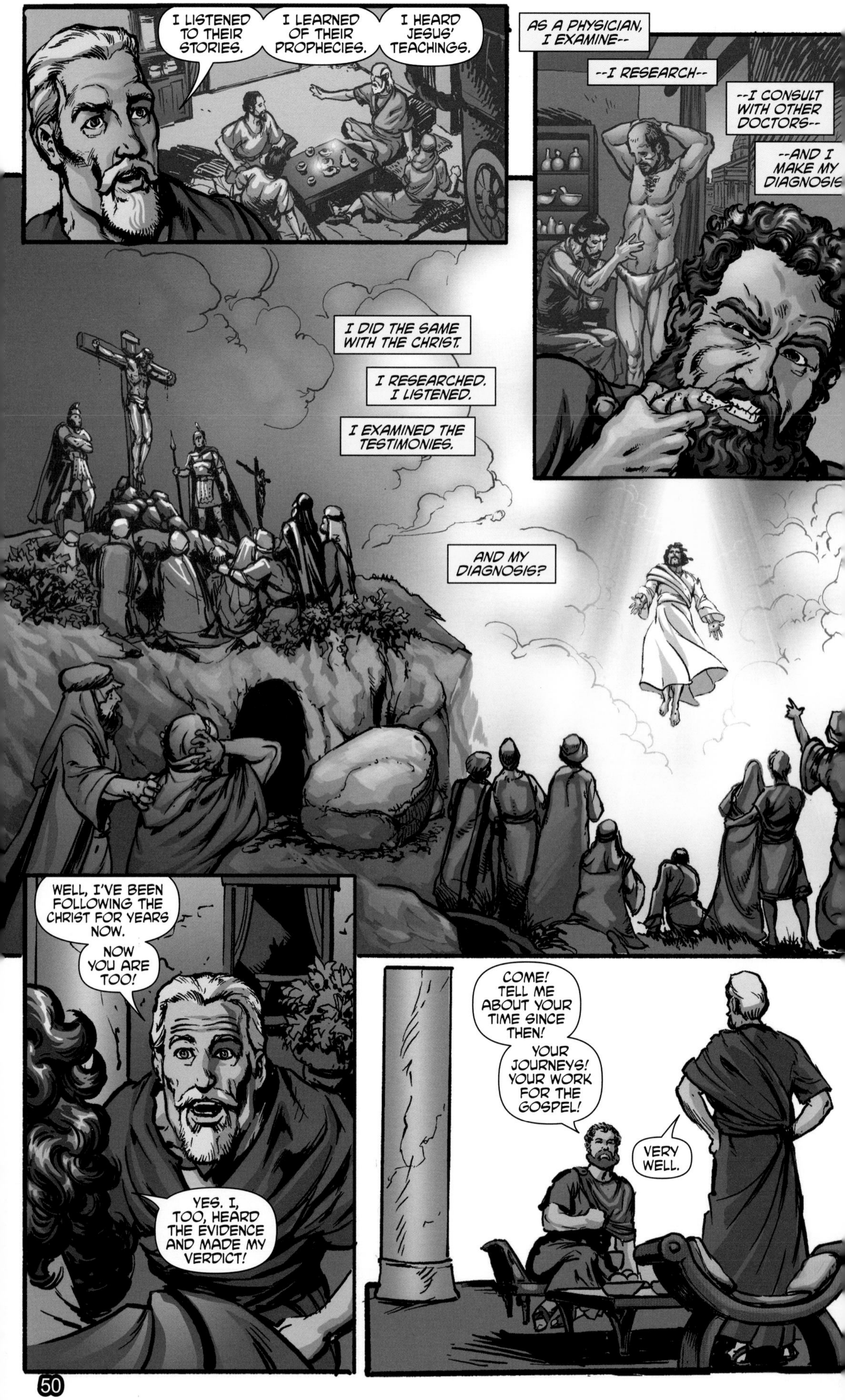

I LISTENED TO THEIR STORIES.
I LEARNED OF THEIR PROPHECIES.
I HEARD JESUS' TEACHINGS.
AS A PHYSICIAN, I EXAMINE--
--I RESEARCH--
--I CONSULT WITH OTHER DOCTORS--
--AND I MAKE MY DIAGNOSIS
I DID THE SAME WITH THE CHRIST.
I RESEARCHED. I LISTENED.
I EXAMINED THE TESTIMONIES.
AND MY DIAGNOSIS?
WELL, I'VE BEEN FOLLOWING THE CHRIST FOR YEARS NOW.
NOW YOU ARE TOO!
YES. I, TOO, HEARD THE EVIDENCE AND MADE MY VERDICT!
COME! TELL ME ABOUT YOUR TIME SINCE THEN!
YOUR JOURNEYS! YOUR WORK FOR THE GOSPEL!
VERY WELL.

I STAYED IN ANTIOCH FOR A WHILE WITH THE BELIEVERS THERE.

EVENTUALLY, I CHOSE TO LEAVE AND BE A MISSIONARY.

AS A LEARNED GREEK WHO ALSO KNEW THE WAYS OF THE JEWS-- --YOU WOULD BE QUITE VALUABLE!

INDEED!

WHAT JESUS DID WAS FOR EVERYONE, JEWS AND GENTILES ALIKE!

BUT IF YOU UNDERSTAND WHAT GOD REVEALED TO THE JEWS IN TIME PAST--

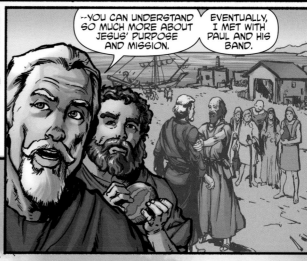

--YOU CAN UNDERSTAND SO MUCH MORE ABOUT JESUS' PURPOSE AND MISSION.

EVENTUALLY, I MET WITH PAUL AND HIS BAND.

AND SOON AFTER THAT, PAUL HAD A VISION.

A MAN FROM MACEDONIA, WHO SAID:

"COME TO MACEDONIA! HELP US!"

THAT WAS WHEN THINGS REALLY STARTED TO HAPPEN.

I HAD OPPORTUNITY TO TRAVEL WITH PAUL.

IT WAS NEVER UNEVENTFUL.

YES? YES? TELL ME MORE!

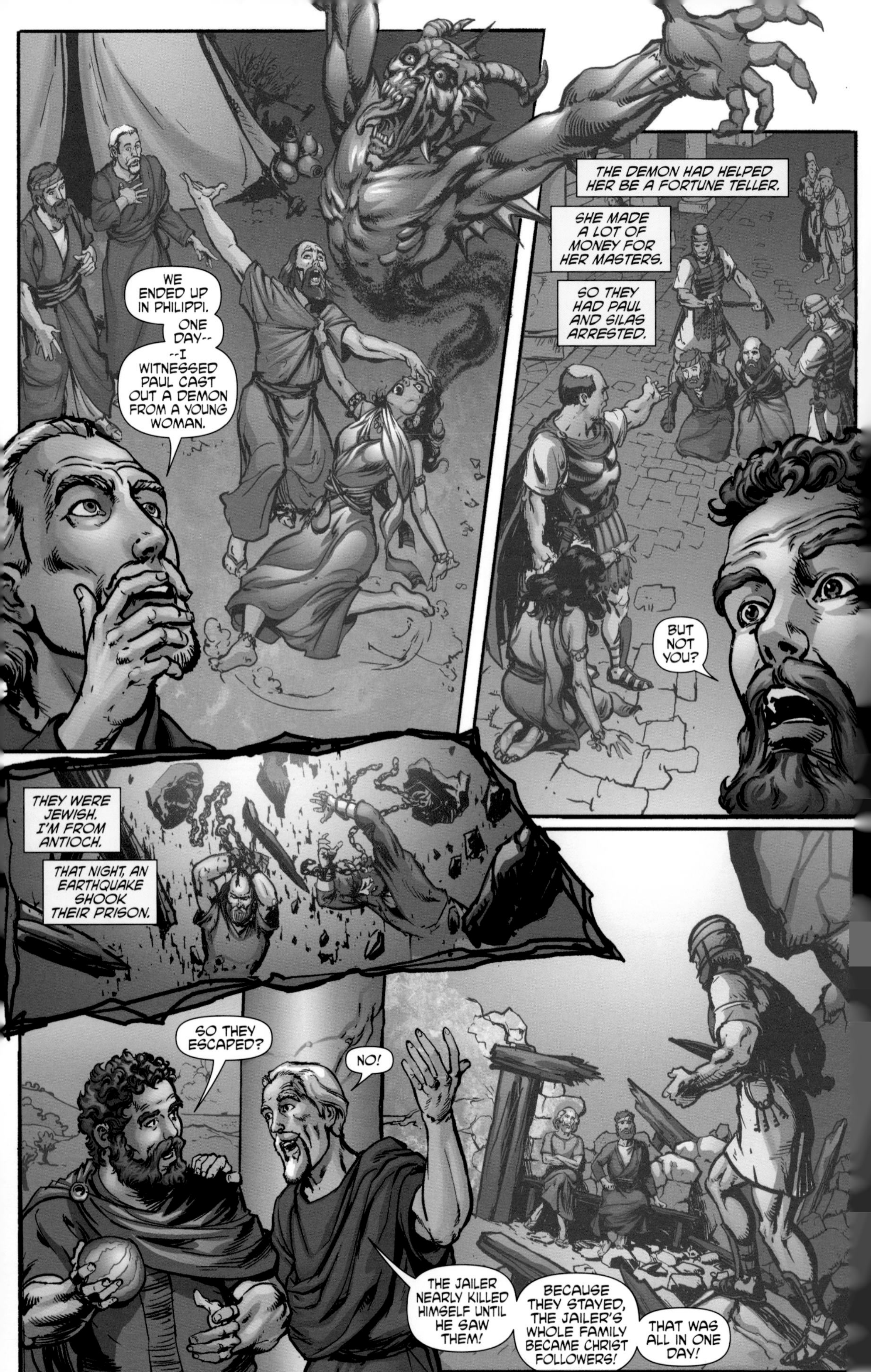

WE ENDED UP IN PHILIPPI.
ONE DAY--
--I WITNESSED PAUL CAST OUT A DEMON FROM A YOUNG WOMAN.
THE DEMON HAD HELPED HER BE A FORTUNE TELLER.
SHE MADE A LOT OF MONEY FOR HER MASTERS.
SO THEY HAD PAUL AND SILAS ARRESTED.
BUT NOT YOU?
THEY WERE JEWISH. I'M FROM ANTIOCH.
THAT NIGHT, AN EARTHQUAKE SHOOK THEIR PRISON.
SO THEY ESCAPED?
NO!
THE JAILER NEARLY KILLED HIMSELF UNTIL HE SAW THEM!
BECAUSE THEY STAYED, THE JAILER'S WHOLE FAMILY BECAME CHRIST FOLLOWERS!
THAT WAS ALL IN ONE DAY!

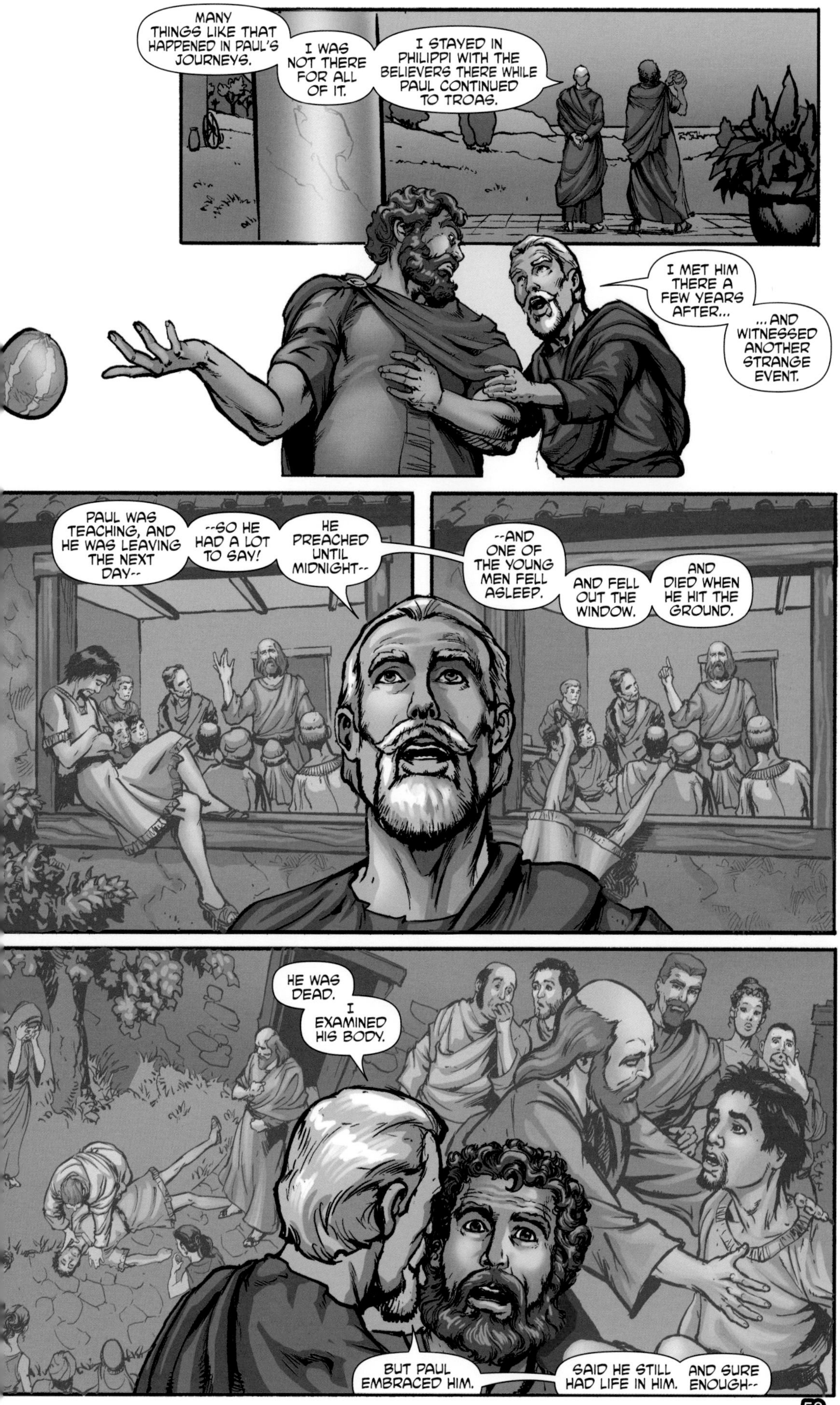
MANY THINGS LIKE THAT HAPPENED IN PAUL'S JOURNEYS.
I WAS NOT THERE FOR ALL OF IT.
I STAYED IN PHILIPPI WITH THE BELIEVERS THERE WHILE PAUL CONTINUED TO TROAS.
I MET HIM THERE A FEW YEARS AFTER...
...AND WITNESSED ANOTHER STRANGE EVENT.
PAUL WAS TEACHING, AND HE WAS LEAVING THE NEXT DAY--
--SO HE HAD A LOT TO SAY!
HE PREACHED UNTIL MIDNIGHT--
--AND ONE OF THE YOUNG MEN FELL ASLEEP.
AND FELL OUT THE WINDOW.
AND DIED WHEN HE HIT THE GROUND.
HE WAS DEAD.
I EXAMINED HIS BODY.
BUT PAUL EMBRACED HIM.
SAID HE STILL HAD LIFE IN HIM.
AND SURE ENOUGH--

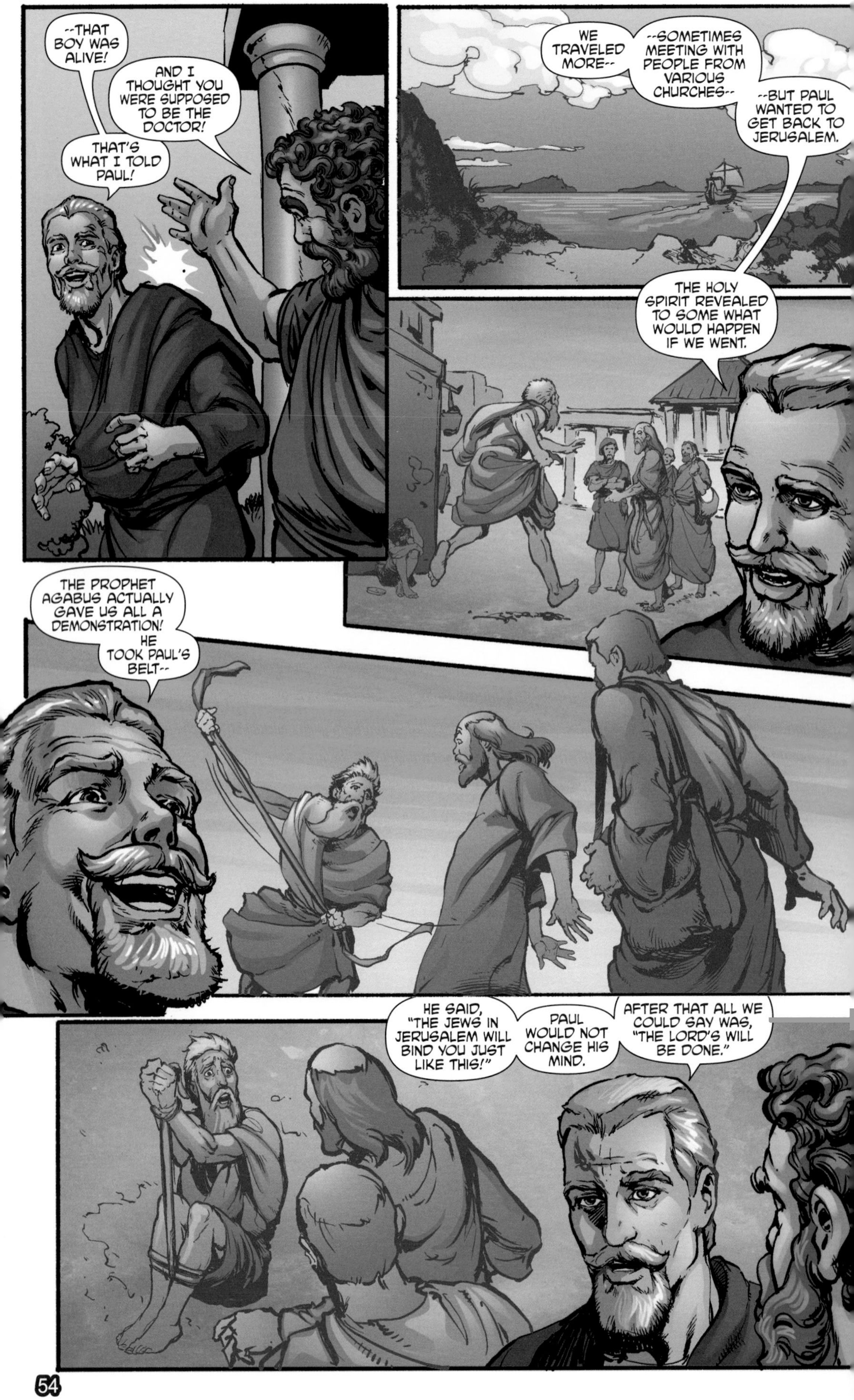
--THAT BOY WAS ALIVE!
AND I THOUGHT YOU WERE SUPPOSED TO BE THE DOCTOR!
THAT'S WHAT I TOLD PAUL!
WE TRAVELED MORE--
--SOMETIMES MEETING WITH PEOPLE FROM VARIOUS CHURCHES--
--BUT PAUL WANTED TO GET BACK TO JERUSALEM.
THE HOLY SPIRIT REVEALED TO SOME WHAT WOULD HAPPEN IF WE WENT.
THE PROPHET AGABUS ACTUALLY GAVE US ALL A DEMONSTRATION!
HE TOOK PAUL'S BELT--
HE SAID, "THE JEWS IN JERUSALEM WILL BIND YOU JUST LIKE THIS!"
PAUL WOULD NOT CHANGE HIS MIND.
AFTER THAT ALL WE COULD SAY WAS, "THE LORD'S WILL BE DONE."

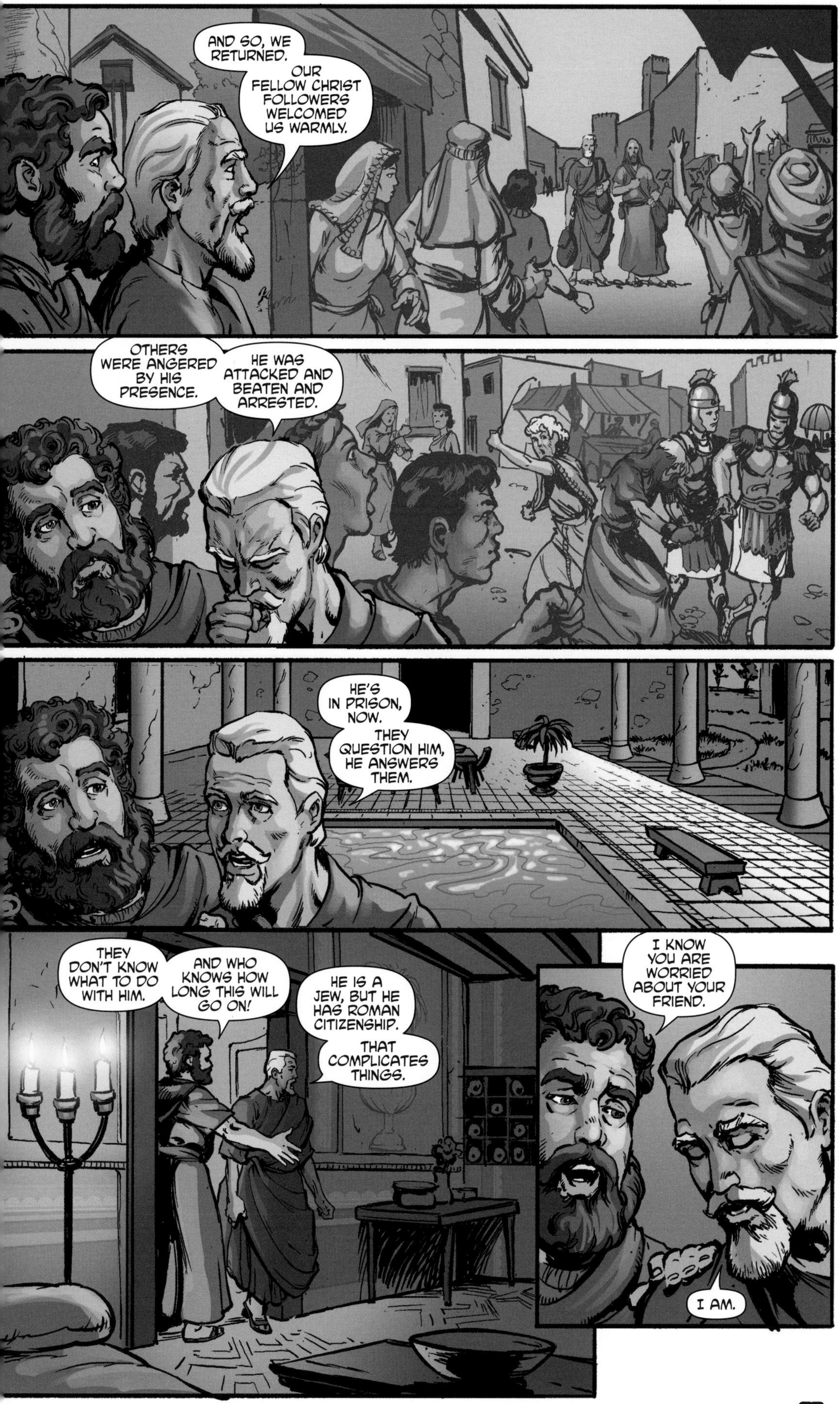

AND SO, WE RETURNED.
OUR FELLOW CHRIST FOLLOWERS WELCOMED US WARMLY.
OTHERS WERE ANGERED BY HIS PRESENCE.
HE WAS ATTACKED AND BEATEN AND ARRESTED.
HE'S IN PRISON, NOW.
THEY QUESTION HIM, HE ANSWERS THEM.
THEY DON'T KNOW WHAT TO DO WITH HIM.
AND WHO KNOWS HOW LONG THIS WILL GO ON!
HE IS A JEW, BUT HE HAS ROMAN CITIZENSHIP.
THAT COMPLICATES THINGS.
I KNOW YOU ARE WORRIED ABOUT YOUR FRIEND.
I AM.

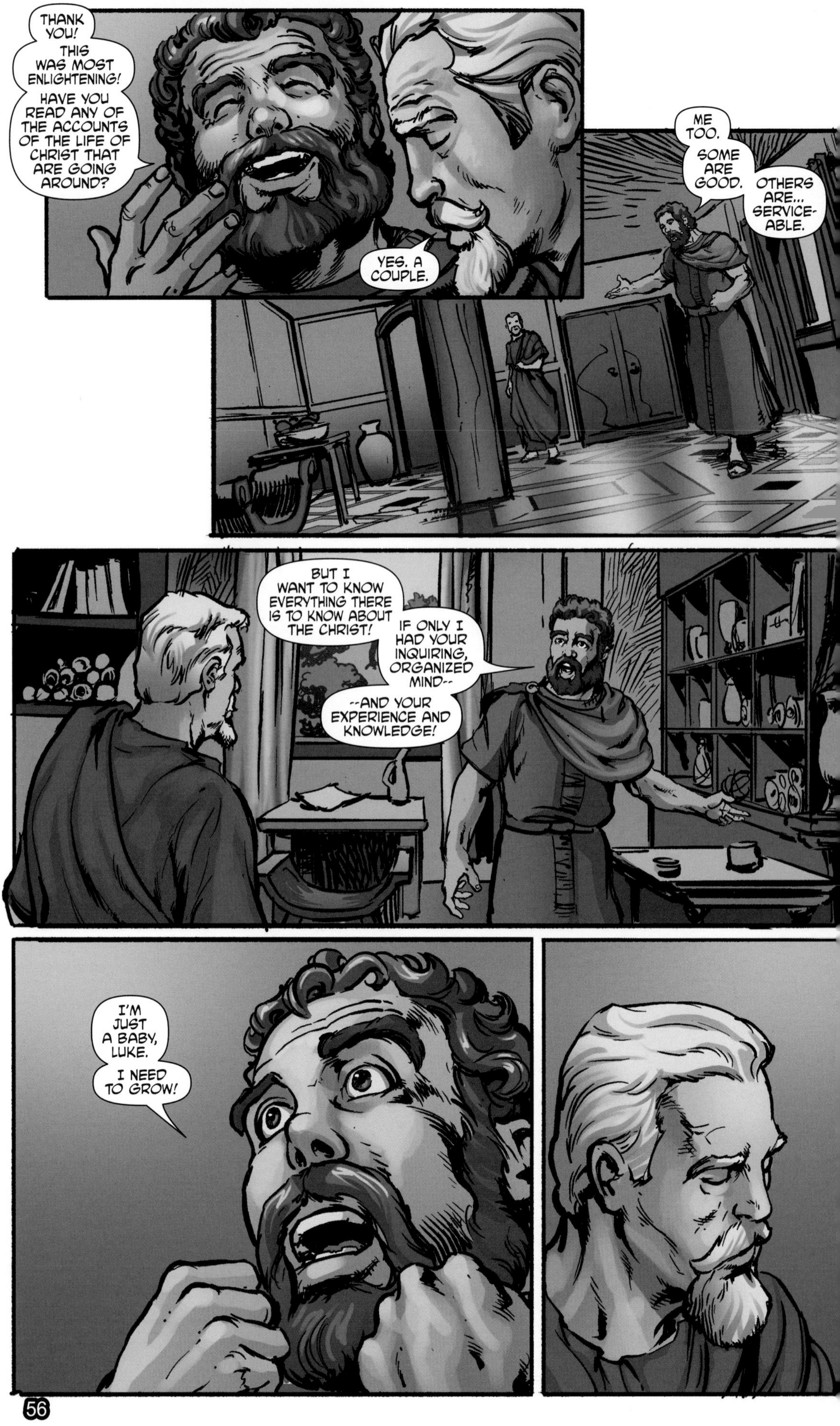
THANK YOU!
THIS WAS MOST ENLIGHTENING!
HAVE YOU READ ANY OF THE ACCOUNTS OF THE LIFE OF CHRIST THAT ARE GOING AROUND?
YES. A COUPLE.
ME TOO.
SOME ARE GOOD.
OTHERS ARE... SERVICE-ABLE.
BUT I WANT TO KNOW EVERYTHING THERE IS TO KNOW ABOUT THE CHRIST!
IF ONLY I HAD YOUR INQUIRING, ORGANIZED MIND--
--AND YOUR EXPERIENCE AND KNOWLEDGE!
I'M JUST A BABY, LUKE.
I NEED TO GROW!

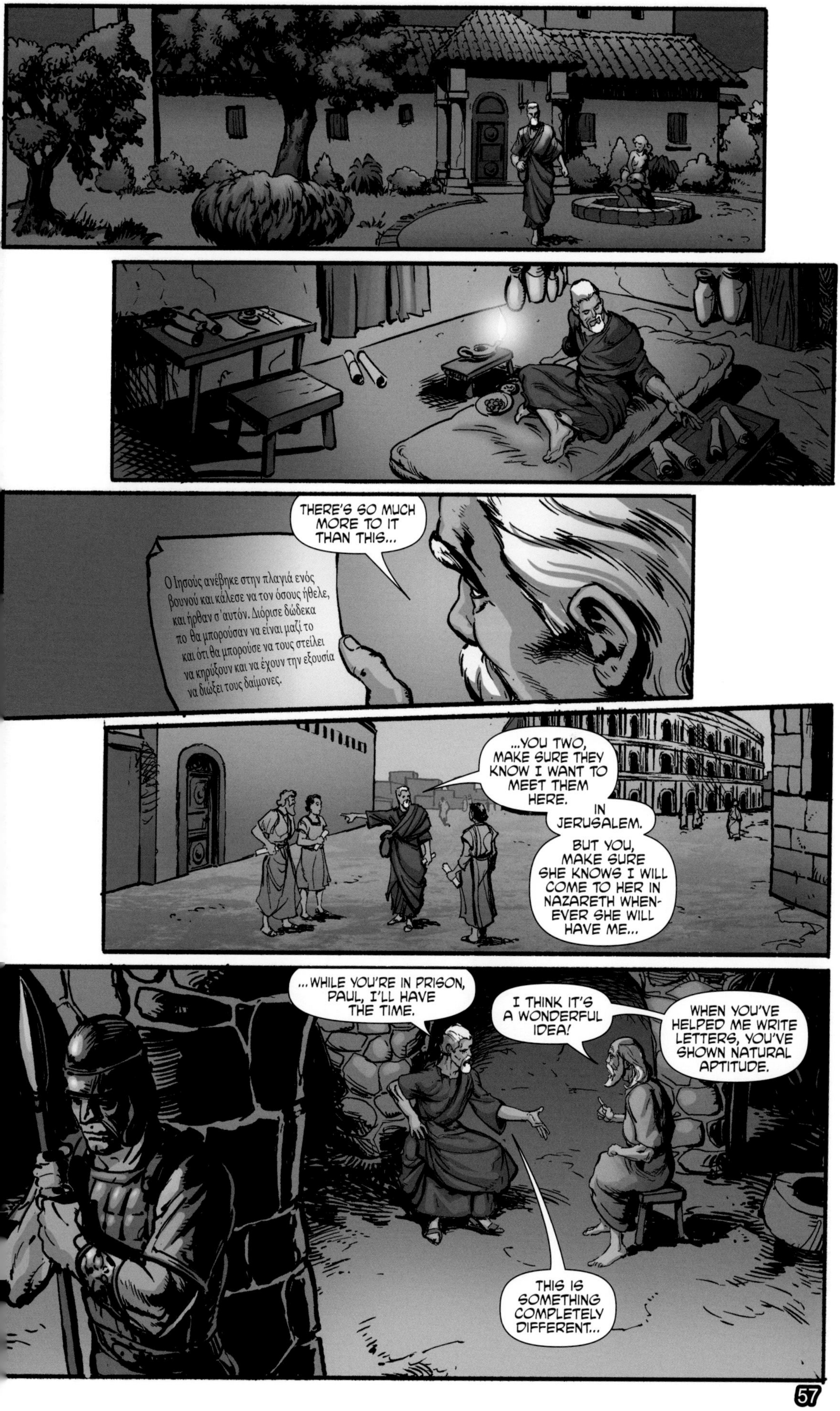

THERE'S SO MUCH MORE TO IT THAN THIS...
Ο Ιησούς ανέβηκε στην πλαγιά ενός
βουνού και κάλεσε να τον όσους ήθελε,
και ήρθαν σ΄αυτόν. Διόρισε δώδεκα
πο θα μπορούσαν να είναι μαζί το
και ότι θα μπορούσε να τους στείλει
να κηρύξουν και να έχουν την εξουσία
να διώξει τους δαίμονες.
...YOU TWO, MAKE SURE THEY KNOW I WANT TO MEET THEM HERE.
IN JERUSALEM.
BUT YOU, MAKE SURE SHE KNOWS I WILL COME TO HER IN NAZARETH WHEN-EVER SHE WILL HAVE ME...
...WHILE YOU'RE IN PRISON, PAUL, I'LL HAVE THE TIME.
I THINK IT'S A WONDERFUL IDEA!
WHEN YOU'VE HELPED ME WRITE LETTERS, YOU'VE SHOWN NATURAL APTITUDE.
THIS IS SOMETHING COMPLETELY DIFFERENT...

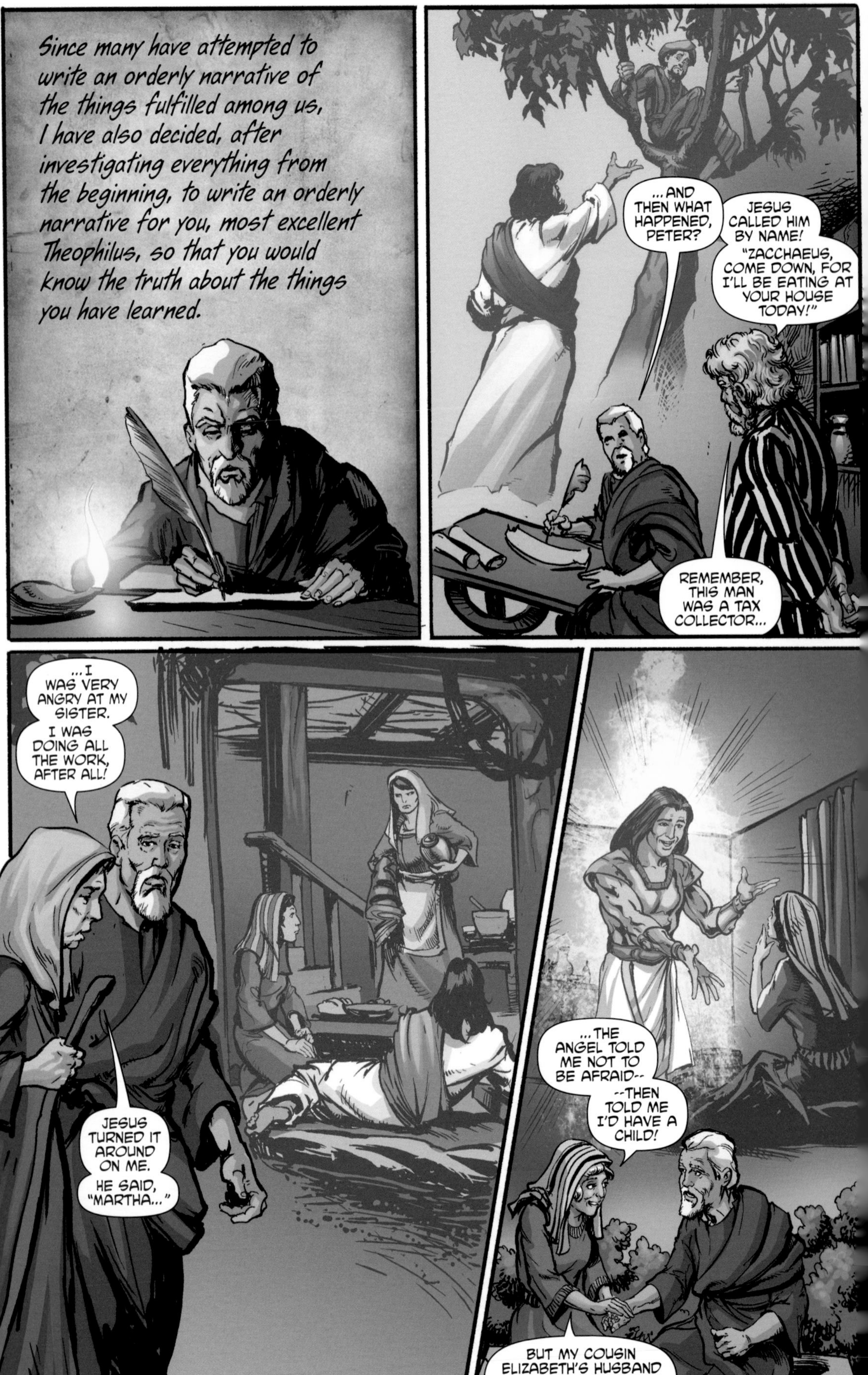
Since many have attempted to write an orderly narrative of the things fulfilled among us, I have also decided, after investigating everything from the beginning, to write an orderly narrative for you, most excellent Theophilus, so that you would know the truth about the things you have learned.
...AND THEN WHAT HAPPENED, PETER?
JESUS CALLED HIM BY NAME! "ZACCHAEUS, COME DOWN, FOR I'LL BE EATING AT YOUR HOUSE TODAY!"
REMEMBER, THIS MAN WAS A TAX COLLECTOR...
...I WAS VERY ANGRY AT MY SISTER. I WAS DOING ALL THE WORK, AFTER ALL!
JESUS TURNED IT AROUND ON ME. HE SAID, "MARTHA..."
...THE ANGEL TOLD ME NOT TO BE AFRAID--
--THEN TOLD ME I'D HAVE A CHILD!
BUT MY COUSIN ELIZABETH'S HUSBAND ALSO HAD AN ANGEL COME WITH A MESSAGE...

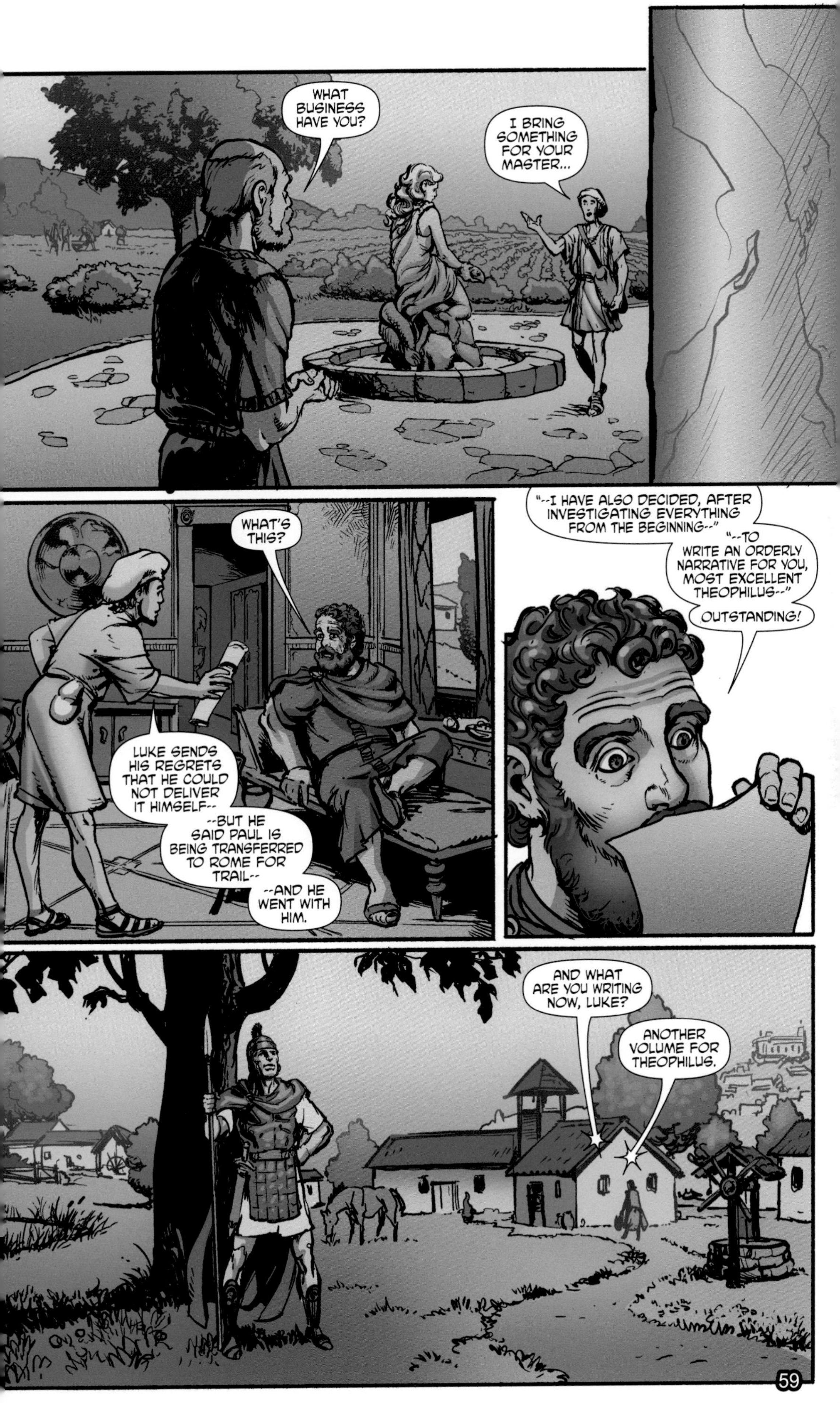
WHAT BUSINESS HAVE YOU?
I BRING SOMETHING FOR YOUR MASTER...
WHAT'S THIS?
LUKE SENDS HIS REGRETS THAT HE COULD NOT DELIVER IT HIMSELF--
--BUT HE SAID PAUL IS BEING TRANSFERRED TO ROME FOR TRAIL--
--AND HE WENT WITH HIM.
"--I HAVE ALSO DECIDED, AFTER INVESTIGATING EVERYTHING FROM THE BEGINNING--"
"--TO WRITE AN ORDERLY NARRATIVE FOR YOU, MOST EXCELLENT THEOPHILUS--"
OUTSTANDING!
AND WHAT ARE YOU WRITING NOW, LUKE?
ANOTHER VOLUME FOR THEOPHILUS.

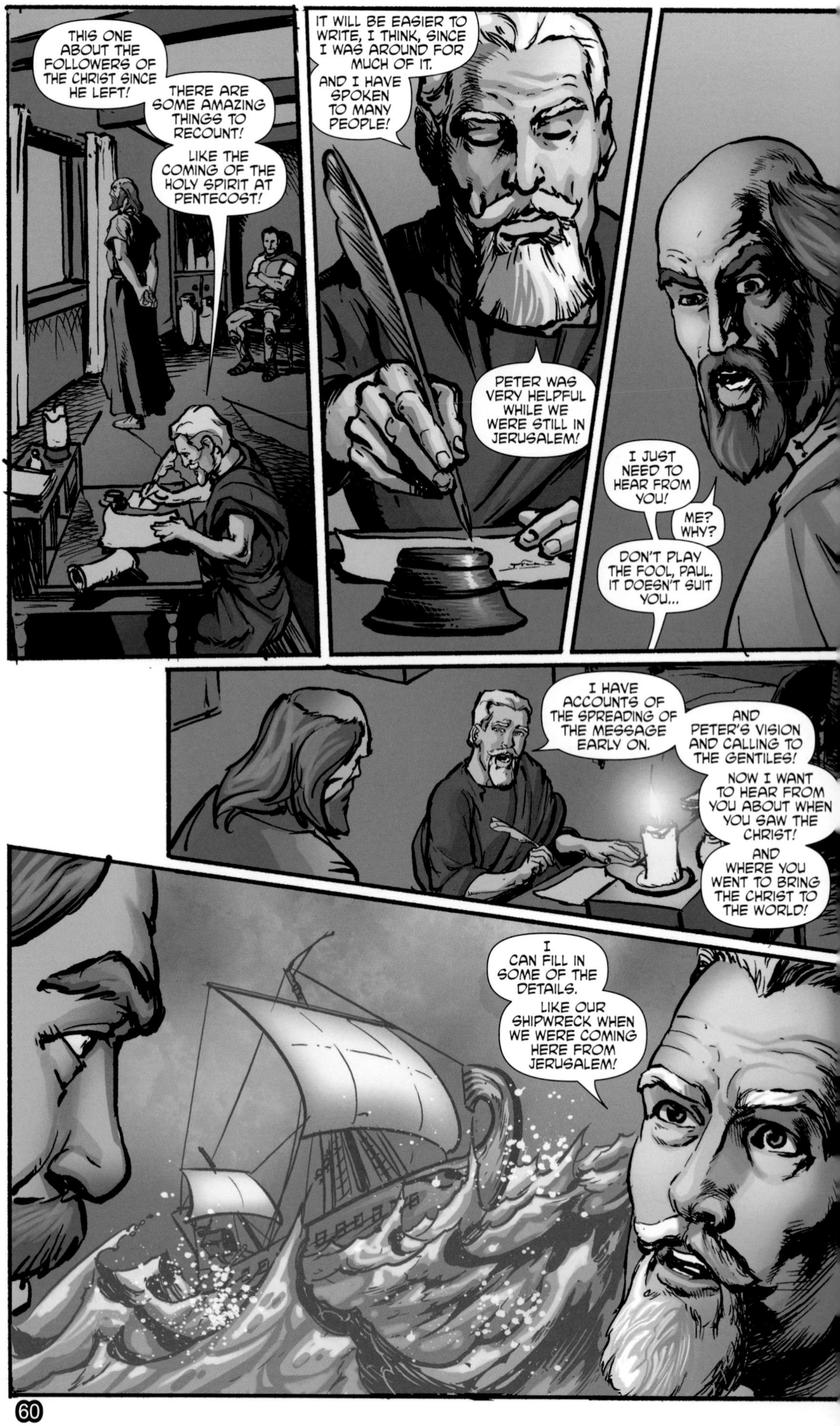

THIS ONE ABOUT THE FOLLOWERS OF THE CHRIST SINCE HE LEFT!
THERE ARE SOME AMAZING THINGS TO RECOUNT!
LIKE THE COMING OF THE HOLY SPIRIT AT PENTECOST!
IT WILL BE EASIER TO WRITE, I THINK, SINCE I WAS AROUND FOR MUCH OF IT.
AND I HAVE SPOKEN TO MANY PEOPLE!
PETER WAS VERY HELPFUL WHILE WE WERE STILL IN JERUSALEM!
I JUST NEED TO HEAR FROM YOU!
ME? WHY?
DON'T PLAY THE FOOL, PAUL. IT DOESN'T SUIT YOU...
I HAVE ACCOUNTS OF THE SPREADING OF THE MESSAGE EARLY ON.
AND PETER'S VISION AND CALLING TO THE GENTILES!
NOW I WANT TO HEAR FROM YOU ABOUT WHEN YOU SAW THE CHRIST!
AND WHERE YOU WENT TO BRING THE CHRIST TO THE WORLD!
I CAN FILL IN SOME OF THE DETAILS.
LIKE OUR SHIPWRECK WHEN WE WERE COMING HERE FROM JERUSALEM!

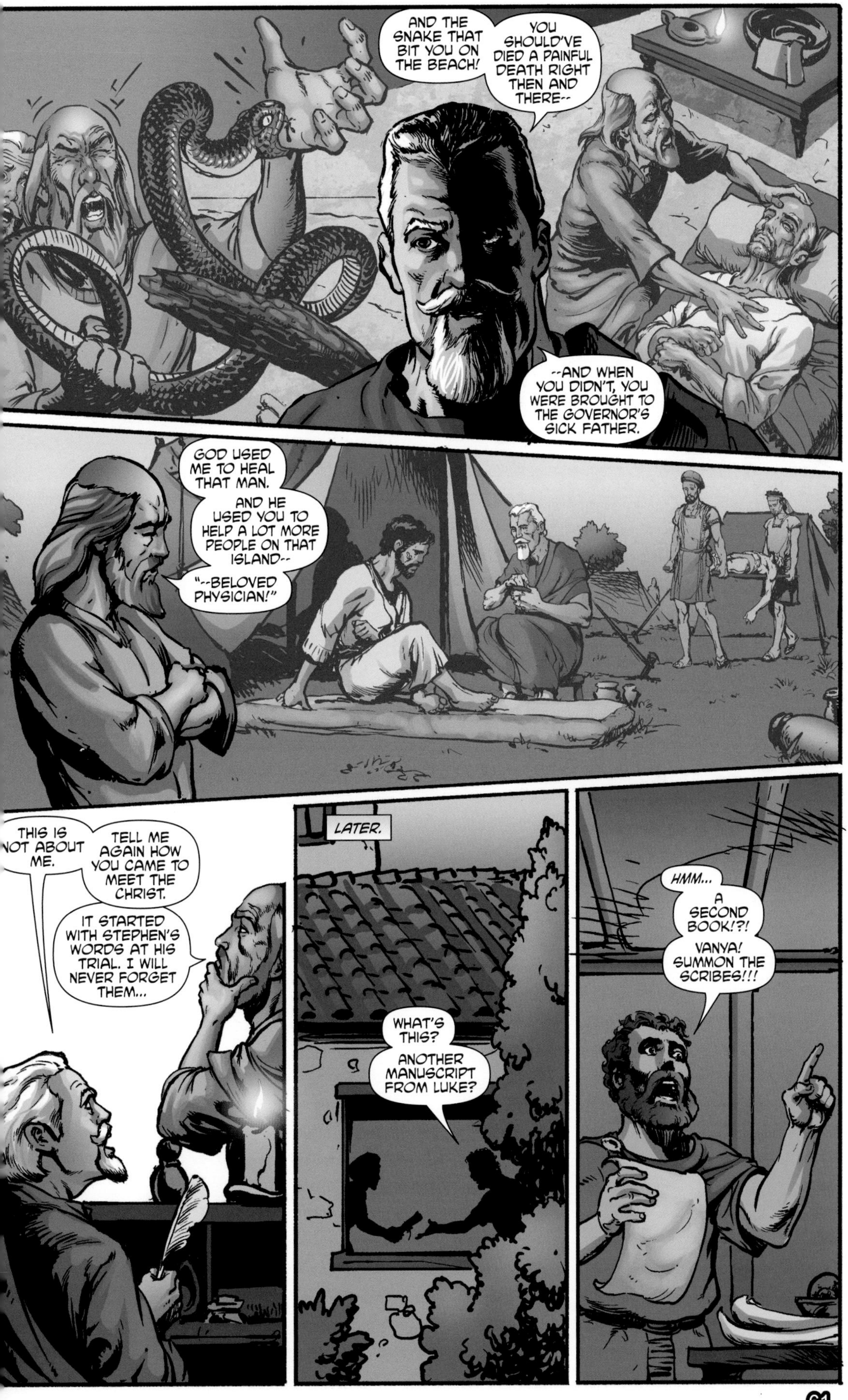
AND THE SNAKE THAT BIT YOU ON THE BEACH!
YOU SHOULD'VE DIED A PAINFUL DEATH RIGHT THEN AND THERE--
--AND WHEN YOU DIDN'T, YOU WERE BROUGHT TO THE GOVERNOR'S SICK FATHER.
GOD USED ME TO HEAL THAT MAN.
AND HE USED YOU TO HELP A LOT MORE PEOPLE ON THAT ISLAND--
"--BELOVED PHYSICIAN!"
THIS IS NOT ABOUT ME.
TELL ME AGAIN HOW YOU CAME TO MEET THE CHRIST.
IT STARTED WITH STEPHEN'S WORDS AT HIS TRIAL. I WILL NEVER FORGET THEM...
LATER.
WHAT'S THIS?
ANOTHER MANUSCRIPT FROM LUKE?
HMM...
A SECOND BOOK!?!
VANYA! SUMMON THE SCRIBES!!!

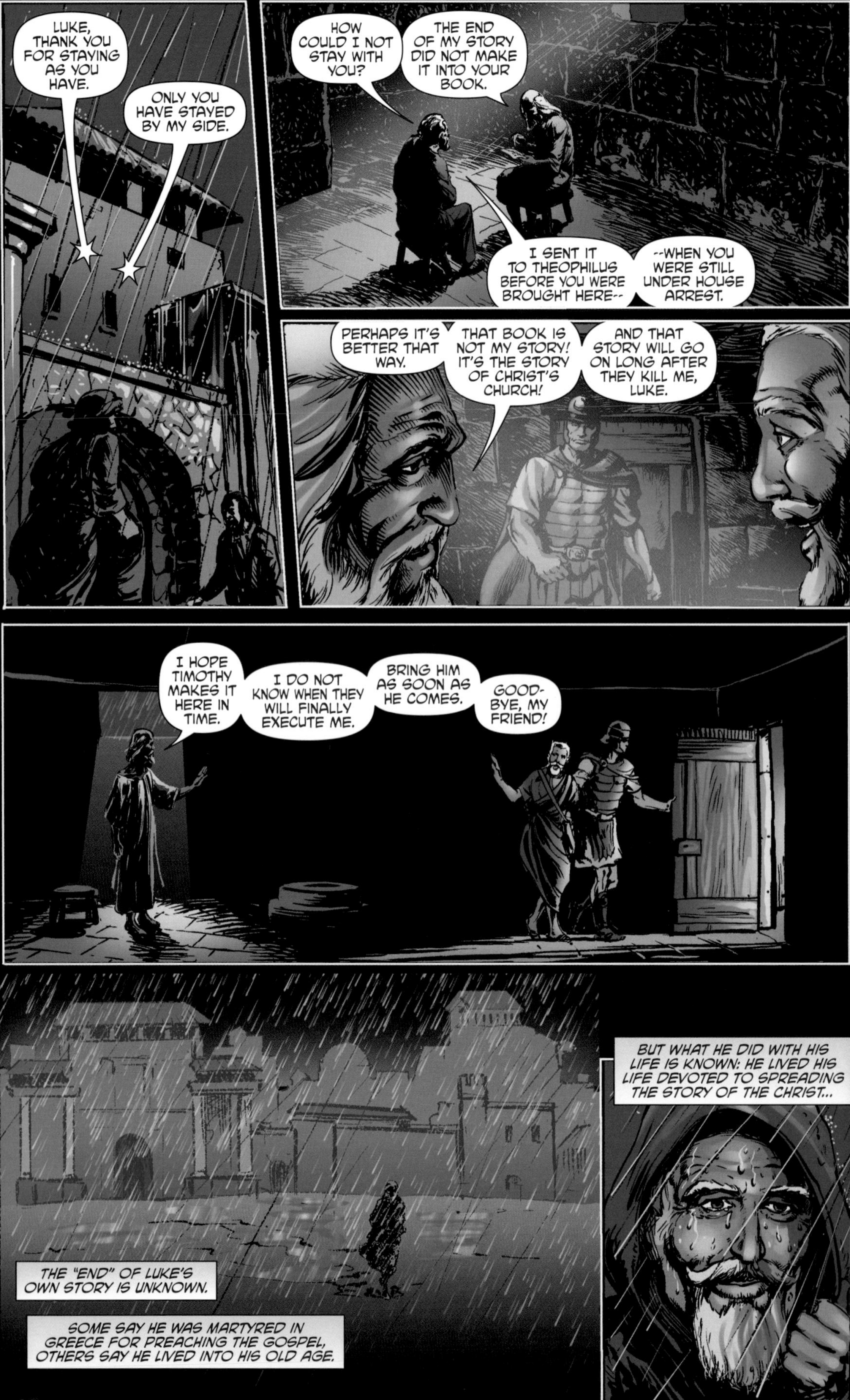

LUKE, THANK YOU FOR STAYING AS YOU HAVE.
ONLY YOU HAVE STAYED BY MY SIDE.
HOW COULD I NOT STAY WITH YOU?
THE END OF MY STORY DID NOT MAKE IT INTO YOUR BOOK.
I SENT IT TO THEOPHILUS BEFORE YOU WERE BROUGHT HERE--
--WHEN YOU WERE STILL UNDER HOUSE ARREST.
PERHAPS IT'S BETTER THAT WAY.
THAT BOOK IS NOT MY STORY! IT'S THE STORY OF CHRIST'S CHURCH!
AND THAT STORY WILL GO ON LONG AFTER THEY KILL ME, LUKE.
I HOPE TIMOTHY MAKES IT HERE IN TIME.
I DO NOT KNOW WHEN THEY WILL FINALLY EXECUTE ME.
BRING HIM AS SOON AS HE COMES.
GOOD-BYE, MY FRIEND!
THE "END" OF LUKE'S OWN STORY IS UNKNOWN.
SOME SAY HE WAS MARTYRED IN GREECE FOR PREACHING THE GOSPEL, OTHERS SAY HE LIVED INTO HIS OLD AGE.
BUT WHAT HE DID WITH HIS LIFE IS KNOWN: HE LIVED HIS LIFE DEVOTED TO SPREADING THE STORY OF THE CHRIST...

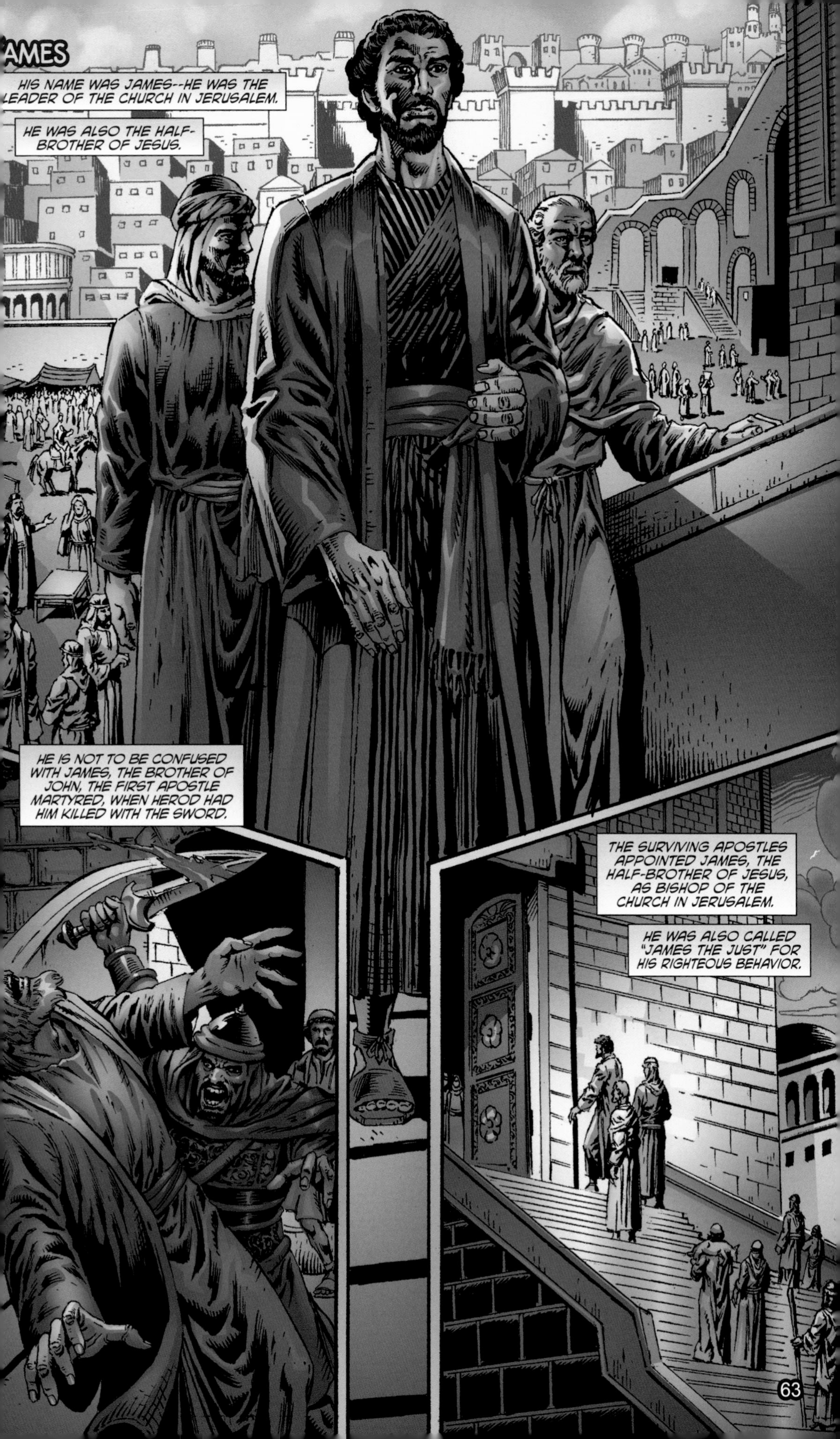
AMES
HIS NAME WAS JAMES--HE WAS THE LEADER OF THE CHURCH IN JERUSALEM.
HE WAS ALSO THE HALF-BROTHER OF JESUS.
HE IS NOT TO BE CONFUSED WITH JAMES, THE BROTHER OF JOHN, THE FIRST APOSTLE MARTYRED, WHEN HEROD HAD HIM KILLED WITH THE SWORD.
THE SURVIVING APOSTLES APPOINTED JAMES, THE HALF-BROTHER OF JESUS, AS BISHOP OF THE CHURCH IN JERUSALEM.
HE WAS ALSO CALLED "JAMES THE JUST" FOR HIS RIGHTEOUS BEHAVIOR.

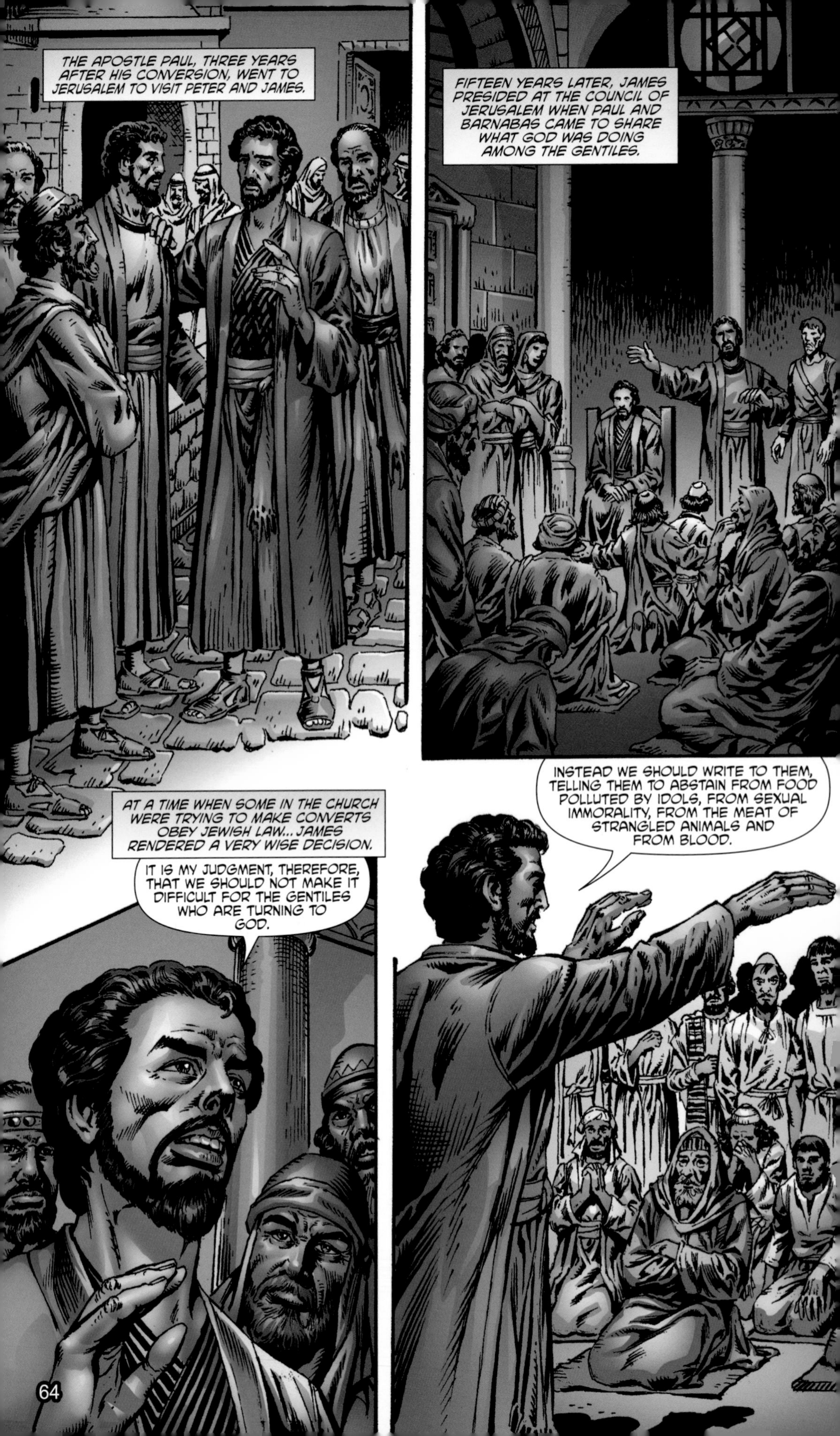
THE APOSTLE PAUL, THREE YEARS AFTER HIS CONVERSION, WENT TO JERUSALEM TO VISIT PETER AND JAMES.
FIFTEEN YEARS LATER, JAMES PRESIDED AT THE COUNCIL OF JERUSALEM WHEN PAUL AND BARNABAS CAME TO SHARE WHAT GOD WAS DOING AMONG THE GENTILES.
AT A TIME WHEN SOME IN THE CHURCH WERE TRYING TO MAKE CONVERTS OBEY JEWISH LAW... JAMES RENDERED A VERY WISE DECISION.
IT IS MY JUDGMENT, THEREFORE, THAT WE SHOULD NOT MAKE IT DIFFICULT FOR THE GENTILES WHO ARE TURNING TO GOD.
INSTEAD WE SHOULD WRITE TO THEM, TELLING THEM TO ABSTAIN FROM FOOD POLLUTED BY IDOLS, FROM SEXUAL IMMORALITY, FROM THE MEAT OF STRANGLED ANIMALS AND FROM BLOOD.

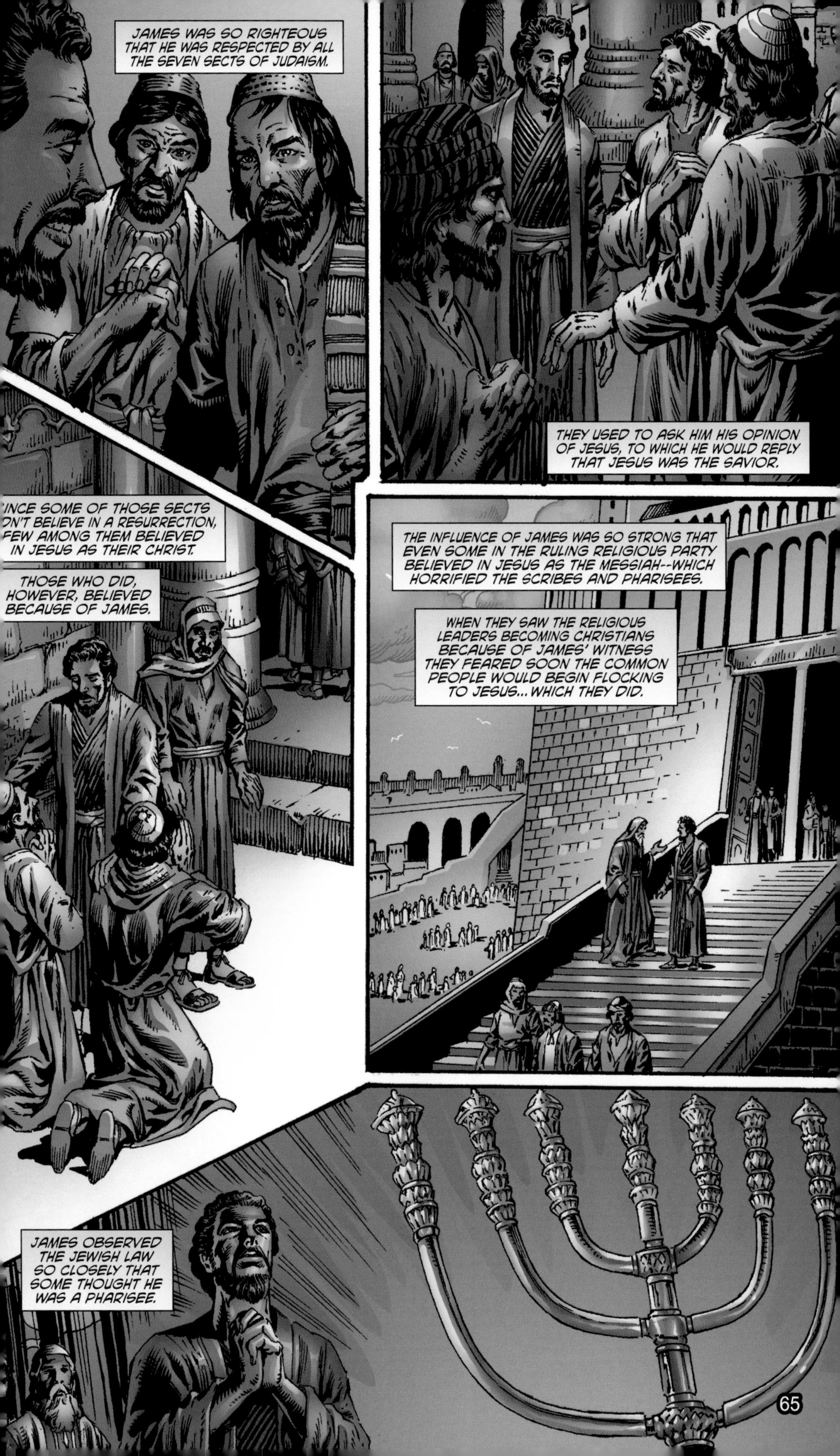
JAMES WAS SO RIGHTEOUS THAT HE WAS RESPECTED BY ALL THE SEVEN SECTS OF JUDAISM.
THEY USED TO ASK HIM HIS OPINION OF JESUS, TO WHICH HE WOULD REPLY THAT JESUS WAS THE SAVIOR.
INCE SOME OF THOSE SECTS ON'T BELIEVE IN A RESURRECTION, FEW AMONG THEM BELIEVED IN JESUS AS THEIR CHRIST.
THOSE WHO DID, HOWEVER, BELIEVED BECAUSE OF JAMES.
THE INFLUENCE OF JAMES WAS SO STRONG THAT EVEN SOME IN THE RULING RELIGIOUS PARTY BELIEVED IN JESUS AS THE MESSIAH--WHICH HORRIFIED THE SCRIBES AND PHARISEES.
WHEN THEY SAW THE RELIGIOUS LEADERS BECOMING CHRISTIANS BECAUSE OF JAMES' WITNESS THEY FEARED SOON THE COMMON PEOPLE WOULD BEGIN FLOCKING TO JESUS... WHICH THEY DID.
JAMES OBSERVED THE JEWISH LAW SO CLOSELY THAT SOME THOUGHT HE WAS A PHARISEE.

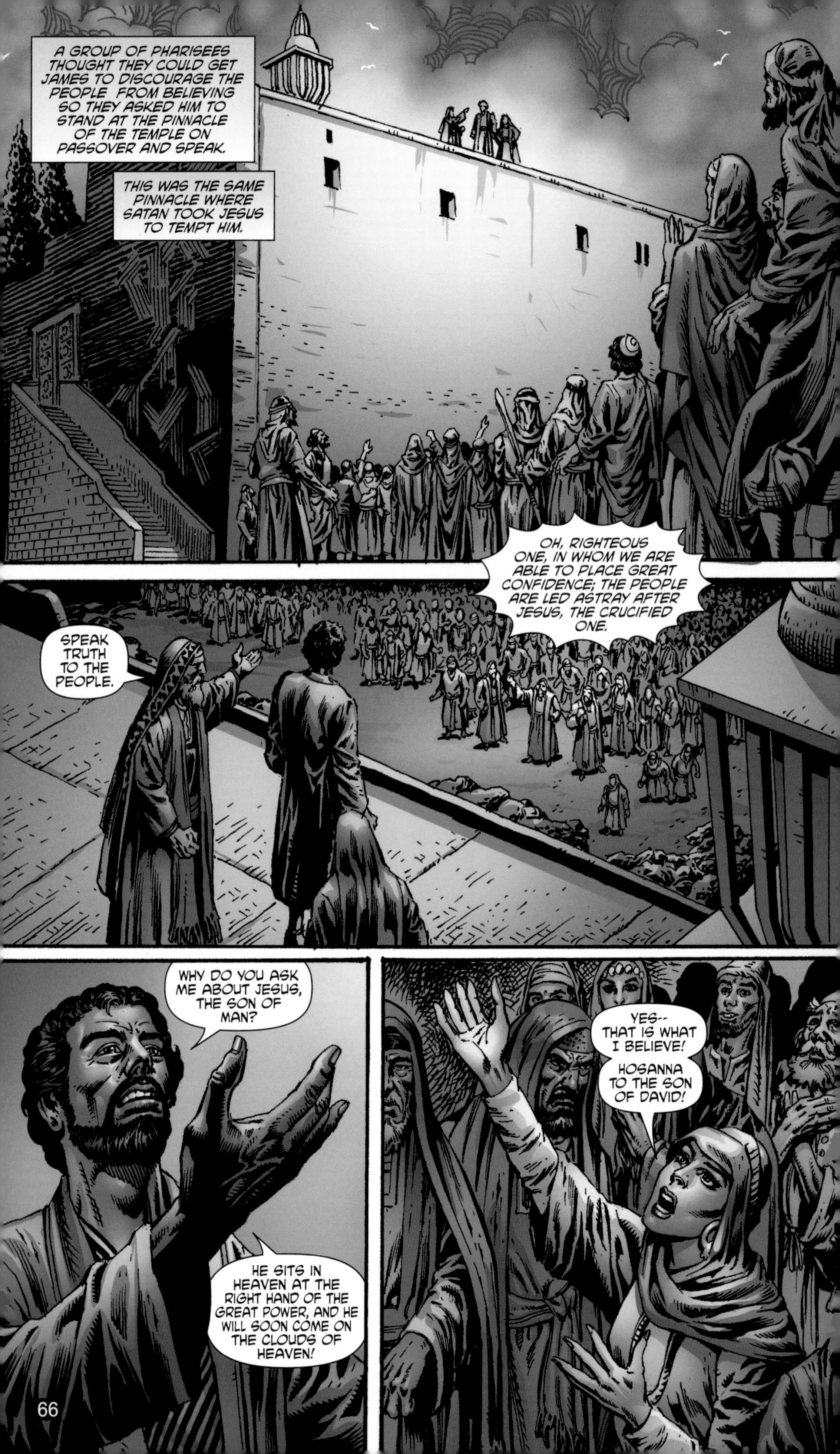

A GROUP OF PHARISEES THOUGHT THEY COULD GET JAMES TO DISCOURAGE THE PEOPLE FROM BELIEVING SO THEY ASKED HIM TO STAND AT THE PINNACLE OF THE TEMPLE ON PASSOVER AND SPEAK.
THIS WAS THE SAME PINNACLE WHERE SATAN TOOK JESUS TO TEMPT HIM.
OH, RIGHTEOUS ONE, IN WHOM WE ARE ABLE TO PLACE GREAT CONFIDENCE; THE PEOPLE ARE LED ASTRAY AFTER JESUS, THE CRUCIFIED ONE.
SPEAK TRUTH TO THE PEOPLE.
WHY DO YOU ASK ME ABOUT JESUS, THE SON OF MAN?
HE SITS IN HEAVEN AT THE RIGHT HAND OF THE GREAT POWER, AND HE WILL SOON COME ON THE CLOUDS OF HEAVEN!
YES-- THAT IS WHAT I BELIEVE!
HOSANNA TO THE SON OF DAVID!

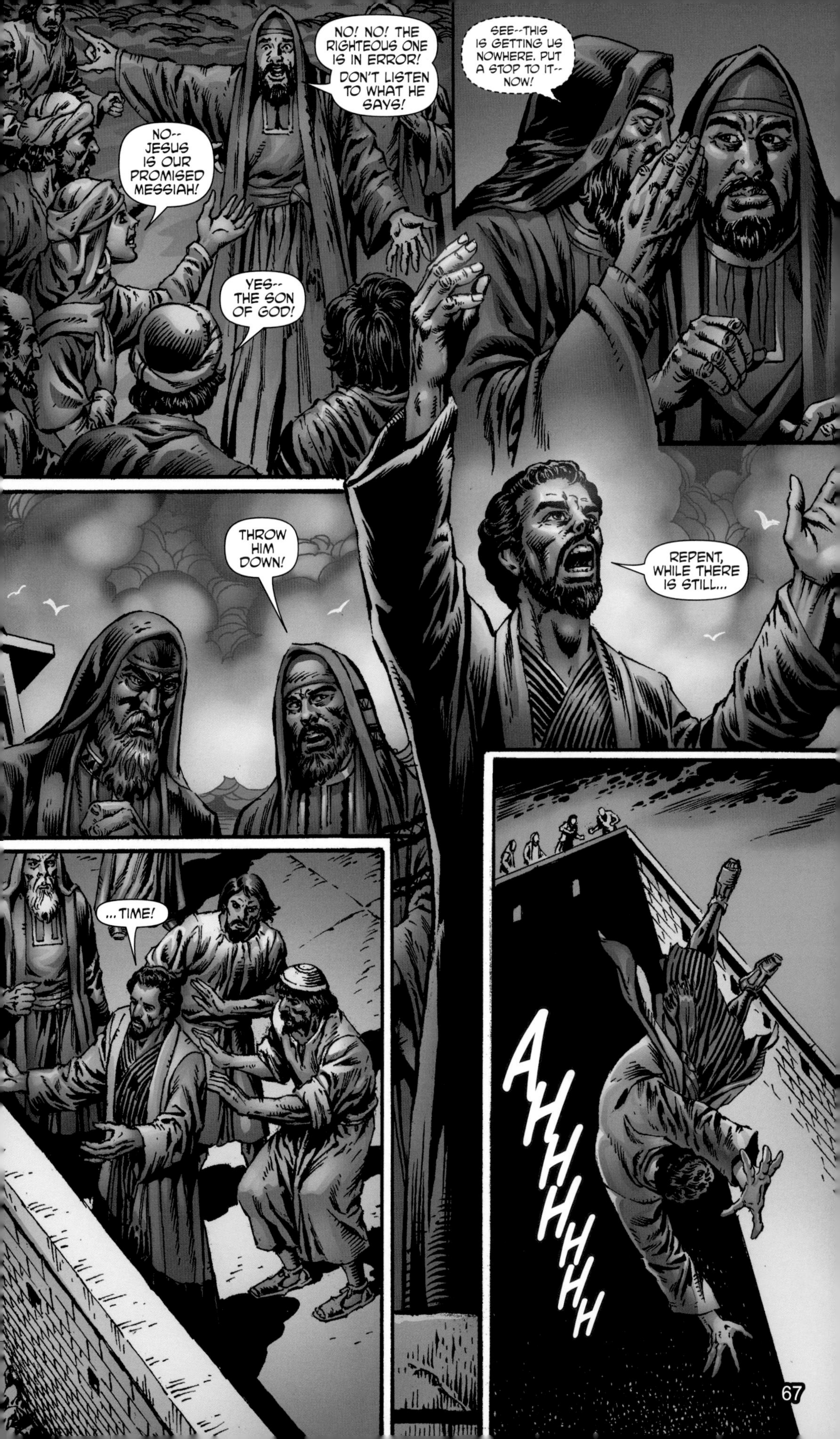
NO! NO! THE RIGHTEOUS ONE IS IN ERROR! DON'T LISTEN TO WHAT HE SAYS!
NO-- JESUS IS OUR PROMISED MESSIAH!
YES-- THE SON OF GOD!
SEE--THIS IS GETTING US NOWHERE. PUT A STOP TO IT-- NOW!
THROW HIM DOWN!
REPENT, WHILE THERE IS STILL...
...TIME!
AHHHHHHHH

I BEG OF YOU, LORD GOD OUR FATHER, FORGIVE THEM! THEY DO NOT KNOW WHAT THEY ARE DOING.

FINISH HIM OFF.

STOP WHAT ARE YOU DOING--

--THE RIGHTEOUS ONE IS PRAYING FOR YOU!

FOR THE LAST TIME--I SAID FINISH HIM.

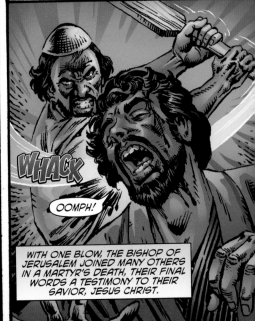

WHACK

OOMPH!

WITH ONE BLOW, THE BISHOP OF JERUSALEM JOINED MANY OTHERS IN A MARTYR'S DEATH, THEIR FINAL WORDS A TESTIMONY TO THEIR SAVIOR, JESUS CHRIST.

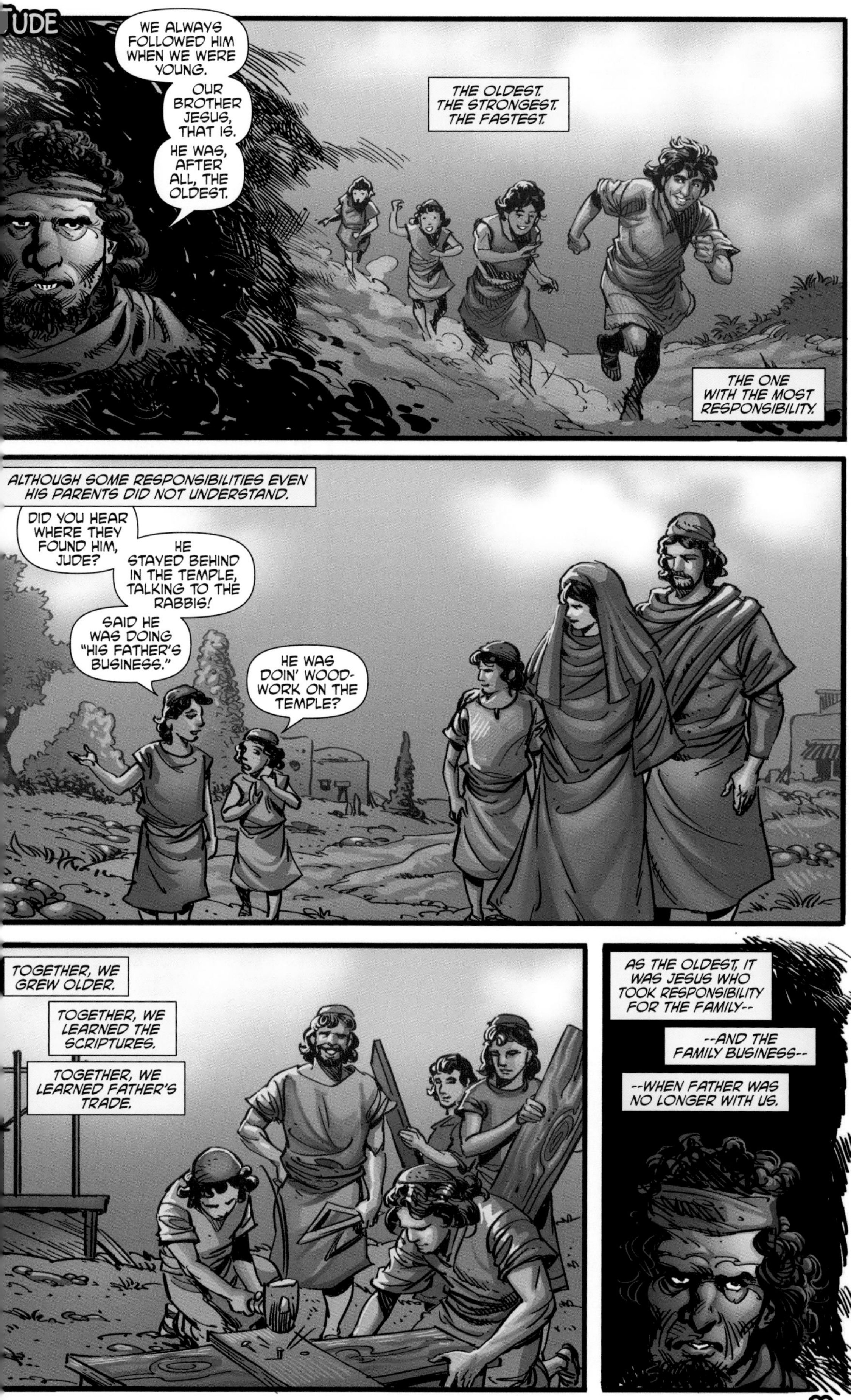
WE ALWAYS FOLLOWED HIM WHEN WE WERE YOUNG.
OUR BROTHER JESUS, THAT IS.
HE WAS, AFTER ALL, THE OLDEST.
THE OLDEST. THE STRONGEST. THE FASTEST.
THE ONE WITH THE MOST RESPONSIBILITY.
ALTHOUGH SOME RESPONSIBILITIES EVEN HIS PARENTS DID NOT UNDERSTAND.
DID YOU HEAR WHERE THEY FOUND HIM, JUDE?
HE STAYED BEHIND IN THE TEMPLE, TALKING TO THE RABBIS!
SAID HE WAS DOING "HIS FATHER'S BUSINESS."
HE WAS DOIN' WOOD-WORK ON THE TEMPLE?
TOGETHER, WE GREW OLDER.
TOGETHER, WE LEARNED THE SCRIPTURES.
TOGETHER, WE LEARNED FATHER'S TRADE.
AS THE OLDEST, IT WAS JESUS WHO TOOK RESPONSIBILITY FOR THE FAMILY--
--AND THE FAMILY BUSINESS--
--WHEN FATHER WAS NO LONGER WITH US.

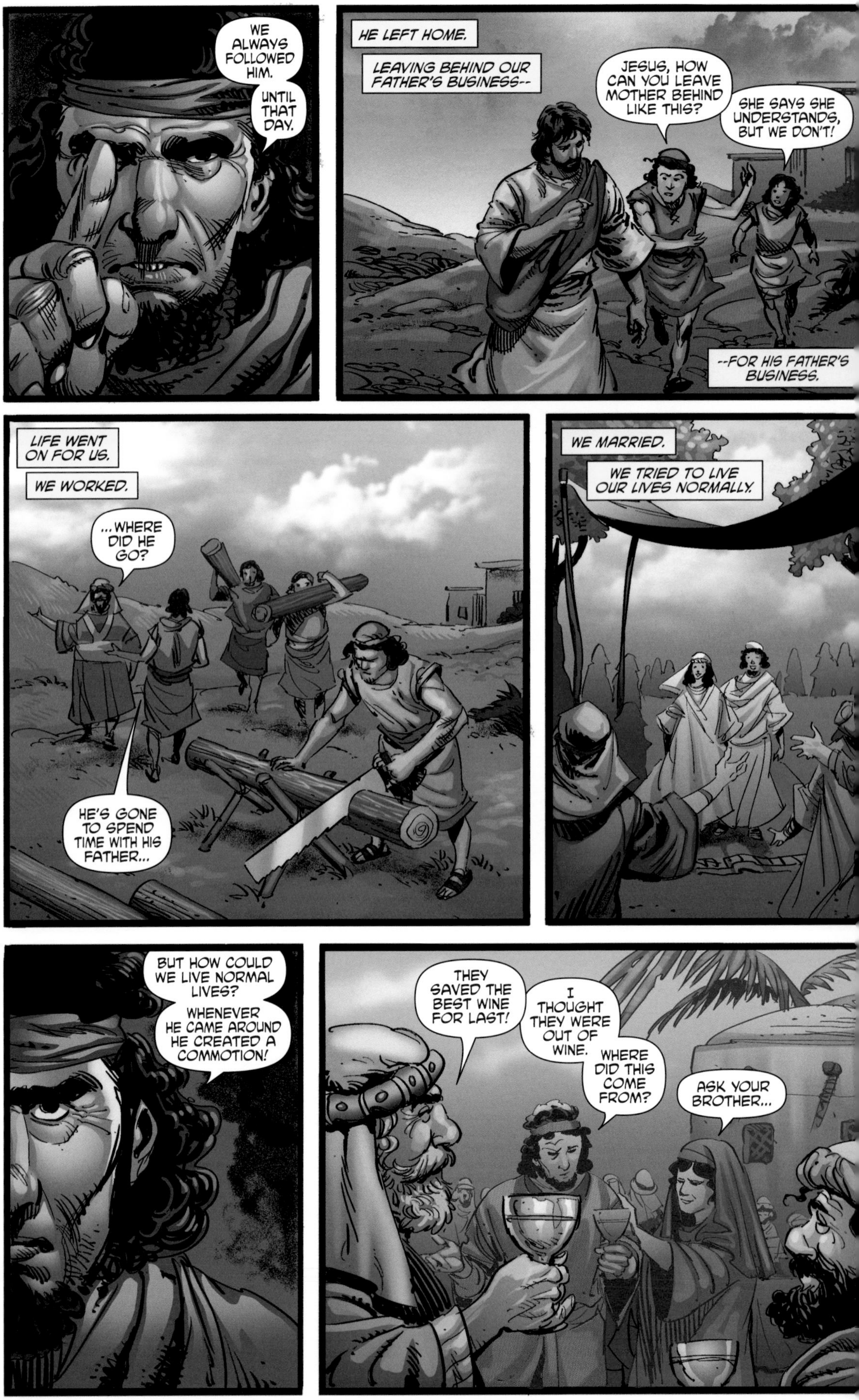
WE ALWAYS FOLLOWED HIM.
UNTIL THAT DAY.
HE LEFT HOME.
LEAVING BEHIND OUR FATHER'S BUSINESS--
JESUS, HOW CAN YOU LEAVE MOTHER BEHIND LIKE THIS?
SHE SAYS SHE UNDERSTANDS, BUT WE DON'T!
--FOR HIS FATHER'S BUSINESS.
LIFE WENT ON FOR US.
WE WORKED.
...WHERE DID HE GO?
HE'S GONE TO SPEND TIME WITH HIS FATHER...
WE MARRIED.
WE TRIED TO LIVE OUR LIVES NORMALLY.
BUT HOW COULD WE LIVE NORMAL LIVES?
WHENEVER HE CAME AROUND HE CREATED A COMMOTION!
THEY SAVED THE BEST WINE FOR LAST!
I THOUGHT THEY WERE OUT OF WINE.
WHERE DID THIS COME FROM?
ASK YOUR BROTHER...

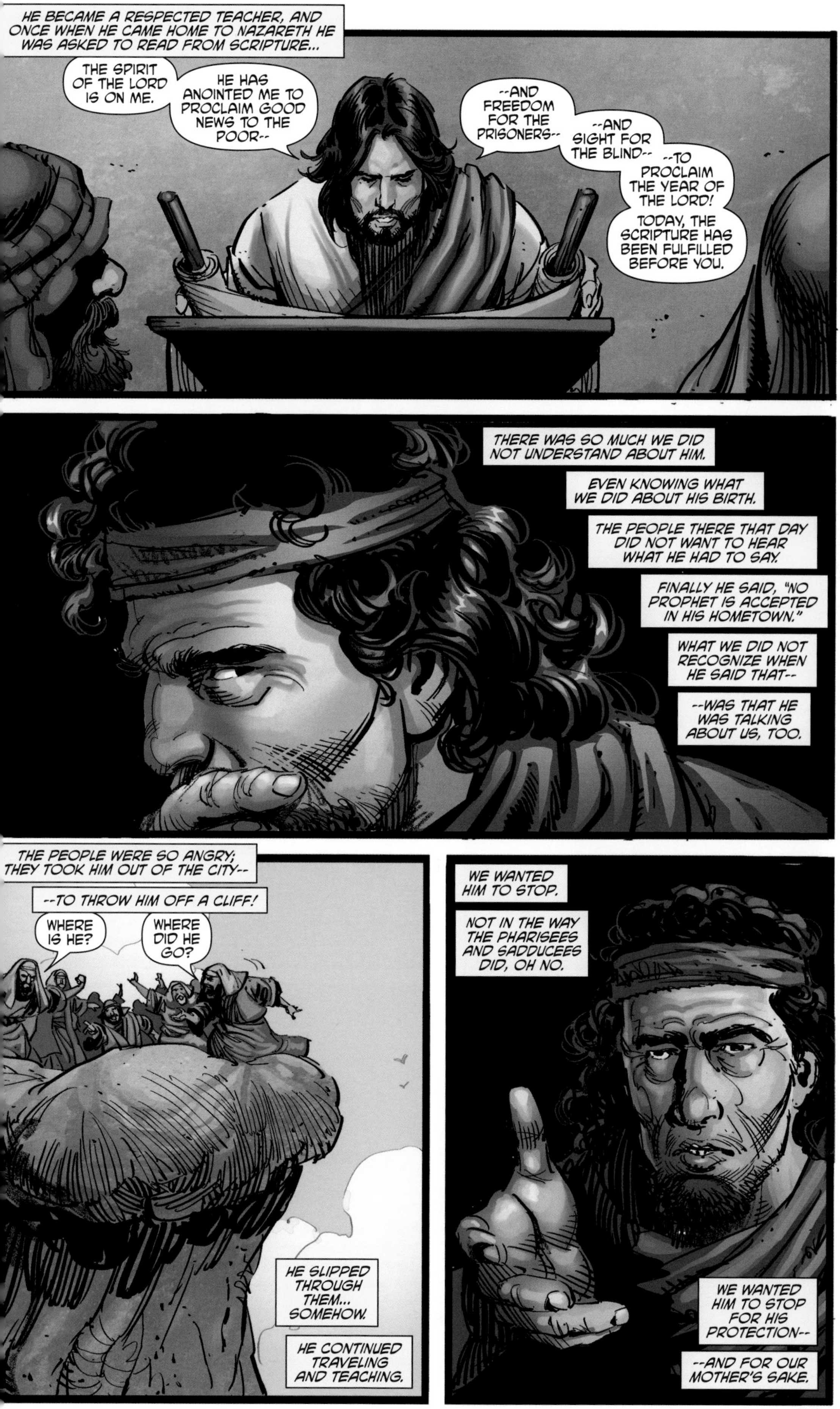
HE BECAME A RESPECTED TEACHER, AND ONCE WHEN HE CAME HOME TO NAZARETH HE WAS ASKED TO READ FROM SCRIPTURE...
THE SPIRIT OF THE LORD IS ON ME.
HE HAS ANOINTED ME TO PROCLAIM GOOD NEWS TO THE POOR--
--AND FREEDOM FOR THE PRISONERS--
--AND SIGHT FOR THE BLIND--
--TO PROCLAIM THE YEAR OF THE LORD!
TODAY, THE SCRIPTURE HAS BEEN FULFILLED BEFORE YOU.
THERE WAS SO MUCH WE DID NOT UNDERSTAND ABOUT HIM.
EVEN KNOWING WHAT WE DID ABOUT HIS BIRTH.
THE PEOPLE THERE THAT DAY DID NOT WANT TO HEAR WHAT HE HAD TO SAY.
FINALLY HE SAID, "NO PROPHET IS ACCEPTED IN HIS HOMETOWN."
WHAT WE DID NOT RECOGNIZE WHEN HE SAID THAT--
--WAS THAT HE WAS TALKING ABOUT US, TOO.
THE PEOPLE WERE SO ANGRY; THEY TOOK HIM OUT OF THE CITY--
--TO THROW HIM OFF A CLIFF!
WHERE IS HE?
WHERE DID HE GO?
HE SLIPPED THROUGH THEM... SOMEHOW.
HE CONTINUED TRAVELING AND TEACHING.
WE WANTED HIM TO STOP.
NOT IN THE WAY THE PHARISEES AND SADDUCEES DID, OH NO.
WE WANTED HIM TO STOP FOR HIS PROTECTION--
--AND FOR OUR MOTHER'S SAKE.

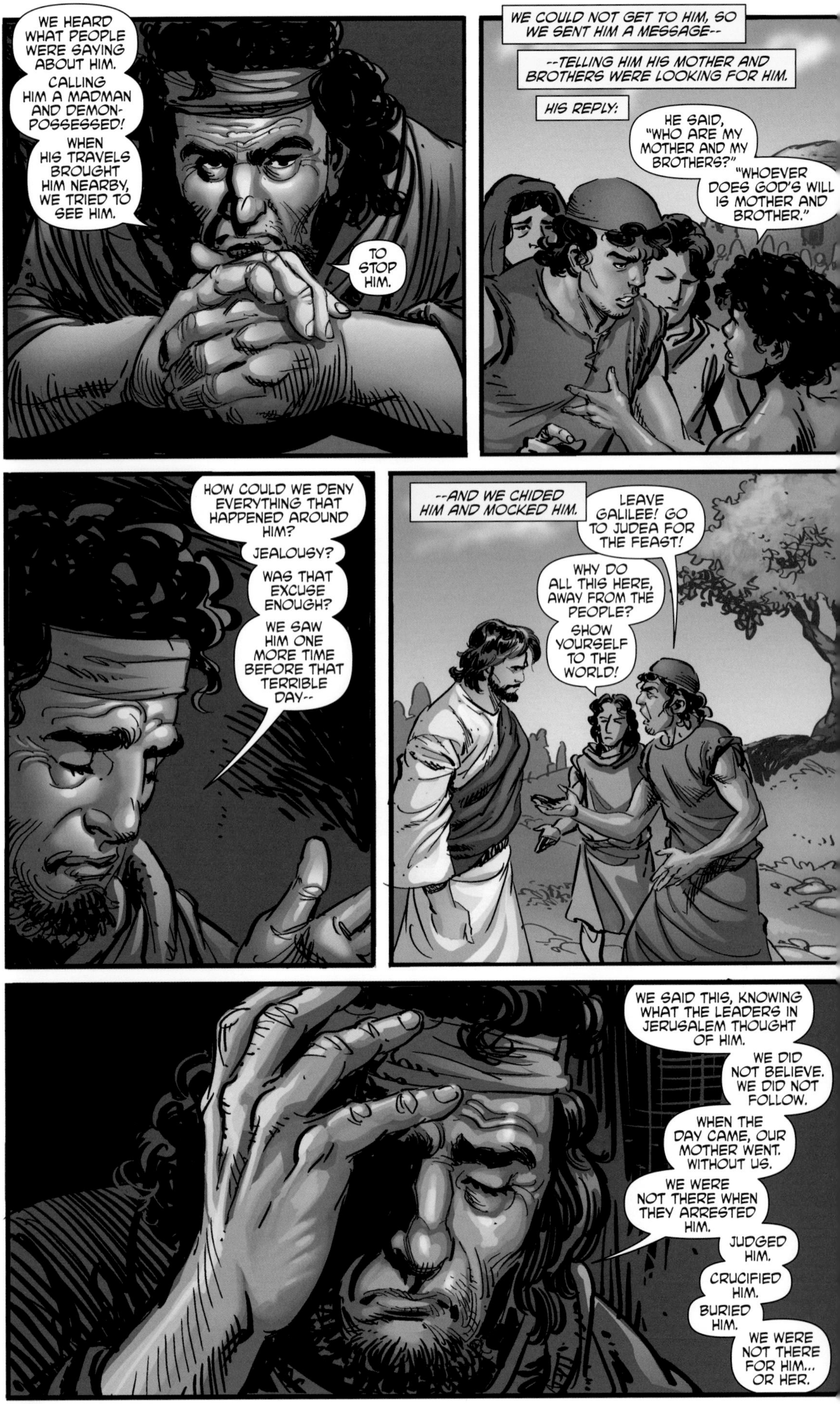
WE HEARD WHAT PEOPLE WERE SAYING ABOUT HIM.
CALLING HIM A MADMAN AND DEMON-POSSESSED!
WHEN HIS TRAVELS BROUGHT HIM NEARBY, WE TRIED TO SEE HIM.
TO STOP HIM.
WE COULD NOT GET TO HIM, SO WE SENT HIM A MESSAGE--
--TELLING HIM HIS MOTHER AND BROTHERS WERE LOOKING FOR HIM.
HIS REPLY:
HE SAID, "WHO ARE MY MOTHER AND MY BROTHERS?"
"WHOEVER DOES GOD'S WILL IS MOTHER AND BROTHER."
HOW COULD WE DENY EVERYTHING THAT HAPPENED AROUND HIM?
JEALOUSY?
WAS THAT EXCUSE ENOUGH?
WE SAW HIM ONE MORE TIME BEFORE THAT TERRIBLE DAY--
--AND WE CHIDED HIM AND MOCKED HIM.
LEAVE GALILEE! GO TO JUDEA FOR THE FEAST!
WHY DO ALL THIS HERE, AWAY FROM THE PEOPLE?
SHOW YOURSELF TO THE WORLD!
WE SAID THIS, KNOWING WHAT THE LEADERS IN JERUSALEM THOUGHT OF HIM.
WE DID NOT BELIEVE. WE DID NOT FOLLOW.
WHEN THE DAY CAME, OUR MOTHER WENT. WITHOUT US.
WE WERE NOT THERE WHEN THEY ARRESTED HIM.
JUDGED HIM.
CRUCIFIED HIM.
BURIED HIM.
WE WERE NOT THERE FOR HIM... OR HER.

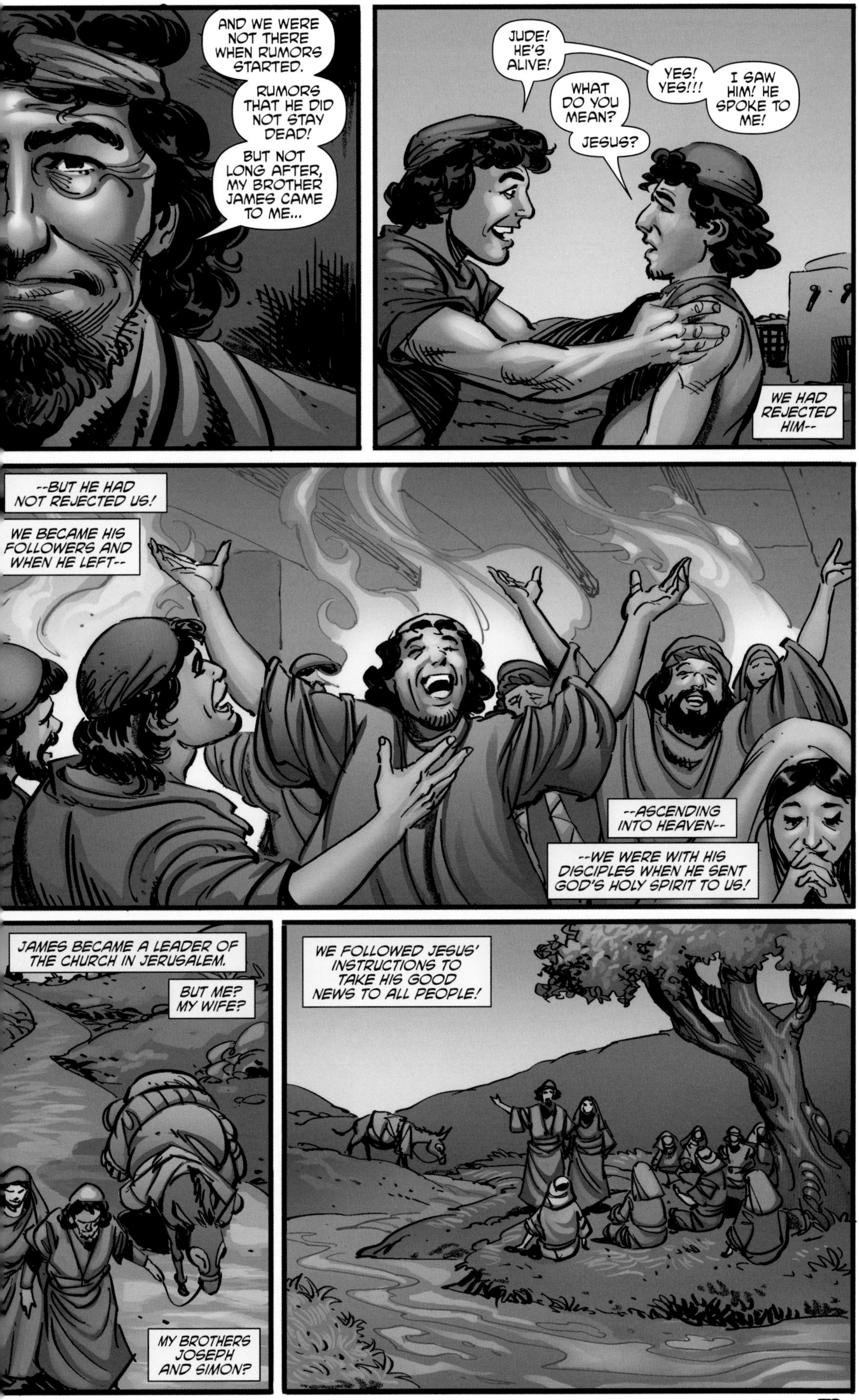
AND WE WERE NOT THERE WHEN RUMORS STARTED.
RUMORS THAT HE DID NOT STAY DEAD!
BUT NOT LONG AFTER, MY BROTHER JAMES CAME TO ME...
JUDE! HE'S ALIVE!
WHAT DO YOU MEAN?
JESUS?
YES! YES!!!
I SAW HIM! HE SPOKE TO ME!
WE HAD REJECTED HIM--
--BUT HE HAD NOT REJECTED US!
WE BECAME HIS FOLLOWERS AND WHEN HE LEFT--
--ASCENDING INTO HEAVEN--
--WE WERE WITH HIS DISCIPLES WHEN HE SENT GOD'S HOLY SPIRIT TO US!
JAMES BECAME A LEADER OF THE CHURCH IN JERUSALEM.
BUT ME? MY WIFE?
MY BROTHERS JOSEPH AND SIMON?
WE FOLLOWED JESUS' INSTRUCTIONS TO TAKE HIS GOOD NEWS TO ALL PEOPLE!

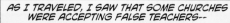

AS I TRAVELED, I SAW THAT SOME CHURCHES WERE ACCEPTING FALSE TEACHERS--

--AND FALSE TEACHINGS.

...YOU CANNOT LISTEN TO PEOPLE DEVOID OF THE SPIRIT!

THEY ARE LIKE WATERLESS CLOUDS BLOWN BY THE WIND...

THEY CAUSE DIVISIONS AMONG US!

I WROTE A LETTER OF MY OWN, WARNING THE CHURCHES AGAINST THIS.

...BUT YOU, BELOVED, BUILD YOURSELF UP ON YOUR HOLY FAITH--

--AND PRAY IN THE HOLY SPIRIT...

AND ENCOURAGING THEM TO REMEMBER THE APOSTLES' TEACHINGS.

"NOW TO HIM WHO IS ABLE TO KEEP YOU FROM FALLING..."

"...TO THE ONLY GOD OUR SAVIOR, THROUGH JESUS CHRIST OUR LORD..."

"...BE ALL GLORY, MAJESTY, AND AUTHORITY FOREVER AND EVER, AMEN."

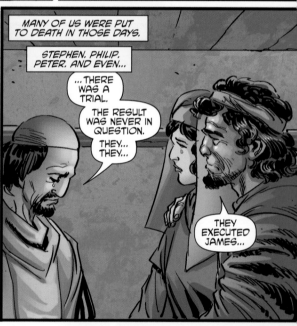

MANY OF US WERE PUT TO DEATH IN THOSE DAYS.

STEPHEN. PHILIP. PETER. AND EVEN...

...THERE WAS A TRIAL.

THE RESULT WAS NEVER IN QUESTION. THEY... THEY...

THEY EXECUTED JAMES...

MY BROTHER. KILLED, AS THEY KILLED OUR LORD.

KILLED FOR FOLLOWING OUR LORD.

FOR YOU SEE, WE HAD FINALLY ACCEPTED HIM.

FINALLY FOLLOWED HIM.

NOT AS BROTHERS, BUT, AS JAMES PUT IT IN HIS LETTER:

"SERVANTS OF OUR LORD JESUS CHRIST!"

THIS STORY WAS BASED ON HINTS AND SUGGESTIONS FOUND IN THE BIBLE (AND OTHER DOCUMENTS) ABOUT JESUS' FAMILY, PARTICULARLY: MATTHEW 12; MARK 6 & MATTHEW 13; JOHN 7; AND GALATIANS 1:9. AND, OF COURSE, THE BOOK OF JUDE, WHICH ARE JUDE'S OWN WORDS!

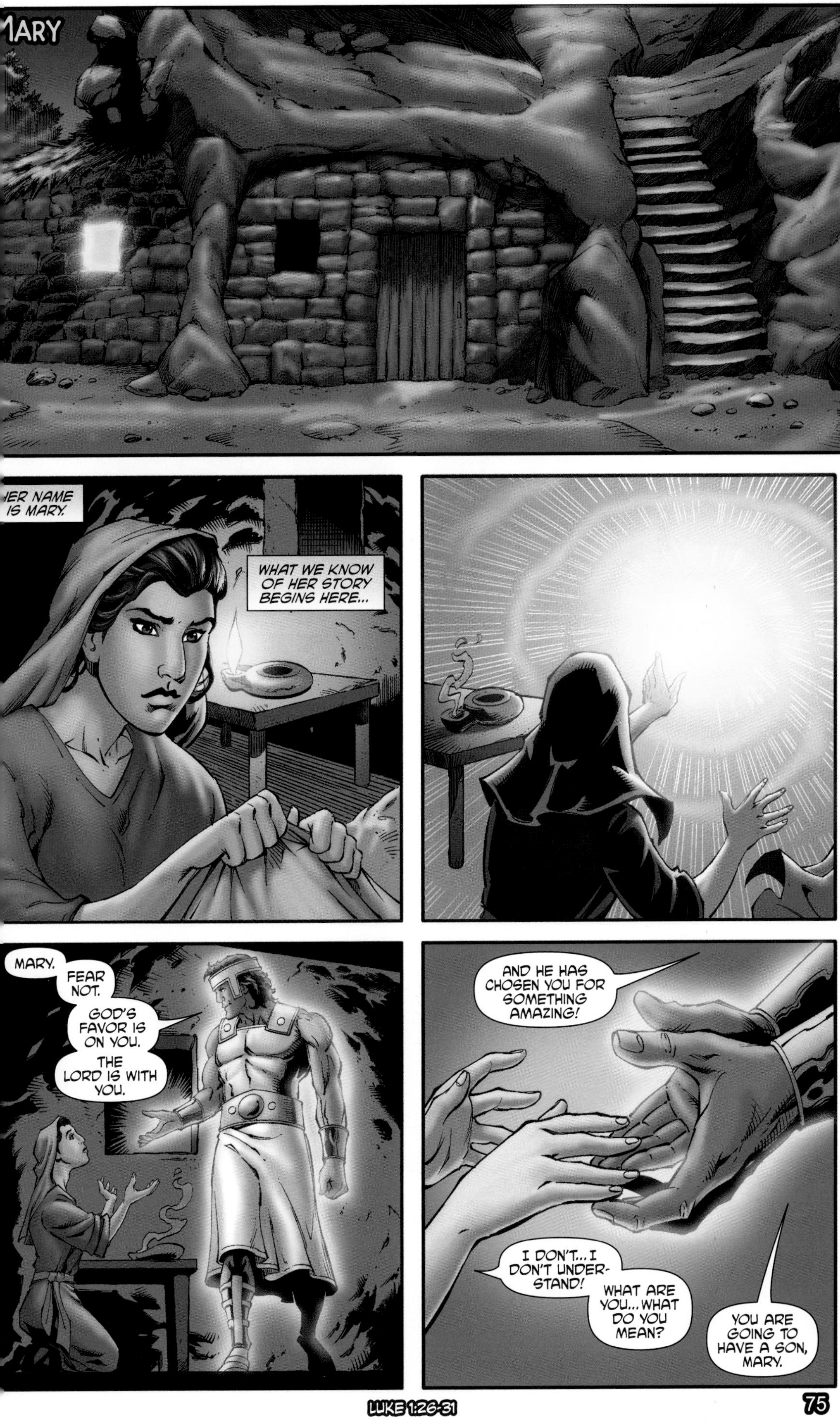
MARY
HER NAME IS MARY.
WHAT WE KNOW OF HER STORY BEGINS HERE...
MARY.
FEAR NOT.
GOD'S FAVOR IS ON YOU.
THE LORD IS WITH YOU.
AND HE HAS CHOSEN YOU FOR SOMETHING AMAZING!
I DON'T... I DON'T UNDER-STAND!
WHAT ARE YOU... WHAT DO YOU MEAN?
YOU ARE GOING TO HAVE A SON, MARY.

LUKE 1:26-31

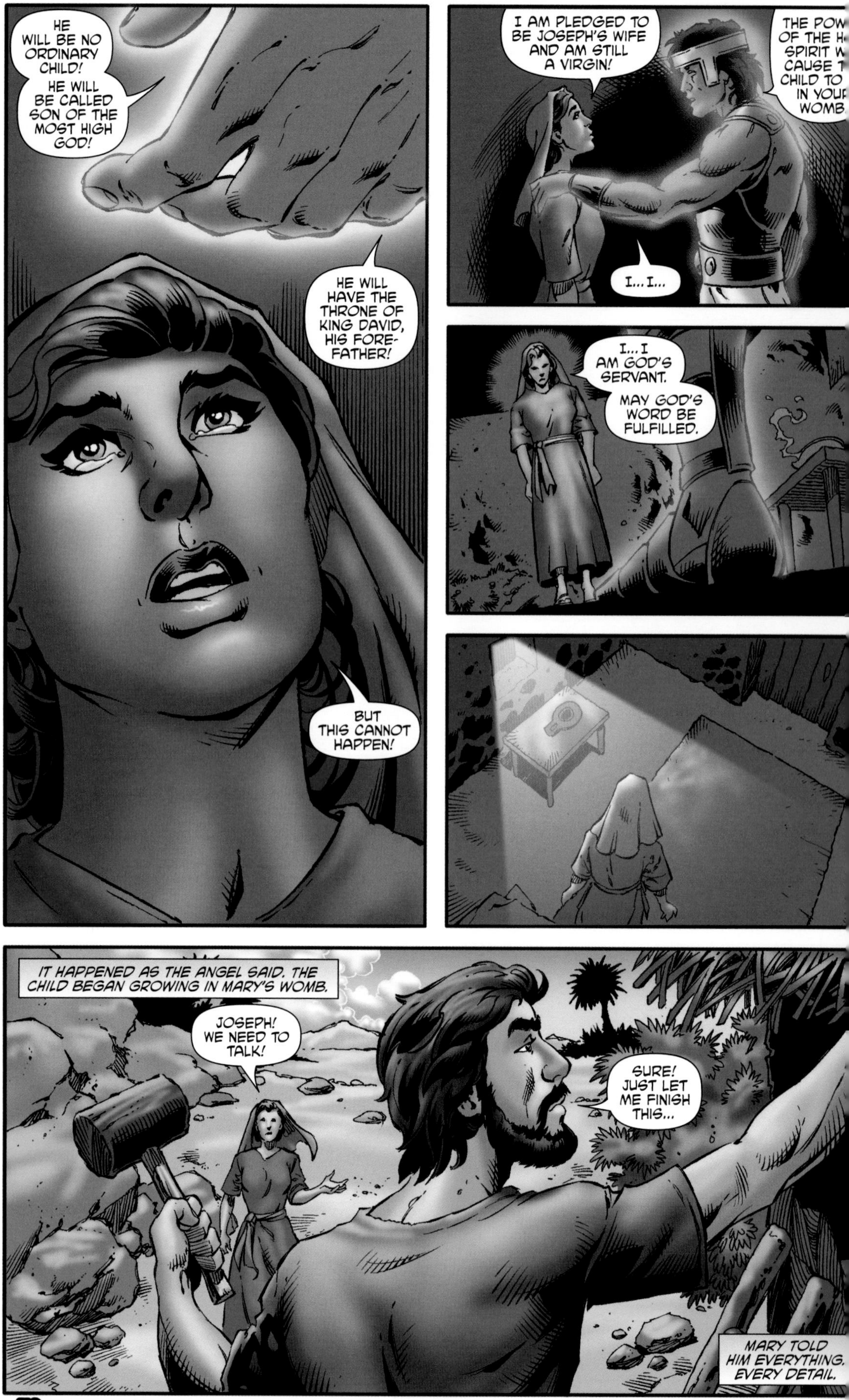
HE WILL BE NO ORDINARY CHILD!
HE WILL BE CALLED SON OF THE MOST HIGH GOD!
HE WILL HAVE THE THRONE OF KING DAVID, HIS FORE-FATHER!
BUT THIS CANNOT HAPPEN!
I AM PLEDGED TO BE JOSEPH'S WIFE AND AM STILL A VIRGIN!
THE POW OF THE H SPIRIT W CAUSE T CHILD TO IN YOUR WOMB
I... I...
I... I AM GOD'S SERVANT.
MAY GOD'S WORD BE FULFILLED.
IT HAPPENED AS THE ANGEL SAID. THE CHILD BEGAN GROWING IN MARY'S WOMB.
JOSEPH! WE NEED TO TALK!
SURE! JUST LET ME FINISH THIS...
MARY TOLD HIM EVERYTHING. EVERY DETAIL.

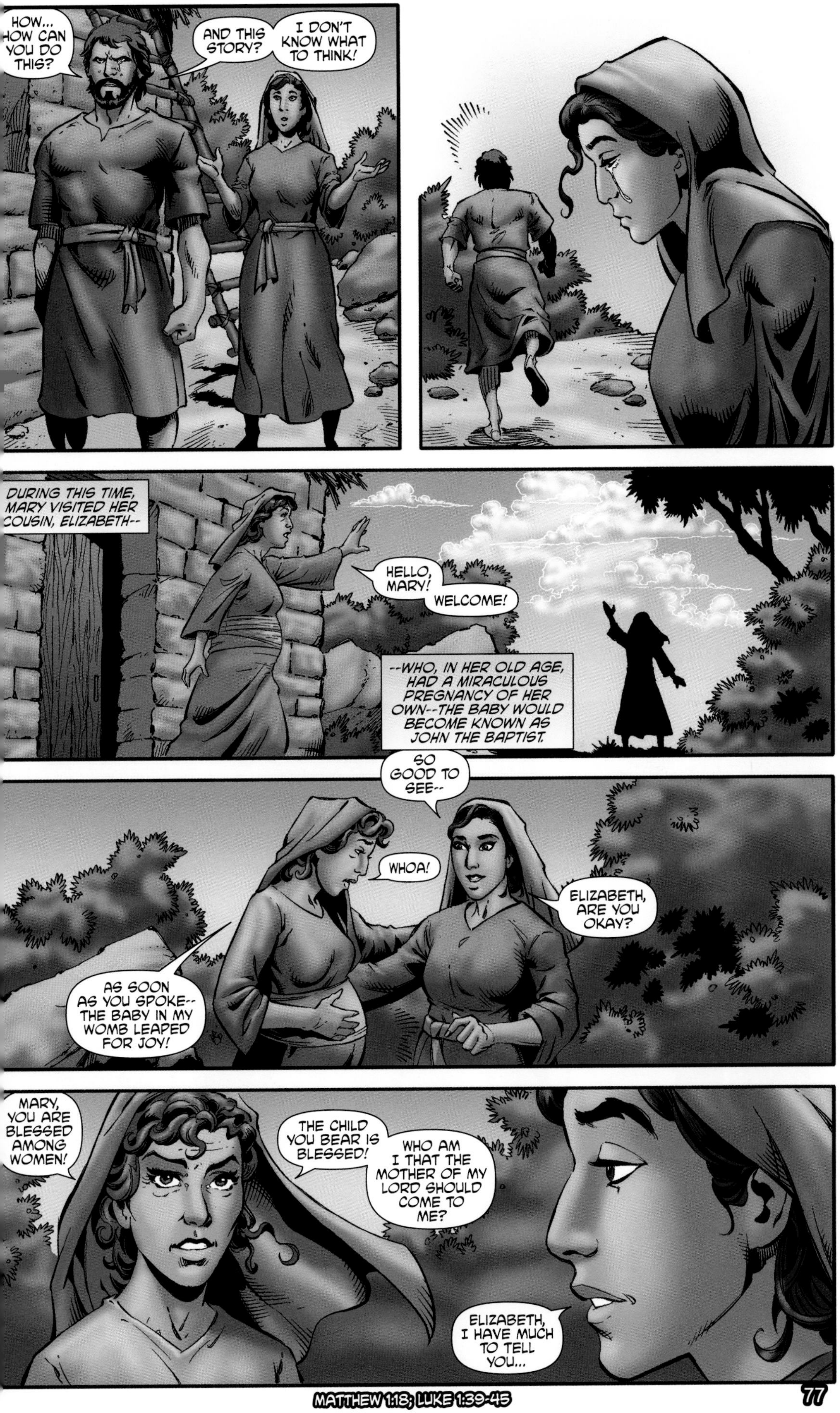
HOW... HOW CAN YOU DO THIS?
AND THIS STORY?
I DON'T KNOW WHAT TO THINK!
DURING THIS TIME, MARY VISITED HER COUSIN, ELIZABETH--
HELLO, MARY!
WELCOME!
--WHO, IN HER OLD AGE, HAD A MIRACULOUS PREGNANCY OF HER OWN--THE BABY WOULD BECOME KNOWN AS JOHN THE BAPTIST.
SO GOOD TO SEE--
WHOA!
ELIZABETH, ARE YOU OKAY?
AS SOON AS YOU SPOKE-- THE BABY IN MY WOMB LEAPED FOR JOY!
MARY, YOU ARE BLESSED AMONG WOMEN!
THE CHILD YOU BEAR IS BLESSED!
WHO AM I THAT THE MOTHER OF MY LORD SHOULD COME TO ME?
ELIZABETH, I HAVE MUCH TO TELL YOU...

MATTHEW 1:18; LUKE 1:39-45

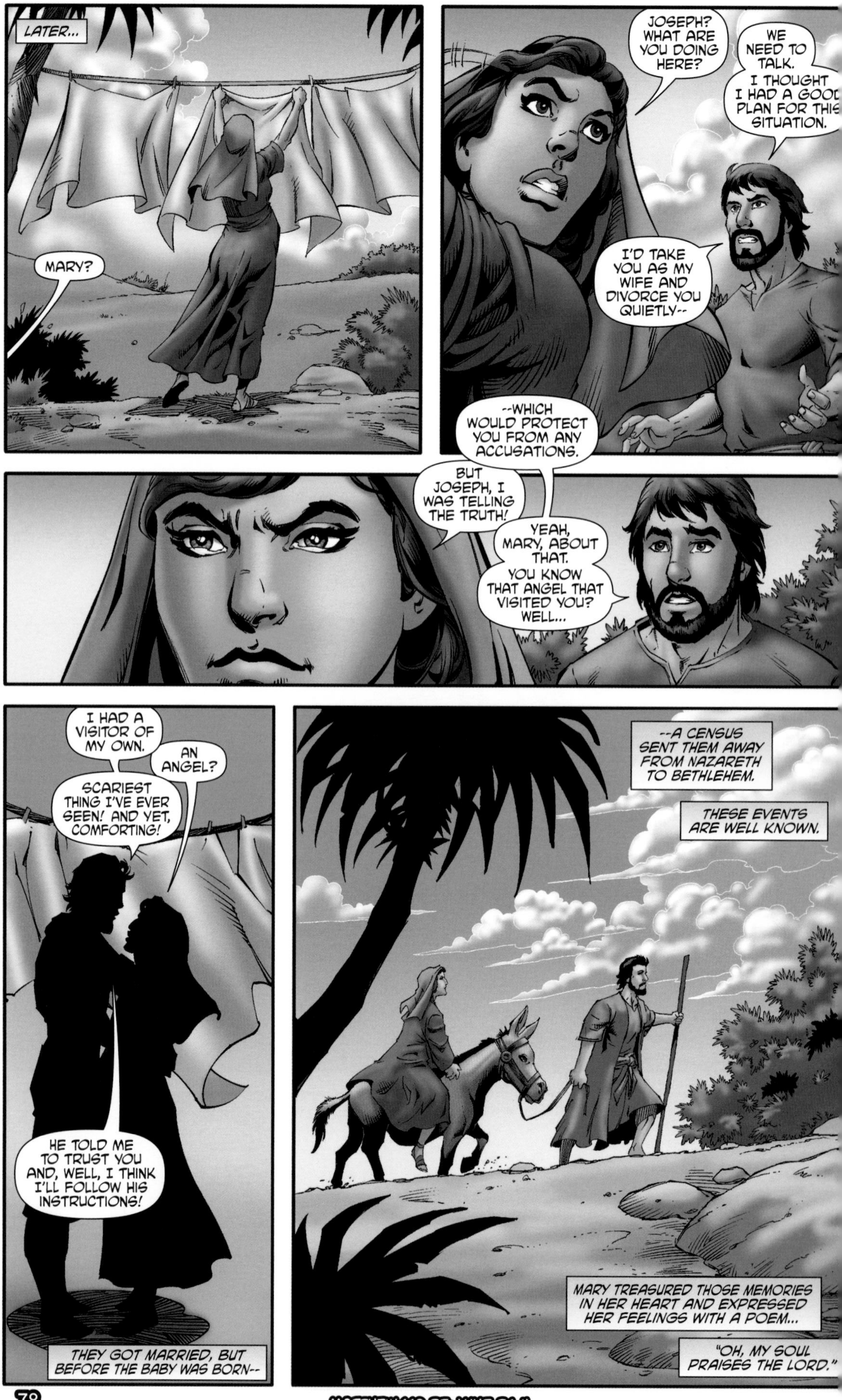
LATER...
MARY?
JOSEPH? WHAT ARE YOU DOING HERE?
WE NEED TO TALK.
I THOUGHT I HAD A GOOD PLAN FOR THIS SITUATION.
I'D TAKE YOU AS MY WIFE AND DIVORCE YOU QUIETLY--
--WHICH WOULD PROTECT YOU FROM ANY ACCUSATIONS.
BUT JOSEPH, I WAS TELLING THE TRUTH!
YEAH, MARY, ABOUT THAT.
YOU KNOW THAT ANGEL THAT VISITED YOU? WELL...
I HAD A VISITOR OF MY OWN.
AN ANGEL?
SCARIEST THING I'VE EVER SEEN! AND YET, COMFORTING!
HE TOLD ME TO TRUST YOU AND, WELL, I THINK I'LL FOLLOW HIS INSTRUCTIONS!
THEY GOT MARRIED, BUT BEFORE THE BABY WAS BORN--
--A CENSUS SENT THEM AWAY FROM NAZARETH TO BETHLEHEM.
THESE EVENTS ARE WELL KNOWN.
MARY TREASURED THOSE MEMORIES IN HER HEART AND EXPRESSED HER FEELINGS WITH A POEM...
"OH, MY SOUL PRAISES THE LORD."

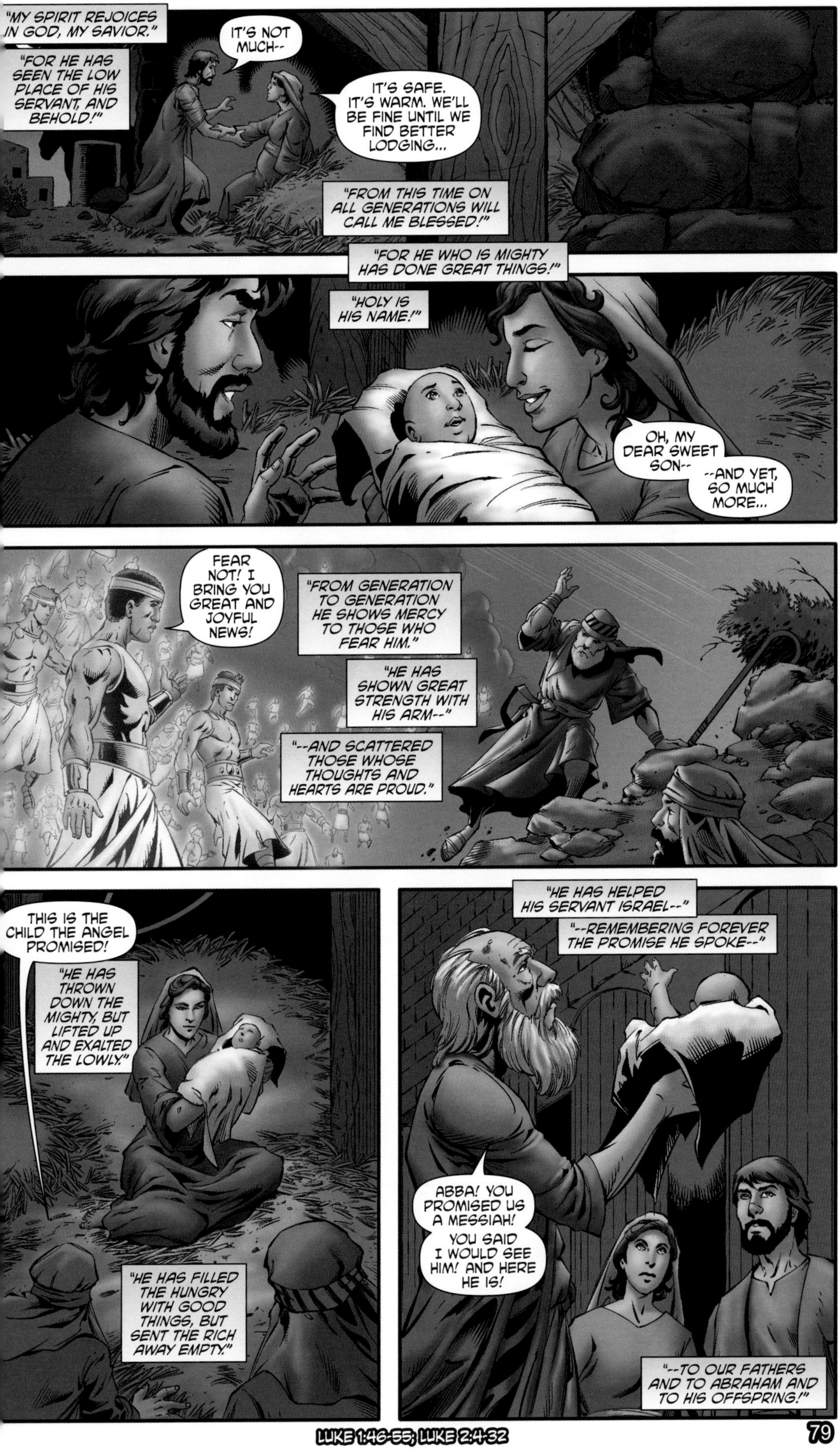
"MY SPIRIT REJOICES IN GOD, MY SAVIOR."
IT'S NOT MUCH--
"FOR HE HAS SEEN THE LOW PLACE OF HIS SERVANT, AND BEHOLD!"
IT'S SAFE. IT'S WARM. WE'LL BE FINE UNTIL WE FIND BETTER LODGING...
"FROM THIS TIME ON ALL GENERATIONS WILL CALL ME BLESSED!"
"FOR HE WHO IS MIGHTY HAS DONE GREAT THINGS!"
"HOLY IS HIS NAME!"
OH, MY DEAR SWEET SON--
--AND YET, SO MUCH MORE...
FEAR NOT! I BRING YOU GREAT AND JOYFUL NEWS!
"FROM GENERATION TO GENERATION HE SHOWS MERCY TO THOSE WHO FEAR HIM."
"HE HAS SHOWN GREAT STRENGTH WITH HIS ARM--"
"--AND SCATTERED THOSE WHOSE THOUGHTS AND HEARTS ARE PROUD."
THIS IS THE CHILD THE ANGEL PROMISED!
"HE HAS THROWN DOWN THE MIGHTY, BUT LIFTED UP AND EXALTED THE LOWLY."
"HE HAS FILLED THE HUNGRY WITH GOOD THINGS, BUT SENT THE RICH AWAY EMPTY."
"HE HAS HELPED HIS SERVANT ISRAEL--"
"--REMEMBERING FOREVER THE PROMISE HE SPOKE--"
ABBA! YOU PROMISED US A MESSIAH!
YOU SAID I WOULD SEE HIM! AND HERE HE IS!
"--TO OUR FATHERS AND TO ABRAHAM AND TO HIS OFFSPRING!"

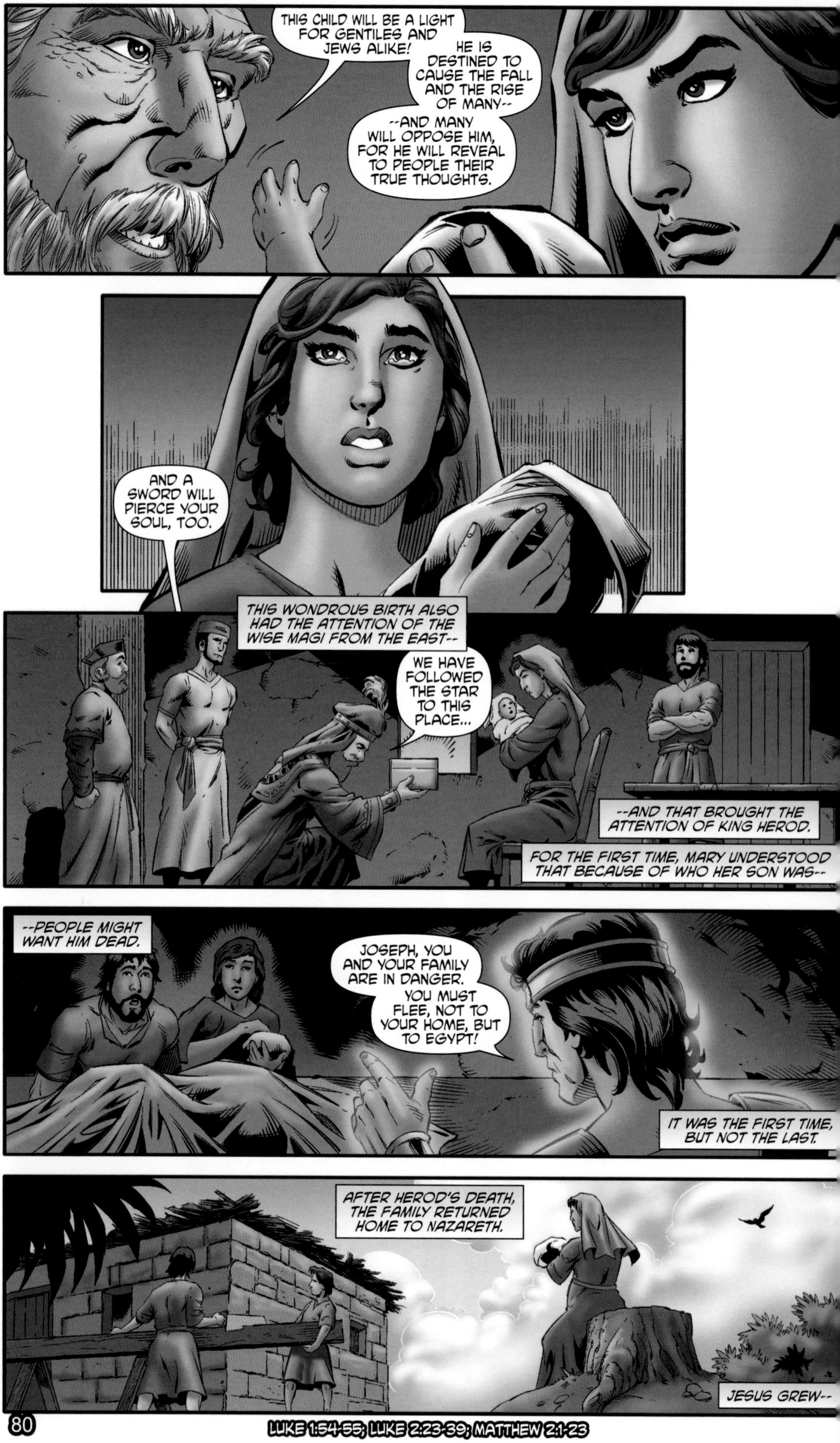
THIS CHILD WILL BE A LIGHT FOR GENTILES AND JEWS ALIKE!
HE IS DESTINED TO CAUSE THE FALL AND THE RISE OF MANY--
--AND MANY WILL OPPOSE HIM, FOR HE WILL REVEAL TO PEOPLE THEIR TRUE THOUGHTS.
AND A SWORD WILL PIERCE YOUR SOUL, TOO.
THIS WONDROUS BIRTH ALSO HAD THE ATTENTION OF THE WISE MAGI FROM THE EAST--
WE HAVE FOLLOWED THE STAR TO THIS PLACE...
--AND THAT BROUGHT THE ATTENTION OF KING HEROD.
FOR THE FIRST TIME, MARY UNDERSTOOD THAT BECAUSE OF WHO HER SON WAS--
--PEOPLE MIGHT WANT HIM DEAD.
JOSEPH, YOU AND YOUR FAMILY ARE IN DANGER.
YOU MUST FLEE, NOT TO YOUR HOME, BUT TO EGYPT!
IT WAS THE FIRST TIME, BUT NOT THE LAST.
AFTER HEROD'S DEATH, THE FAMILY RETURNED HOME TO NAZARETH.
JESUS GREW--

LUKE 1:54-55; LUKE 2:23-39; MATTHEW 2:1-23

--AND SO DID THEIR FAMILY.

JESUS WAS MARY'S FIRSTBORN SON--

--HER OTHER SONS WERE JOSEPH, JAMES, JUDAS, AND SIMON.

HIS SISTERS' NAMES WERE NOT RECORDED.

MOST OF JESUS' CHILDHOOD IS EITHER LOST TO THE MEMORIES OF THOSE WHO WERE THERE--

--OR LEFT TO THE IMAGINATIONS OF THOSE WHO WERE NOT.

ONE EVENT, HOWEVER, WAS RECORDED.

ON THE ROAD FROM JERUSALEM TO NAZARETH, AFTER THE PASSOVER FEAST...

JOSEPH! I CANNOT FIND JESUS!

I HAVEN'T SEEN HIM SINCE BEFORE WE LEFT THE CITY!

AND SO MARY AND JOSEPH RETURNED TO JERUSALEM.

...I JUST THOUGHT HE WAS WITH YOU AND THE MEN!

HE'S OLD ENOUGH NOW.

AND I FIGURED HE WAS WITH YOU AND THE OTHER KIDS...

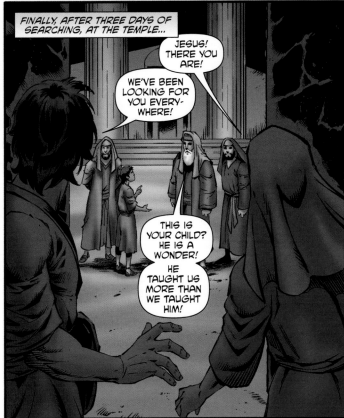

FINALLY, AFTER THREE DAYS OF SEARCHING, AT THE TEMPLE...

JESUS! THERE YOU ARE!

WE'VE BEEN LOOKING FOR YOU EVERY-WHERE!

THIS IS YOUR CHILD? HE IS A WONDER!

HE TAUGHT US MORE THAN WE TAUGHT HIM!

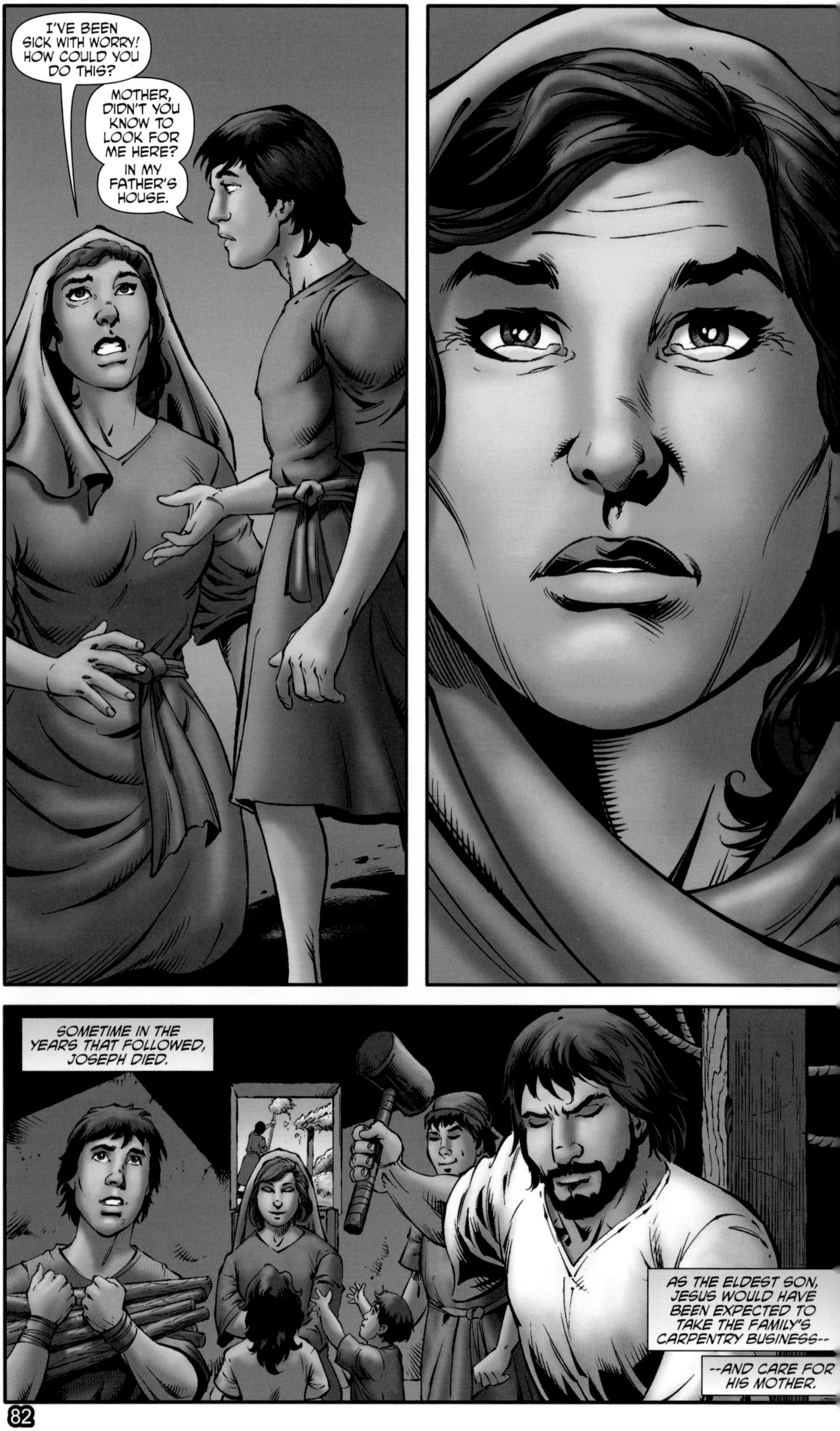
I'VE BEEN SICK WITH WORRY! HOW COULD YOU DO THIS?
MOTHER, DIDN'T YOU KNOW TO LOOK FOR ME HERE?
IN MY FATHER'S HOUSE.
SOMETIME IN THE YEARS THAT FOLLOWED, JOSEPH DIED.
AS THE ELDEST SON, JESUS WOULD HAVE BEEN EXPECTED TO TAKE THE FAMILY'S CARPENTRY BUSINESS--
--AND CARE FOR HIS MOTHER.

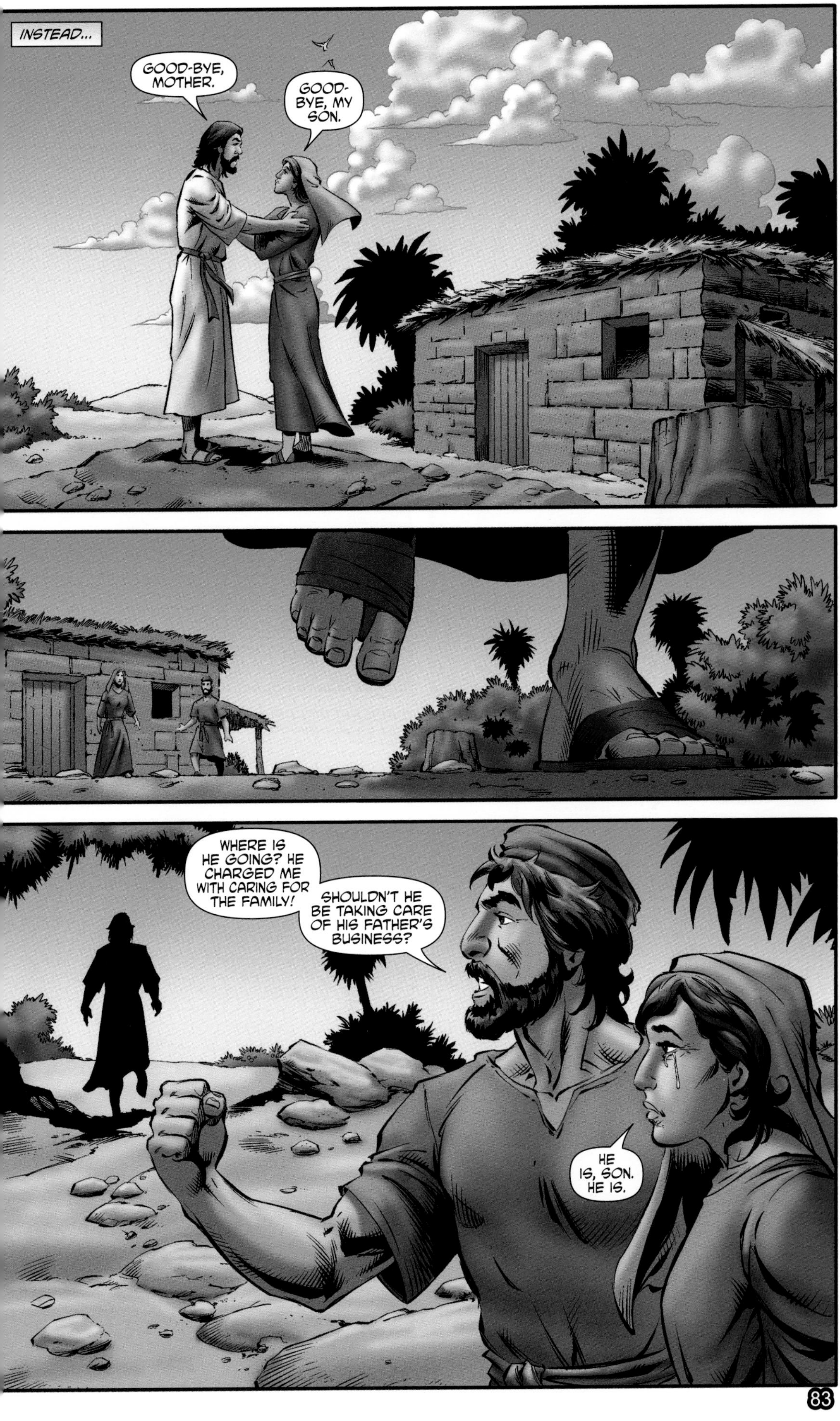
INSTEAD...
GOOD-BYE, MOTHER.
GOOD-BYE, MY SON.
WHERE IS HE GOING? HE CHARGED ME WITH CARING FOR THE FAMILY!
SHOULDN'T HE BE TAKING CARE OF HIS FATHER'S BUSINESS?
HE IS, SON. HE IS.

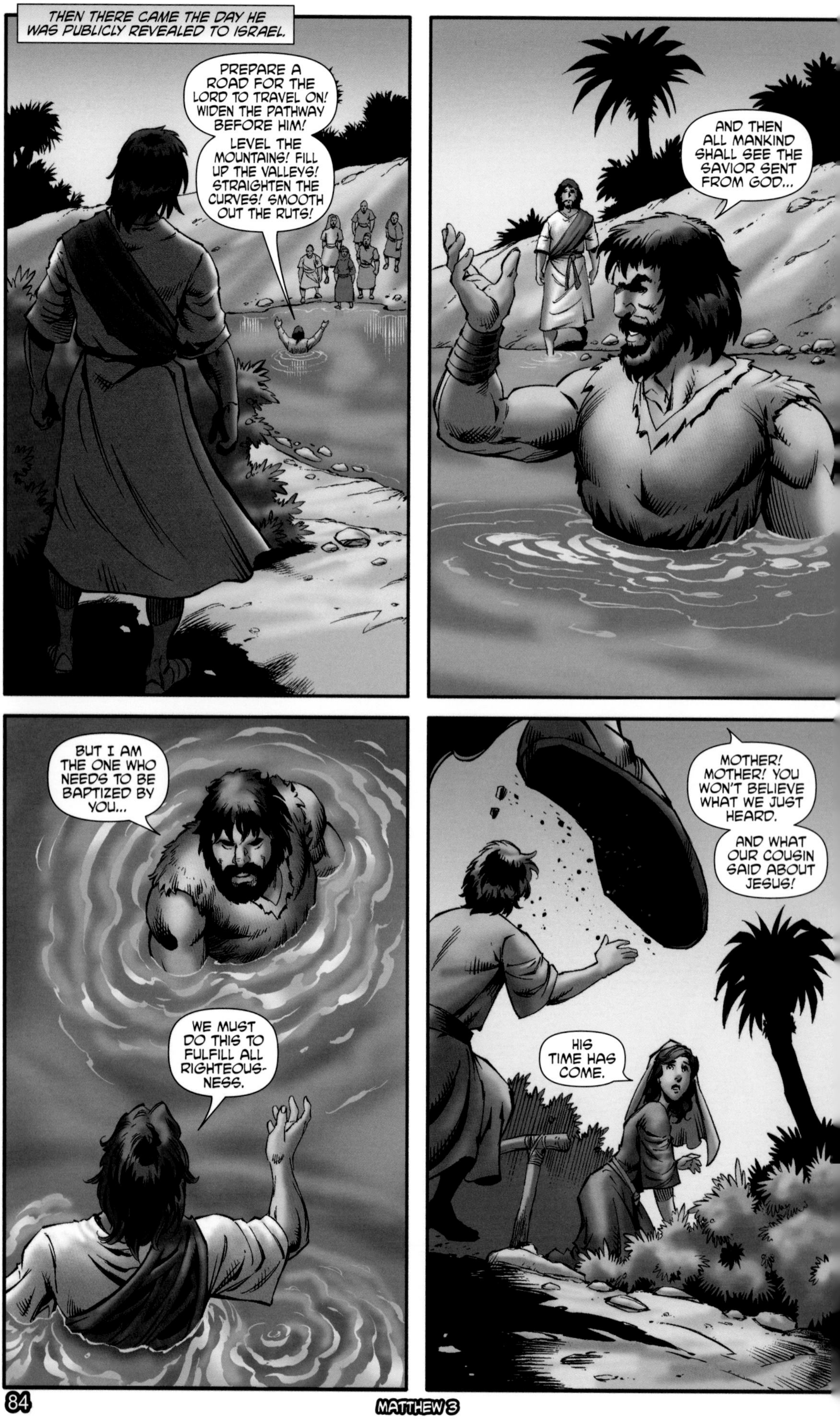

THEN THERE CAME THE DAY HE WAS PUBLICLY REVEALED TO ISRAEL.
PREPARE A ROAD FOR THE LORD TO TRAVEL ON! WIDEN THE PATHWAY BEFORE HIM!
LEVEL THE MOUNTAINS! FILL UP THE VALLEYS! STRAIGHTEN THE CURVES! SMOOTH OUT THE RUTS!
AND THEN ALL MANKIND SHALL SEE THE SAVIOR SENT FROM GOD...
BUT I AM THE ONE WHO NEEDS TO BE BAPTIZED BY YOU...
WE MUST DO THIS TO FULFILL ALL RIGHTEOUS-NESS.
MOTHER! MOTHER! YOU WON'T BELIEVE WHAT WE JUST HEARD.
AND WHAT OUR COUSIN SAID ABOUT JESUS!
HIS TIME HAS COME.

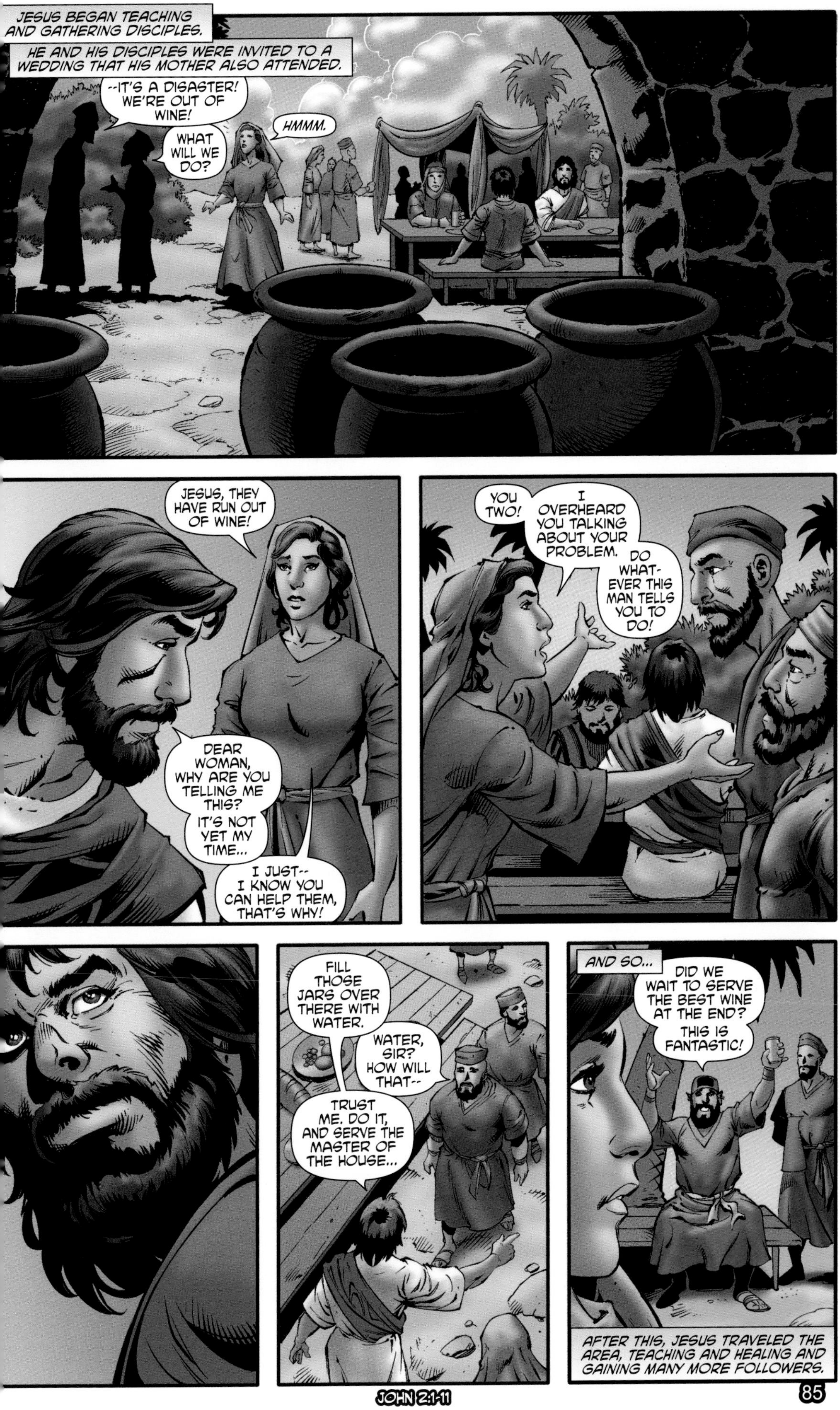

JESUS BEGAN TEACHING AND GATHERING DISCIPLES.
HE AND HIS DISCIPLES WERE INVITED TO A WEDDING THAT HIS MOTHER ALSO ATTENDED.
--IT'S A DISASTER! WE'RE OUT OF WINE!
WHAT WILL WE DO?
HMMM.
JESUS, THEY HAVE RUN OUT OF WINE!
DEAR WOMAN, WHY ARE YOU TELLING ME THIS?
IT'S NOT YET MY TIME...
I JUST-- I KNOW YOU CAN HELP THEM, THAT'S WHY!
YOU TWO!
I OVERHEARD YOU TALKING ABOUT YOUR PROBLEM.
DO WHATEVER THIS MAN TELLS YOU TO DO!
FILL THOSE JARS OVER THERE WITH WATER.
WATER, SIR? HOW WILL THAT--
TRUST ME. DO IT, AND SERVE THE MASTER OF THE HOUSE...
AND SO...
DID WE WAIT TO SERVE THE BEST WINE AT THE END?
THIS IS FANTASTIC!
AFTER THIS, JESUS TRAVELED THE AREA, TEACHING AND HEALING AND GAINING MANY MORE FOLLOWERS.

JOHN 2:1-11

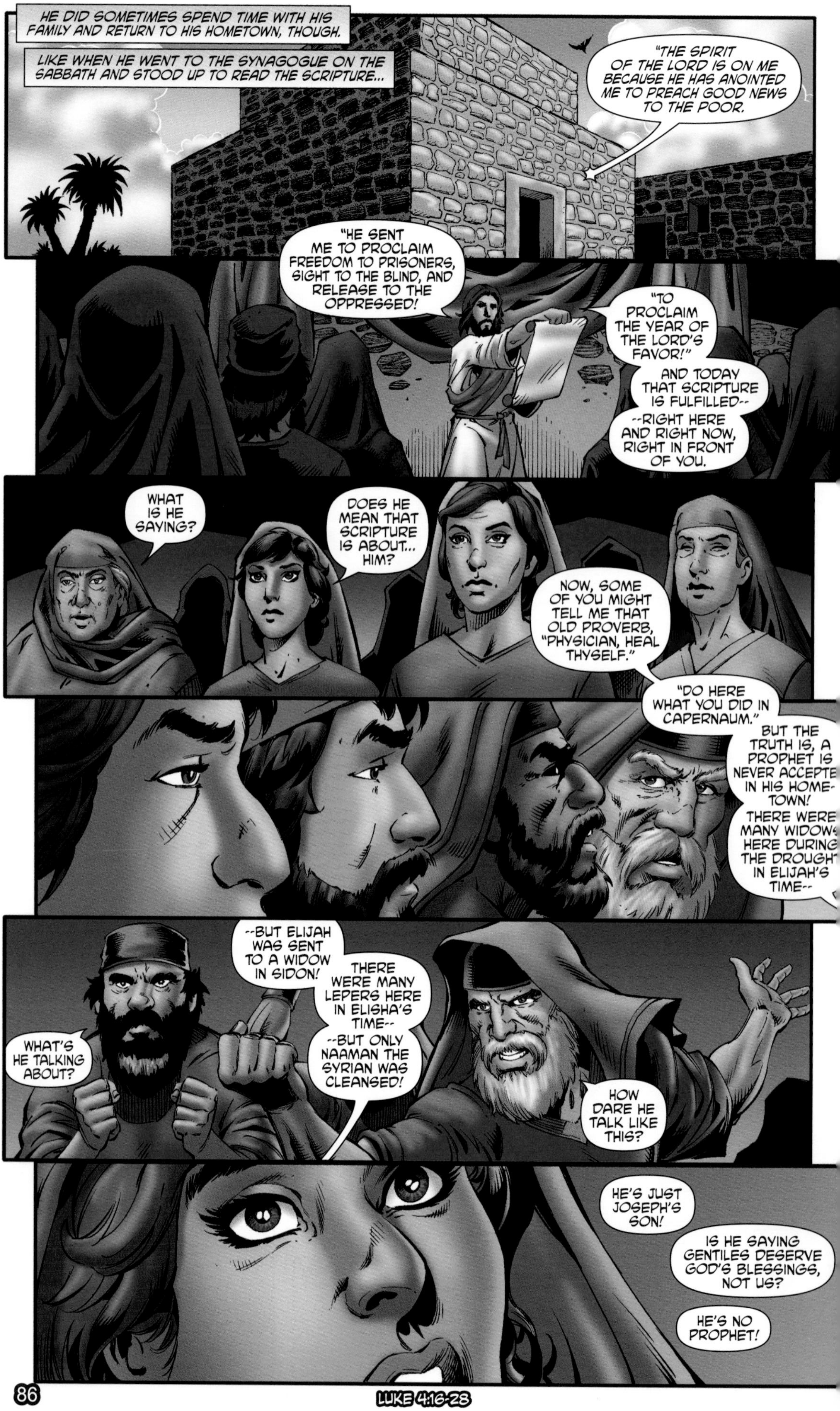
HE DID SOMETIMES SPEND TIME WITH HIS FAMILY AND RETURN TO HIS HOMETOWN, THOUGH.
LIKE WHEN HE WENT TO THE SYNAGOGUE ON THE SABBATH AND STOOD UP TO READ THE SCRIPTURE...
"THE SPIRIT OF THE LORD IS ON ME BECAUSE HE HAS ANOINTED ME TO PREACH GOOD NEWS TO THE POOR.
"HE SENT ME TO PROCLAIM FREEDOM TO PRISONERS, SIGHT TO THE BLIND, AND RELEASE TO THE OPPRESSED!
"TO PROCLAIM THE YEAR OF THE LORD'S FAVOR!"
AND TODAY THAT SCRIPTURE IS FULFILLED--
--RIGHT HERE AND RIGHT NOW, RIGHT IN FRONT OF YOU.
WHAT IS HE SAYING?
DOES HE MEAN THAT SCRIPTURE IS ABOUT... HIM?
NOW, SOME OF YOU MIGHT TELL ME THAT OLD PROVERB, "PHYSICIAN, HEAL THYSELF."
"DO HERE WHAT YOU DID IN CAPERNAUM."
BUT THE TRUTH IS, A PROPHET IS NEVER ACCEPTE IN HIS HOME-TOWN!
THERE WERE MANY WIDOW HERE DURING THE DROUGHT IN ELIJAH'S TIME--
--BUT ELIJAH WAS SENT TO A WIDOW IN SIDON!
THERE WERE MANY LEPERS HERE IN ELISHA'S TIME--
--BUT ONLY NAAMAN THE SYRIAN WAS CLEANSED!
WHAT'S HE TALKING ABOUT?
HOW DARE HE TALK LIKE THIS?
HE'S JUST JOSEPH'S SON!
IS HE SAYING GENTILES DESERVE GOD'S BLESSINGS, NOT US?
HE'S NO PROPHET!

LUKE 4:16-28

WHAT ARE THEY DOING?

WHERE ARE THEY TAKING HIM?

MOTHER, DON'T COME ANY CLOSER!

WHAT ARE THEY DOING WITH HIM?

THEY MEAN TO THROW HIM OVER THE CLIFF! DON'T LOOK!

WHO'S THAT?

THEY HAVEN'T NOTICED THAT HE SLIPPED AWAY!

HOW'D HE MANAGE THAT!

JUDE, YOU STILL DON'T UNDERSTAND WHO HE IS, DO YOU?

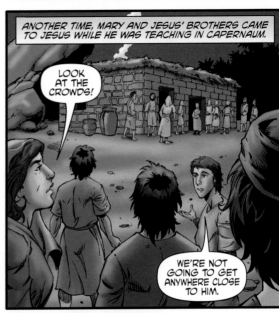

ANOTHER TIME, MARY AND JESUS' BROTHERS CAME TO JESUS WHILE HE WAS TEACHING IN CAPERNAUM.

LOOK AT THE CROWDS!

WE'RE NOT GOING TO GET ANYWHERE CLOSE TO HIM.

EXCUSE ME... COULD YOU TELL THE MAN WHO IS SPEAKING INSIDE THAT HIS MOTHER AND BROTHERS WANT TO SEE HIM?

YOU'RE JESUS' MOTHER? SURE! I'LL HELP YOU OUT!

MOTHER, DO YOU REALLY BELIEVE HE IS THE MESSIAH?

YOU STILL DON'T UNDERSTAND, AFTER ALL YOU'VE SEEN AND HEARD?

WITH ALL THESE PEOPLE I CAN'T SEE OR HEAR ANYTHING!

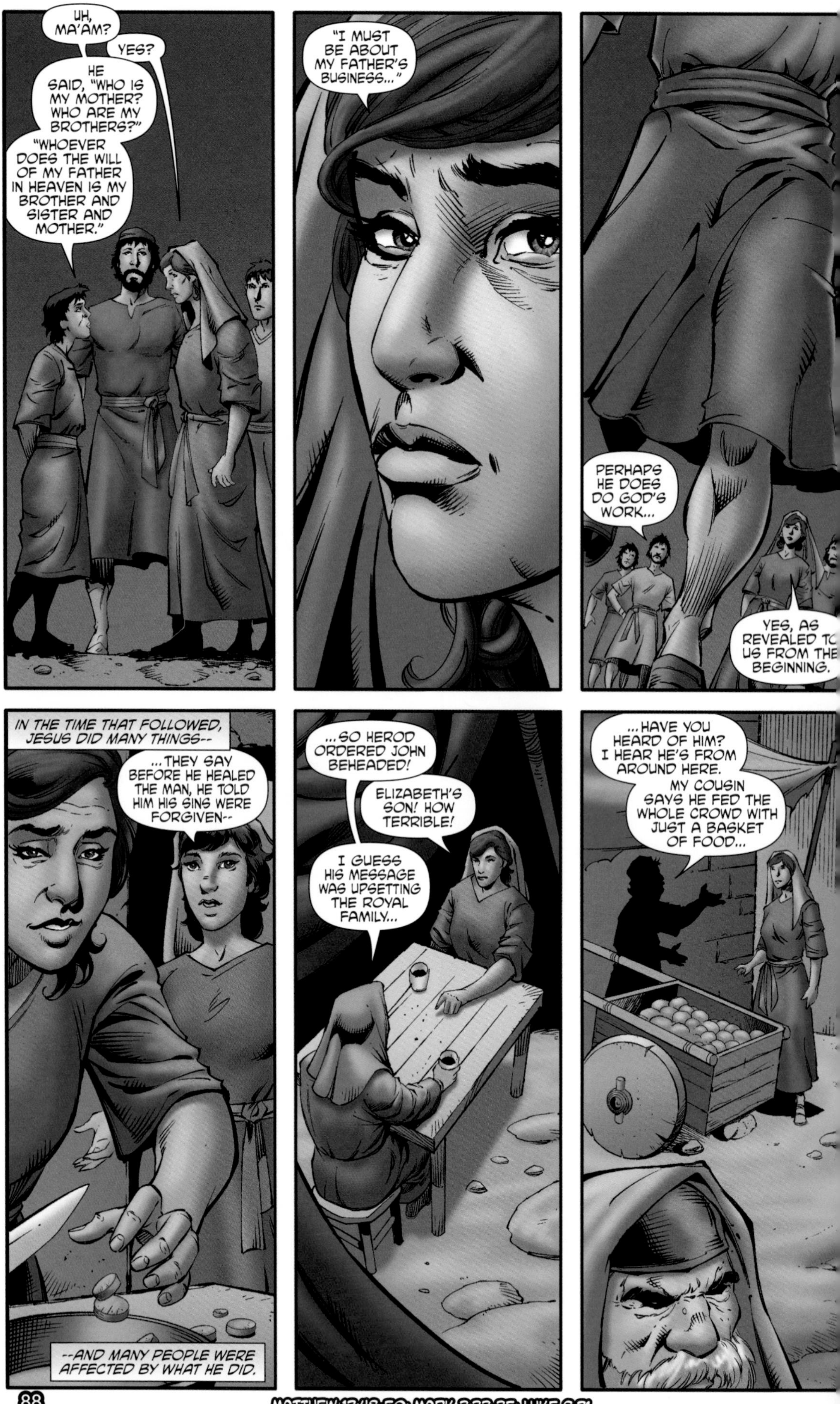
UH, MA'AM?
YES?
HE SAID, "WHO IS MY MOTHER? WHO ARE MY BROTHERS?"
"WHOEVER DOES THE WILL OF MY FATHER IN HEAVEN IS MY BROTHER AND SISTER AND MOTHER."
"I MUST BE ABOUT MY FATHER'S BUSINESS..."
PERHAPS HE DOES DO GOD'S WORK...
YES, AS REVEALED TO US FROM THE BEGINNING.
IN THE TIME THAT FOLLOWED, JESUS DID MANY THINGS--
...THEY SAY BEFORE HE HEALED THE MAN, HE TOLD HIM HIS SINS WERE FORGIVEN--
--AND MANY PEOPLE WERE AFFECTED BY WHAT HE DID.
...SO HEROD ORDERED JOHN BEHEADED!
ELIZABETH'S SON! HOW TERRIBLE!
I GUESS HIS MESSAGE WAS UPSETTING THE ROYAL FAMILY...
...HAVE YOU HEARD OF HIM? I HEAR HE'S FROM AROUND HERE.
MY COUSIN SAYS HE FED THE WHOLE CROWD WITH JUST A BASKET OF FOOD...

MATTHEW 12:48-50; MARK 3:33-35; LUKE 8:21

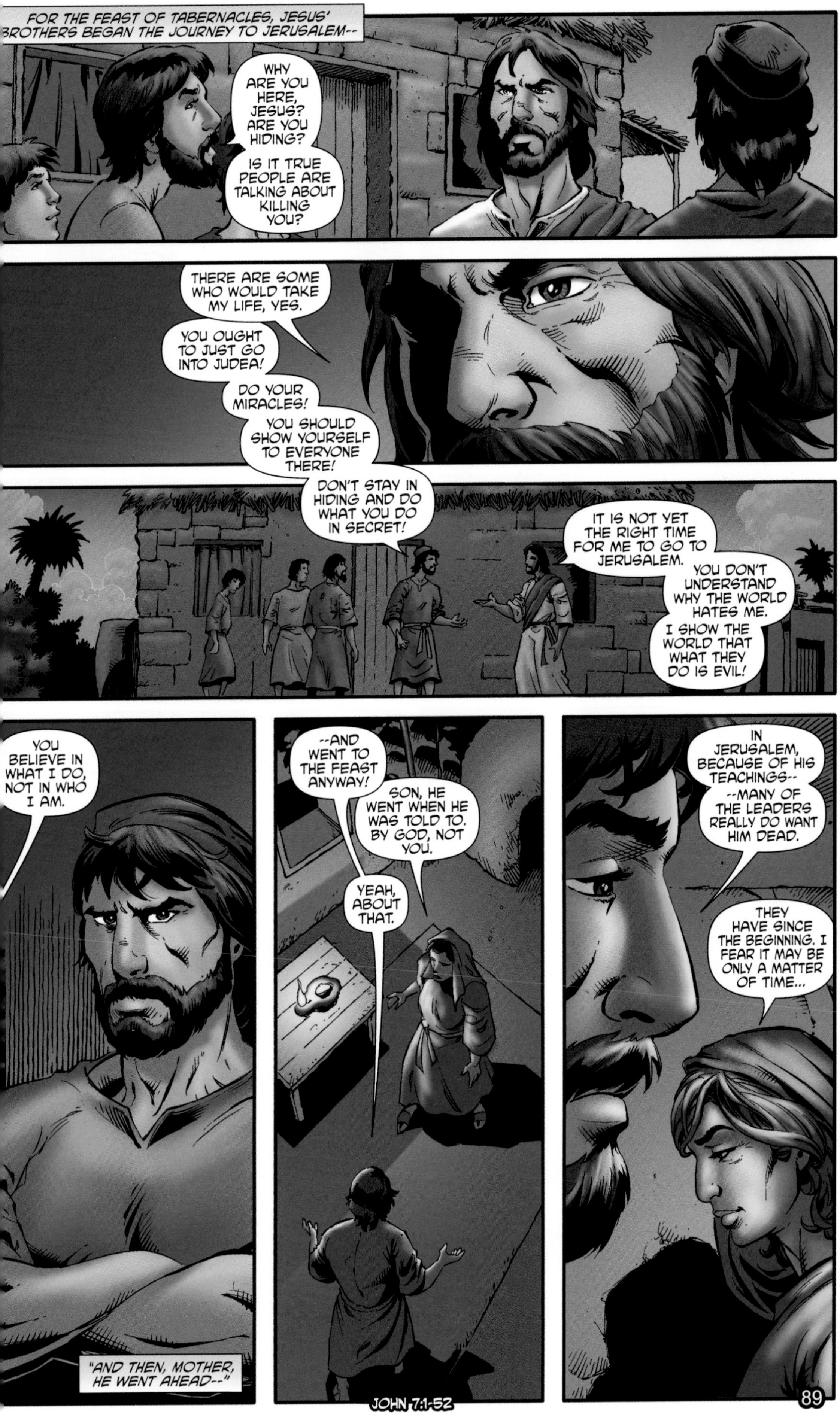
FOR THE FEAST OF TABERNACLES, JESUS' BROTHERS BEGAN THE JOURNEY TO JERUSALEM--
WHY ARE YOU HERE, JESUS? ARE YOU HIDING?
IS IT TRUE PEOPLE ARE TALKING ABOUT KILLING YOU?
THERE ARE SOME WHO WOULD TAKE MY LIFE, YES.
YOU OUGHT TO JUST GO INTO JUDEA!
DO YOUR MIRACLES!
YOU SHOULD SHOW YOURSELF TO EVERYONE THERE!
DON'T STAY IN HIDING AND DO WHAT YOU DO IN SECRET!
IT IS NOT YET THE RIGHT TIME FOR ME TO GO TO JERUSALEM.
YOU DON'T UNDERSTAND WHY THE WORLD HATES ME.
I SHOW THE WORLD THAT WHAT THEY DO IS EVIL!
YOU BELIEVE IN WHAT I DO, NOT IN WHO I AM.
"AND THEN, MOTHER, HE WENT AHEAD--"
--AND WENT TO THE FEAST ANYWAY!
SON, HE WENT WHEN HE WAS TOLD TO. BY GOD, NOT YOU.
YEAH, ABOUT THAT.
IN JERUSALEM, BECAUSE OF HIS TEACHINGS--
--MANY OF THE LEADERS REALLY DO WANT HIM DEAD.
THEY HAVE SINCE THE BEGINNING. I FEAR IT MAY BE ONLY A MATTER OF TIME...

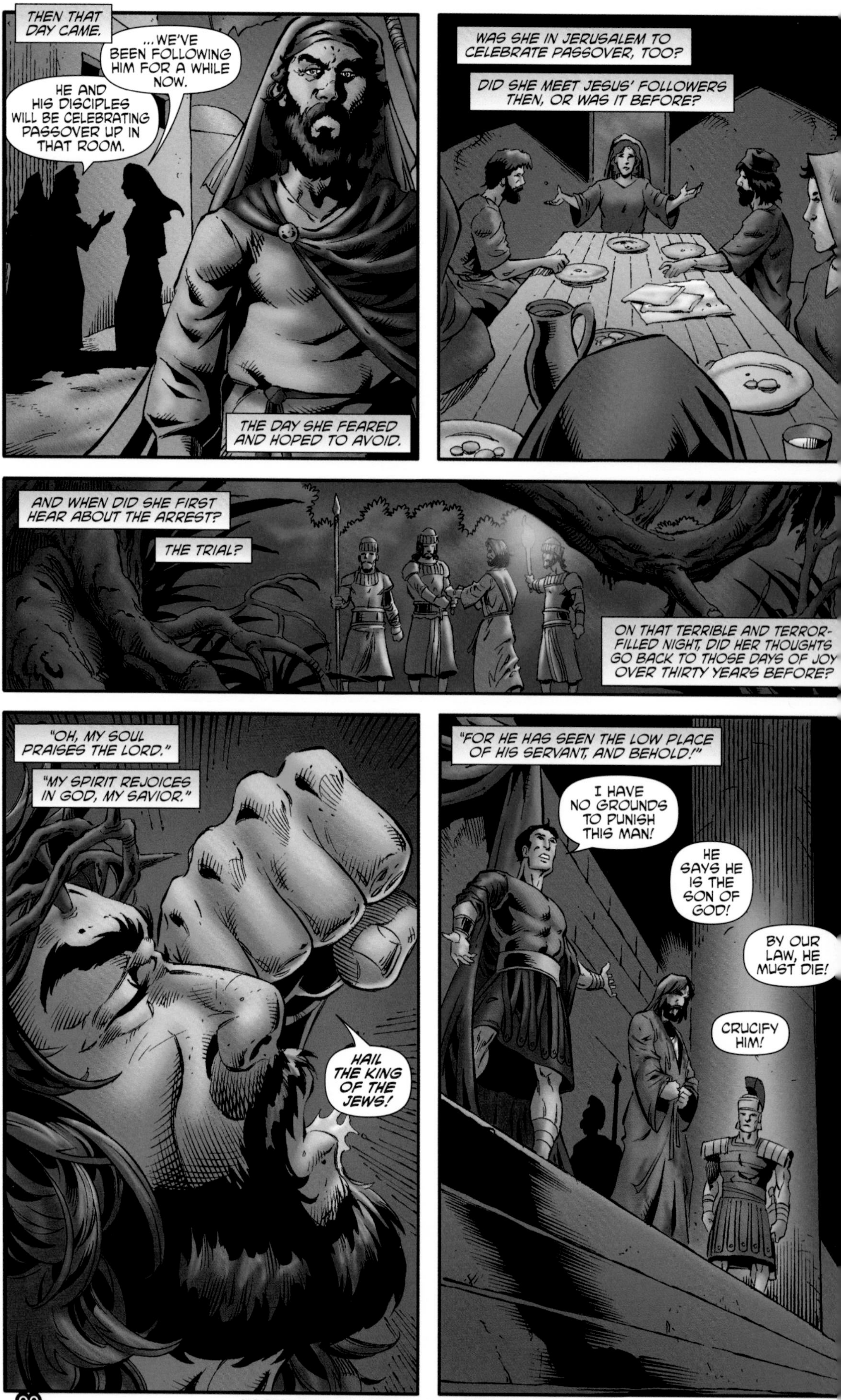
THEN THAT DAY CAME.
...WE'VE BEEN FOLLOWING HIM FOR A WHILE NOW.
HE AND HIS DISCIPLES WILL BE CELEBRATING PASSOVER UP IN THAT ROOM.
THE DAY SHE FEARED AND HOPED TO AVOID.
WAS SHE IN JERUSALEM TO CELEBRATE PASSOVER, TOO?
DID SHE MEET JESUS' FOLLOWERS THEN, OR WAS IT BEFORE?
AND WHEN DID SHE FIRST HEAR ABOUT THE ARREST?
THE TRIAL?
ON THAT TERRIBLE AND TERROR-FILLED NIGHT, DID HER THOUGHTS GO BACK TO THOSE DAYS OF JOY OVER THIRTY YEARS BEFORE?
"OH, MY SOUL PRAISES THE LORD."
"MY SPIRIT REJOICES IN GOD, MY SAVIOR."
HAIL THE KING OF THE JEWS!
"FOR HE HAS SEEN THE LOW PLACE OF HIS SERVANT, AND BEHOLD!"
I HAVE NO GROUNDS TO PUNISH THIS MAN!
HE SAYS HE IS THE SON OF GOD!
BY OUR LAW, HE MUST DIE!
CRUCIFY HIM!

MATTHEW 26-27; MARK 14-15; LUKE 22-23; JOHN 13-19

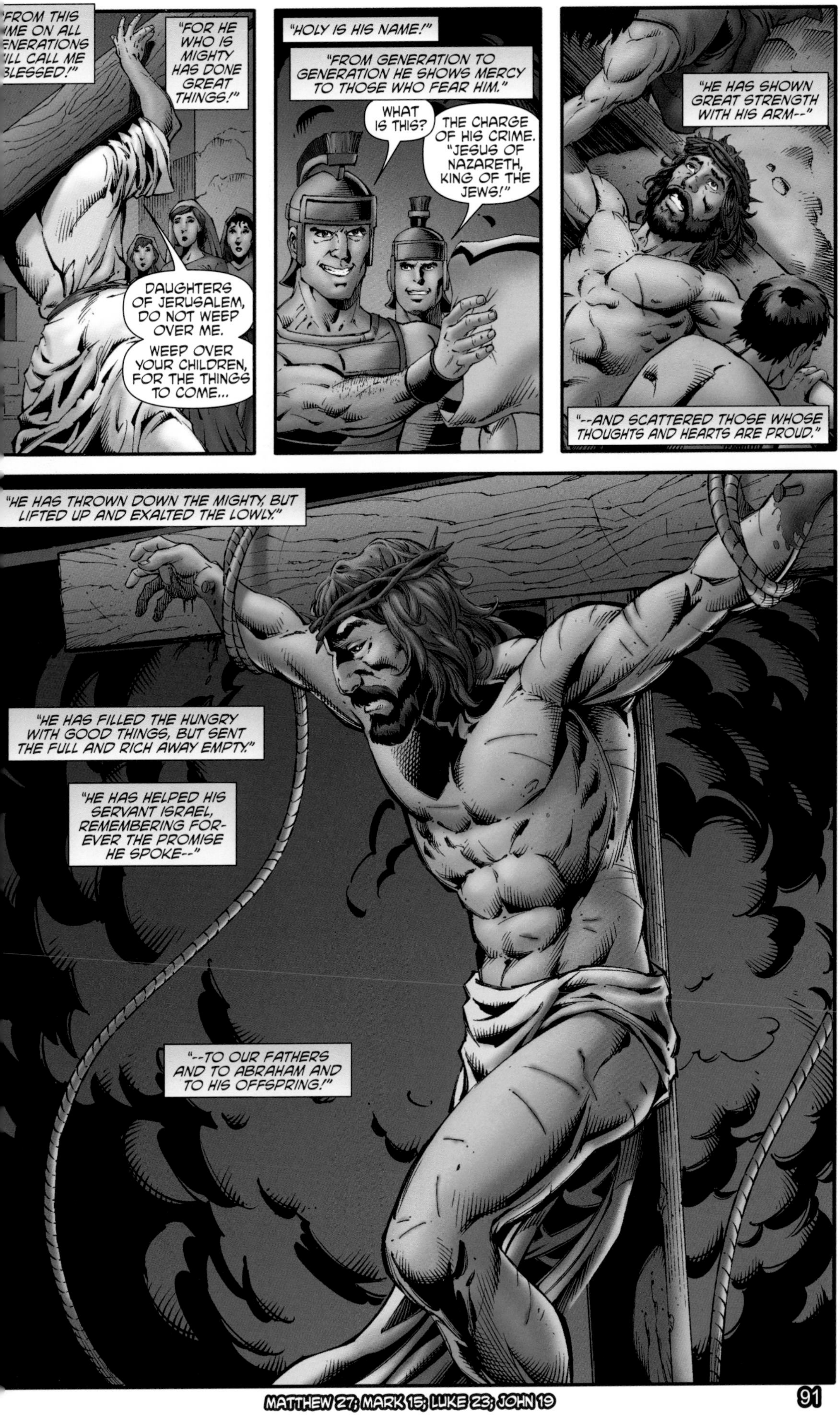

"FROM THIS
...ME ON ALL
...ENERATIONS
...ILL CALL ME
...LESSED!"
"FOR HE WHO IS MIGHTY HAS DONE GREAT THINGS!"
DAUGHTERS OF JERUSALEM, DO NOT WEEP OVER ME.
WEEP OVER YOUR CHILDREN, FOR THE THINGS TO COME...
"HOLY IS HIS NAME!"
"FROM GENERATION TO GENERATION HE SHOWS MERCY TO THOSE WHO FEAR HIM."
WHAT IS THIS?
THE CHARGE OF HIS CRIME. "JESUS OF NAZARETH, KING OF THE JEWS!"
"HE HAS SHOWN GREAT STRENGTH WITH HIS ARM--"
"--AND SCATTERED THOSE WHOSE THOUGHTS AND HEARTS ARE PROUD."
"HE HAS THROWN DOWN THE MIGHTY, BUT LIFTED UP AND EXALTED THE LOWLY."
"HE HAS FILLED THE HUNGRY WITH GOOD THINGS, BUT SENT THE FULL AND RICH AWAY EMPTY."
"HE HAS HELPED HIS SERVANT ISRAEL, REMEMBERING FOREVER THE PROMISE HE SPOKE--"
"--TO OUR FATHERS AND TO ABRAHAM AND TO HIS OFFSPRING!"

MATTHEW 27; MARK 15; LUKE 23; JOHN 19

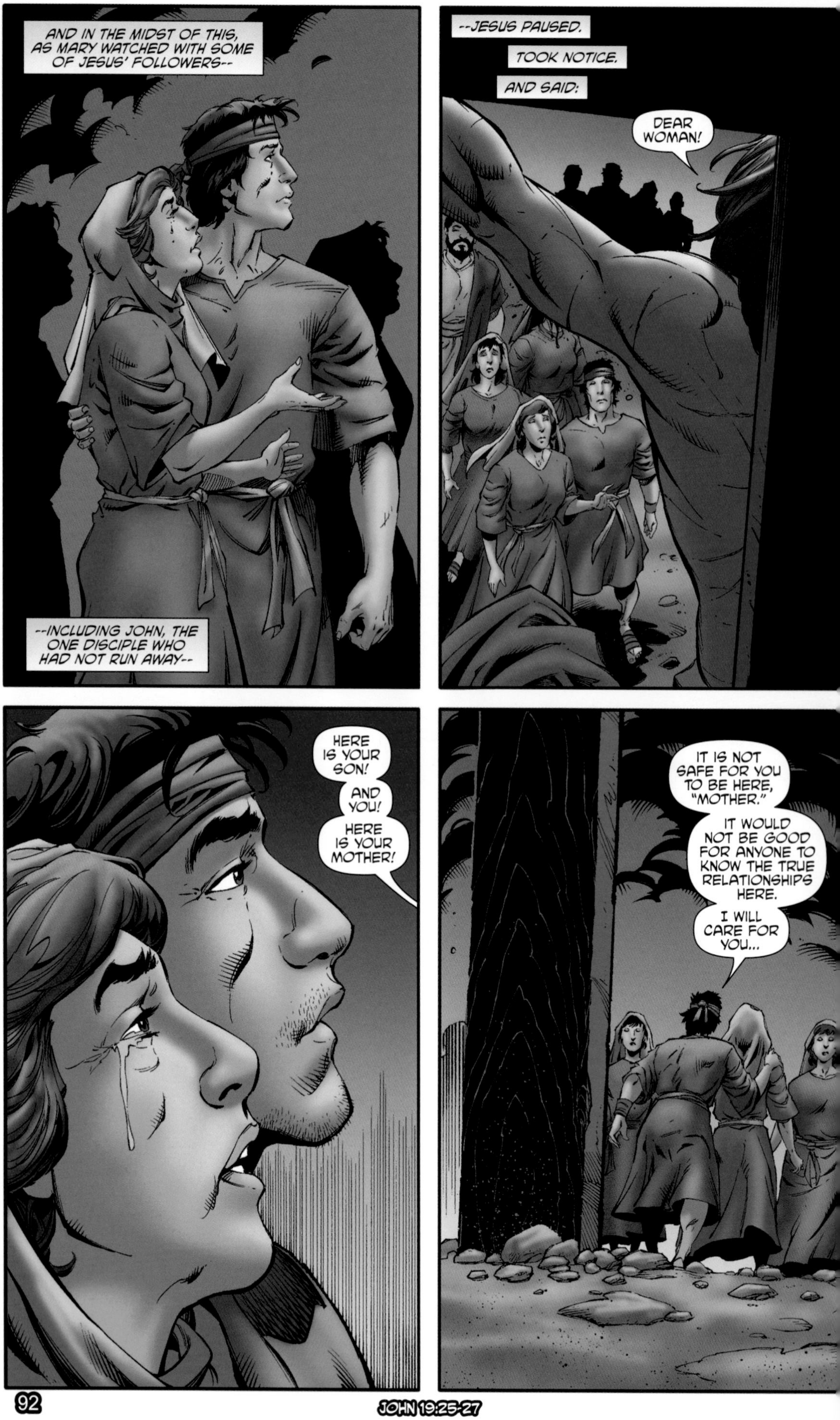
AND IN THE MIDST OF THIS, AS MARY WATCHED WITH SOME OF JESUS' FOLLOWERS--
--INCLUDING JOHN, THE ONE DISCIPLE WHO HAD NOT RUN AWAY--
--JESUS PAUSED.
TOOK NOTICE.
AND SAID:
DEAR WOMAN!
HERE IS YOUR SON!
AND YOU!
HERE IS YOUR MOTHER!
IT IS NOT SAFE FOR YOU TO BE HERE, "MOTHER."
IT WOULD NOT BE GOOD FOR ANYONE TO KNOW THE TRUE RELATIONSHIPS HERE.
I WILL CARE FOR YOU...

JOHN 19:25-27

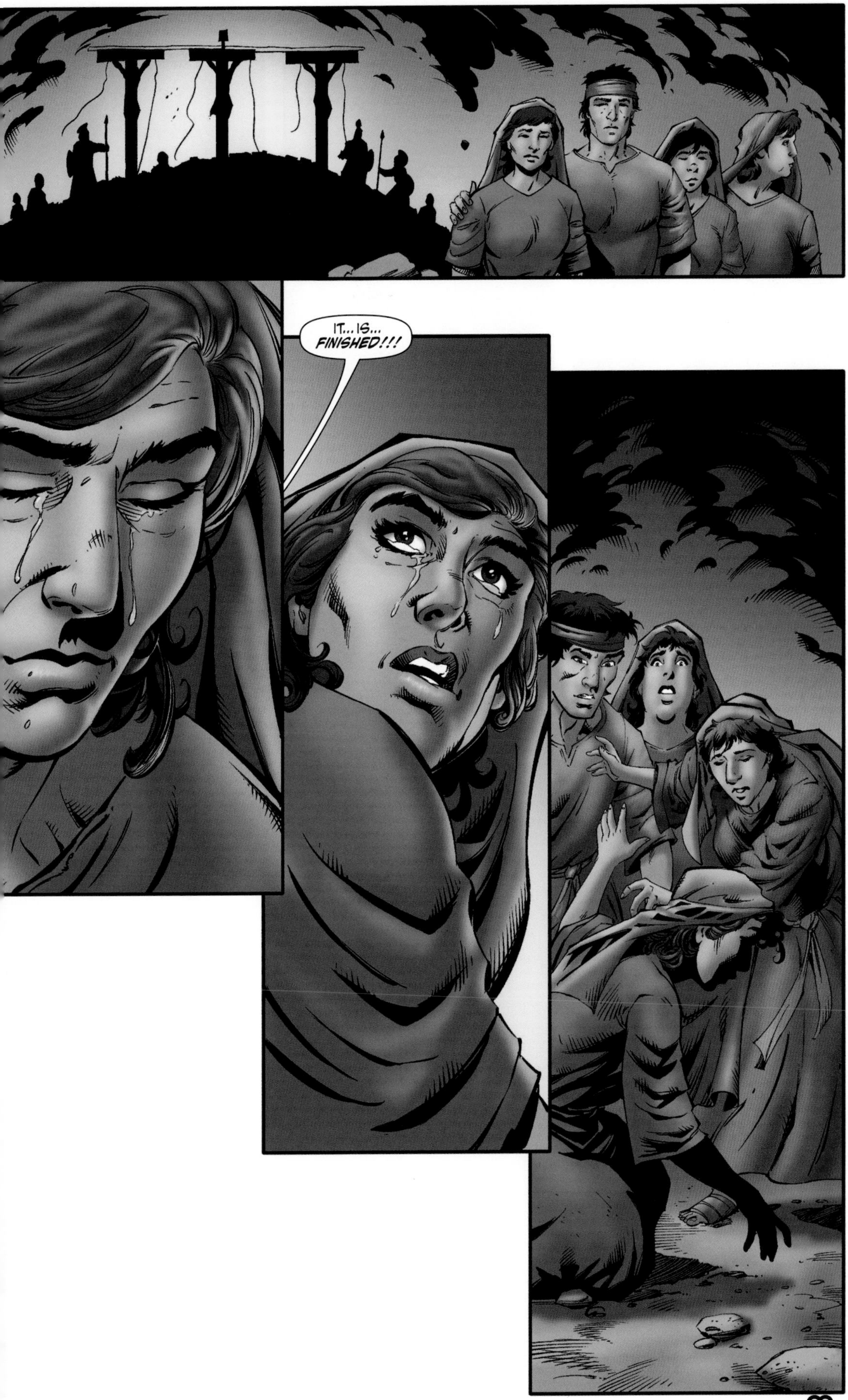
IT... IS... FINISHED!!!

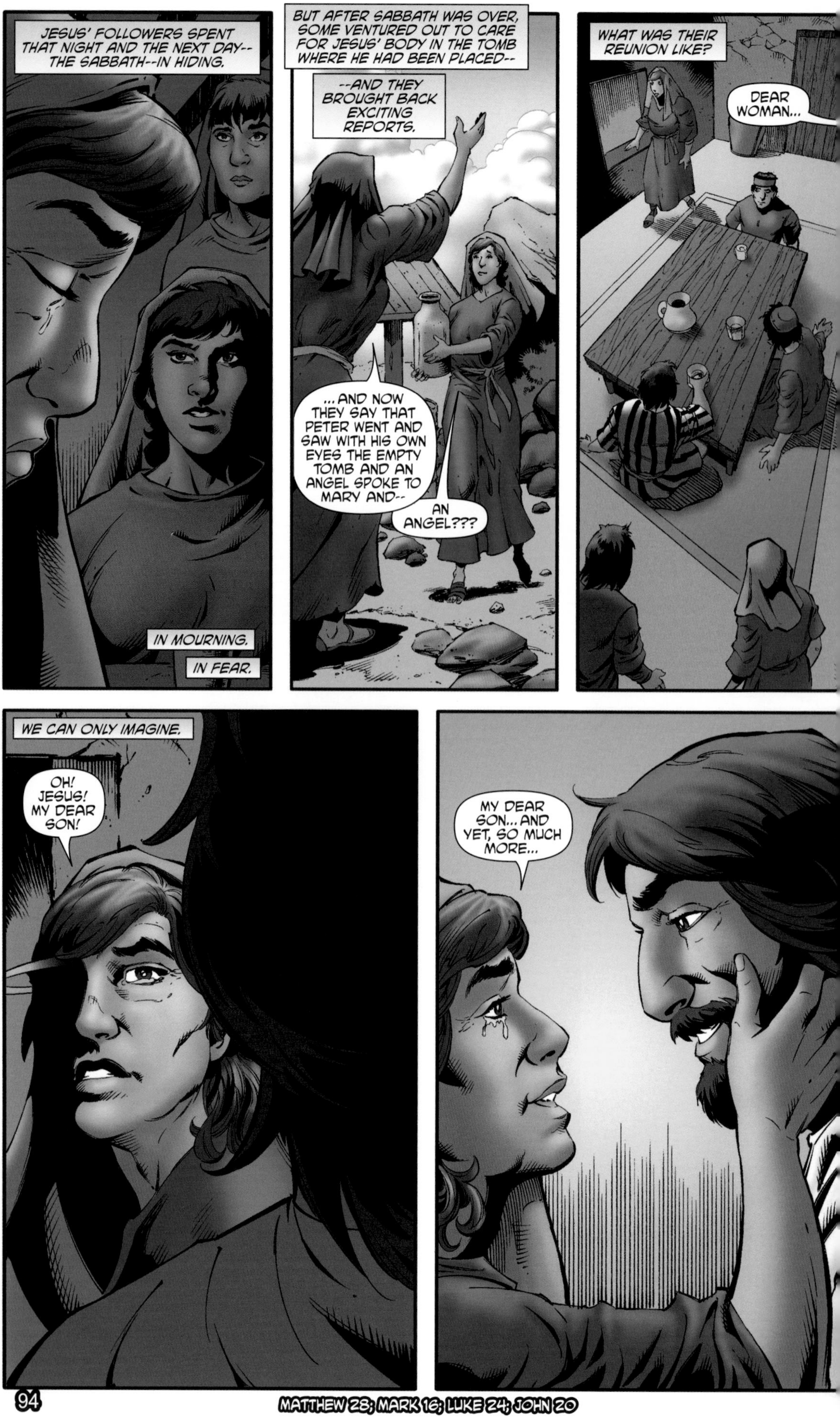
JESUS' FOLLOWERS SPENT THAT NIGHT AND THE NEXT DAY--THE SABBATH--IN HIDING.
IN MOURNING.
IN FEAR.
BUT AFTER SABBATH WAS OVER, SOME VENTURED OUT TO CARE FOR JESUS' BODY IN THE TOMB WHERE HE HAD BEEN PLACED--
--AND THEY BROUGHT BACK EXCITING REPORTS.
...AND NOW THEY SAY THAT PETER WENT AND SAW WITH HIS OWN EYES THE EMPTY TOMB AND AN ANGEL SPOKE TO MARY AND--
AN ANGEL???
WHAT WAS THEIR REUNION LIKE?
DEAR WOMAN...
WE CAN ONLY IMAGINE.
OH! JESUS! MY DEAR SON!
MY DEAR SON... AND YET, SO MUCH MORE...

MATTHEW 28; MARK 16; LUKE 24; JOHN 20

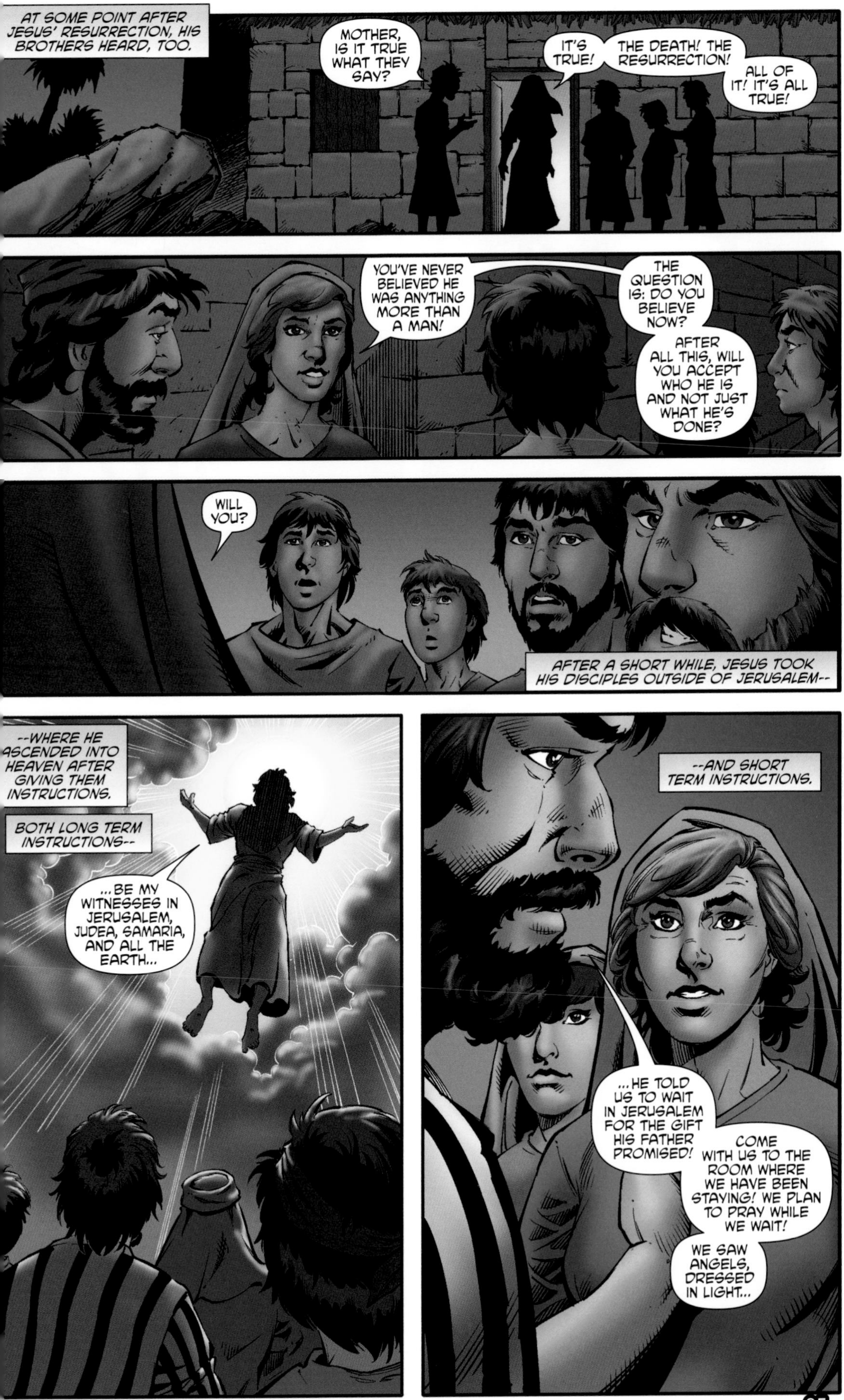
AT SOME POINT AFTER JESUS' RESURRECTION, HIS BROTHERS HEARD, TOO.
MOTHER, IS IT TRUE WHAT THEY SAY?
IT'S TRUE!
THE DEATH! THE RESURRECTION!
ALL OF IT! IT'S ALL TRUE!
YOU'VE NEVER BELIEVED HE WAS ANYTHING MORE THAN A MAN!
THE QUESTION IS: DO YOU BELIEVE NOW?
AFTER ALL THIS, WILL YOU ACCEPT WHO HE IS AND NOT JUST WHAT HE'S DONE?
WILL YOU?
AFTER A SHORT WHILE, JESUS TOOK HIS DISCIPLES OUTSIDE OF JERUSALEM--
--WHERE HE ASCENDED INTO HEAVEN AFTER GIVING THEM INSTRUCTIONS.
BOTH LONG TERM INSTRUCTIONS--
...BE MY WITNESSES IN JERUSALEM, JUDEA, SAMARIA, AND ALL THE EARTH...
--AND SHORT TERM INSTRUCTIONS.
...HE TOLD US TO WAIT IN JERUSALEM FOR THE GIFT HIS FATHER PROMISED!
COME WITH US TO THE ROOM WHERE WE HAVE BEEN STAYING! WE PLAN TO PRAY WHILE WE WAIT!
WE SAW ANGELS, DRESSED IN LIGHT...

HER NAME IS MARY.

AND WHAT WE KNOW OF HER STORY ENDS HERE.

ONCE MORE WITH ANGELS AND A PROMISE OF A GREAT GIFT FROM GOD.

WE NEED A REPLACEMENT FOR THE ONE WHO BETRAYED JESUS.

IT SHOULD BE SOMEONE WHO WAS WITH US FROM THE BEGINNING!

FROM THE BAPTISM WITH JOHN TO THE RESURRECTION OF JESUS TO NOW!

THE BEGINNING...

WE DON'T KNOW WHEN HER OTHER SONS BECAME FOLLOWERS OF THEIR BROTHER--

--BUT THEY, TOO, WERE IN THAT ROOM, WAITING AND PRAYING.

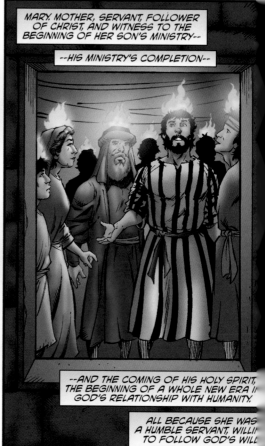

MARY. MOTHER, SERVANT, FOLLOWER OF CHRIST, AND WITNESS TO THE BEGINNING OF HER SON'S MINISTRY--

--HIS MINISTRY'S COMPLETION--

--AND THE COMING OF HIS HOLY SPIRIT, THE BEGINNING OF A WHOLE NEW ERA IN GOD'S RELATIONSHIP WITH HUMANITY.

ALL BECAUSE SHE WAS A HUMBLE SERVANT, WILLING TO FOLLOW GOD'S WILL.

ACTS 2

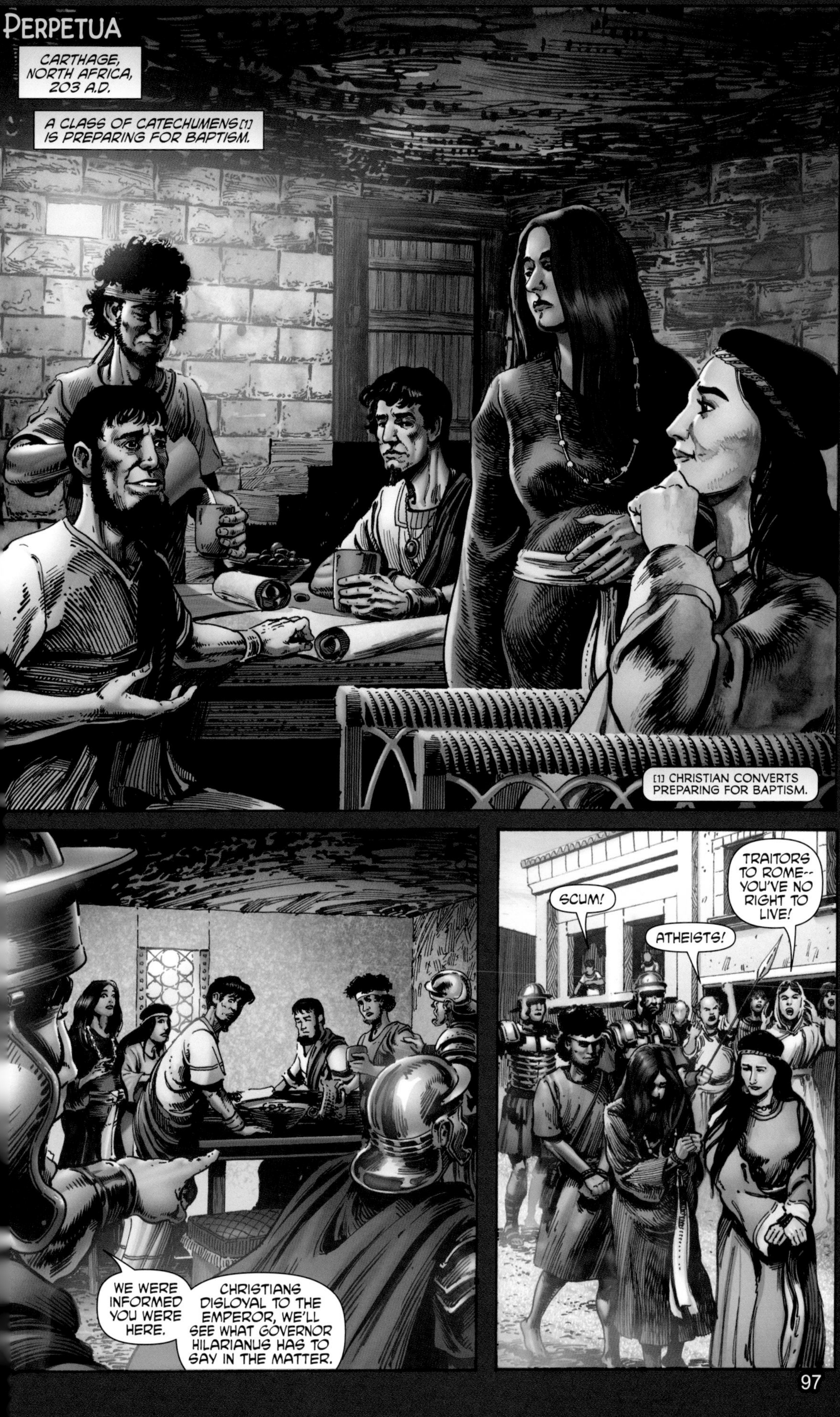
PERPETUA
CARTHAGE, NORTH AFRICA, 203 A.D.
A CLASS OF CATECHUMENS[1] IS PREPARING FOR BAPTISM.
[1] CHRISTIAN CONVERTS PREPARING FOR BAPTISM.
WE WERE INFORMED YOU WERE HERE.
CHRISTIANS DISLOYAL TO THE EMPEROR, WE'LL SEE WHAT GOVERNOR HILARIANUS HAS TO SAY IN THE MATTER.
SCUM!
ATHEISTS!
TRAITORS TO ROME-- YOU'VE NO RIGHT TO LIVE!

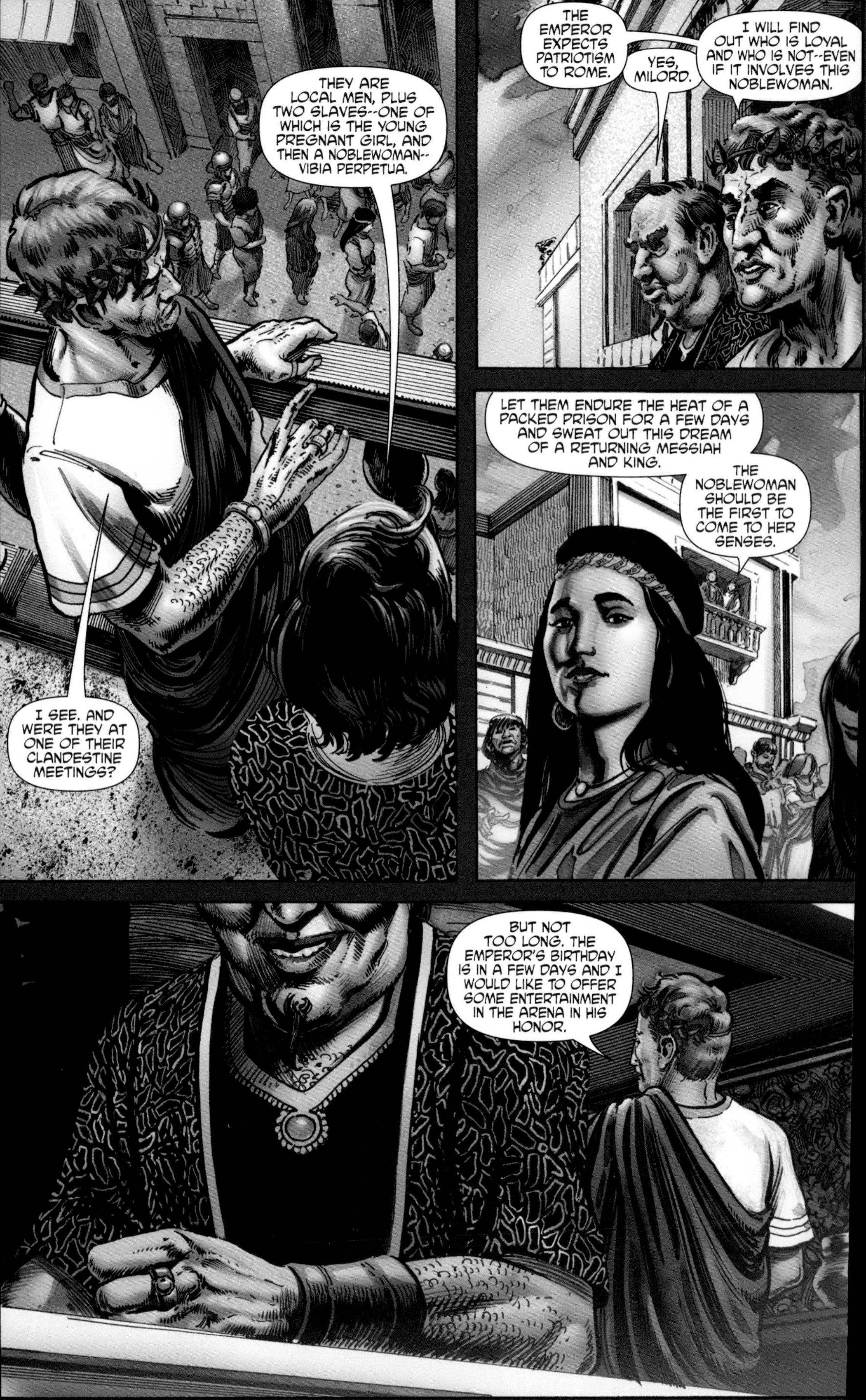
THEY ARE LOCAL MEN, PLUS TWO SLAVES--ONE OF WHICH IS THE YOUNG PREGNANT GIRL, AND THEN A NOBLEWOMAN--VIBIA PERPETUA.
I SEE. AND WERE THEY AT ONE OF THEIR CLANDESTINE MEETINGS?
THE EMPEROR EXPECTS PATRIOTISM TO ROME.
YES, MILORD.
I WILL FIND OUT WHO IS LOYAL AND WHO IS NOT--EVEN IF IT INVOLVES THIS NOBLEWOMAN.
LET THEM ENDURE THE HEAT OF A PACKED PRISON FOR A FEW DAYS AND SWEAT OUT THIS DREAM OF A RETURNING MESSIAH AND KING.
THE NOBLEWOMAN SHOULD BE THE FIRST TO COME TO HER SENSES.
BUT NOT TOO LONG. THE EMPEROR'S BIRTHDAY IS IN A FEW DAYS AND I WOULD LIKE TO OFFER SOME ENTERTAINMENT IN THE ARENA IN HIS HONOR.

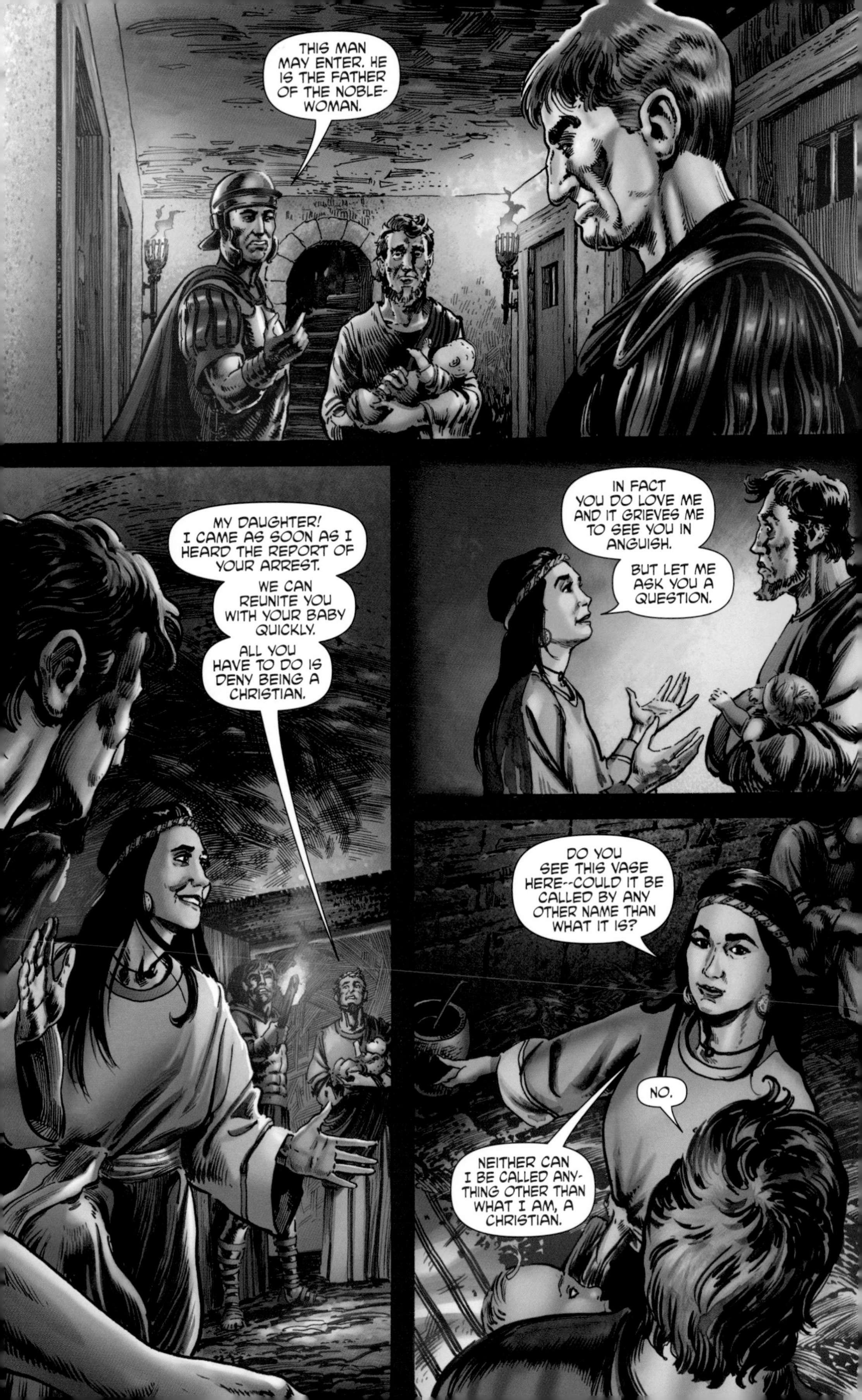
THIS MAN MAY ENTER. HE IS THE FATHER OF THE NOBLE-WOMAN.
MY DAUGHTER! I CAME AS SOON AS I HEARD THE REPORT OF YOUR ARREST.
WE CAN REUNITE YOU WITH YOUR BABY QUICKLY.
ALL YOU HAVE TO DO IS DENY BEING A CHRISTIAN.
IN FACT YOU DO LOVE ME AND IT GRIEVES ME TO SEE YOU IN ANGUISH.
BUT LET ME ASK YOU A QUESTION.
DO YOU SEE THIS VASE HERE--COULD IT BE CALLED BY ANY OTHER NAME THAN WHAT IT IS?
NO.
NEITHER CAN I BE CALLED ANY-THING OTHER THAN WHAT I AM, A CHRISTIAN.

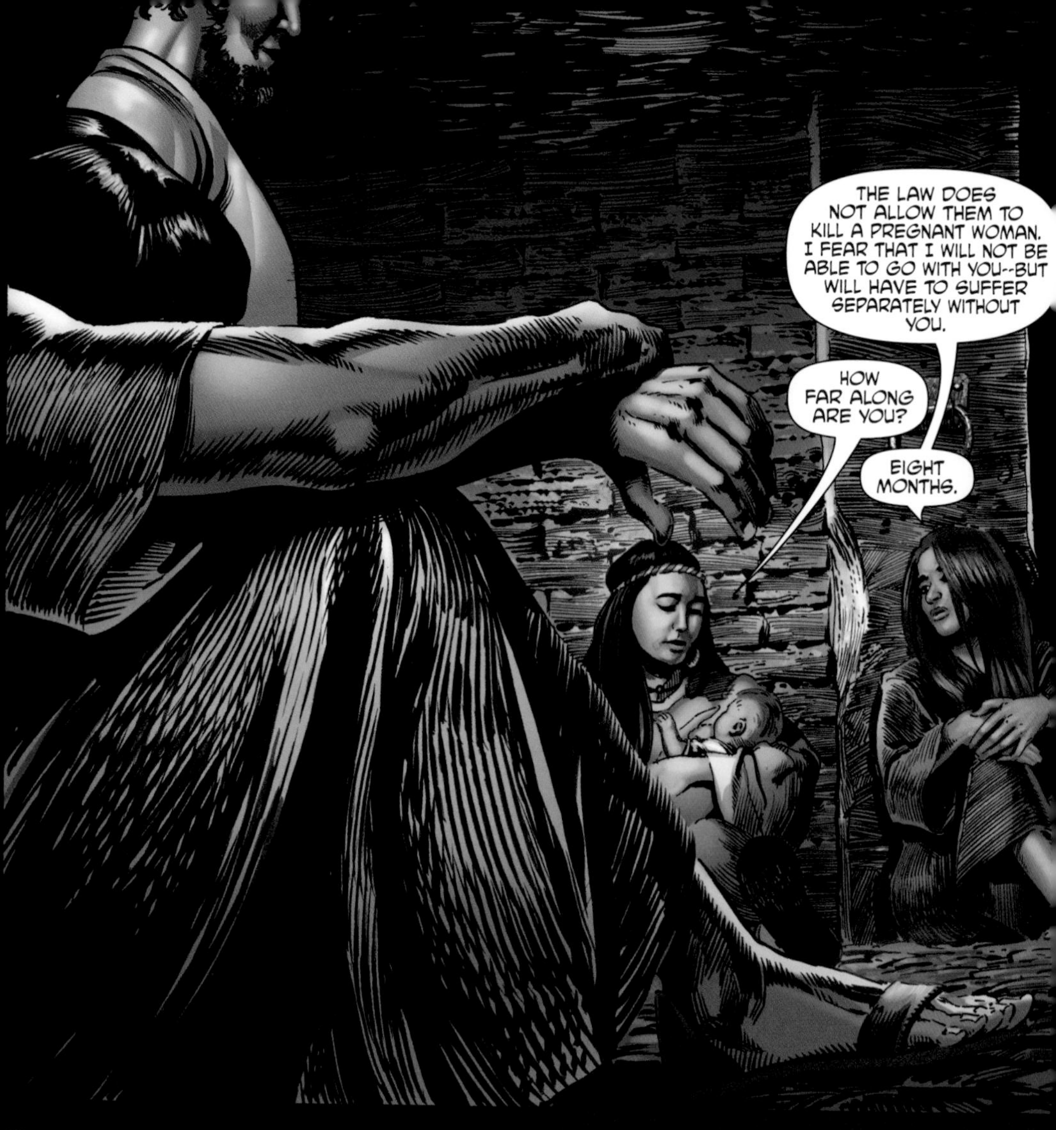
THE LAW DOES NOT ALLOW THEM TO KILL A PREGNANT WOMAN. I FEAR THAT I WILL NOT BE ABLE TO GO WITH YOU--BUT WILL HAVE TO SUFFER SEPARATELY WITHOUT YOU.
HOW FAR ALONG ARE YOU?
EIGHT MONTHS.

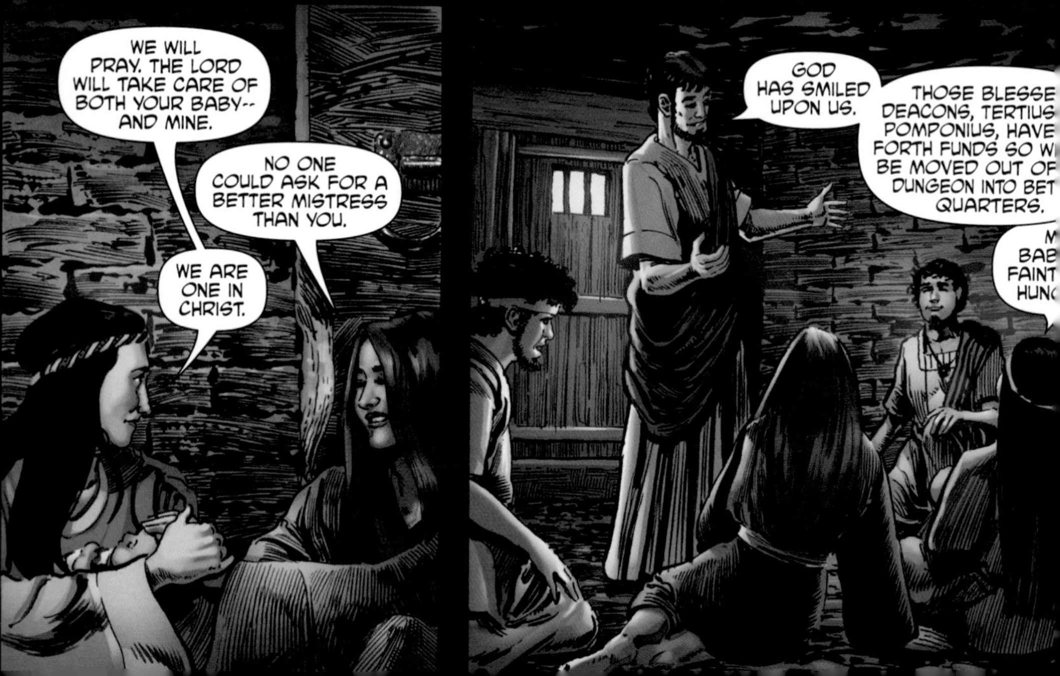
WE WILL PRAY. THE LORD WILL TAKE CARE OF BOTH YOUR BABY-- AND MINE.
NO ONE COULD ASK FOR A BETTER MISTRESS THAN YOU.
WE ARE ONE IN CHRIST.
GOD HAS SMILED UPON US.
THOSE BLESSE DEACONS, TERTIUS POMPONIUS, HAVE FORTH FUNDS SO W BE MOVED OUT OF DUNGEON INTO BET QUARTERS.
BAB FAINT HUN

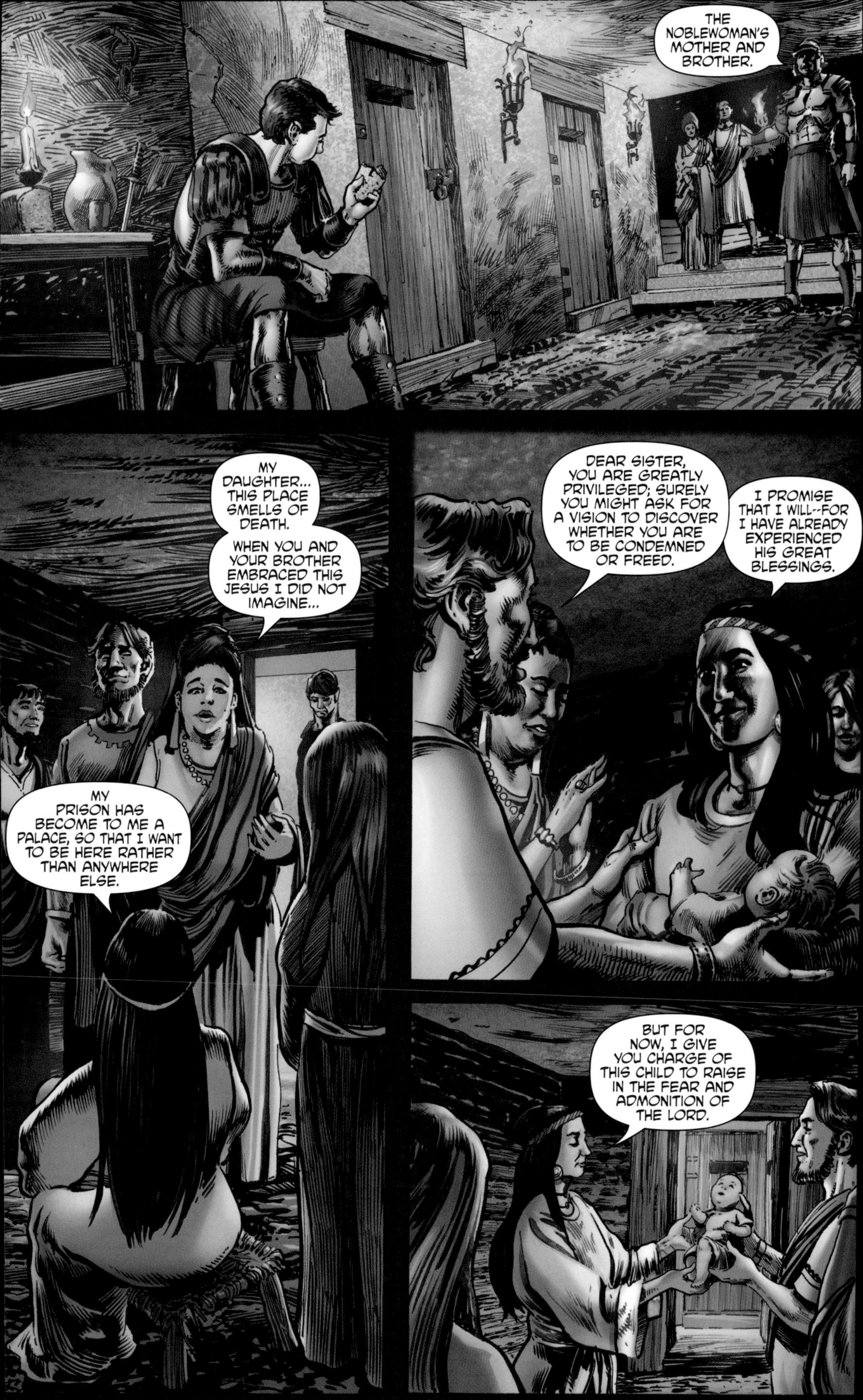
THE NOBLEWOMAN'S MOTHER AND BROTHER.
MY DAUGHTER... THIS PLACE SMELLS OF DEATH.
WHEN YOU AND YOUR BROTHER EMBRACED THIS JESUS I DID NOT IMAGINE...
MY PRISON HAS BECOME TO ME A PALACE, SO THAT I WANT TO BE HERE RATHER THAN ANYWHERE ELSE.
DEAR SISTER, YOU ARE GREATLY PRIVILEGED; SURELY YOU MIGHT ASK FOR A VISION TO DISCOVER WHETHER YOU ARE TO BE CONDEMNED OR FREED.
I PROMISE THAT I WILL--FOR I HAVE ALREADY EXPERIENCED HIS GREAT BLESSINGS.
BUT FOR NOW, I GIVE YOU CHARGE OF THIS CHILD TO RAISE IN THE FEAR AND ADMONITION OF THE LORD.

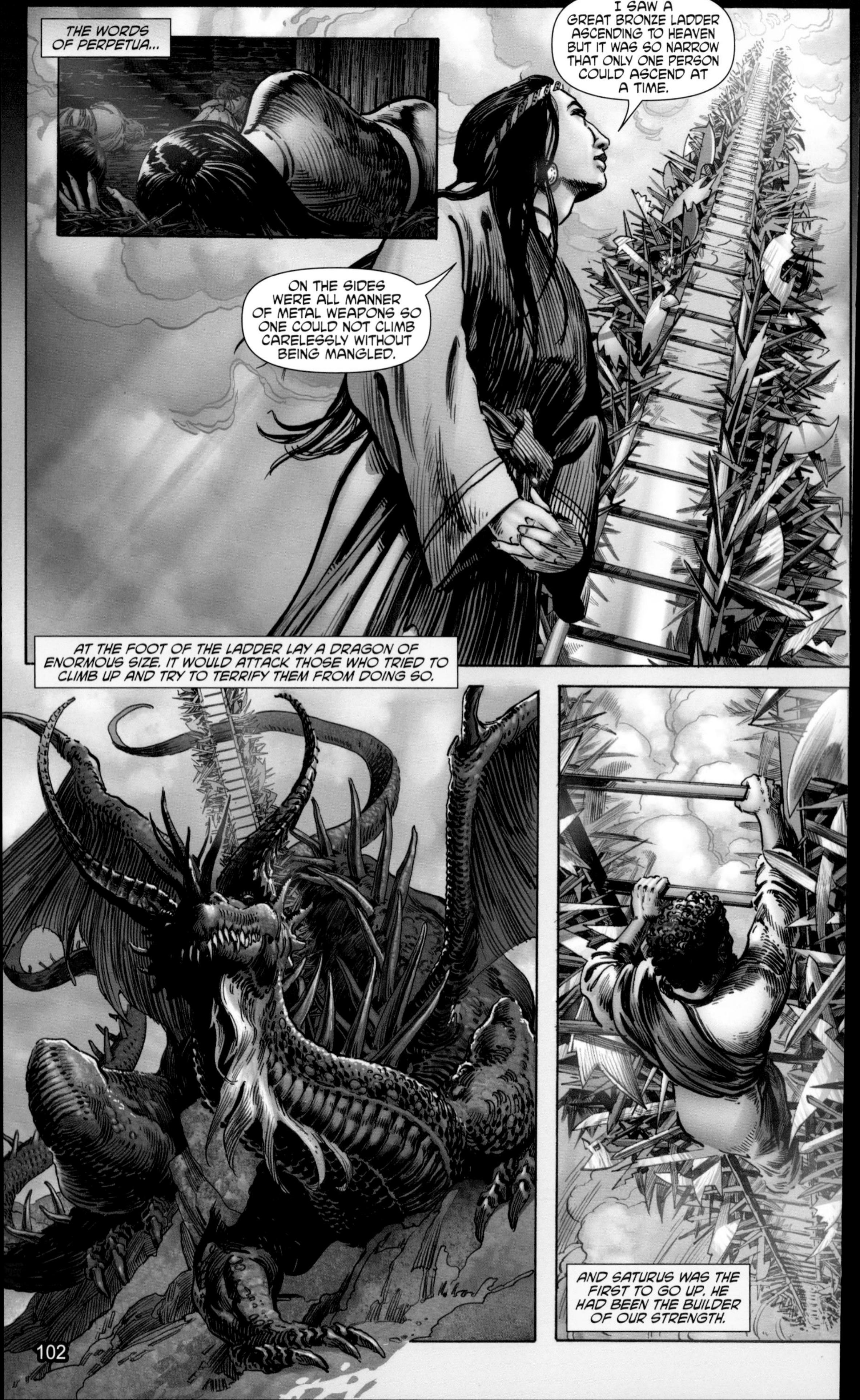
THE WORDS OF PERPETUA...
I SAW A GREAT BRONZE LADDER ASCENDING TO HEAVEN BUT IT WAS SO NARROW THAT ONLY ONE PERSON COULD ASCEND AT A TIME.
ON THE SIDES WERE ALL MANNER OF METAL WEAPONS SO ONE COULD NOT CLIMB CARELESSLY WITHOUT BEING MANGLED.
AT THE FOOT OF THE LADDER LAY A DRAGON OF ENORMOUS SIZE. IT WOULD ATTACK THOSE WHO TRIED TO CLIMB UP AND TRY TO TERRIFY THEM FROM DOING SO.
AND SATURUS WAS THE FIRST TO GO UP. HE HAD BEEN THE BUILDER OF OUR STRENGTH.

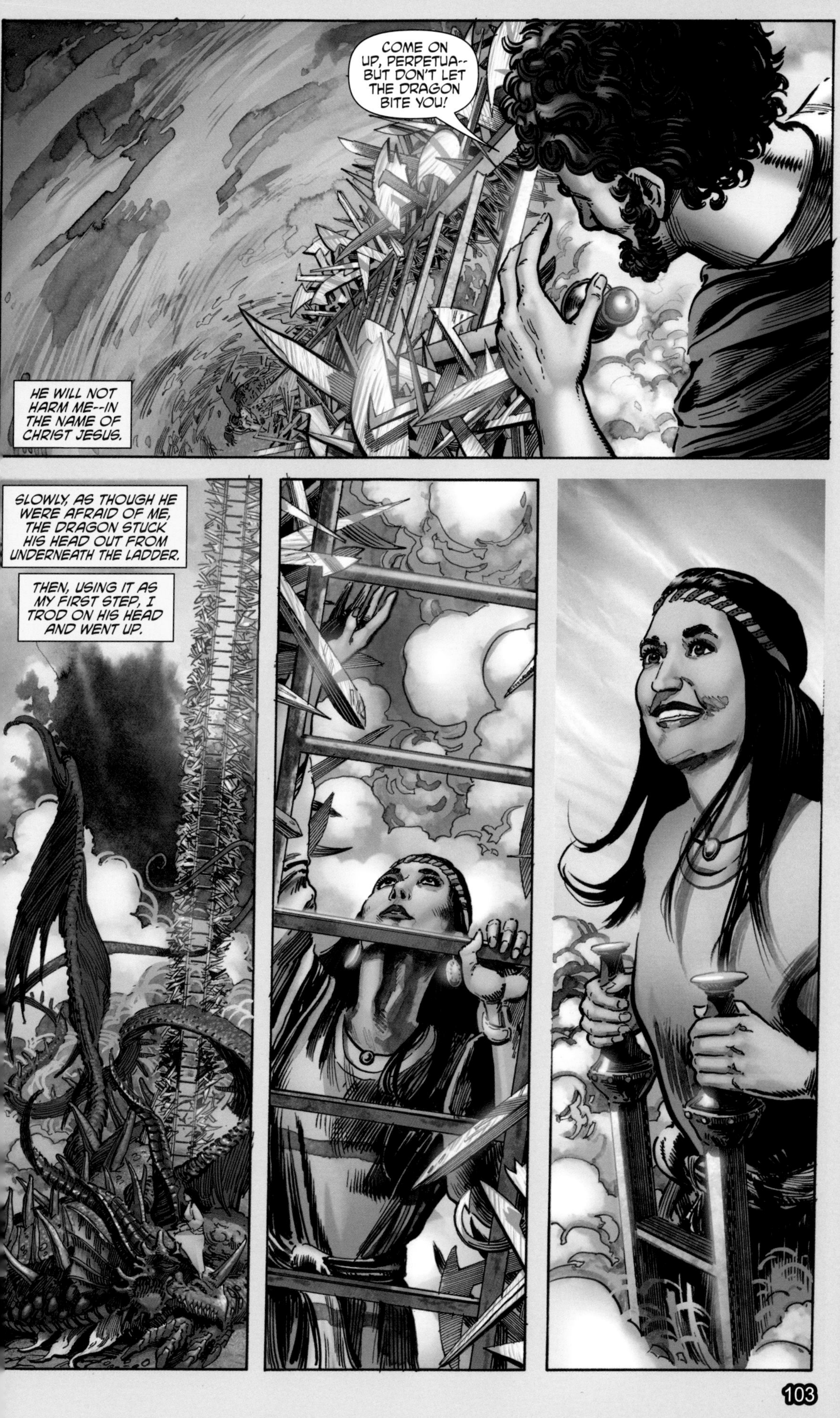
COME ON UP, PERPETUA--BUT DON'T LET THE DRAGON BITE YOU!
HE WILL NOT HARM ME--IN THE NAME OF CHRIST JESUS.
SLOWLY, AS THOUGH HE WERE AFRAID OF ME, THE DRAGON STUCK HIS HEAD OUT FROM UNDERNEATH THE LADDER.
THEN, USING IT AS MY FIRST STEP, I TROD ON HIS HEAD AND WENT UP.

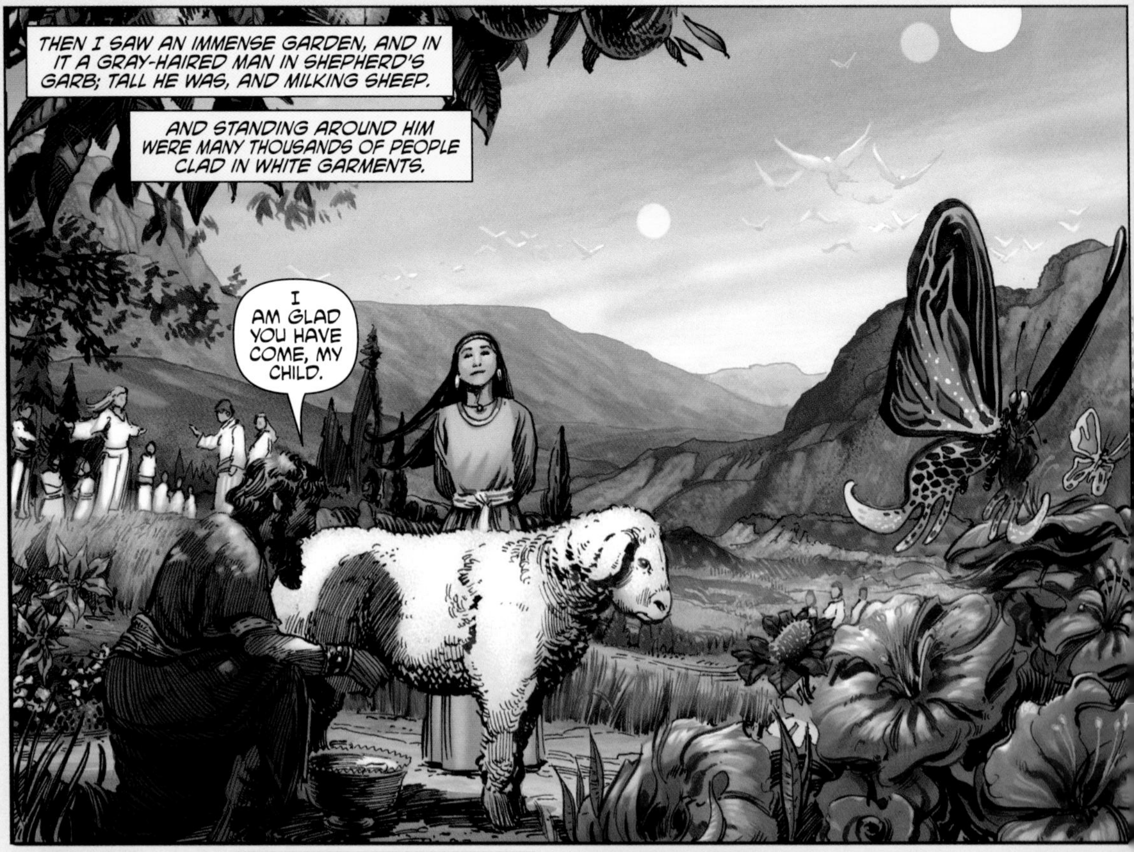
THEN I SAW AN IMMENSE GARDEN, AND IN IT A GRAY-HAIRED MAN IN SHEPHERD'S GARB; TALL HE WAS, AND MILKING SHEEP.
AND STANDING AROUND HIM WERE MANY THOUSANDS OF PEOPLE CLAD IN WHITE GARMENTS.
I AM GLAD YOU HAVE COME, MY CHILD.

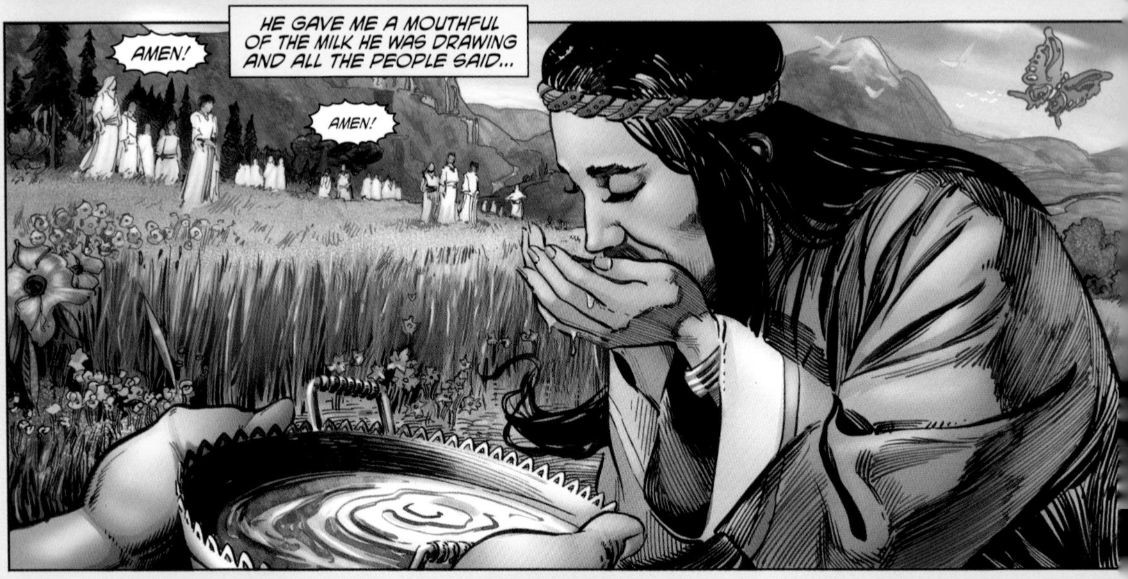
HE GAVE ME A MOUTHFUL OF THE MILK HE WAS DRAWING AND ALL THE PEOPLE SAID...
AMEN!
AMEN!

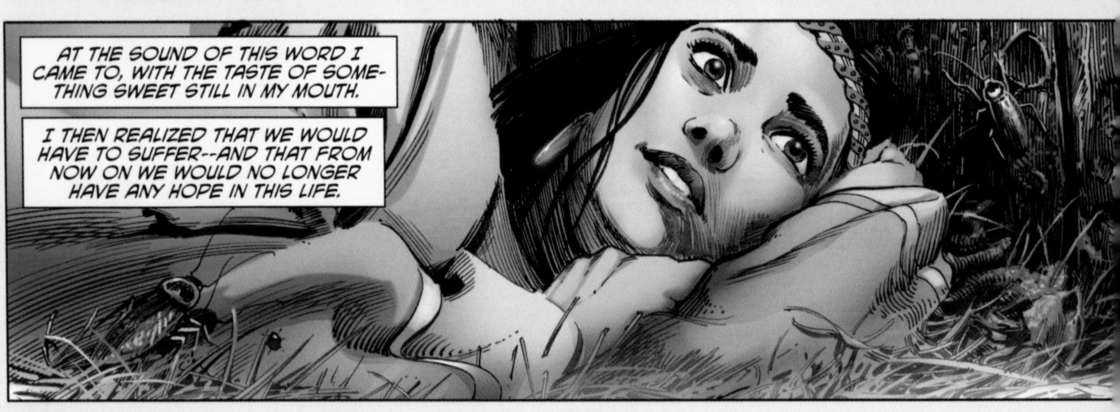
AT THE SOUND OF THIS WORD I CAME TO, WITH THE TASTE OF SOMETHING SWEET STILL IN MY MOUTH.
I THEN REALIZED THAT WE WOULD HAVE TO SUFFER--AND THAT FROM NOW ON WE WOULD NO LONGER HAVE ANY HOPE IN THIS LIFE.

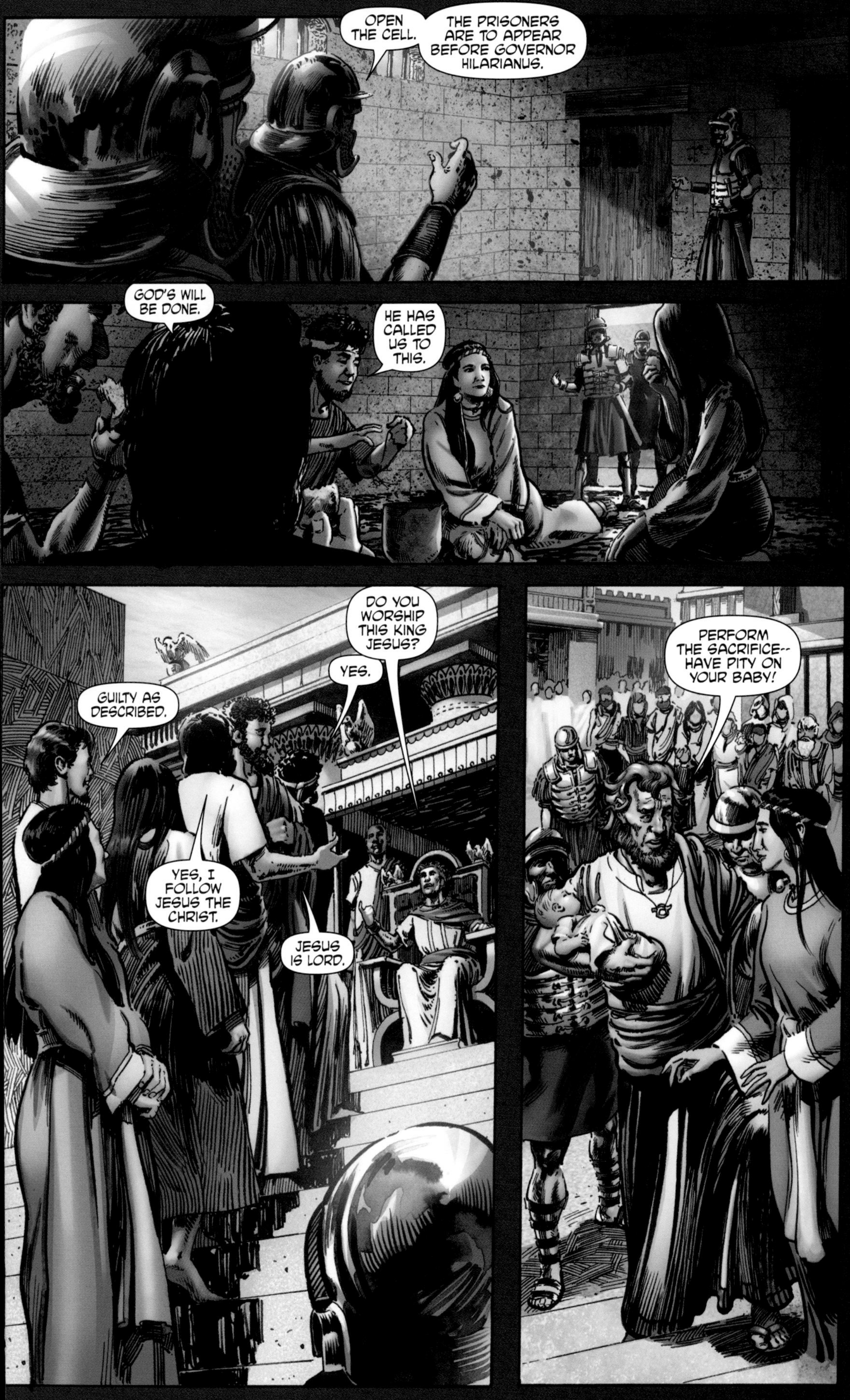
OPEN THE CELL.
THE PRISONERS ARE TO APPEAR BEFORE GOVERNOR HILARIANUS.
GOD'S WILL BE DONE.
HE HAS CALLED US TO THIS.
DO YOU WORSHIP THIS KING JESUS?
YES.
GUILTY AS DESCRIBED.
YES, I FOLLOW JESUS THE CHRIST.
JESUS IS LORD.
PERFORM THE SACRIFICE-- HAVE PITY ON YOUR BABY!

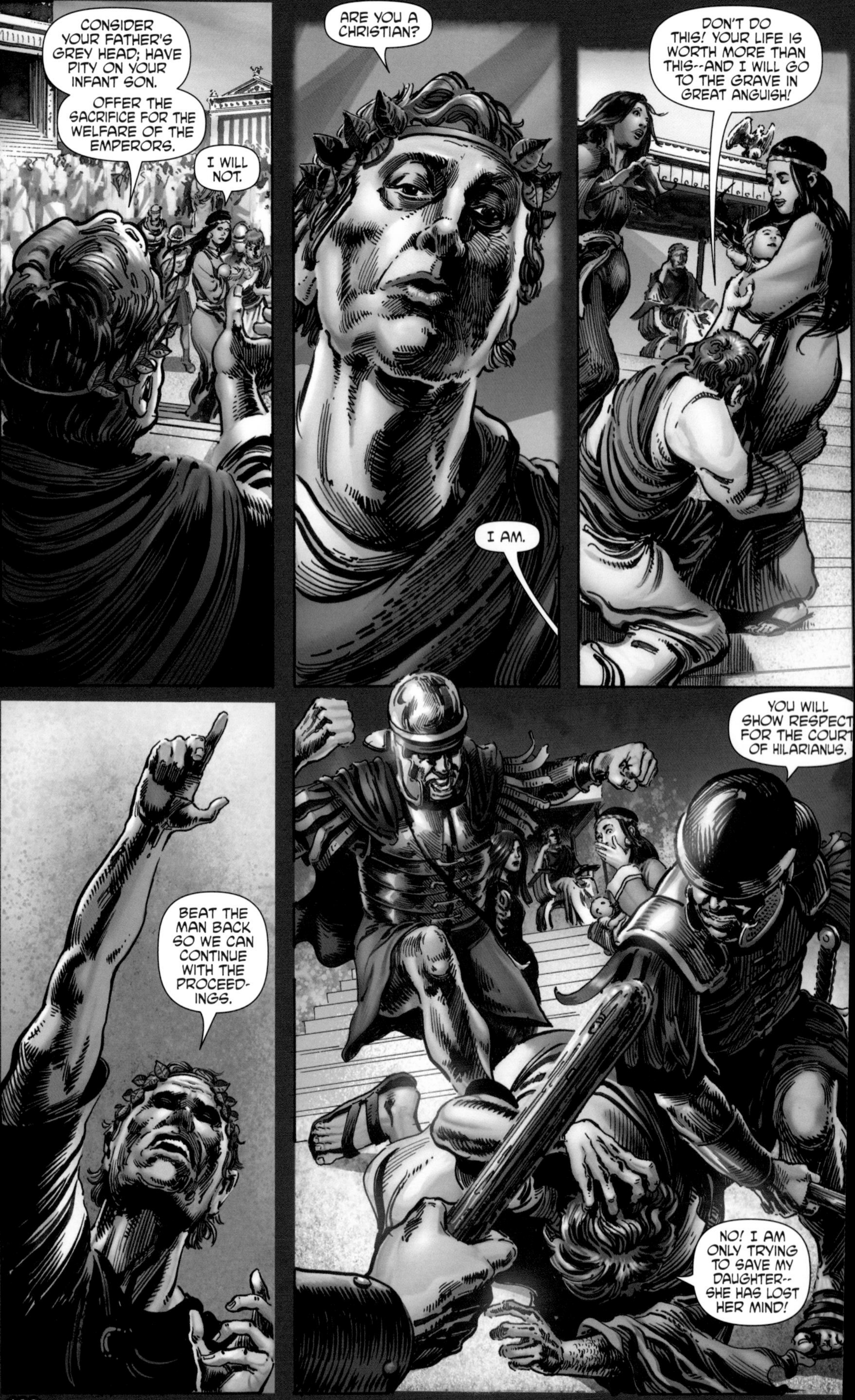
CONSIDER YOUR FATHER'S GREY HEAD; HAVE PITY ON YOUR INFANT SON.
OFFER THE SACRIFICE FOR THE WELFARE OF THE EMPERORS.
I WILL NOT.
ARE YOU A CHRISTIAN?
I AM.
DON'T DO THIS! YOUR LIFE IS WORTH MORE THAN THIS--AND I WILL GO TO THE GRAVE IN GREAT ANGUISH!
BEAT THE MAN BACK SO WE CAN CONTINUE WITH THE PROCEED-INGS.
YOU WILL SHOW RESPECT FOR THE COURT OF HILARIANUS.
NO! I AM ONLY TRYING TO SAVE MY DAUGHTER-- SHE HAS LOST HER MIND!

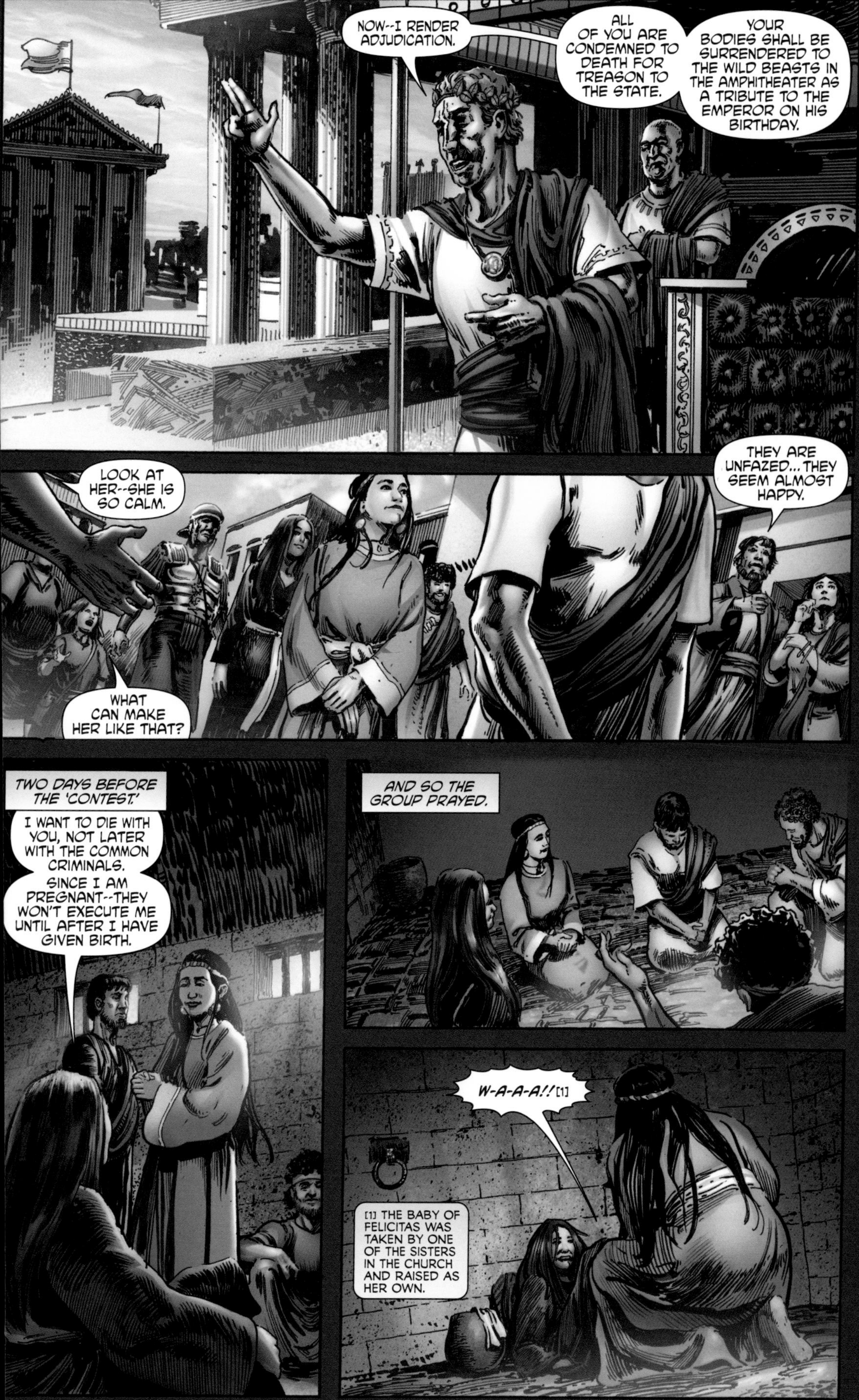
NOW--I RENDER ADJUDICATION.
ALL OF YOU ARE CONDEMNED TO DEATH FOR TREASON TO THE STATE.
YOUR BODIES SHALL BE SURRENDERED TO THE WILD BEASTS IN THE AMPHITHEATER AS A TRIBUTE TO THE EMPEROR ON HIS BIRTHDAY.
LOOK AT HER--SHE IS SO CALM.
WHAT CAN MAKE HER LIKE THAT?
THEY ARE UNFAZED...THEY SEEM ALMOST HAPPY.
TWO DAYS BEFORE THE 'CONTEST.'
I WANT TO DIE WITH YOU, NOT LATER WITH THE COMMON CRIMINALS.
SINCE I AM PREGNANT--THEY WON'T EXECUTE ME UNTIL AFTER I HAVE GIVEN BIRTH.
AND SO THE GROUP PRAYED.
W-A-A-A!! [1]
[1] THE BABY OF FELICITAS WAS TAKEN BY ONE OF THE SISTERS IN THE CHURCH AND RAISED AS HER OWN.

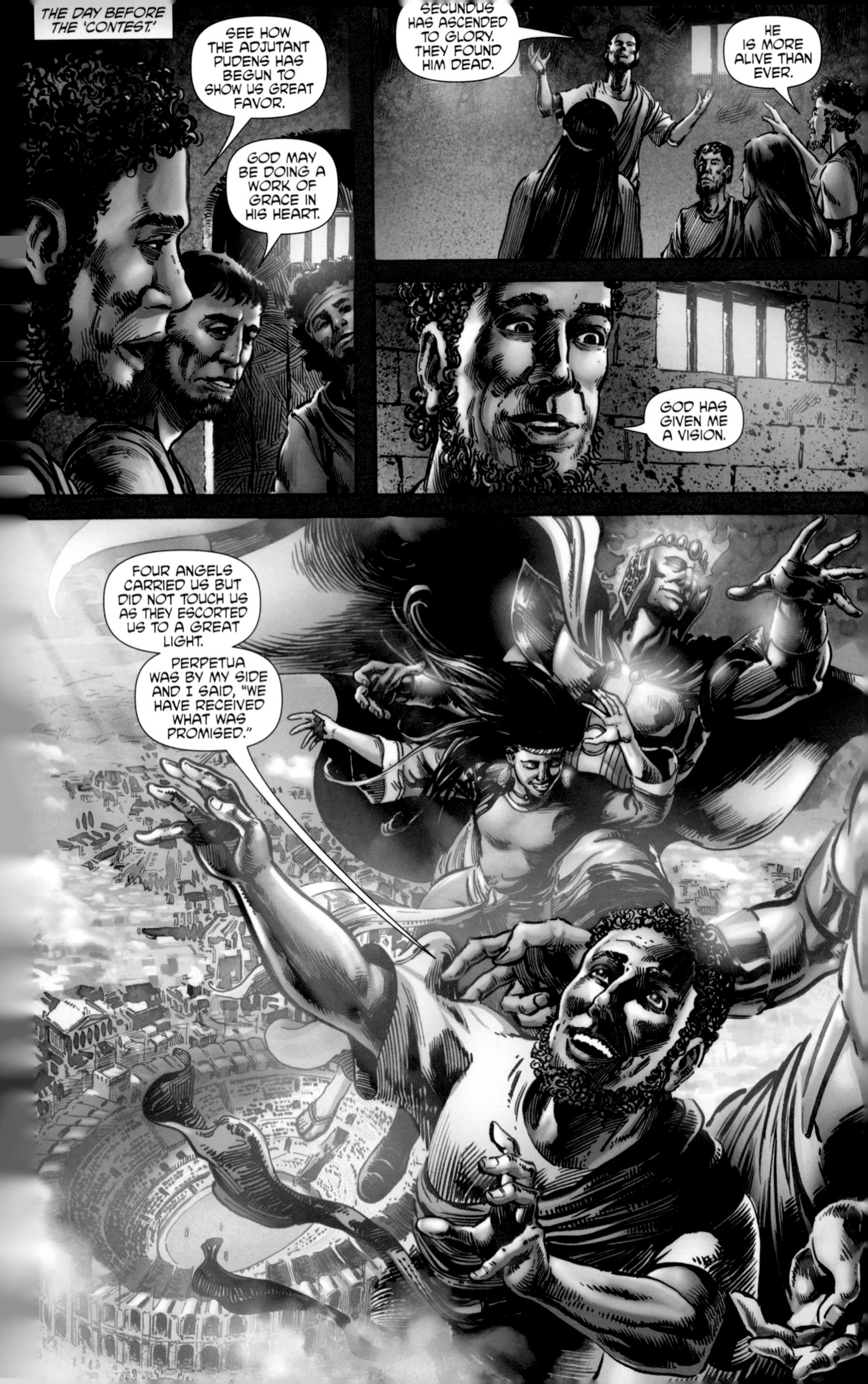
THE DAY BEFORE THE 'CONTEST.'
SEE HOW THE ADJUTANT PUDENS HAS BEGUN TO SHOW US GREAT FAVOR.
GOD MAY BE DOING A WORK OF GRACE IN HIS HEART.
SECUNDUS HAS ASCENDED TO GLORY. THEY FOUND HIM DEAD.
HE IS MORE ALIVE THAN EVER.
GOD HAS GIVEN ME A VISION.
FOUR ANGELS CARRIED US BUT DID NOT TOUCH US AS THEY ESCORTED US TO A GREAT LIGHT.
PERPETUA WAS BY MY SIDE AND I SAID, "WE HAVE RECEIVED WHAT WAS PROMISED."

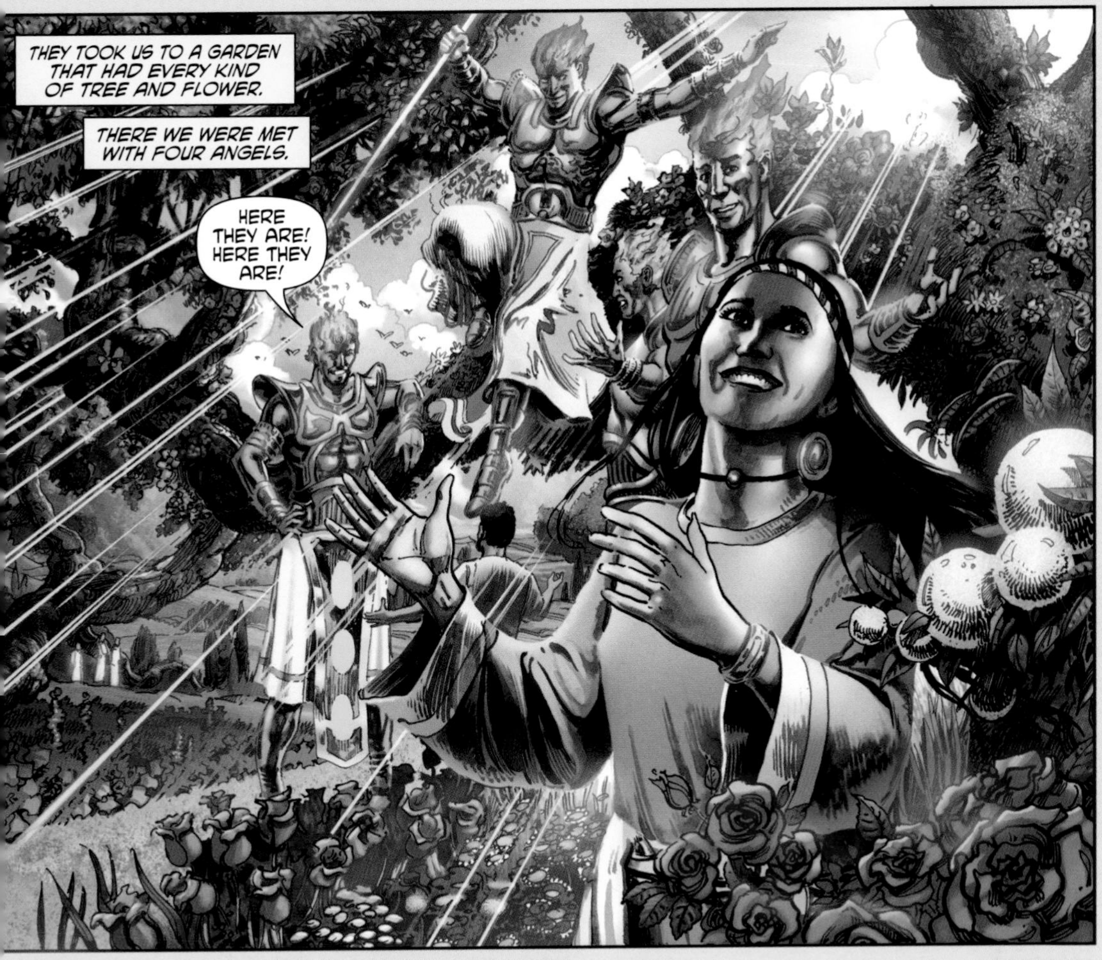
THEY TOOK US TO A GARDEN THAT HAD EVERY KIND OF TREE AND FLOWER.
THERE WE WERE MET WITH FOUR ANGELS.
HERE THEY ARE! HERE THEY ARE!

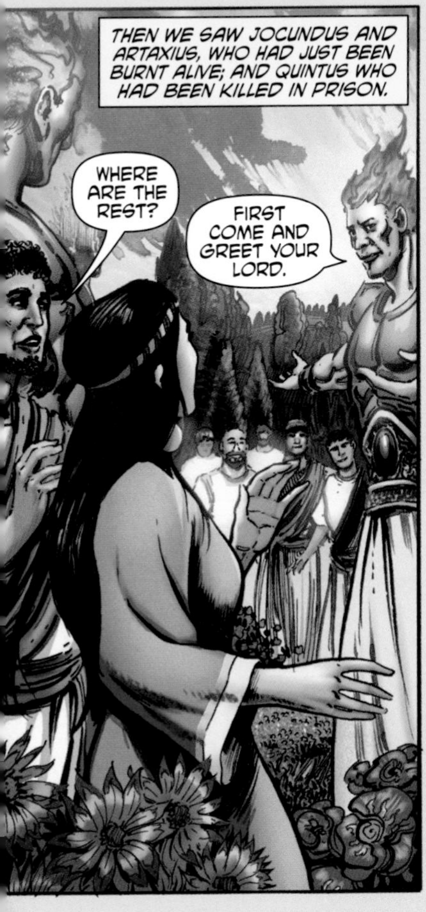
THEN WE SAW JOCUNDUS AND ARTAXIUS, WHO HAD JUST BEEN BURNT ALIVE; AND QUINTUS WHO HAD BEEN KILLED IN PRISON.
WHERE ARE THE REST?
FIRST COME AND GREET YOUR LORD.

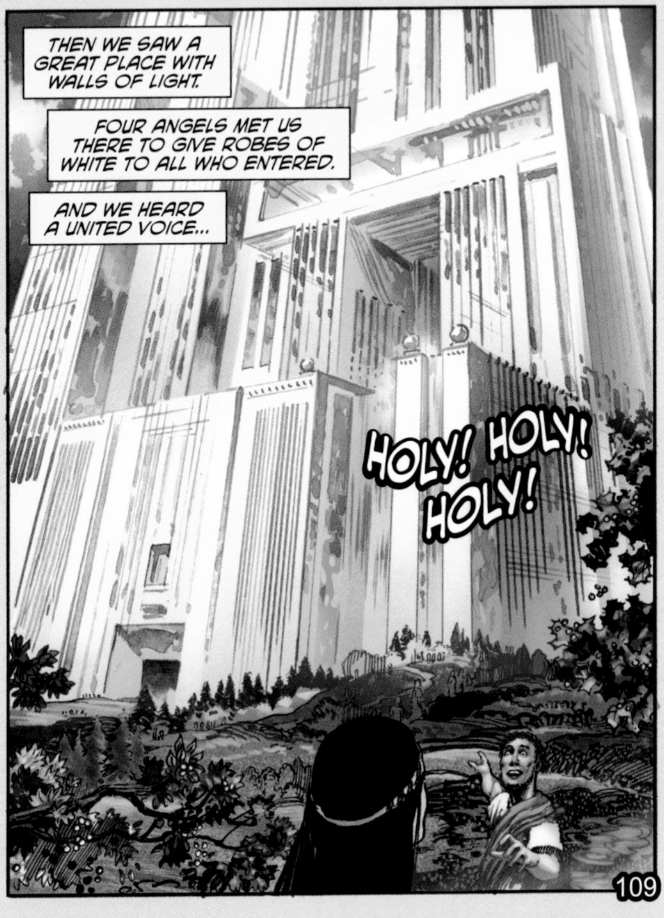
THEN WE SAW A GREAT PLACE WITH WALLS OF LIGHT.
FOUR ANGELS MET US THERE TO GIVE ROBES OF WHITE TO ALL WHO ENTERED.
AND WE HEARD A UNITED VOICE...
HOLY! HOLY! HOLY!

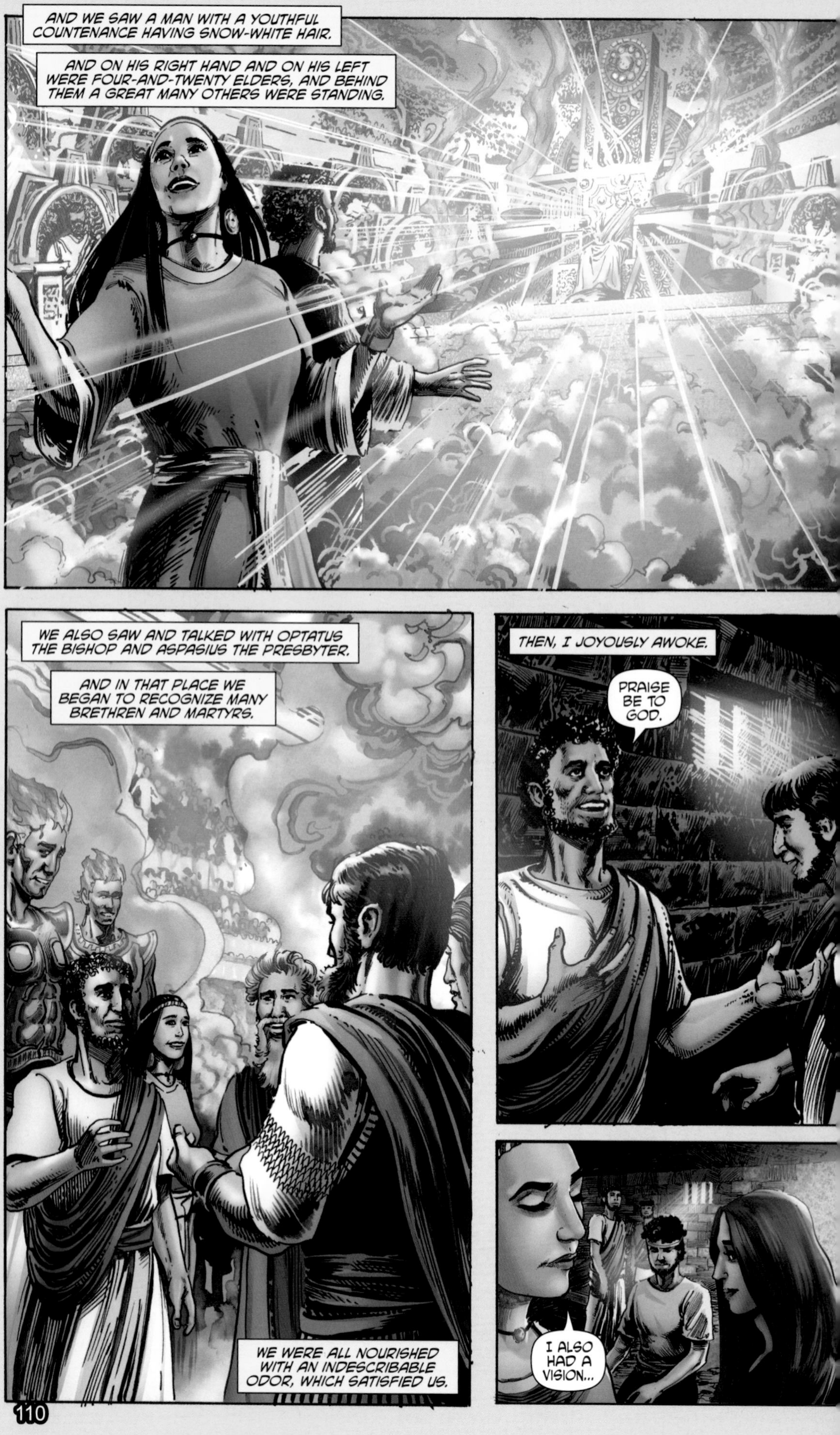
AND WE SAW A MAN WITH A YOUTHFUL COUNTENANCE HAVING SNOW-WHITE HAIR.
AND ON HIS RIGHT HAND AND ON HIS LEFT WERE FOUR-AND-TWENTY ELDERS, AND BEHIND THEM A GREAT MANY OTHERS WERE STANDING.
WE ALSO SAW AND TALKED WITH OPTATUS THE BISHOP AND ASPASIUS THE PRESBYTER.
AND IN THAT PLACE WE BEGAN TO RECOGNIZE MANY BRETHREN AND MARTYRS.
WE WERE ALL NOURISHED WITH AN INDESCRIBABLE ODOR, WHICH SATISFIED US.
THEN, I JOYOUSLY AWOKE.
PRAISE BE TO GOD.
I ALSO HAD A VISION...

IN MY VISION, THE DEACON POMPONIUS MET ME AT THE PRISON GATES.

HE TOOK ME TO THE AMPHITHEATER.

DO NOT BE AFRAID. I AM HERE, STRUGGLING WITH YOU.

THEN HE LEFT.

I LOOKED AT THE ENORMOUS CROWD WHO WATCHED IN ASTONISHMENT.

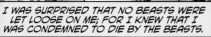

I WAS SURPRISED THAT NO BEASTS WERE LET LOOSE ON ME; FOR I KNEW THAT I WAS CONDEMNED TO DIE BY THE BEASTS.

THEN OUT CAME AN EGYPTIAN AGAINST ME, OF VICIOUS APPEARANCE, TOGETHER WITH HIS SECONDS, TO FIGHT WITH ME.

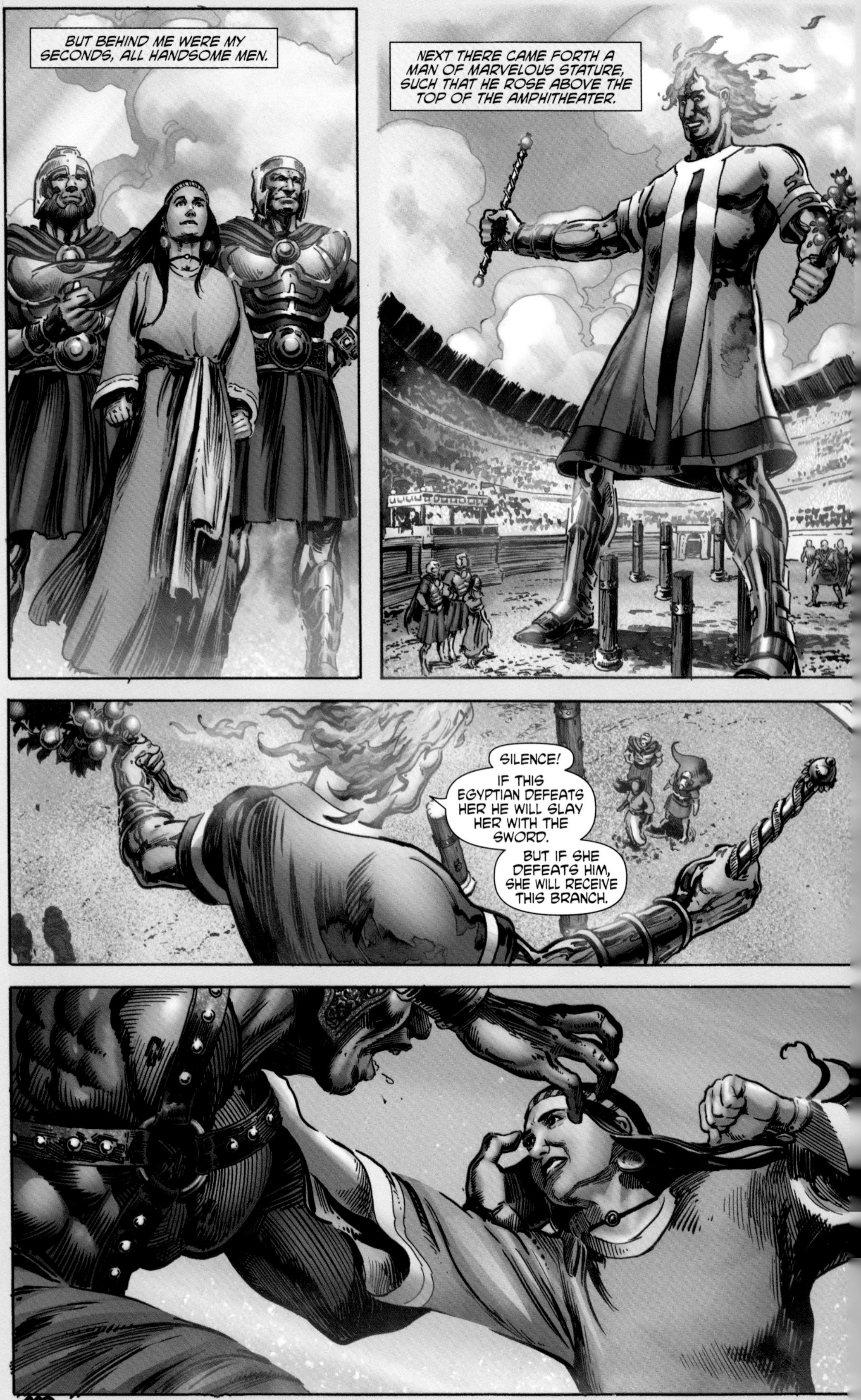

BUT BEHIND ME WERE MY SECONDS, ALL HANDSOME MEN.
NEXT THERE CAME FORTH A MAN OF MARVELOUS STATURE, SUCH THAT HE ROSE ABOVE THE TOP OF THE AMPHITHEATER.
SILENCE!
IF THIS EGYPTIAN DEFEATS HER HE WILL SLAY HER WITH THE SWORD.
BUT IF SHE DEFEATS HIM, SHE WILL RECEIVE THIS BRANCH.

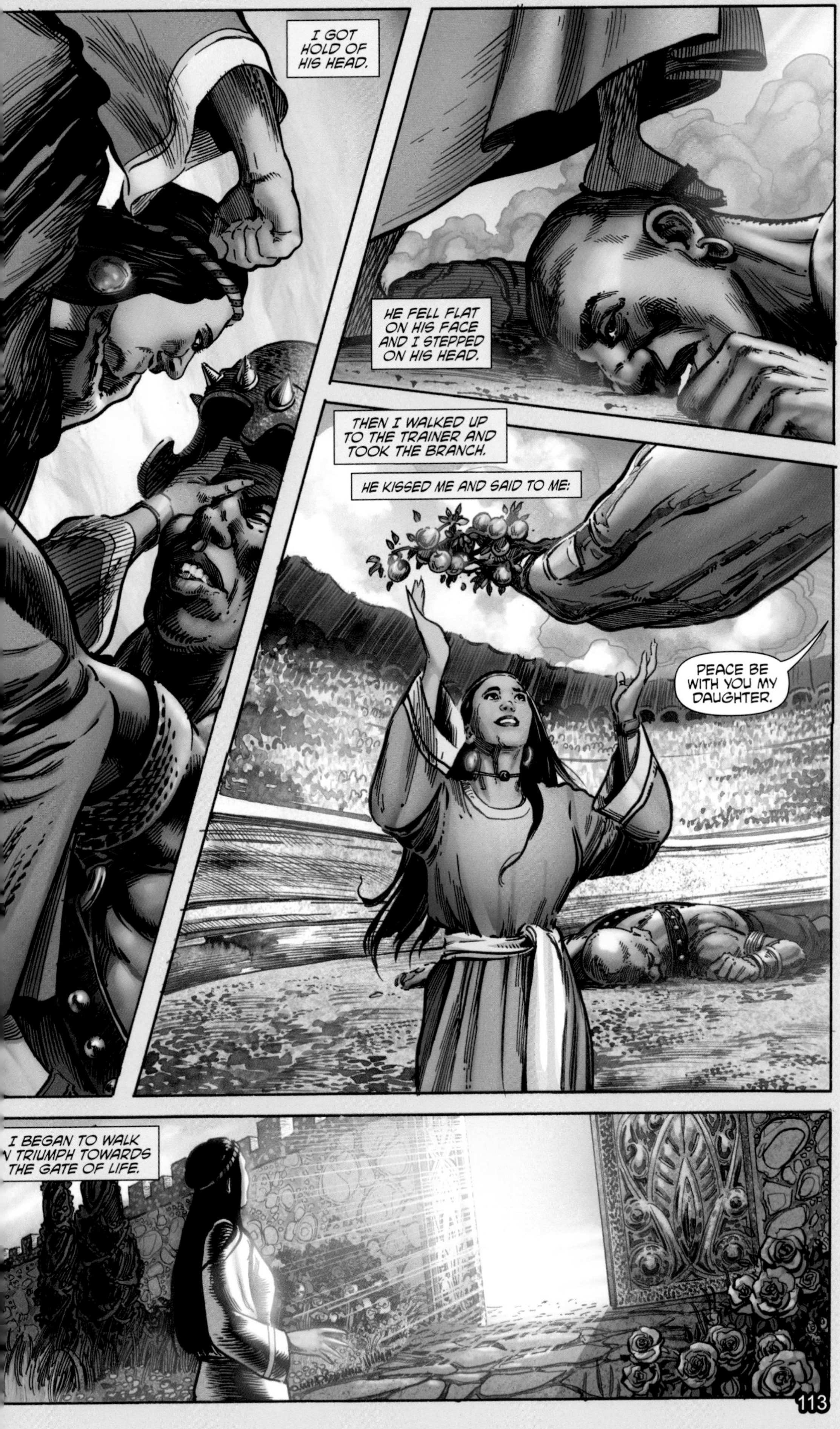
I GOT HOLD OF HIS HEAD.
HE FELL FLAT ON HIS FACE AND I STEPPED ON HIS HEAD.
THEN I WALKED UP TO THE TRAINER AND TOOK THE BRANCH.
HE KISSED ME AND SAID TO ME:
PEACE BE WITH YOU MY DAUGHTER.
I BEGAN TO WALK
N TRIUMPH TOWARDS
THE GATE OF LIFE.

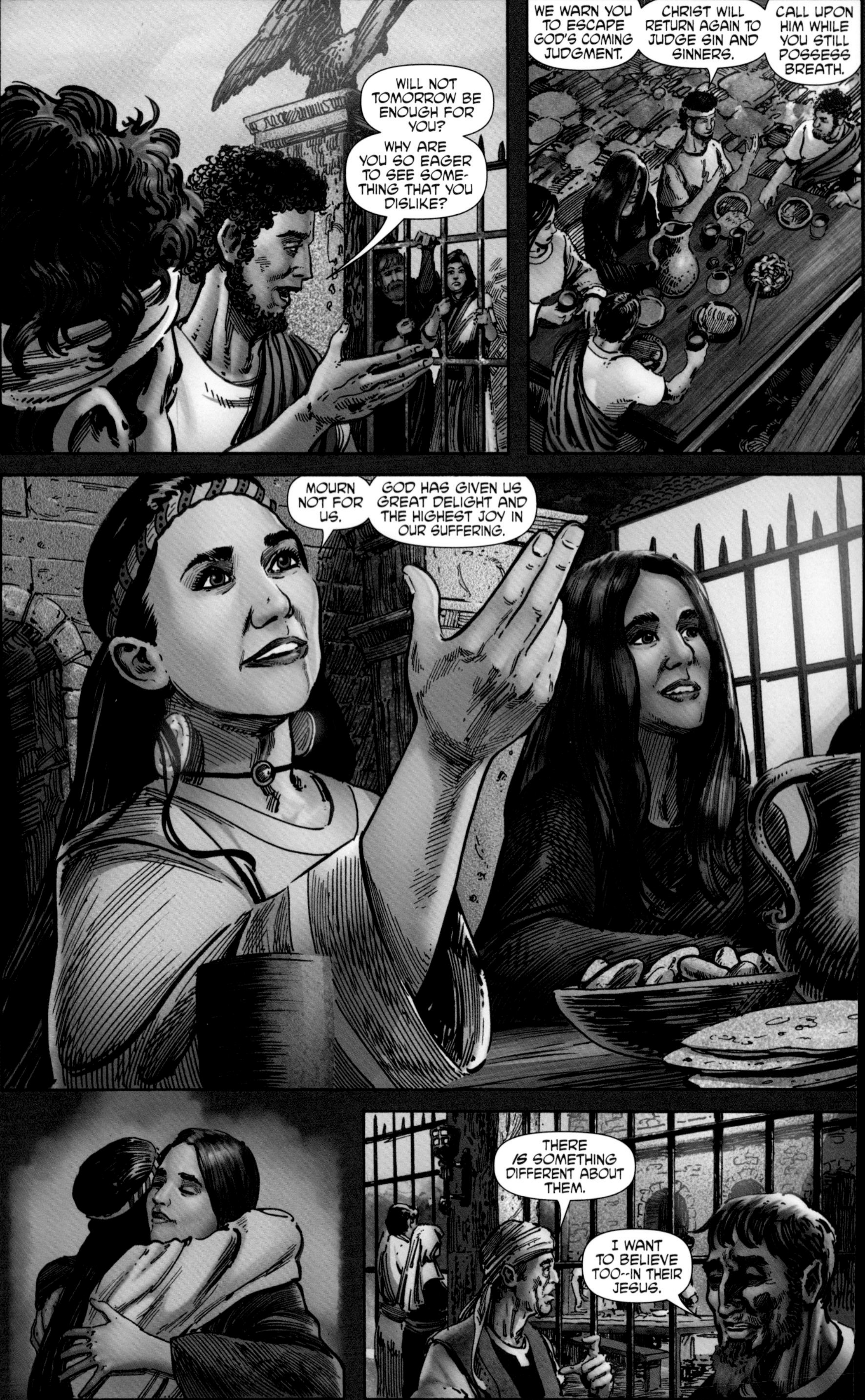
WILL NOT TOMORROW BE ENOUGH FOR YOU?
WHY ARE YOU SO EAGER TO SEE SOME-THING THAT YOU DISLIKE?
WE WARN YOU TO ESCAPE GOD'S COMING JUDGMENT.
CHRIST WILL RETURN AGAIN TO JUDGE SIN AND SINNERS.
CALL UPON HIM WHILE YOU STILL POSSESS BREATH.
MOURN NOT FOR US.
GOD HAS GIVEN US GREAT DELIGHT AND THE HIGHEST JOY IN OUR SUFFERING.
THERE *IS* SOMETHING DIFFERENT ABOUT THEM.
I WANT TO BELIEVE TOO--IN THEIR JESUS.

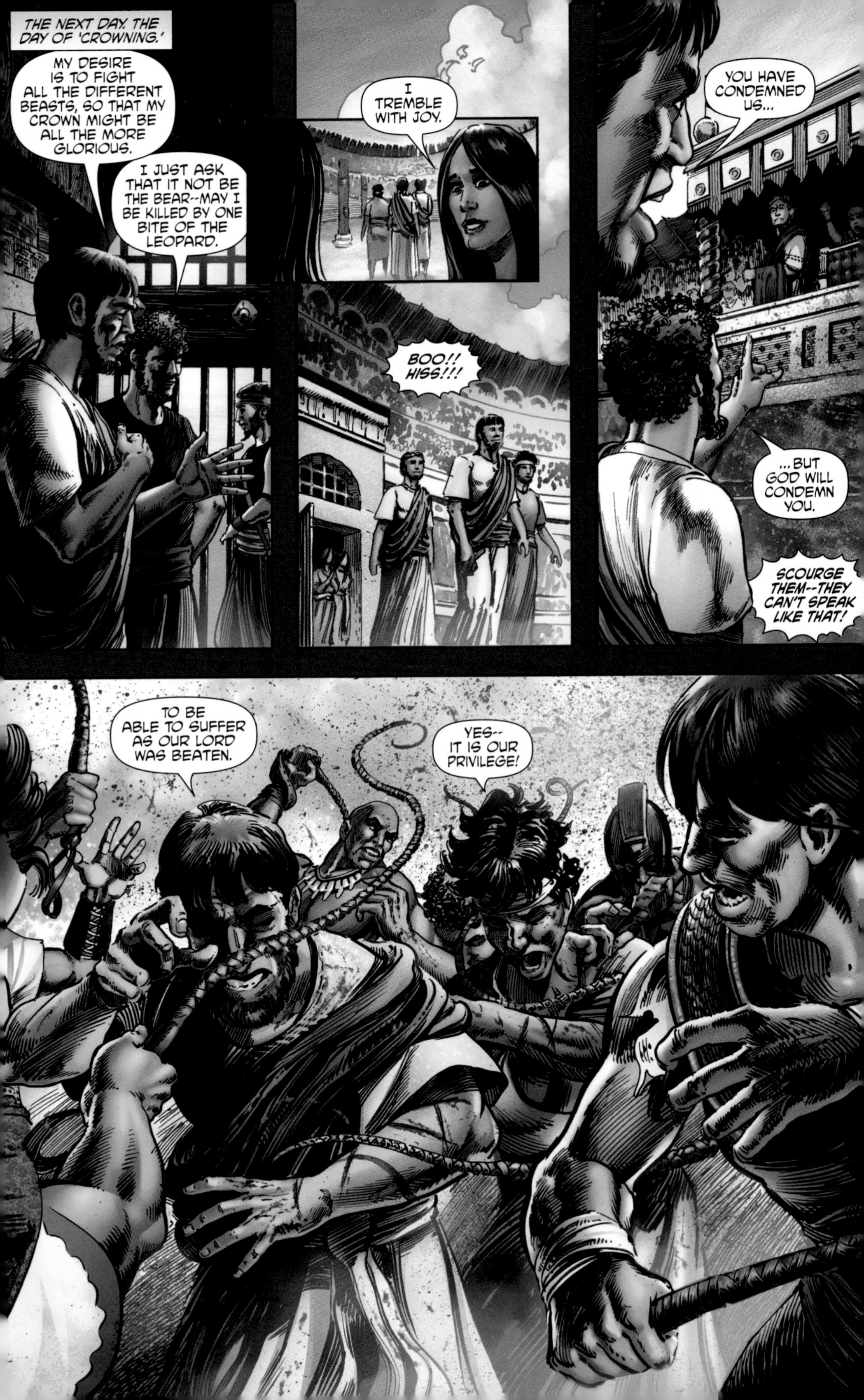

THE NEXT DAY. THE DAY OF 'CROWNING.'
MY DESIRE IS TO FIGHT ALL THE DIFFERENT BEASTS, SO THAT MY CROWN MIGHT BE ALL THE MORE GLORIOUS.
I JUST ASK THAT IT NOT BE THE BEAR--MAY I BE KILLED BY ONE BITE OF THE LEOPARD.
I TREMBLE WITH JOY.
BOO!! HISS!!!
YOU HAVE CONDEMNED US...
...BUT GOD WILL CONDEMN YOU.
SCOURGE THEM--THEY CAN'T SPEAK LIKE THAT!
TO BE ABLE TO SUFFER AS OUR LORD WAS BEATEN.
YES-- IT IS OUR PRIVILEGE!

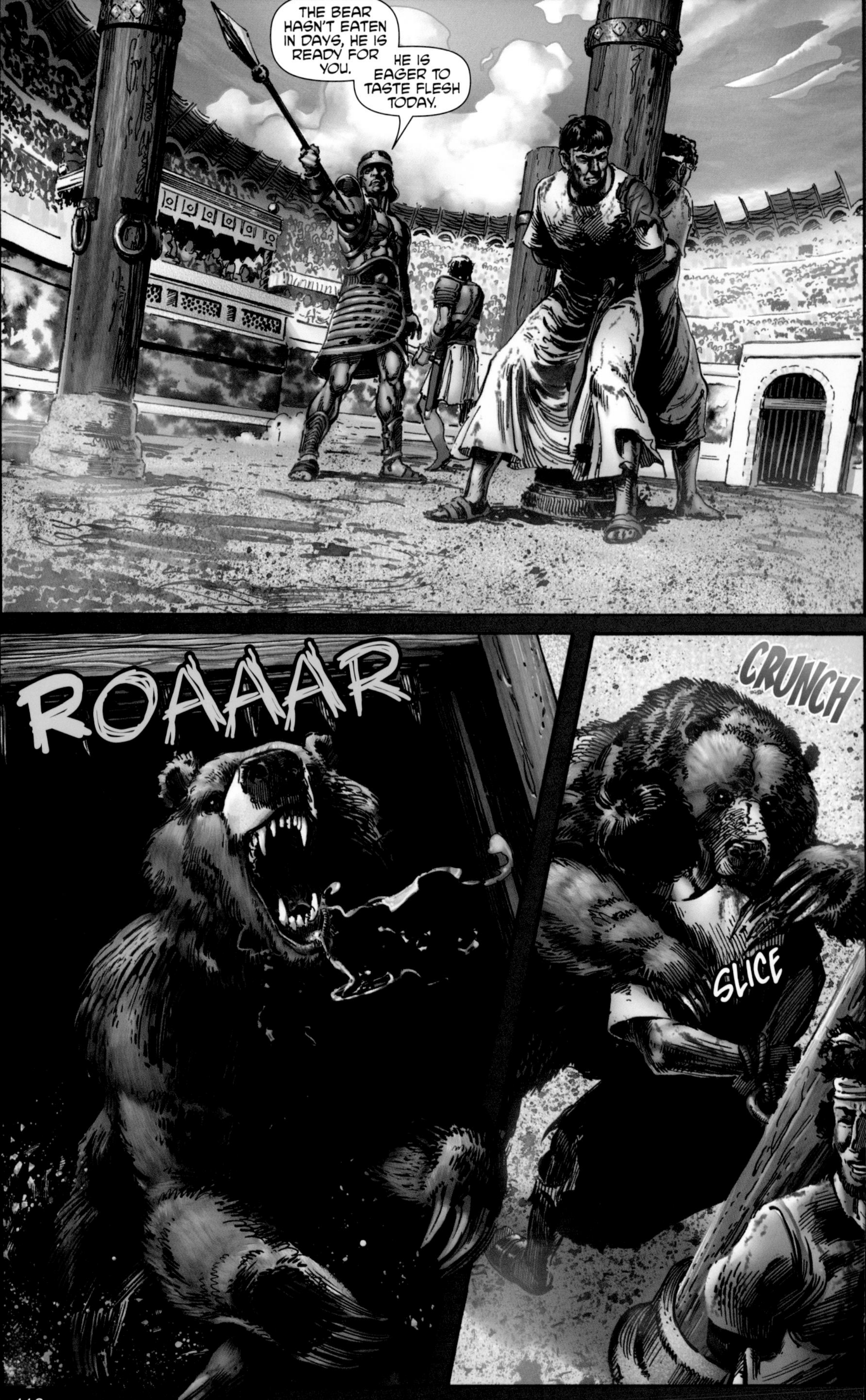
THE BEAR HASN'T EATEN IN DAYS, HE IS READY FOR YOU.
HE IS EAGER TO TASTE FLESH TODAY.
ROAAAR
CRUNCH
SLICE

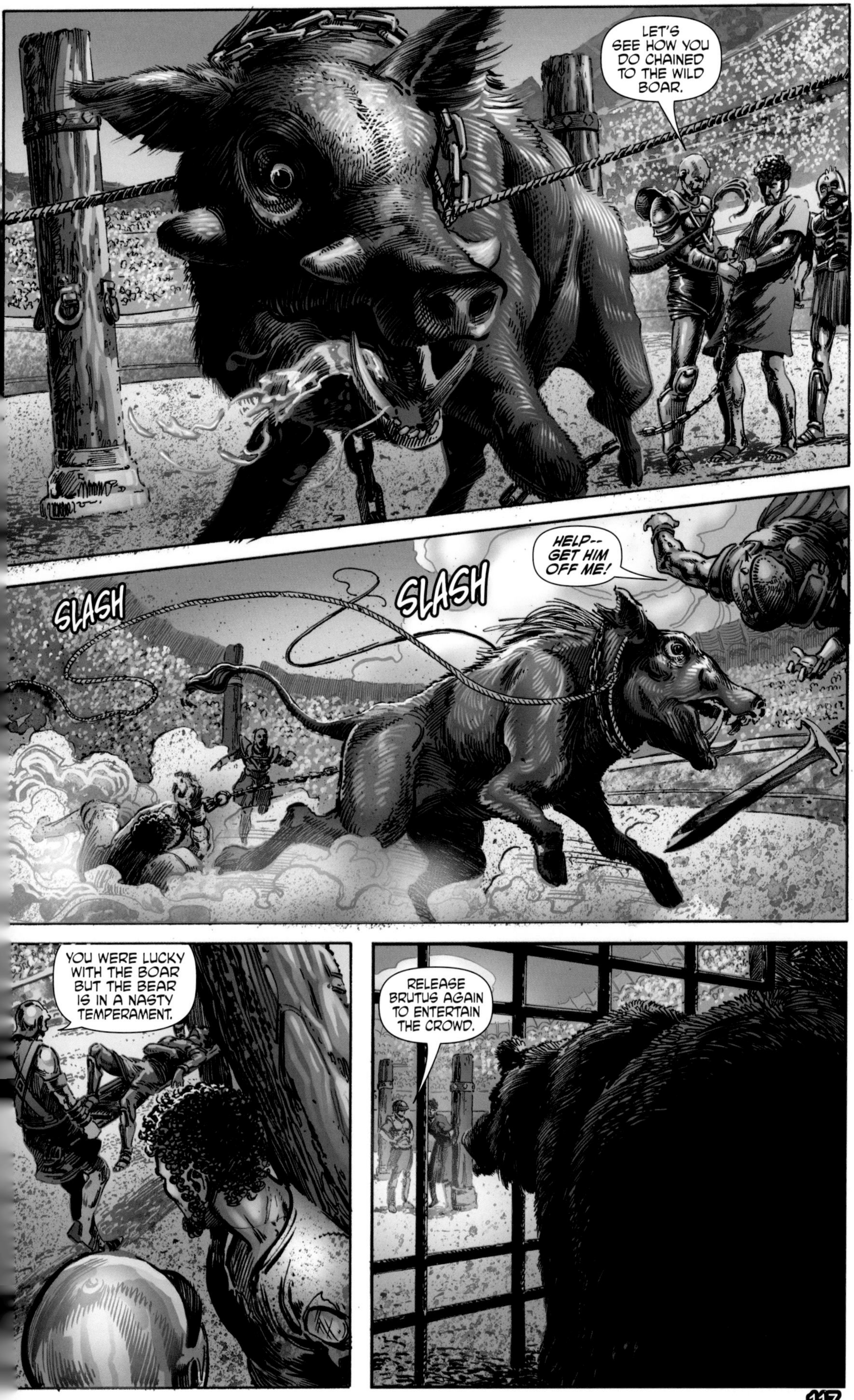
LET'S SEE HOW YOU DO CHAINED TO THE WILD BOAR.
SLASH
SLASH
HELP-- GET HIM OFF ME!
YOU WERE LUCKY WITH THE BOAR BUT THE BEAR IS IN A NASTY TEMPERAMENT.
RELEASE BRUTUS AGAIN TO ENTERTAIN THE CROWD.

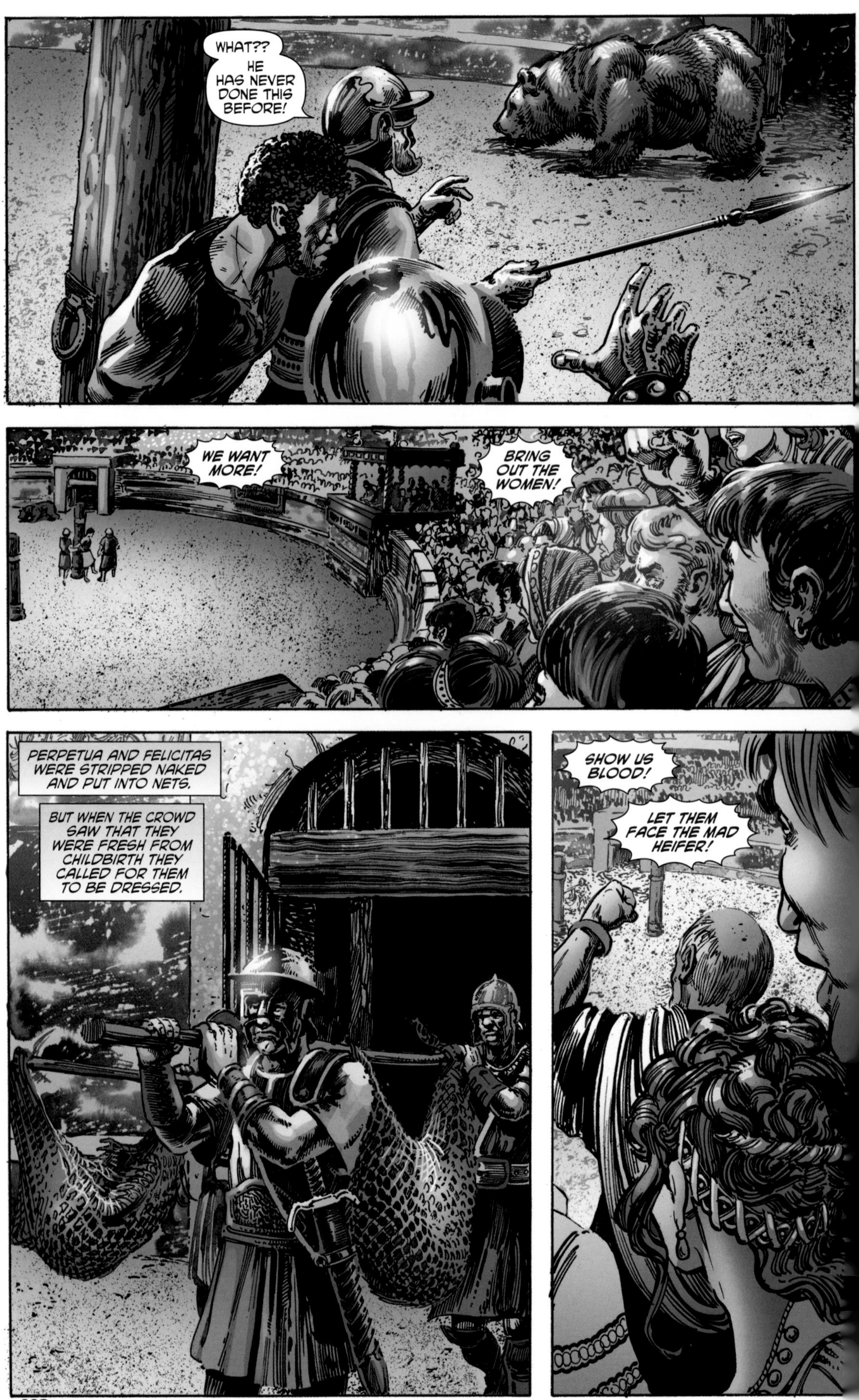
WHAT?? HE HAS NEVER DONE THIS BEFORE!
WE WANT MORE!
BRING OUT THE WOMEN!
PERPETUA AND FELICITAS WERE STRIPPED NAKED AND PUT INTO NETS.
BUT WHEN THE CROWD SAW THAT THEY WERE FRESH FROM CHILDBIRTH THEY CALLED FOR THEM TO BE DRESSED.
SHOW US BLOOD!
LET THEM FACE THE MAD HEIFER!

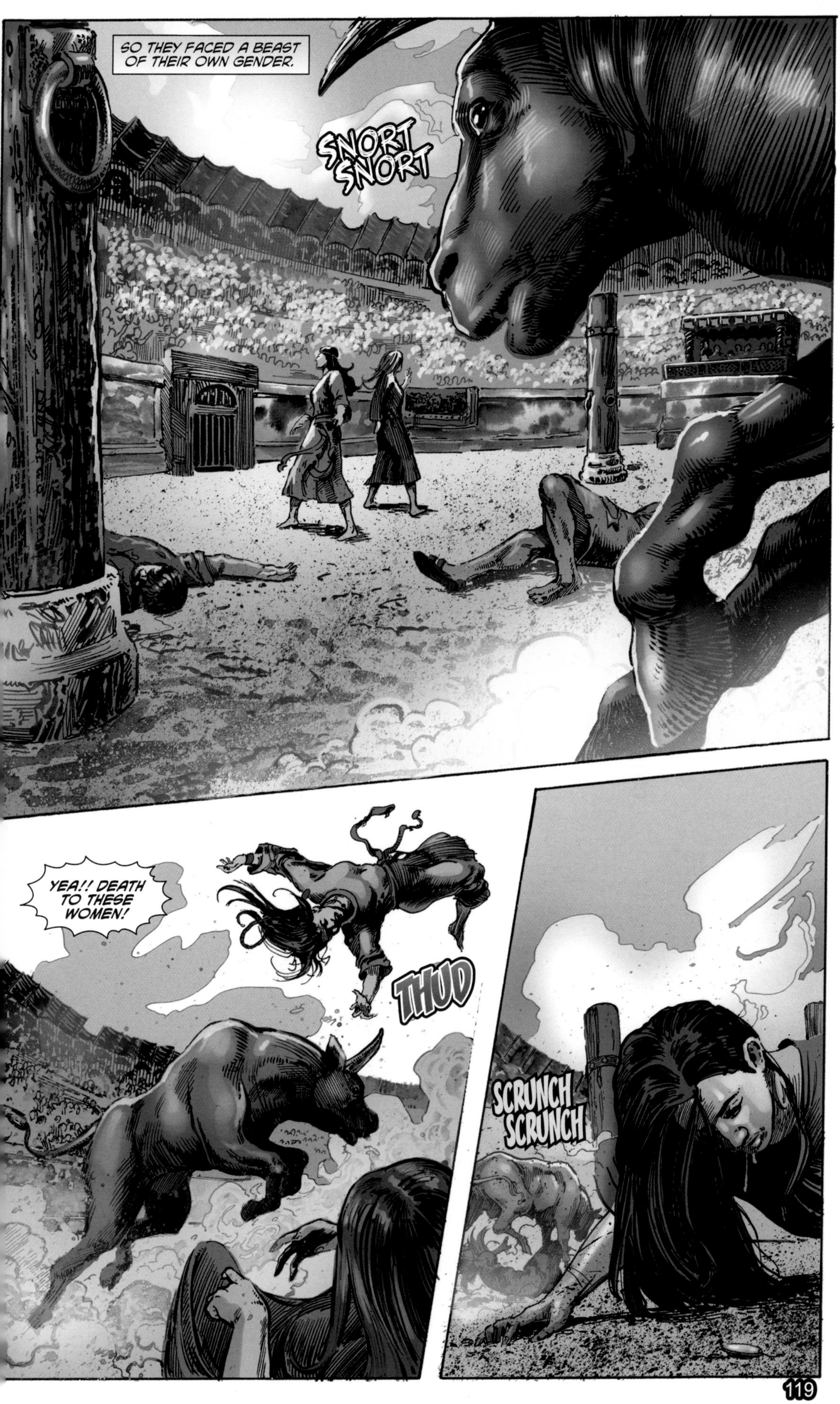
SO THEY FACED A BEAST OF THEIR OWN GENDER.
SNORT SNORT
YEA!! DEATH TO THESE WOMEN!
THUD
SCRUNCH SCRUNCH

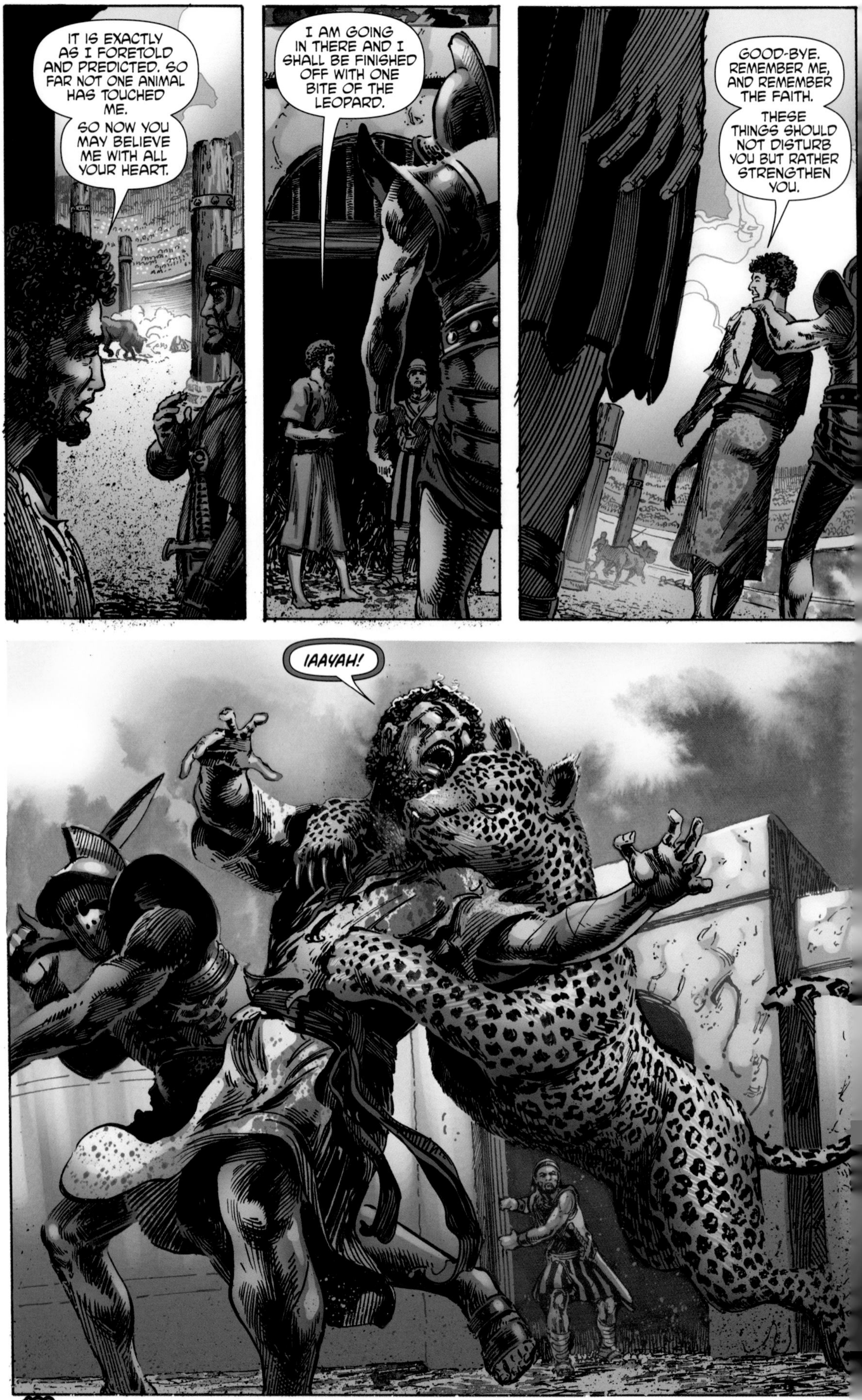
IT IS EXACTLY AS I FORETOLD AND PREDICTED. SO FAR NOT ONE ANIMAL HAS TOUCHED ME.
SO NOW YOU MAY BELIEVE ME WITH ALL YOUR HEART.
I AM GOING IN THERE AND I SHALL BE FINISHED OFF WITH ONE BITE OF THE LEOPARD.
GOOD-BYE. REMEMBER ME, AND REMEMBER THE FAITH.
THESE THINGS SHOULD NOT DISTURB YOU BUT RATHER STRENGTHEN YOU.
¡AAYAH!

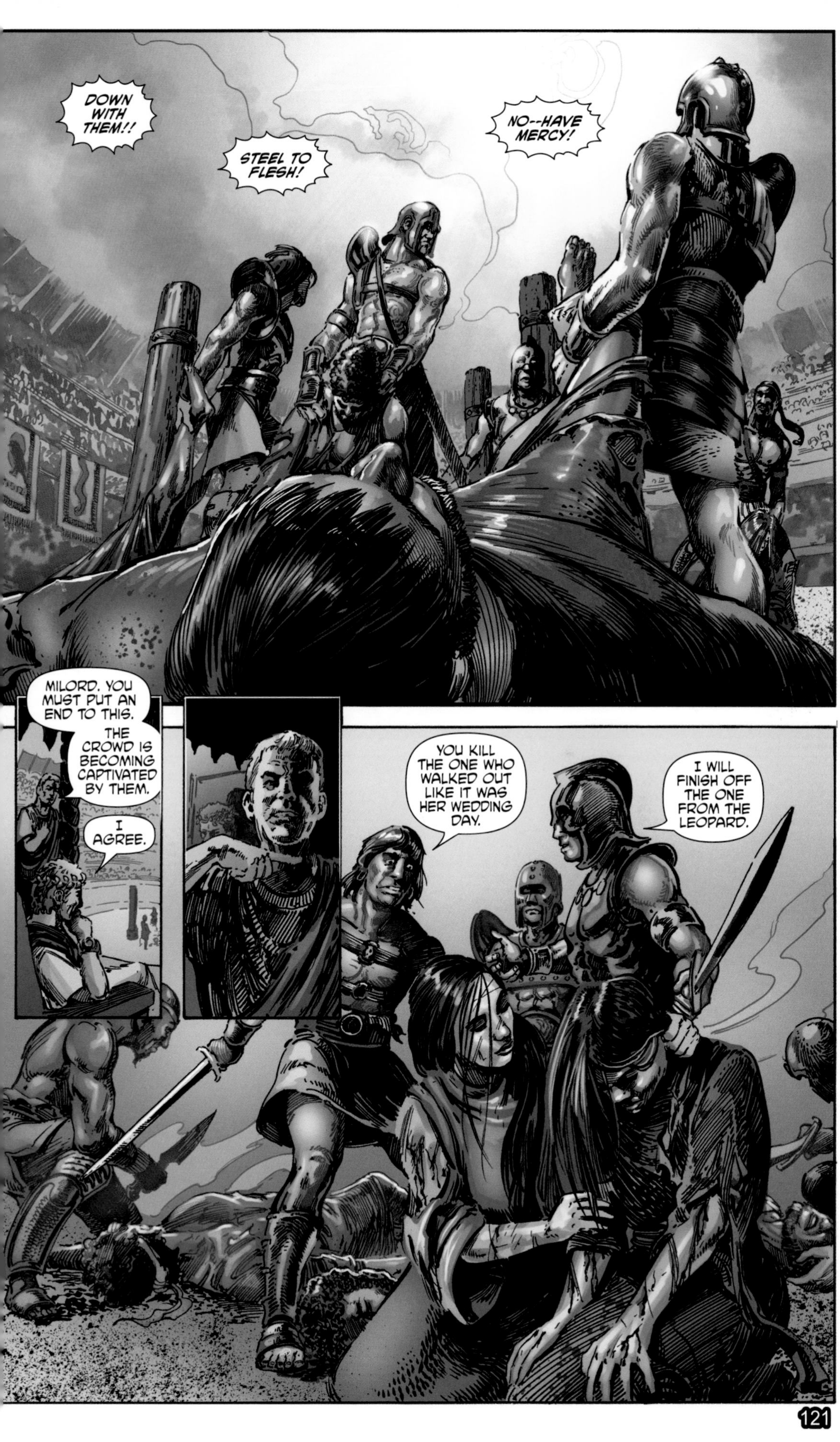
DOWN WITH THEM!!
STEEL TO FLESH!
NO--HAVE MERCY!
MILORD. YOU MUST PUT AN END TO THIS.
THE CROWD IS BECOMING CAPTIVATED BY THEM.
I AGREE.
YOU KILL THE ONE WHO WALKED OUT LIKE IT WAS HER WEDDING DAY.
I WILL FINISH OFF THE ONE FROM THE LEOPARD.

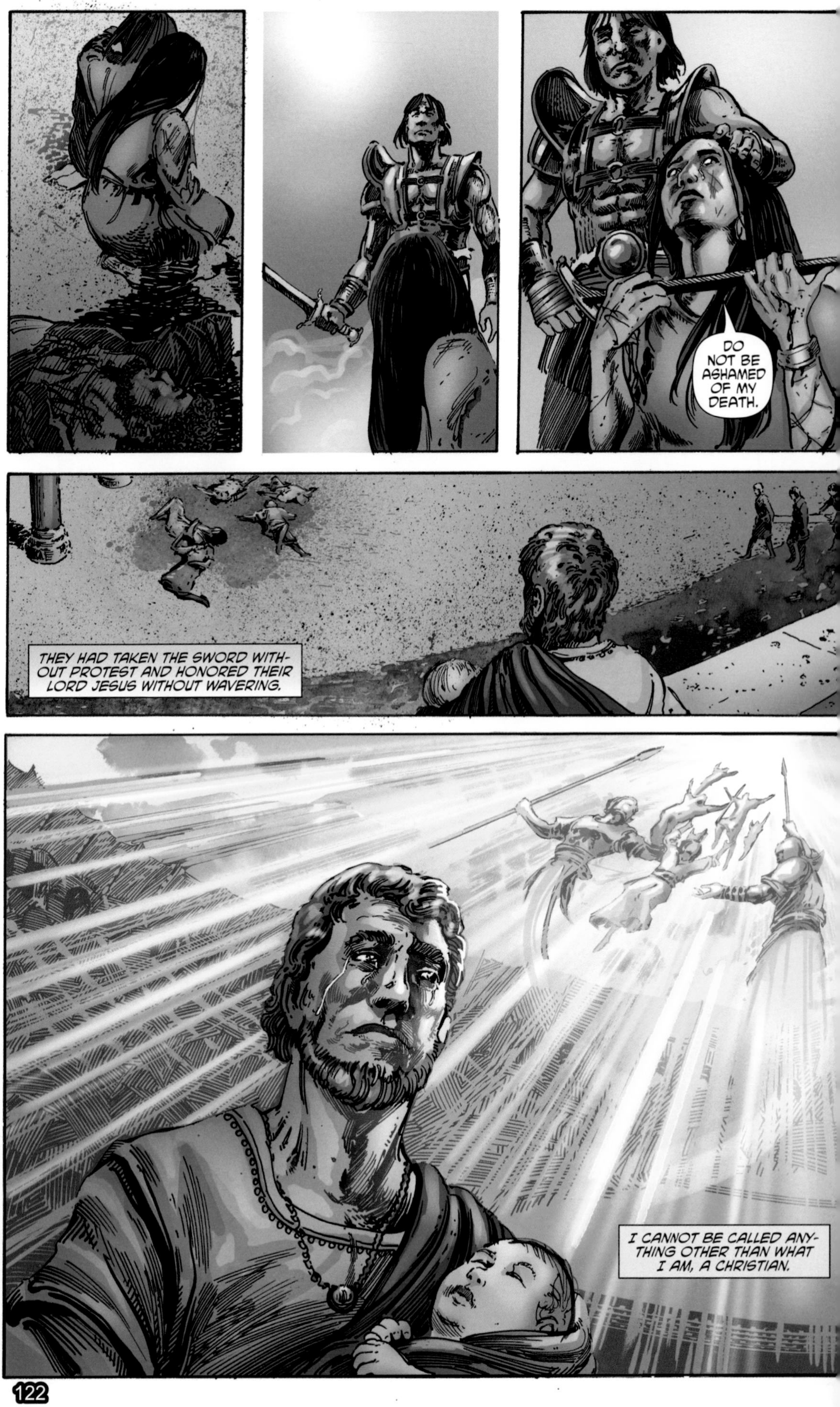
DO NOT BE ASHAMED OF MY DEATH.
THEY HAD TAKEN THE SWORD WITHOUT PROTEST AND HONORED THEIR LORD JESUS WITHOUT WAVERING.
I CANNOT BE CALLED ANYTHING OTHER THAN WHAT I AM, A CHRISTIAN.

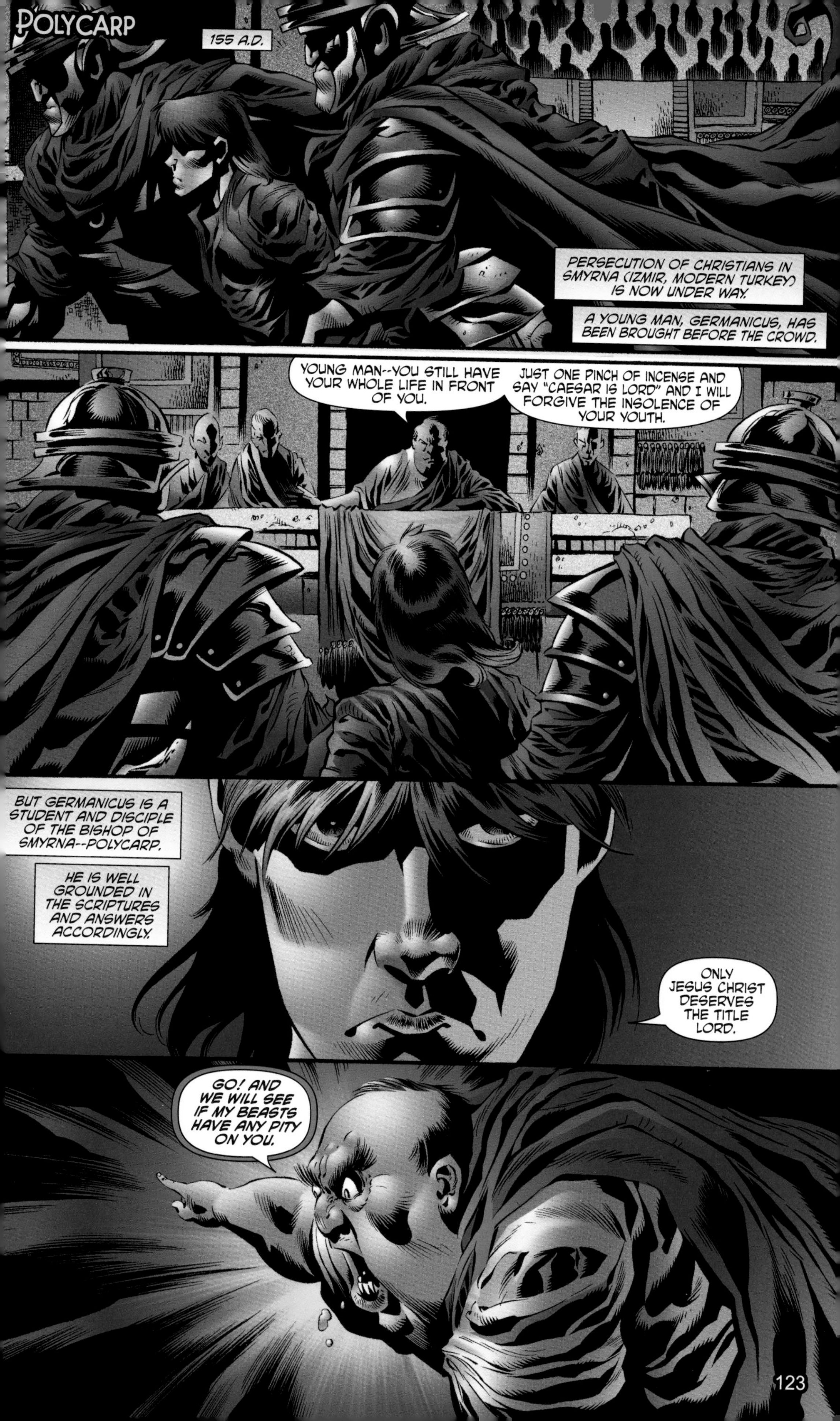
POLYCARP
155 A.D.
PERSECUTION OF CHRISTIANS IN SMYRNA (IZMIR, MODERN TURKEY) IS NOW UNDER WAY.
A YOUNG MAN, GERMANICUS, HAS BEEN BROUGHT BEFORE THE CROWD.
YOUNG MAN--YOU STILL HAVE YOUR WHOLE LIFE IN FRONT OF YOU.
JUST ONE PINCH OF INCENSE AND SAY "CAESAR IS LORD" AND I WILL FORGIVE THE INSOLENCE OF YOUR YOUTH.
BUT GERMANICUS IS A STUDENT AND DISCIPLE OF THE BISHOP OF SMYRNA--POLYCARP.
HE IS WELL GROUNDED IN THE SCRIPTURES AND ANSWERS ACCORDINGLY.
ONLY JESUS CHRIST DESERVES THE TITLE LORD.
GO! AND WE WILL SEE IF MY BEASTS HAVE ANY PITY ON YOU.

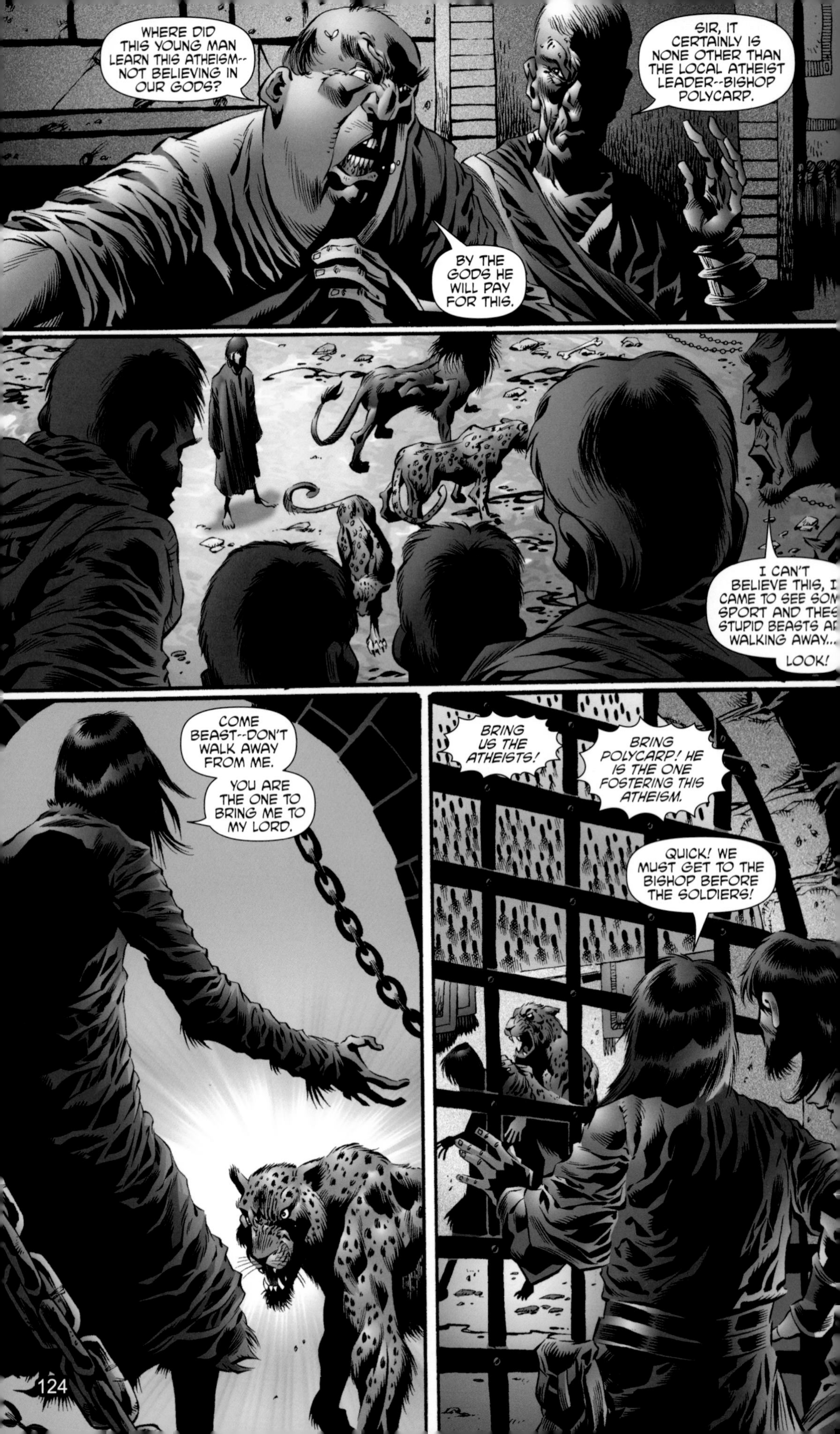
WHERE DID THIS YOUNG MAN LEARN THIS ATHEISM--NOT BELIEVING IN OUR GODS?
SIR, IT CERTAINLY IS NONE OTHER THAN THE LOCAL ATHEIST LEADER--BISHOP POLYCARP.
BY THE GODS HE WILL PAY FOR THIS.
I CAN'T BELIEVE THIS, I CAME TO SEE SOM SPORT AND THES STUPID BEASTS AR WALKING AWAY...
LOOK!
COME BEAST--DON'T WALK AWAY FROM ME.
YOU ARE THE ONE TO BRING ME TO MY LORD.
BRING US THE ATHEISTS!
BRING POLYCARP! HE IS THE ONE FOSTERING THIS ATHEISM.
QUICK! WE MUST GET TO THE BISHOP BEFORE THE SOLDIERS!

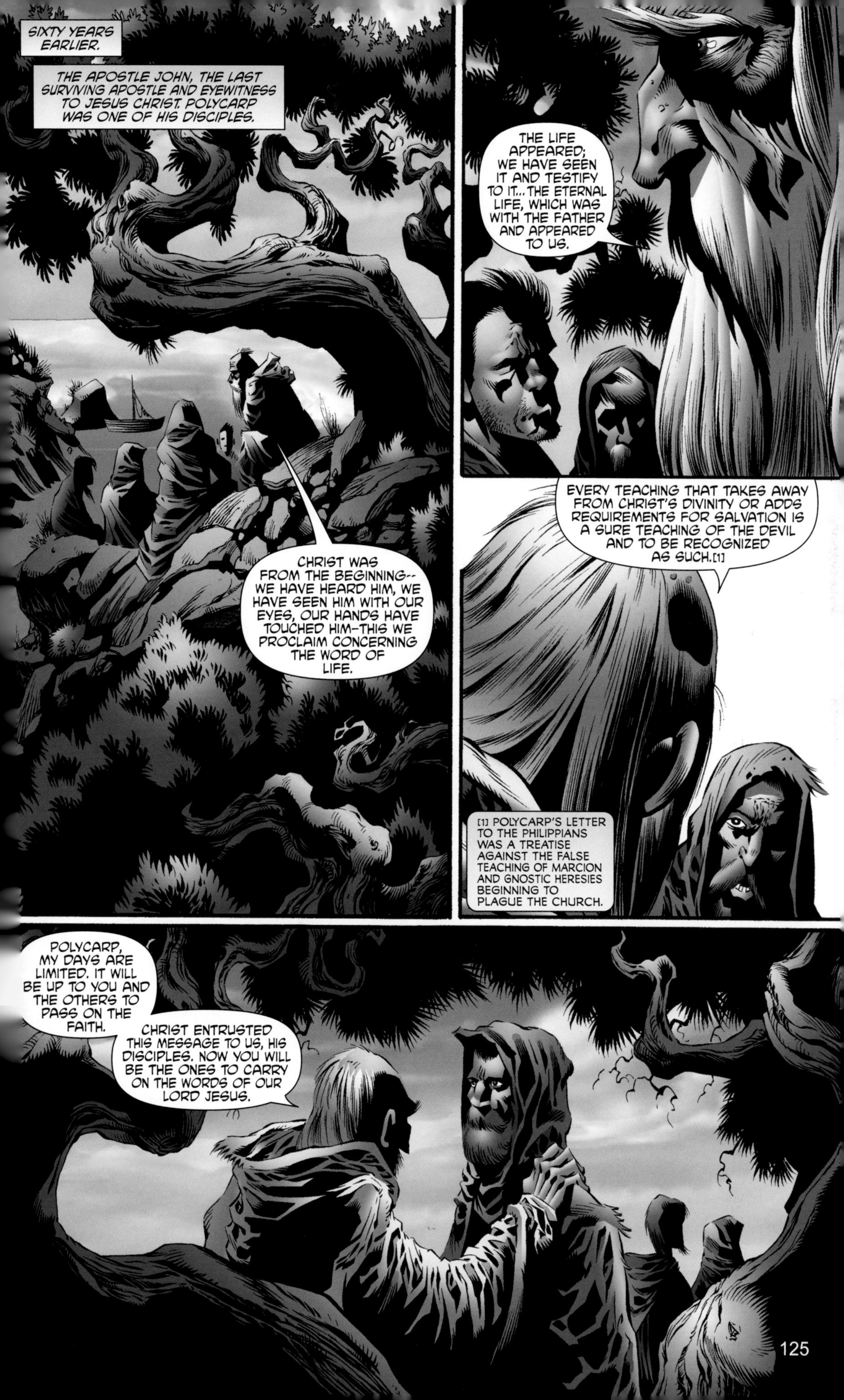

SIXTY YEARS EARLIER.
THE APOSTLE JOHN, THE LAST SURVIVING APOSTLE AND EYEWITNESS TO JESUS CHRIST. POLYCARP WAS ONE OF HIS DISCIPLES.
CHRIST WAS FROM THE BEGINNING-- WE HAVE HEARD HIM, WE HAVE SEEN HIM WITH OUR EYES, OUR HANDS HAVE TOUCHED HIM–THIS WE PROCLAIM CONCERNING THE WORD OF LIFE.
THE LIFE APPEARED; WE HAVE SEEN IT AND TESTIFY TO IT... THE ETERNAL LIFE, WHICH WAS WITH THE FATHER AND APPEARED TO US.
EVERY TEACHING THAT TAKES AWAY FROM CHRIST'S DIVINITY OR ADDS REQUIREMENTS FOR SALVATION IS A SURE TEACHING OF THE DEVIL AND TO BE RECOGNIZED AS SUCH.[1]
[1] POLYCARP'S LETTER TO THE PHILIPPIANS WAS A TREATISE AGAINST THE FALSE TEACHING OF MARCION AND GNOSTIC HERESIES BEGINNING TO PLAGUE THE CHURCH.
POLYCARP, MY DAYS ARE LIMITED. IT WILL BE UP TO YOU AND THE OTHERS TO PASS ON THE FAITH.
CHRIST ENTRUSTED THIS MESSAGE TO US, HIS DISCIPLES. NOW YOU WILL BE THE ONES TO CARRY ON THE WORDS OF OUR LORD JESUS.

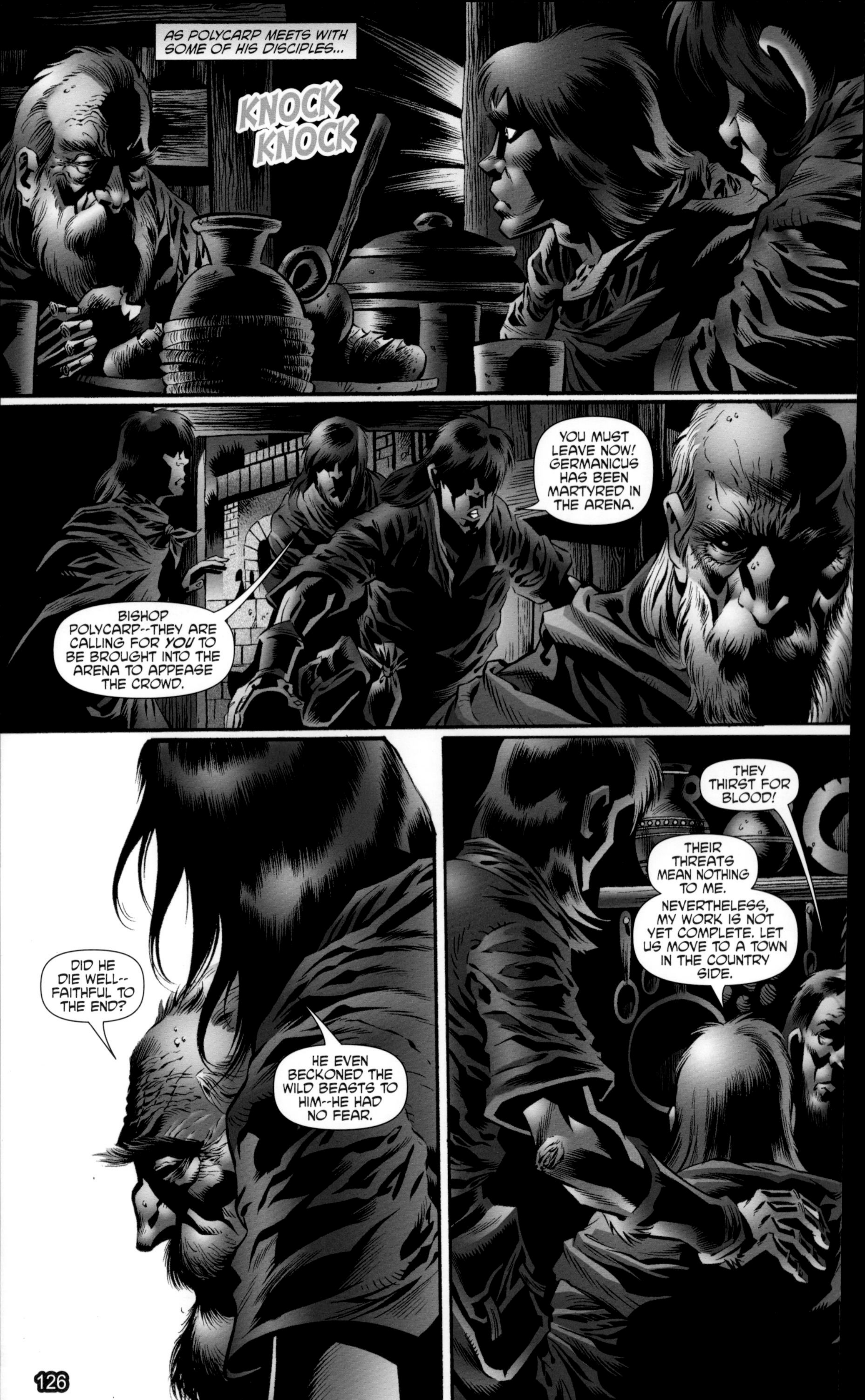
AS POLYCARP MEETS WITH SOME OF HIS DISCIPLES...
KNOCK KNOCK
YOU MUST LEAVE NOW! GERMANICUS HAS BEEN MARTYRED IN THE ARENA.
BISHOP POLYCARP--THEY ARE CALLING FOR YOU TO BE BROUGHT INTO THE ARENA TO APPEASE THE CROWD.
DID HE DIE WELL--FAITHFUL TO THE END?
HE EVEN BECKONED THE WILD BEASTS TO HIM--HE HAD NO FEAR.
THEY THIRST FOR BLOOD!
THEIR THREATS MEAN NOTHING TO ME.
NEVERTHELESS, MY WORK IS NOT YET COMPLETE. LET US MOVE TO A TOWN IN THE COUNTRY SIDE.

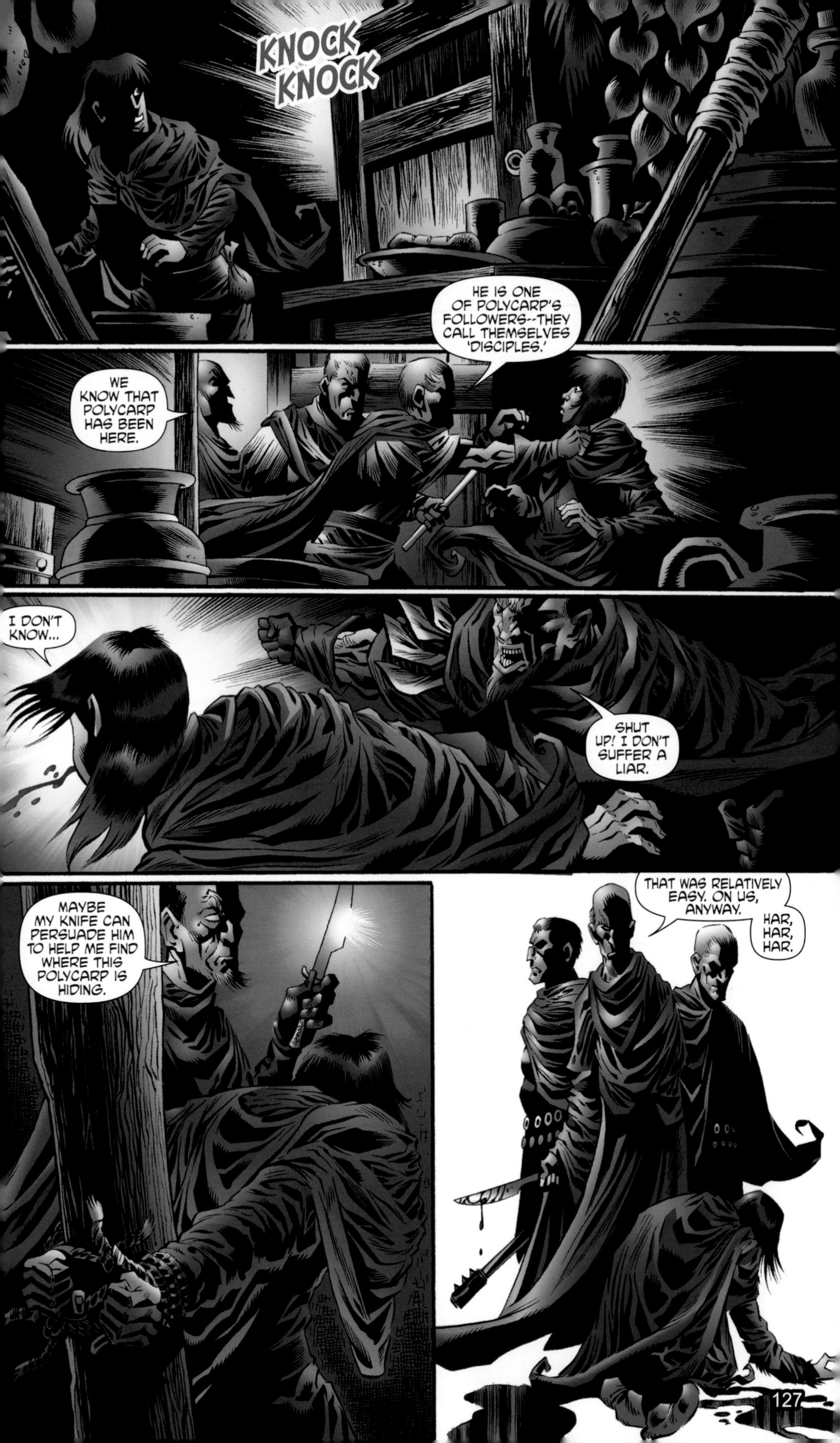
KNOCK KNOCK
HE IS ONE OF POLYCARP'S FOLLOWERS--THEY CALL THEMSELVES 'DISCIPLES.'
WE KNOW THAT POLYCARP HAS BEEN HERE.
I DON'T KNOW...
SHUT UP! I DON'T SUFFER A LIAR.
MAYBE MY KNIFE CAN PERSUADE HIM TO HELP ME FIND WHERE THIS POLYCARP IS HIDING.
THAT WAS RELATIVELY EASY. ON US, ANYWAY.
HAR, HAR, HAR.

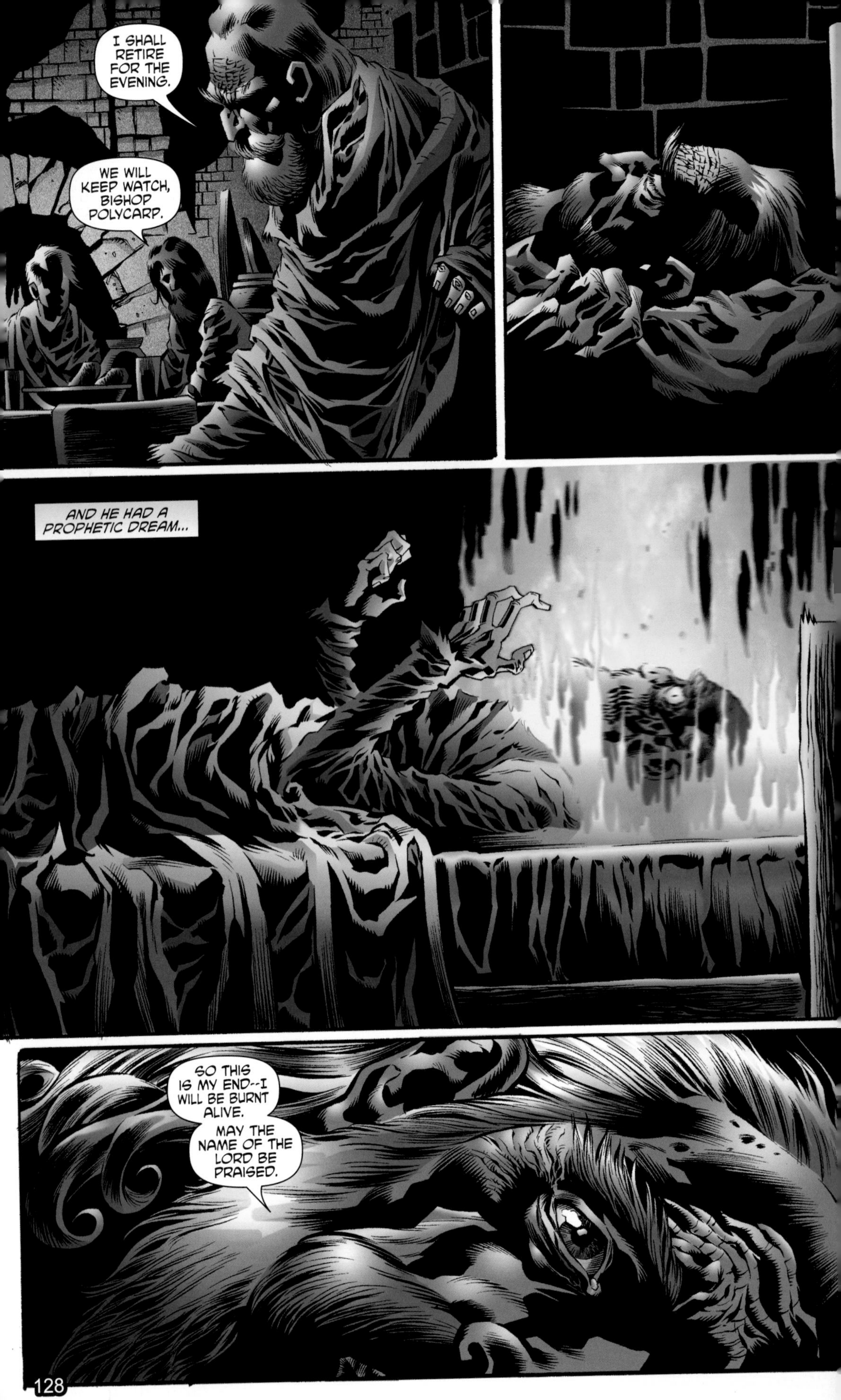
I SHALL RETIRE FOR THE EVENING.
WE WILL KEEP WATCH, BISHOP POLYCARP.
AND HE HAD A PROPHETIC DREAM...
SO THIS IS MY END--I WILL BE BURNT ALIVE.
MAY THE NAME OF THE LORD BE PRAISED.

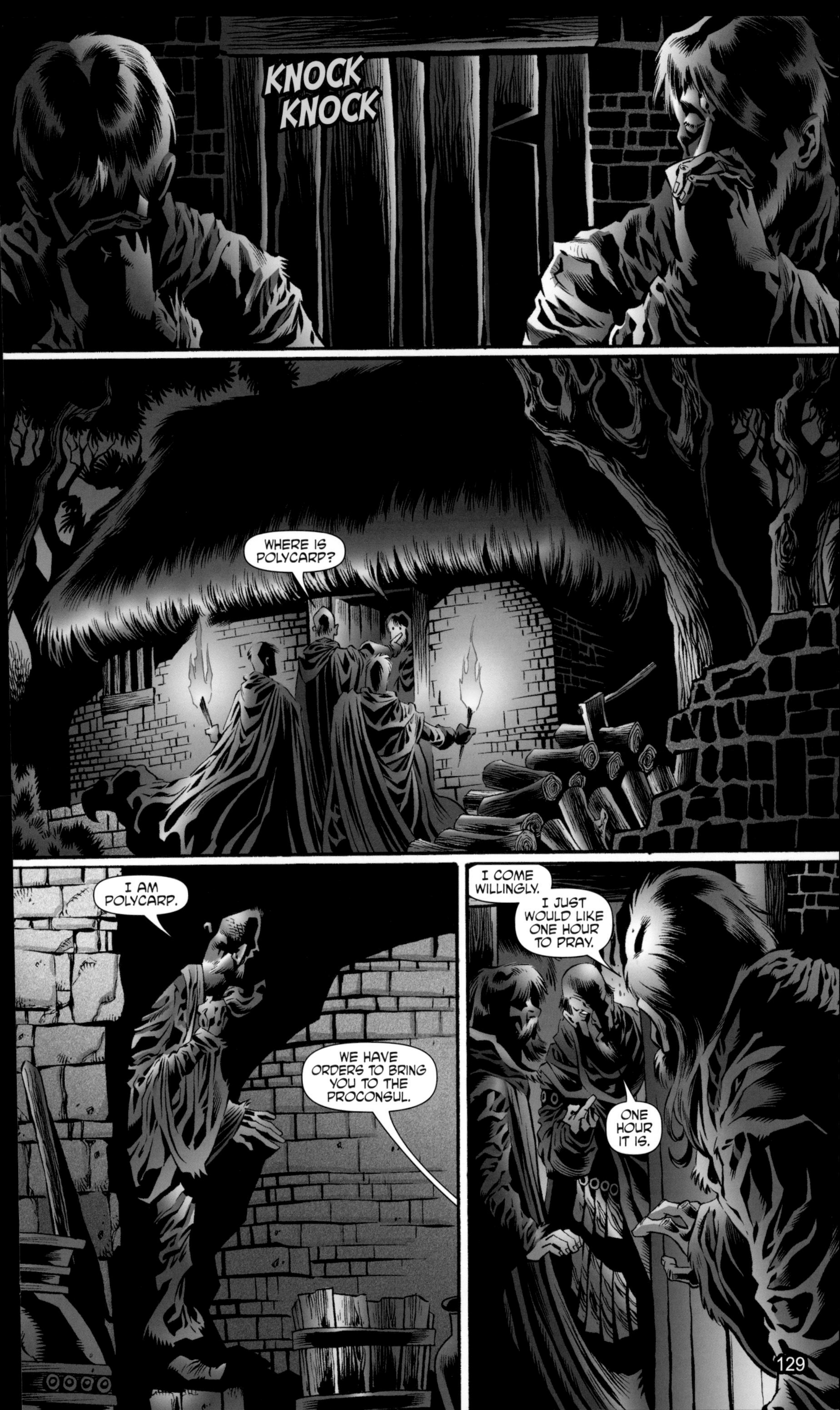
KNOCK KNOCK
WHERE IS POLYCARP?
I AM POLYCARP.
WE HAVE ORDERS TO BRING YOU TO THE PROCONSUL.
I COME WILLINGLY.
I JUST WOULD LIKE ONE HOUR TO PRAY.
ONE HOUR IT IS.

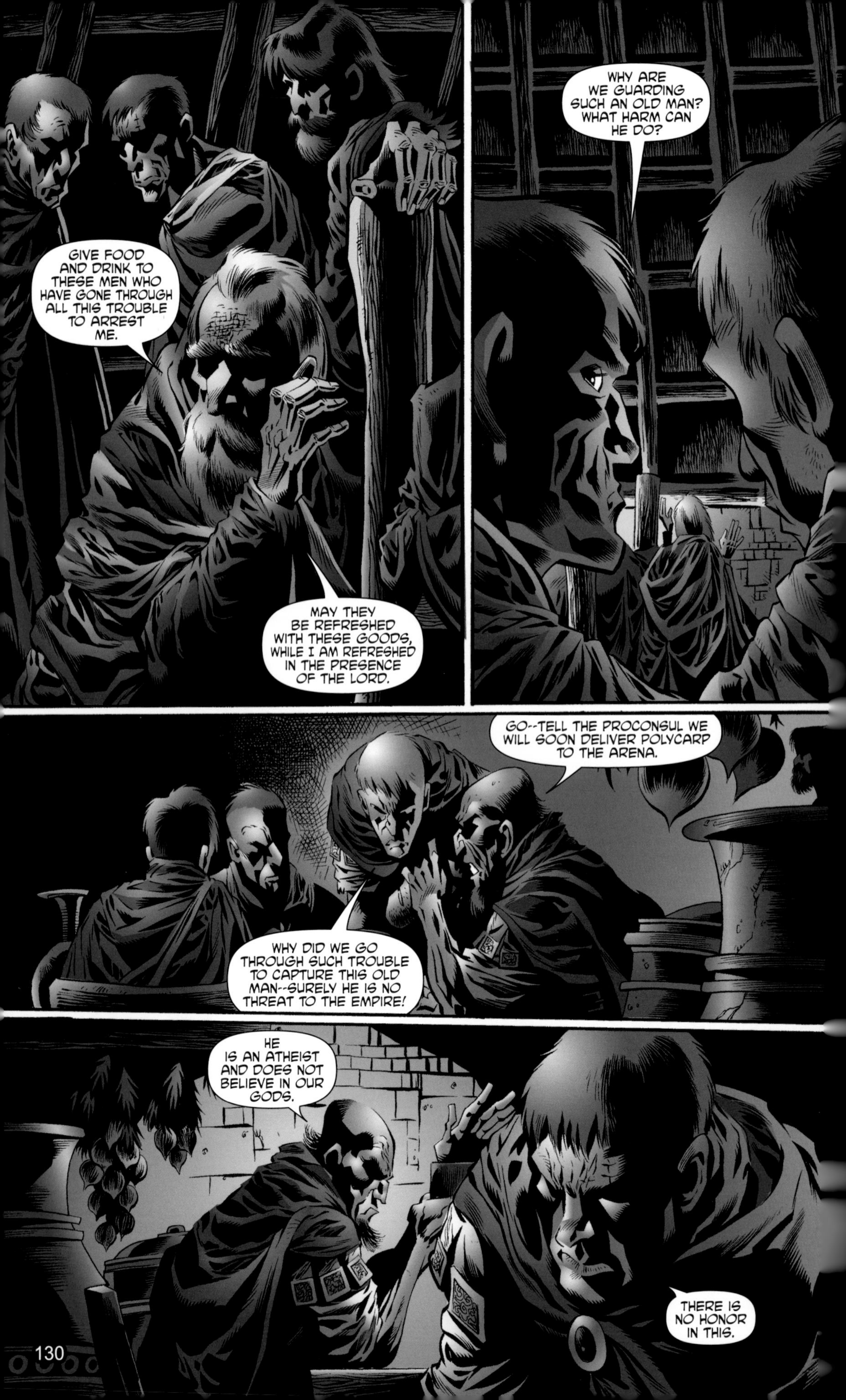
GIVE FOOD AND DRINK TO THESE MEN WHO HAVE GONE THROUGH ALL THIS TROUBLE TO ARREST ME.
MAY THEY BE REFRESHED WITH THESE GOODS, WHILE I AM REFRESHED IN THE PRESENCE OF THE LORD.
WHY ARE WE GUARDING SUCH AN OLD MAN? WHAT HARM CAN HE DO?
GO--TELL THE PROCONSUL WE WILL SOON DELIVER POLYCARP TO THE ARENA.
WHY DID WE GO THROUGH SUCH TROUBLE TO CAPTURE THIS OLD MAN--SURELY HE IS NO THREAT TO THE EMPIRE!
HE IS AN ATHEIST AND DOES NOT BELIEVE IN OUR GODS.
THERE IS NO HONOR IN THIS.

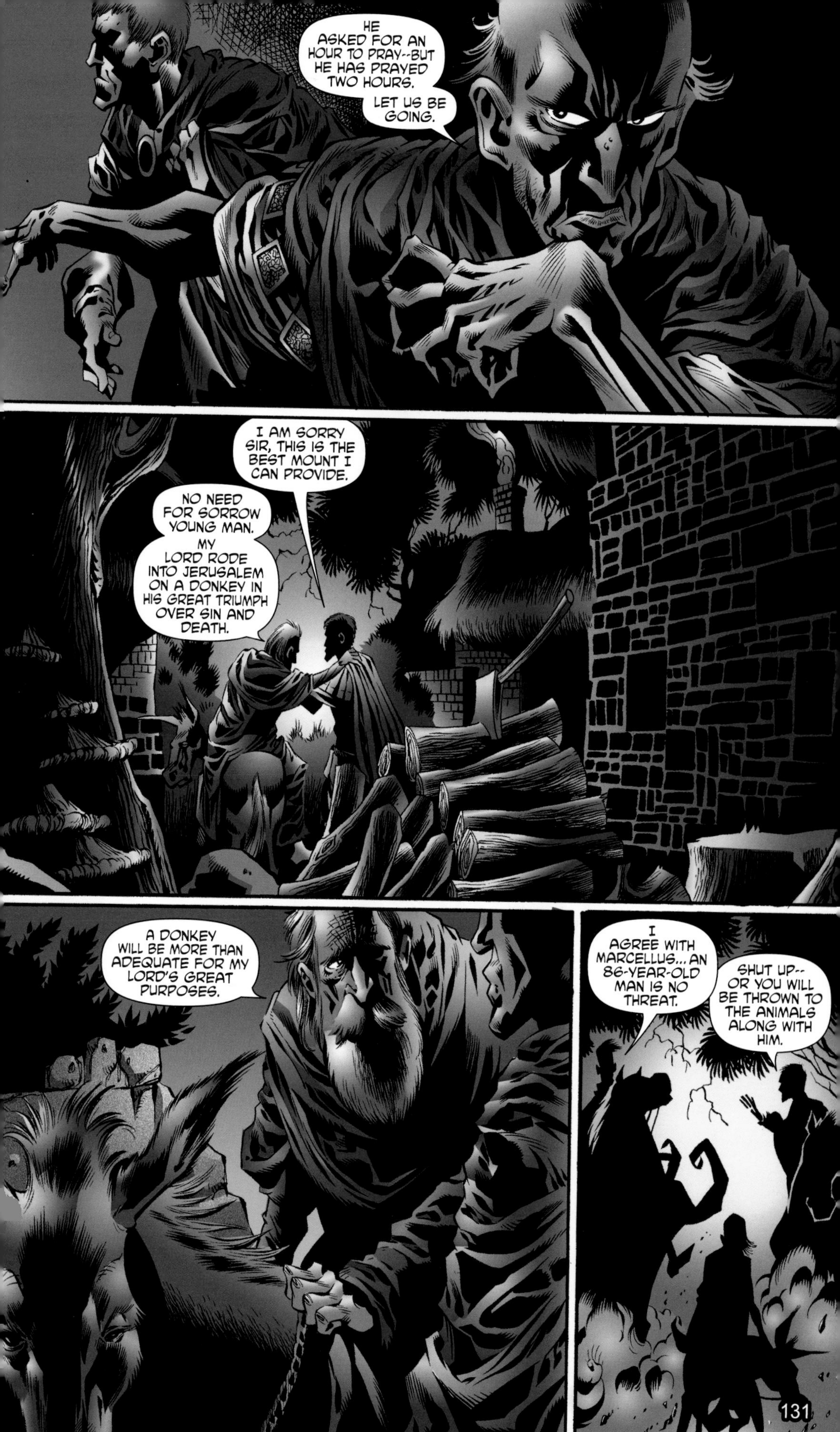
HE ASKED FOR AN HOUR TO PRAY--BUT HE HAS PRAYED TWO HOURS.
LET US BE GOING.
I AM SORRY SIR, THIS IS THE BEST MOUNT I CAN PROVIDE.
NO NEED FOR SORROW YOUNG MAN.
MY LORD RODE INTO JERUSALEM ON A DONKEY IN HIS GREAT TRIUMPH OVER SIN AND DEATH.
A DONKEY WILL BE MORE THAN ADEQUATE FOR MY LORD'S GREAT PURPOSES.
I AGREE WITH MARCELLUS... AN 86-YEAR-OLD MAN IS NO THREAT.
SHUT UP-- OR YOU WILL BE THROWN TO THE ANIMALS ALONG WITH HIM.

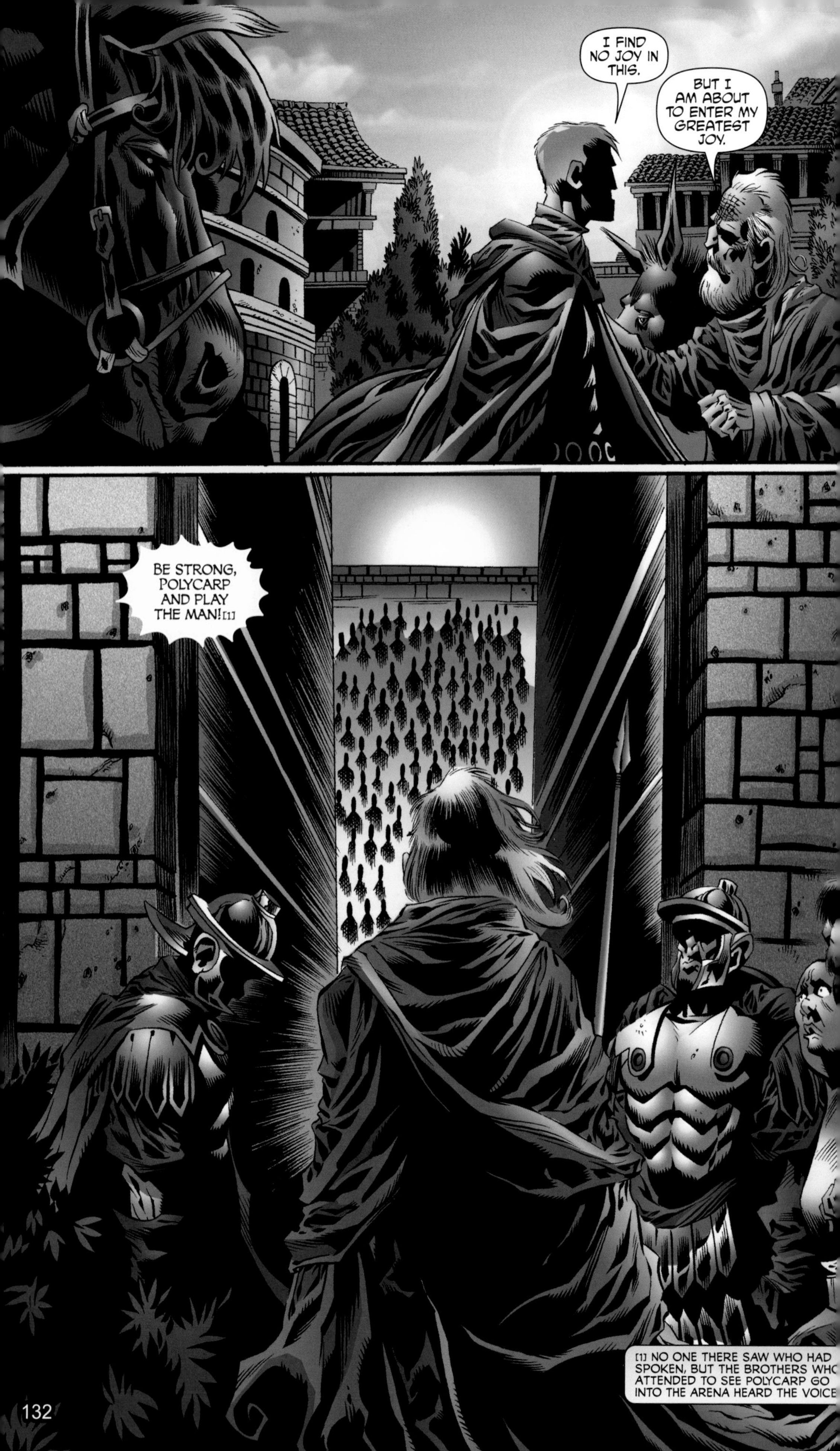
I FIND NO JOY IN THIS.
BUT I AM ABOUT TO ENTER MY GREATEST JOY.
BE STRONG, POLYCARP AND PLAY THE MAN![1]
[1] NO ONE THERE SAW WHO HAD SPOKEN, BUT THE BROTHERS WHO ATTENDED TO SEE POLYCARP GO INTO THE ARENA HEARD THE VOICE

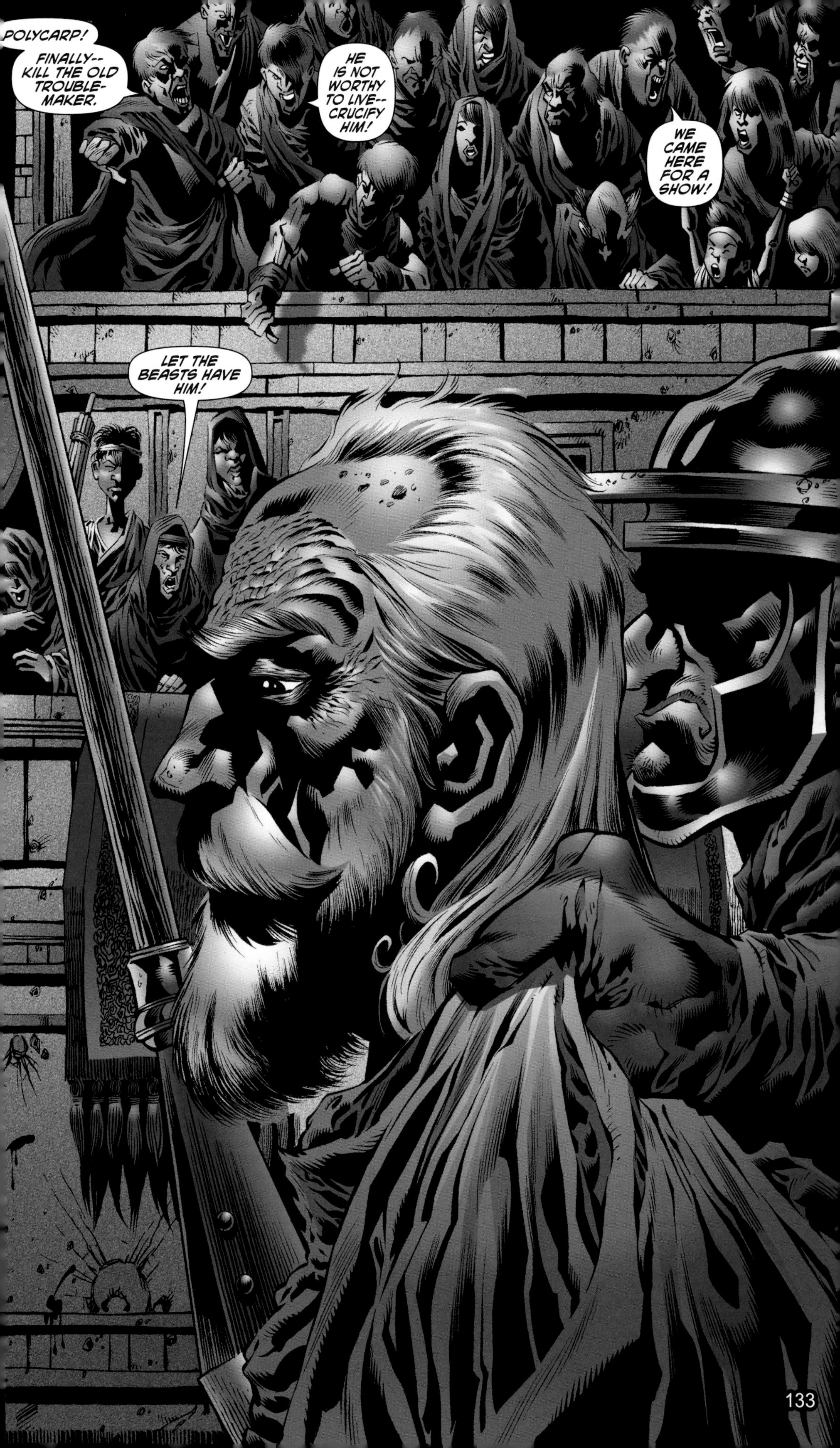
POLYCARP!
FINALLY-- KILL THE OLD TROUBLE-MAKER.
HE IS NOT WORTHY TO LIVE-- CRUCIFY HIM!
WE CAME HERE FOR A SHOW!
LET THE BEASTS HAVE HIM!

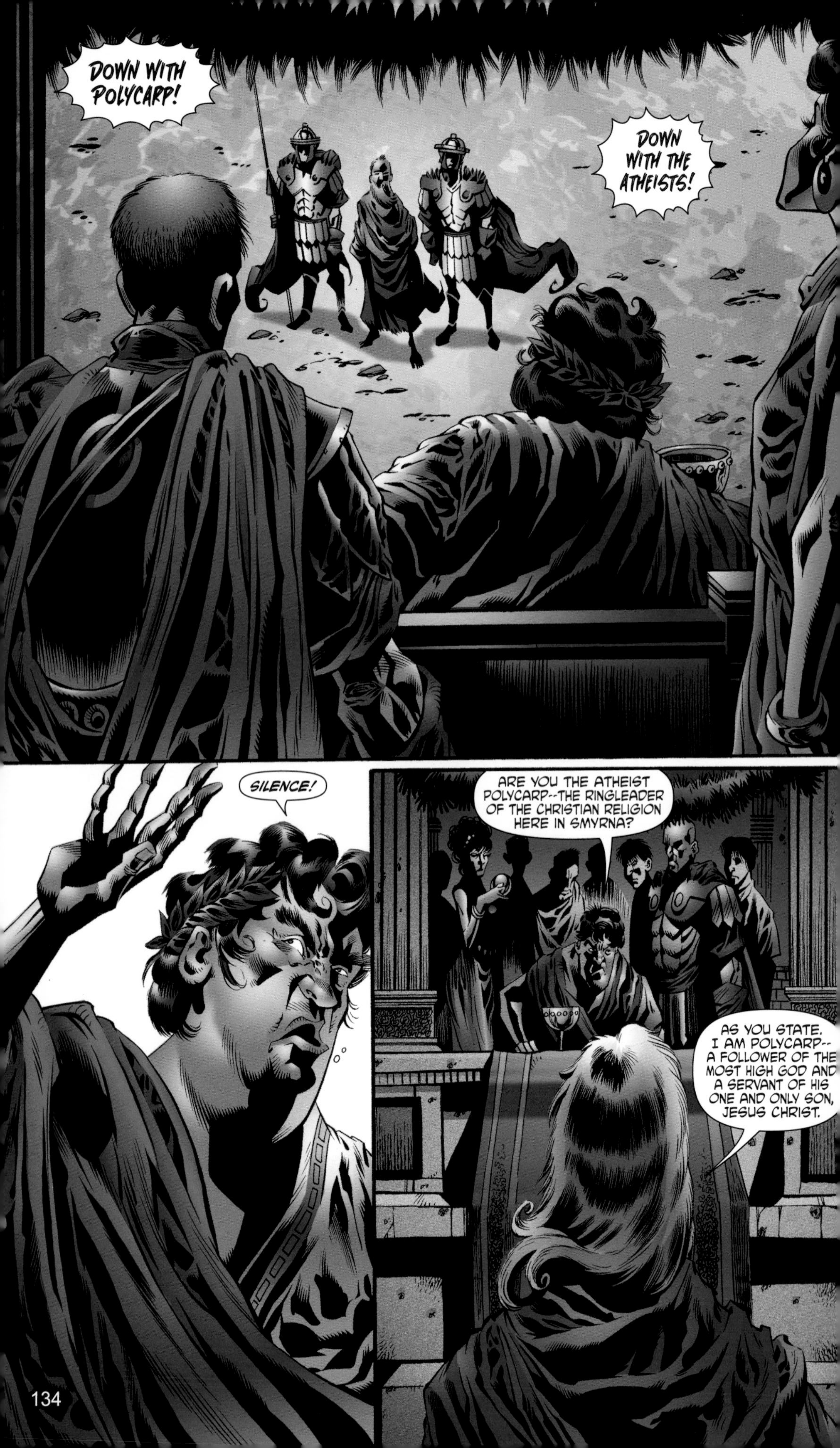
DOWN WITH POLYCARP!
DOWN WITH THE ATHEISTS!
SILENCE!
ARE YOU THE ATHEIST POLYCARP--THE RINGLEADER OF THE CHRISTIAN RELIGION HERE IN SMYRNA?
AS YOU STATE. I AM POLYCARP-- A FOLLOWER OF THE MOST HIGH GOD AND A SERVANT OF HIS ONE AND ONLY SON, JESUS CHRIST.

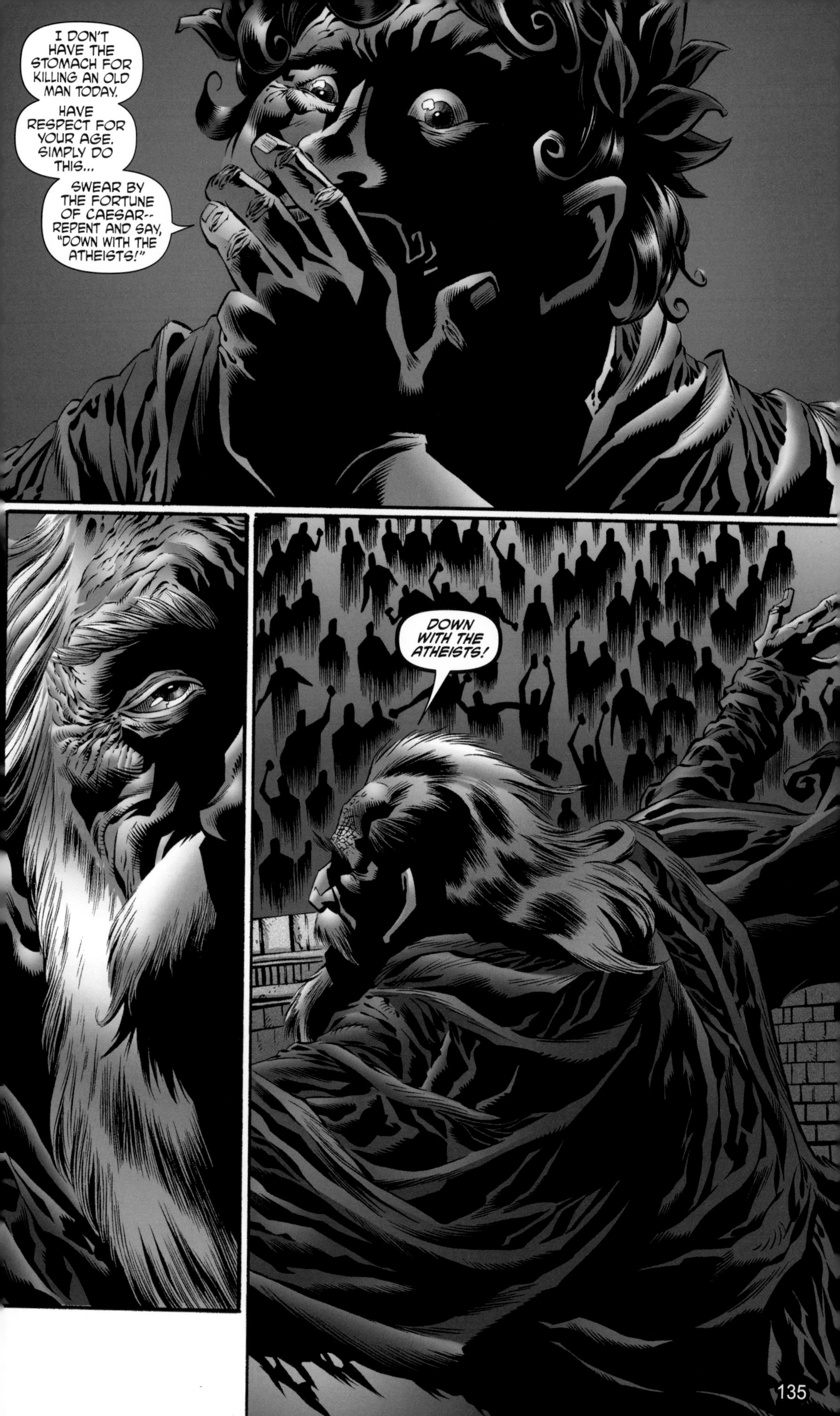
I DON'T HAVE THE STOMACH FOR KILLING AN OLD MAN TODAY.
HAVE RESPECT FOR YOUR AGE. SIMPLY DO THIS...
SWEAR BY THE FORTUNE OF CAESAR-- REPENT AND SAY, "DOWN WITH THE ATHEISTS!"
DOWN WITH THE ATHEISTS!

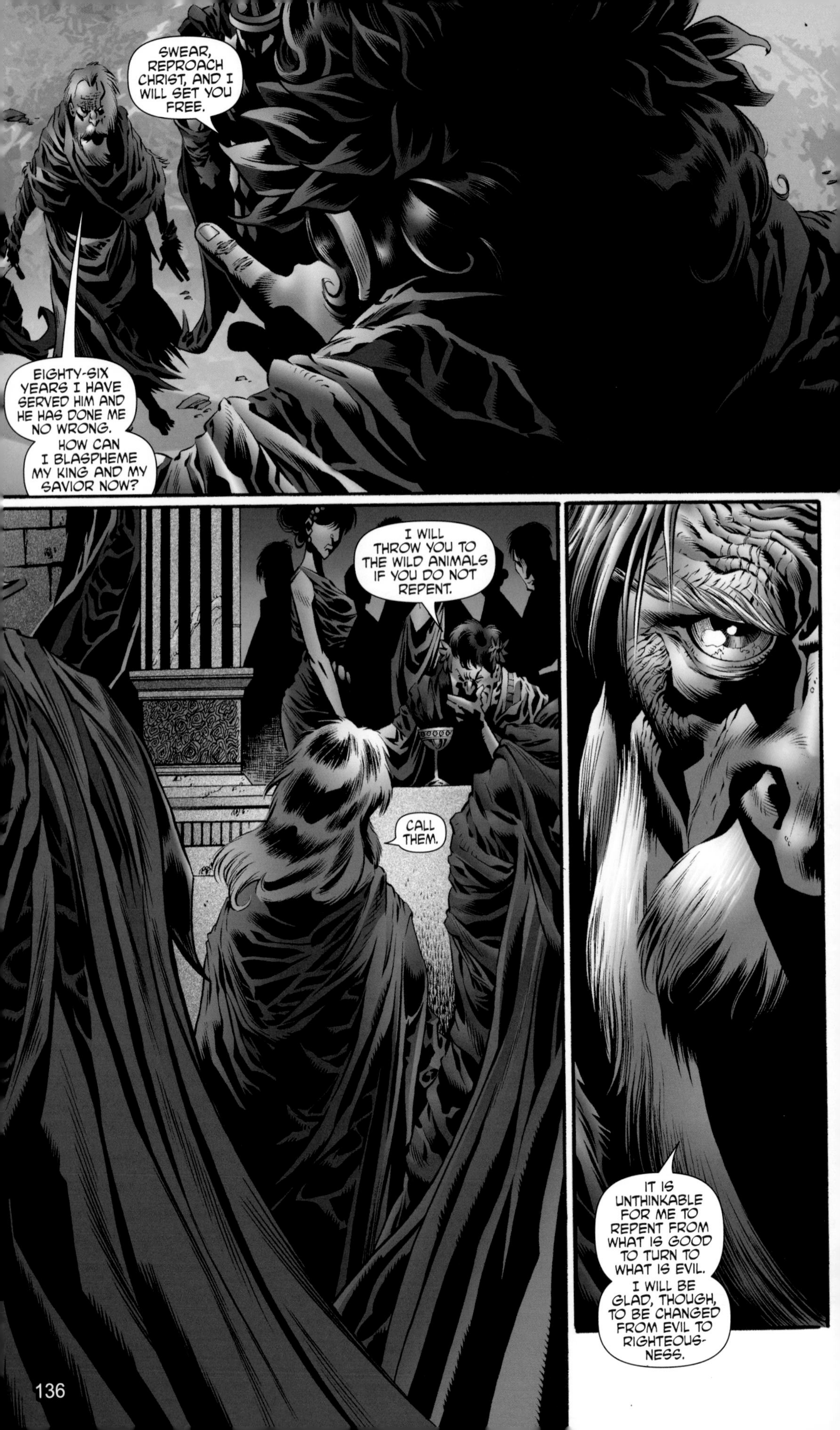
SWEAR, REPROACH CHRIST, AND I WILL SET YOU FREE.
EIGHTY-SIX YEARS I HAVE SERVED HIM AND HE HAS DONE ME NO WRONG.
HOW CAN I BLASPHEME MY KING AND MY SAVIOR NOW?
I WILL THROW YOU TO THE WILD ANIMALS IF YOU DO NOT REPENT.
CALL THEM.
IT IS UNTHINKABLE FOR ME TO REPENT FROM WHAT IS GOOD TO TURN TO WHAT IS EVIL.
I WILL BE GLAD, THOUGH, TO BE CHANGED FROM EVIL TO RIGHTEOUS-NESS.

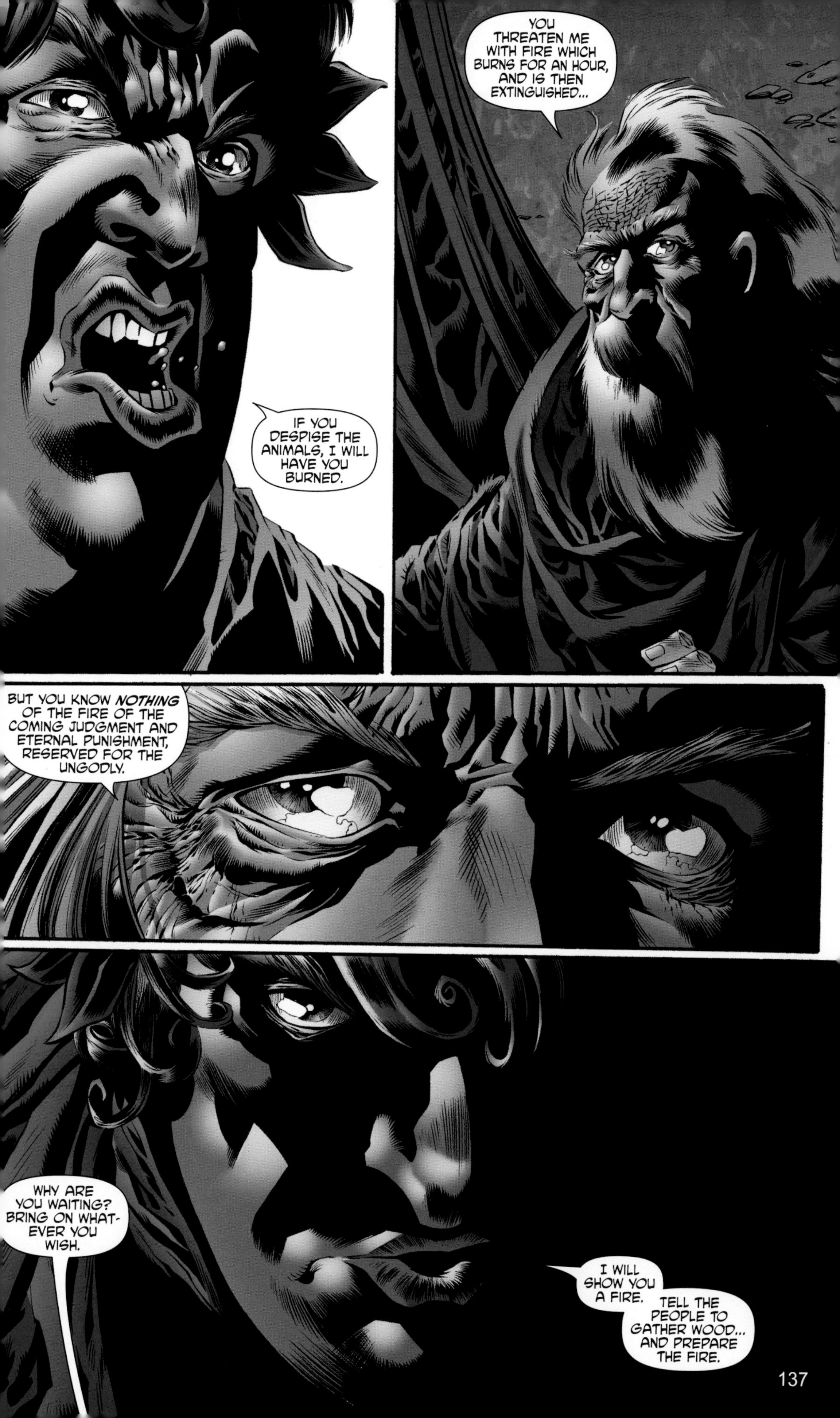
IF YOU DESPISE THE ANIMALS, I WILL HAVE YOU BURNED.
YOU THREATEN ME WITH FIRE WHICH BURNS FOR AN HOUR, AND IS THEN EXTINGUISHED...
BUT YOU KNOW *NOTHING* OF THE FIRE OF THE COMING JUDGMENT AND ETERNAL PUNISHMENT, RESERVED FOR THE UNGODLY.
WHY ARE YOU WAITING? BRING ON WHAT-EVER YOU WISH.
I WILL SHOW YOU A FIRE.
TELL THE PEOPLE TO GATHER WOOD... AND PREPARE THE FIRE.

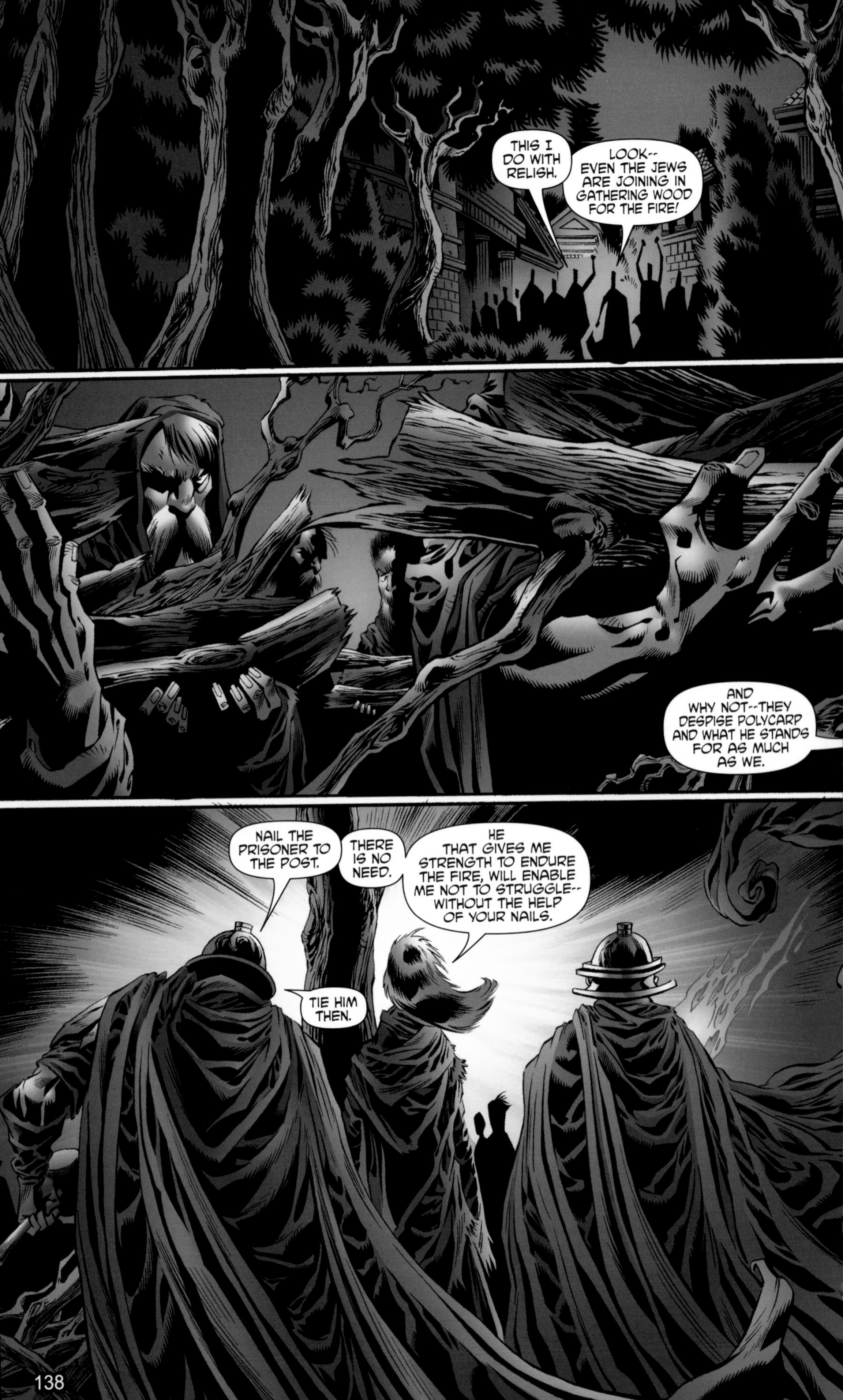
THIS I DO WITH RELISH.
LOOK-- EVEN THE JEWS ARE JOINING IN GATHERING WOOD FOR THE FIRE!
AND WHY NOT--THEY DESPISE POLYCARP AND WHAT HE STANDS FOR AS MUCH AS WE.
NAIL THE PRISONER TO THE POST.
THERE IS NO NEED.
HE THAT GIVES ME STRENGTH TO ENDURE THE FIRE, WILL ENABLE ME NOT TO STRUGGLE-- WITHOUT THE HELP OF YOUR NAILS.
TIE HIM THEN.

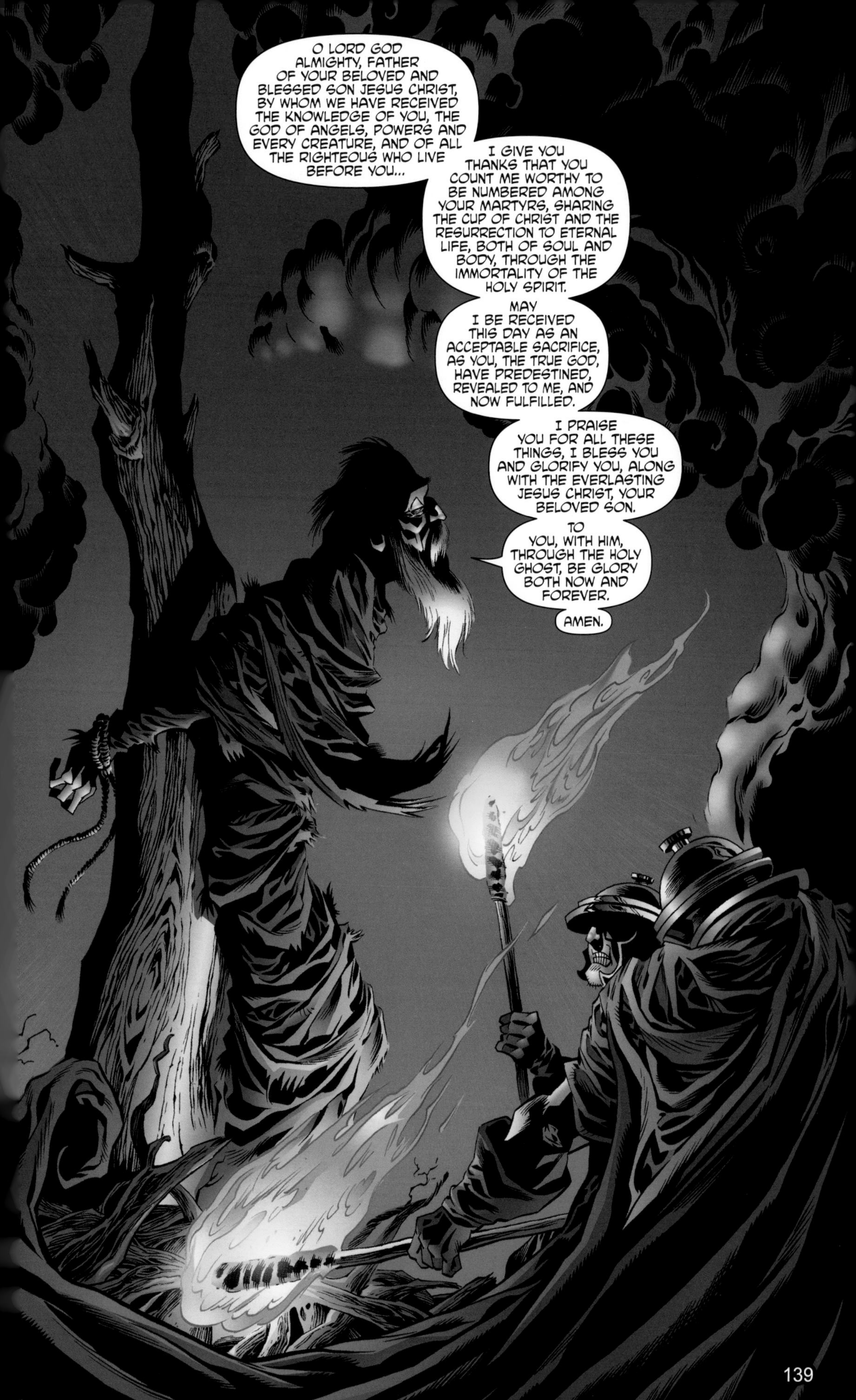
O LORD GOD ALMIGHTY, FATHER OF YOUR BELOVED AND BLESSED SON JESUS CHRIST, BY WHOM WE HAVE RECEIVED THE KNOWLEDGE OF YOU, THE GOD OF ANGELS, POWERS AND EVERY CREATURE, AND OF ALL THE RIGHTEOUS WHO LIVE BEFORE YOU...
I GIVE YOU THANKS THAT YOU COUNT ME WORTHY TO BE NUMBERED AMONG YOUR MARTYRS, SHARING THE CUP OF CHRIST AND THE RESURRECTION TO ETERNAL LIFE, BOTH OF SOUL AND BODY, THROUGH THE IMMORTALITY OF THE HOLY SPIRIT.
MAY I BE RECEIVED THIS DAY AS AN ACCEPTABLE SACRIFICE, AS YOU, THE TRUE GOD, HAVE PREDESTINED, REVEALED TO ME, AND NOW FULFILLED.
I PRAISE YOU FOR ALL THESE THINGS, I BLESS YOU AND GLORIFY YOU, ALONG WITH THE EVERLASTING JESUS CHRIST, YOUR BELOVED SON.
TO YOU, WITH HIM, THROUGH THE HOLY GHOST, BE GLORY BOTH NOW AND FOREVER.
AMEN.

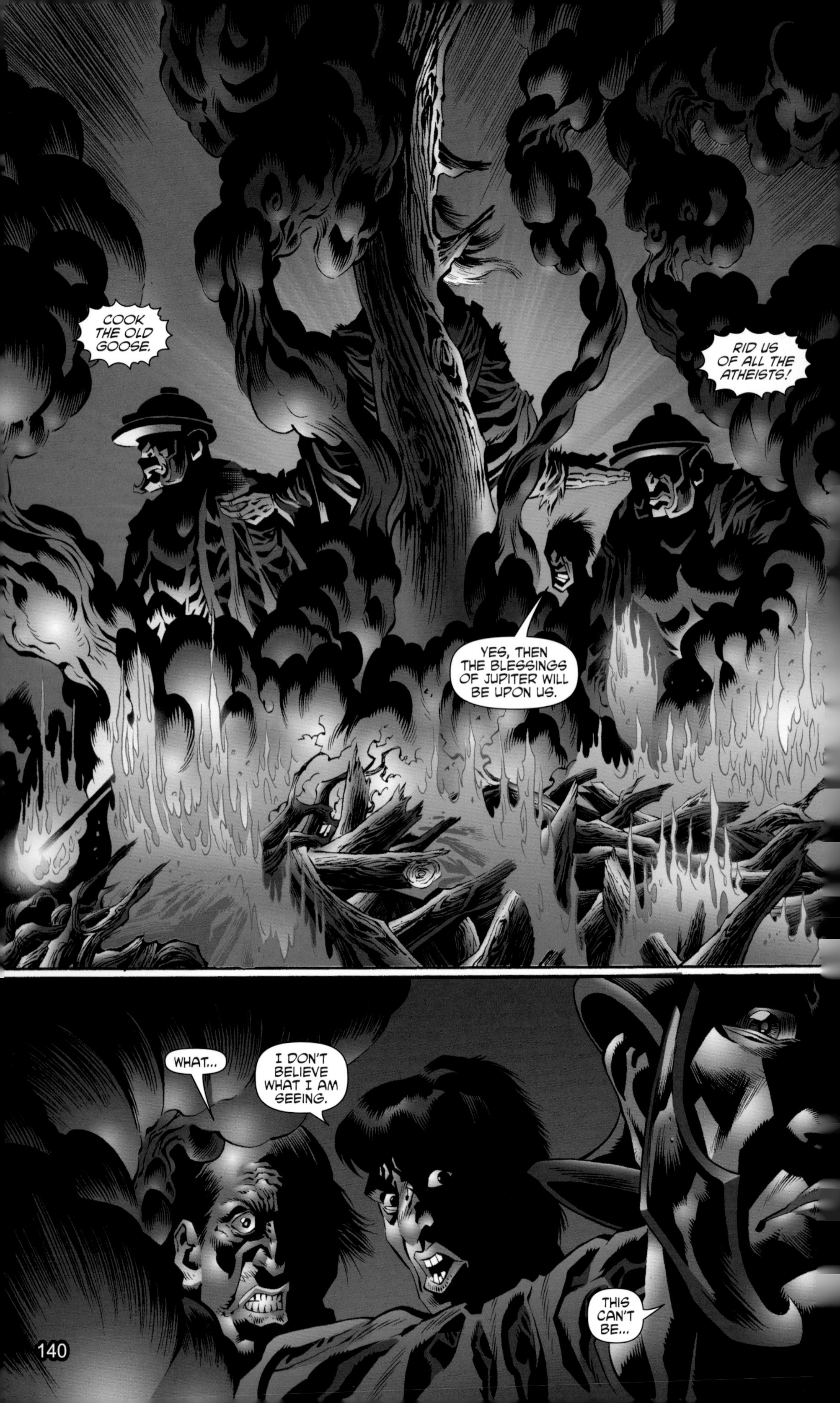
COOK THE OLD GOOSE.
RID US OF ALL THE ATHEISTS!
YES, THEN THE BLESSINGS OF JUPITER WILL BE UPON US.
WHAT...
I DON'T BELIEVE WHAT I AM SEEING.
THIS CAN'T BE...

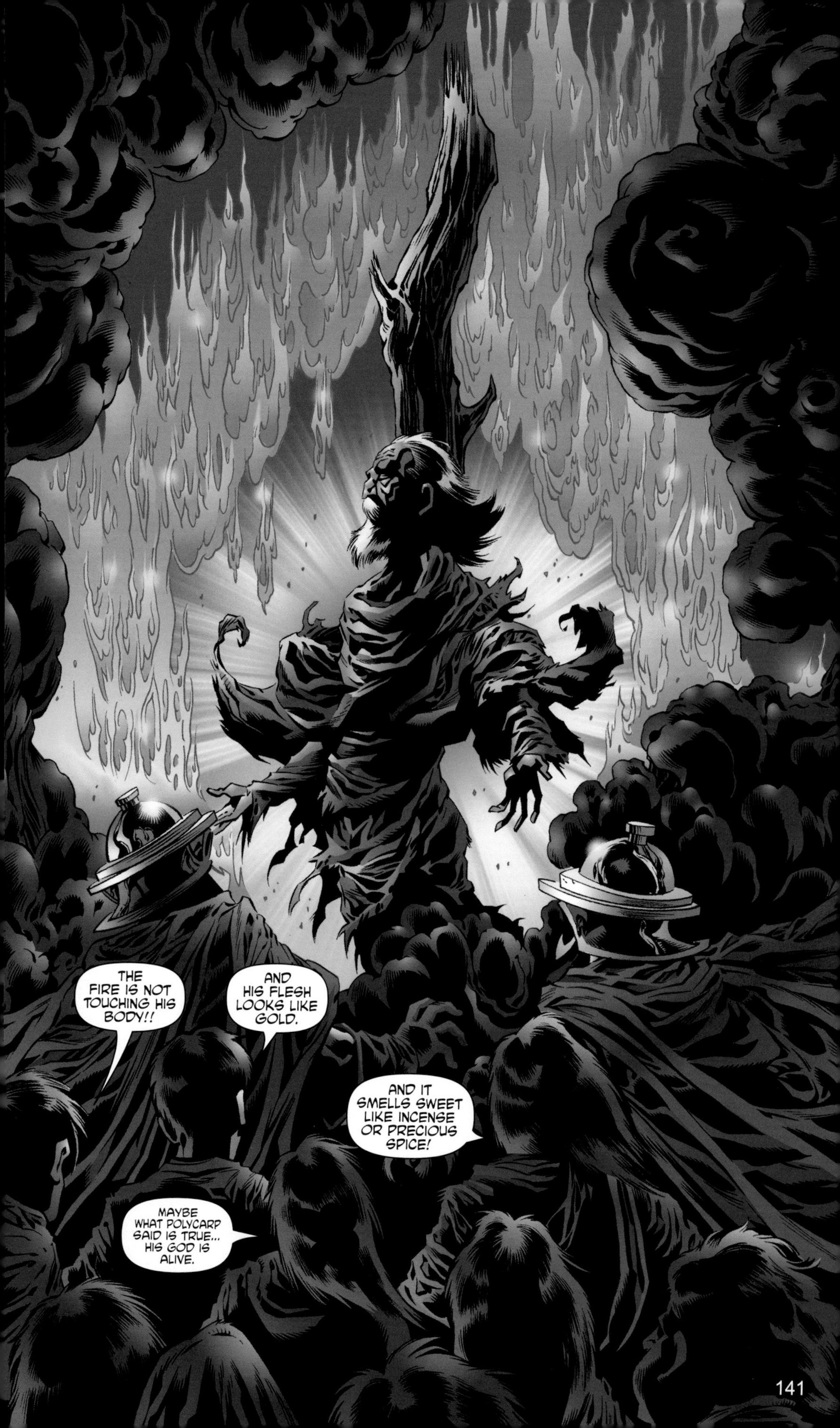
THE FIRE IS NOT TOUCHING HIS BODY!!
AND HIS FLESH LOOKS LIKE GOLD.
AND IT SMELLS SWEET LIKE INCENSE OR PRECIOUS SPICE!
MAYBE WHAT POLYCARP SAID IS TRUE... HIS GOD IS ALIVE.

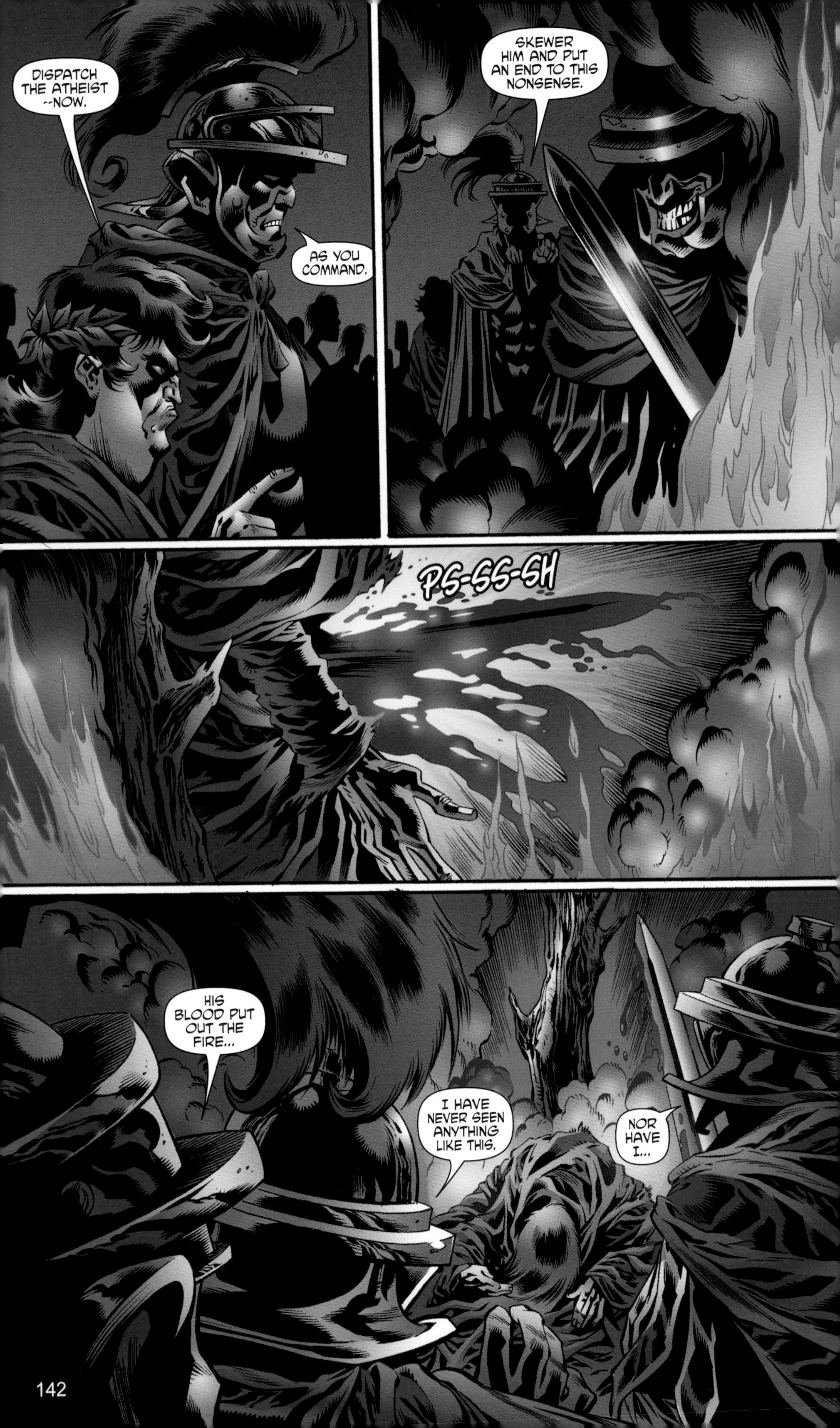
DISPATCH THE ATHEIST --NOW.
AS YOU COMMAND.
SKEWER HIM AND PUT AN END TO THIS NONSENSE.
PS-SS-SH
HIS BLOOD PUT OUT THE FIRE...
I HAVE NEVER SEEN ANYTHING LIKE THIS.
NOR HAVE I...

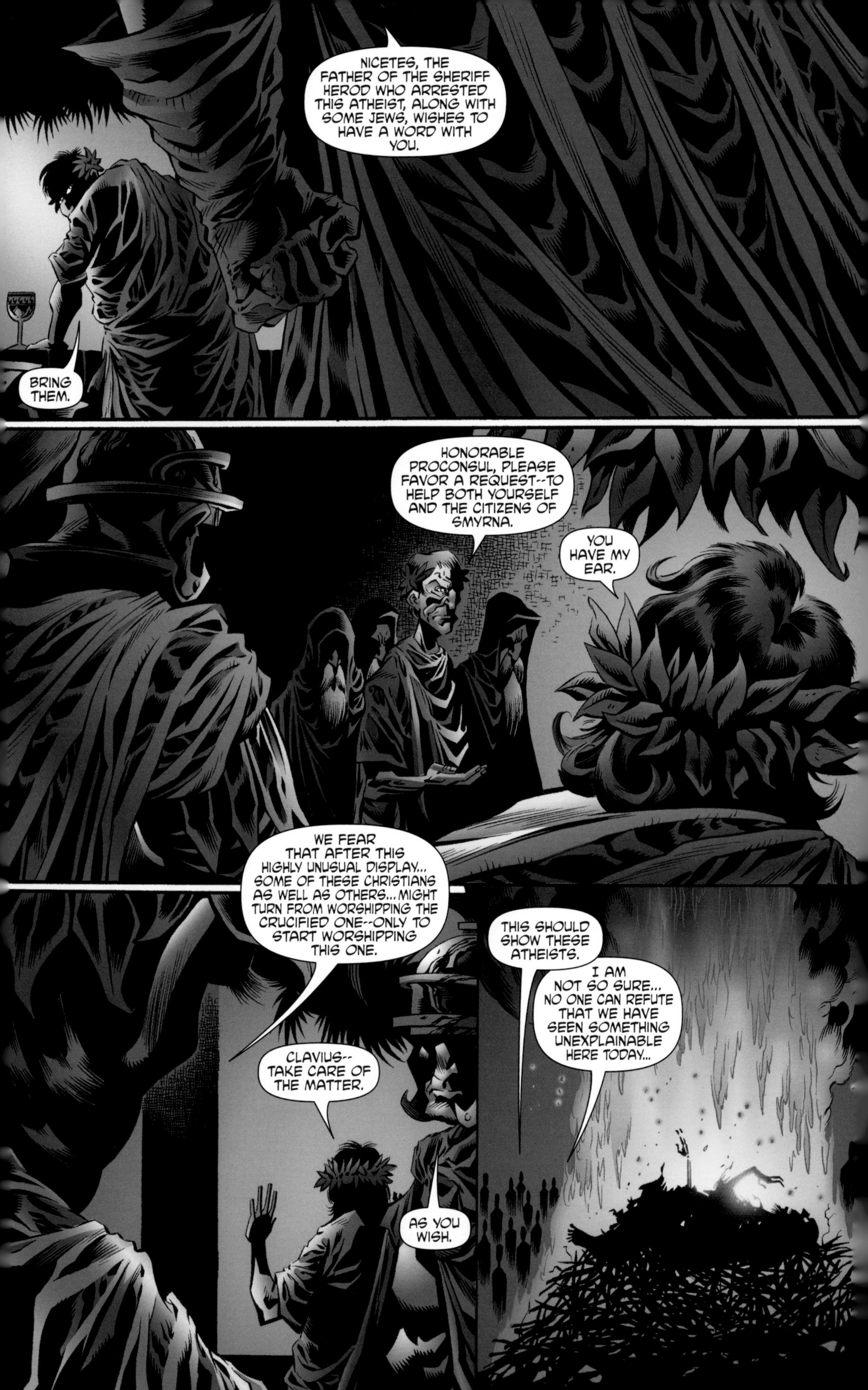
NICETES, THE FATHER OF THE SHERIFF HEROD WHO ARRESTED THIS ATHEIST, ALONG WITH SOME JEWS, WISHES TO HAVE A WORD WITH YOU.
BRING THEM.
HONORABLE PROCONSUL, PLEASE FAVOR A REQUEST--TO HELP BOTH YOURSELF AND THE CITIZENS OF SMYRNA.
YOU HAVE MY EAR.
WE FEAR THAT AFTER THIS HIGHLY UNUSUAL DISPLAY... SOME OF THESE CHRISTIANS AS WELL AS OTHERS... MIGHT TURN FROM WORSHIPPING THE CRUCIFIED ONE--ONLY TO START WORSHIPPING THIS ONE.
CLAVIUS-- TAKE CARE OF THE MATTER.
AS YOU WISH.
THIS SHOULD SHOW THESE ATHEISTS.
I AM NOT SO SURE... NO ONE CAN REFUTE THAT WE HAVE SEEN SOMETHING UNEXPLAINABLE HERE TODAY...

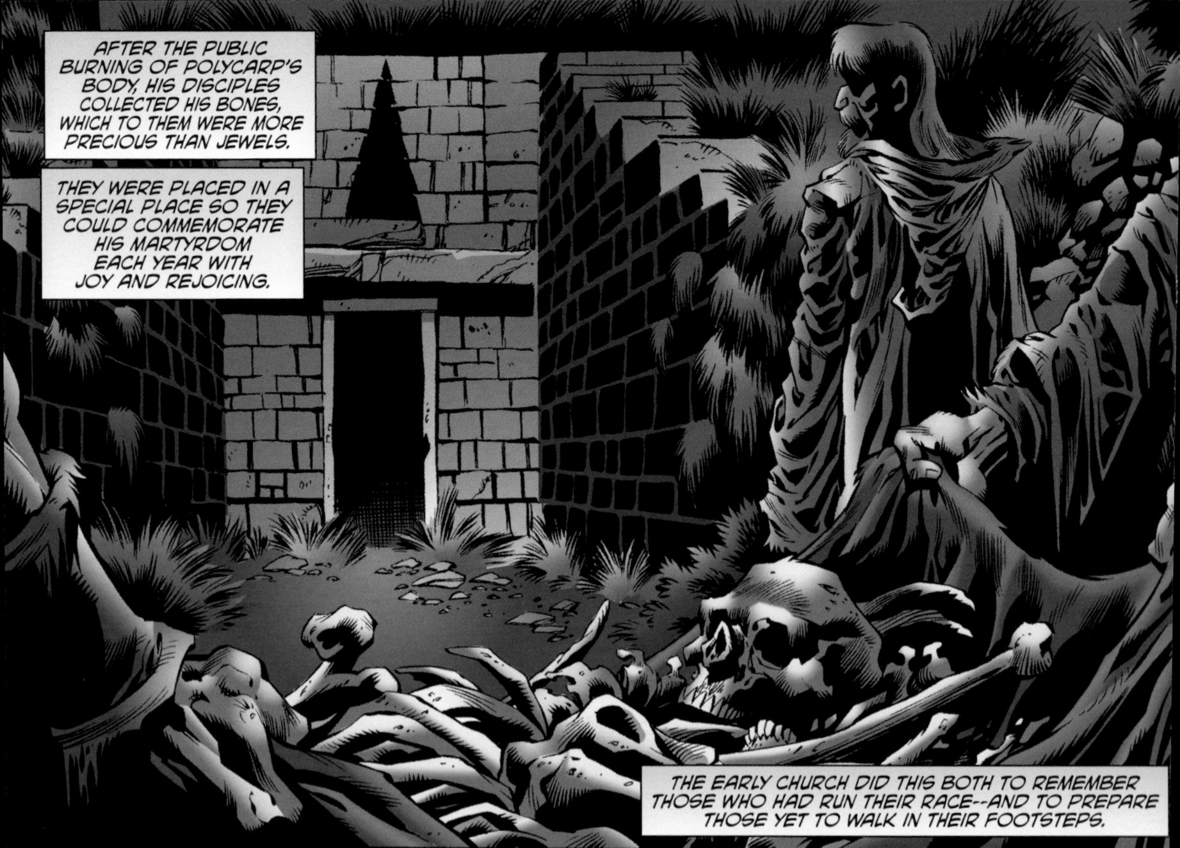
AFTER THE PUBLIC BURNING OF POLYCARP'S BODY, HIS DISCIPLES COLLECTED HIS BONES, WHICH TO THEM WERE MORE PRECIOUS THAN JEWELS.
THEY WERE PLACED IN A SPECIAL PLACE SO THEY COULD COMMEMORATE HIS MARTYRDOM EACH YEAR WITH JOY AND REJOICING.
THE EARLY CHURCH DID THIS BOTH TO REMEMBER THOSE WHO HAD RUN THEIR RACE--AND TO PREPARE THOSE YET TO WALK IN THEIR FOOTSTEPS.

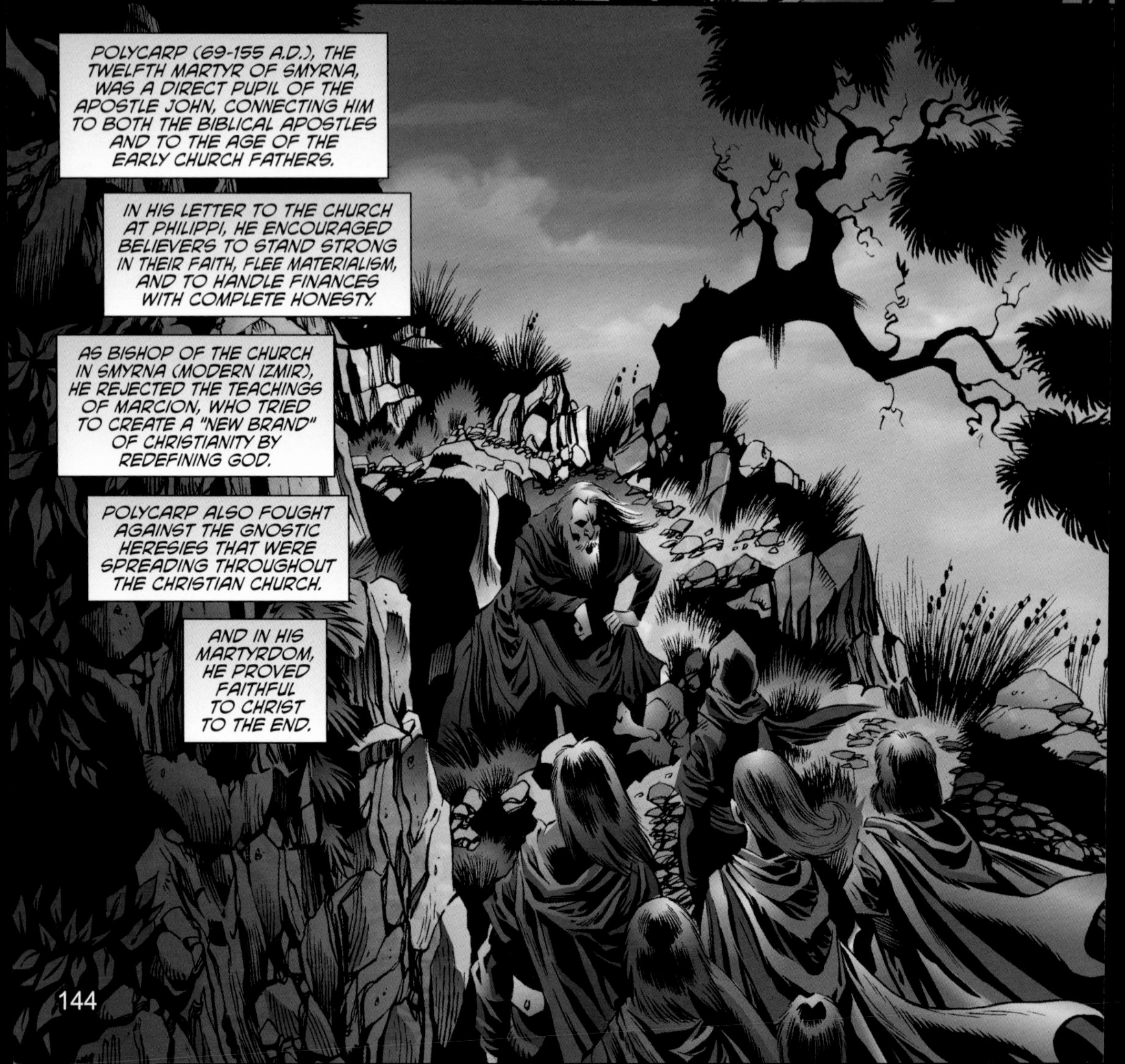
POLYCARP (69-155 A.D.), THE TWELFTH MARTYR OF SMYRNA, WAS A DIRECT PUPIL OF THE APOSTLE JOHN, CONNECTING HIM TO BOTH THE BIBLICAL APOSTLES AND TO THE AGE OF THE EARLY CHURCH FATHERS.
IN HIS LETTER TO THE CHURCH AT PHILIPPI, HE ENCOURAGED BELIEVERS TO STAND STRONG IN THEIR FAITH, FLEE MATERIALISM, AND TO HANDLE FINANCES WITH COMPLETE HONESTY.
AS BISHOP OF THE CHURCH IN SMYRNA (MODERN IZMIR), HE REJECTED THE TEACHINGS OF MARCION, WHO TRIED TO CREATE A "NEW BRAND" OF CHRISTIANITY BY REDEFINING GOD.
POLYCARP ALSO FOUGHT AGAINST THE GNOSTIC HERESIES THAT WERE SPREADING THROUGHOUT THE CHRISTIAN CHURCH.
AND IN HIS MARTYRDOM, HE PROVED FAITHFUL TO CHRIST TO THE END.

JUSTIN MARTYR

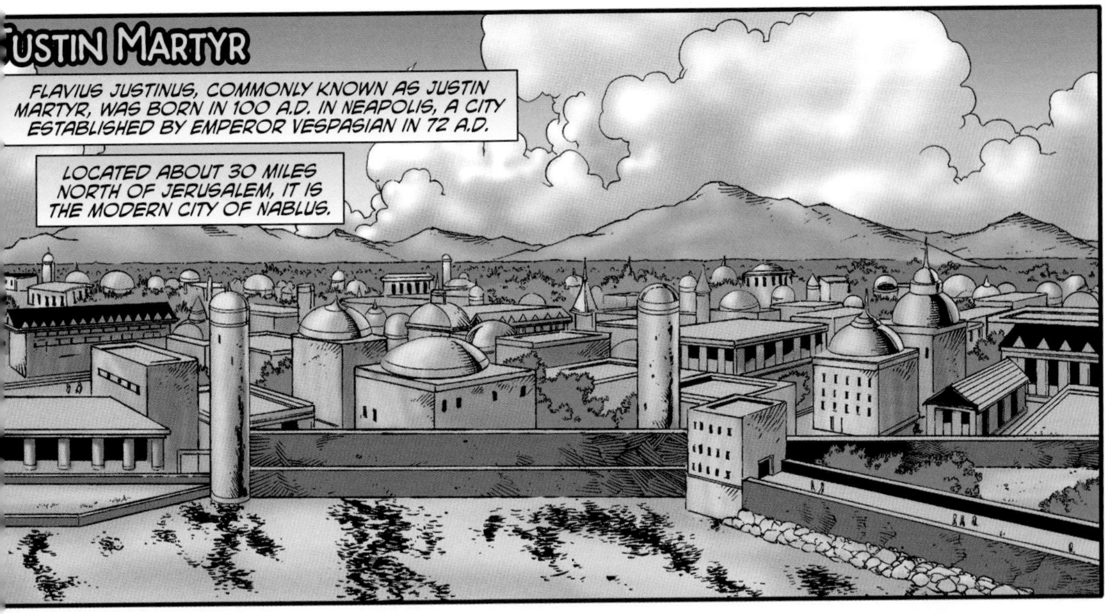

FLAVIUS JUSTINUS, COMMONLY KNOWN AS JUSTIN MARTYR, WAS BORN IN 100 A.D. IN NEAPOLIS, A CITY ESTABLISHED BY EMPEROR VESPASIAN IN 72 A.D.
LOCATED ABOUT 30 MILES NORTH OF JERUSALEM, IT IS THE MODERN CITY OF NABLUS.

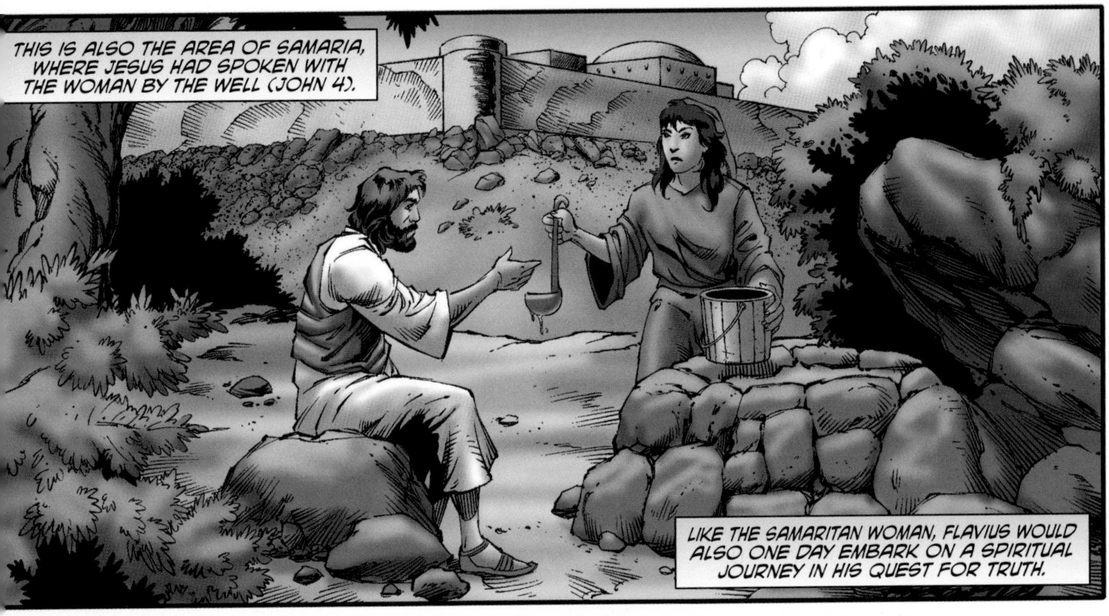

THIS IS ALSO THE AREA OF SAMARIA, WHERE JESUS HAD SPOKEN WITH THE WOMAN BY THE WELL (JOHN 4).
LIKE THE SAMARITAN WOMAN, FLAVIUS WOULD ALSO ONE DAY EMBARK ON A SPIRITUAL JOURNEY IN HIS QUEST FOR TRUTH.

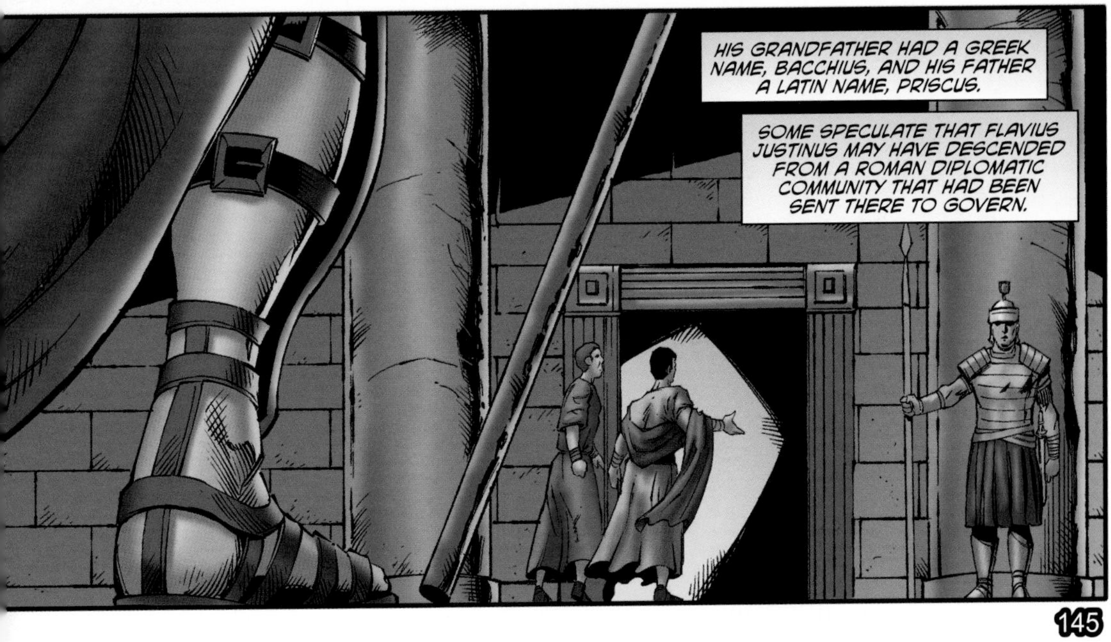

HIS GRANDFATHER HAD A GREEK NAME, BACCHIUS, AND HIS FATHER A LATIN NAME, PRISCUS.
SOME SPECULATE THAT FLAVIUS JUSTINUS MAY HAVE DESCENDED FROM A ROMAN DIPLOMATIC COMMUNITY THAT HAD BEEN SENT THERE TO GOVERN.

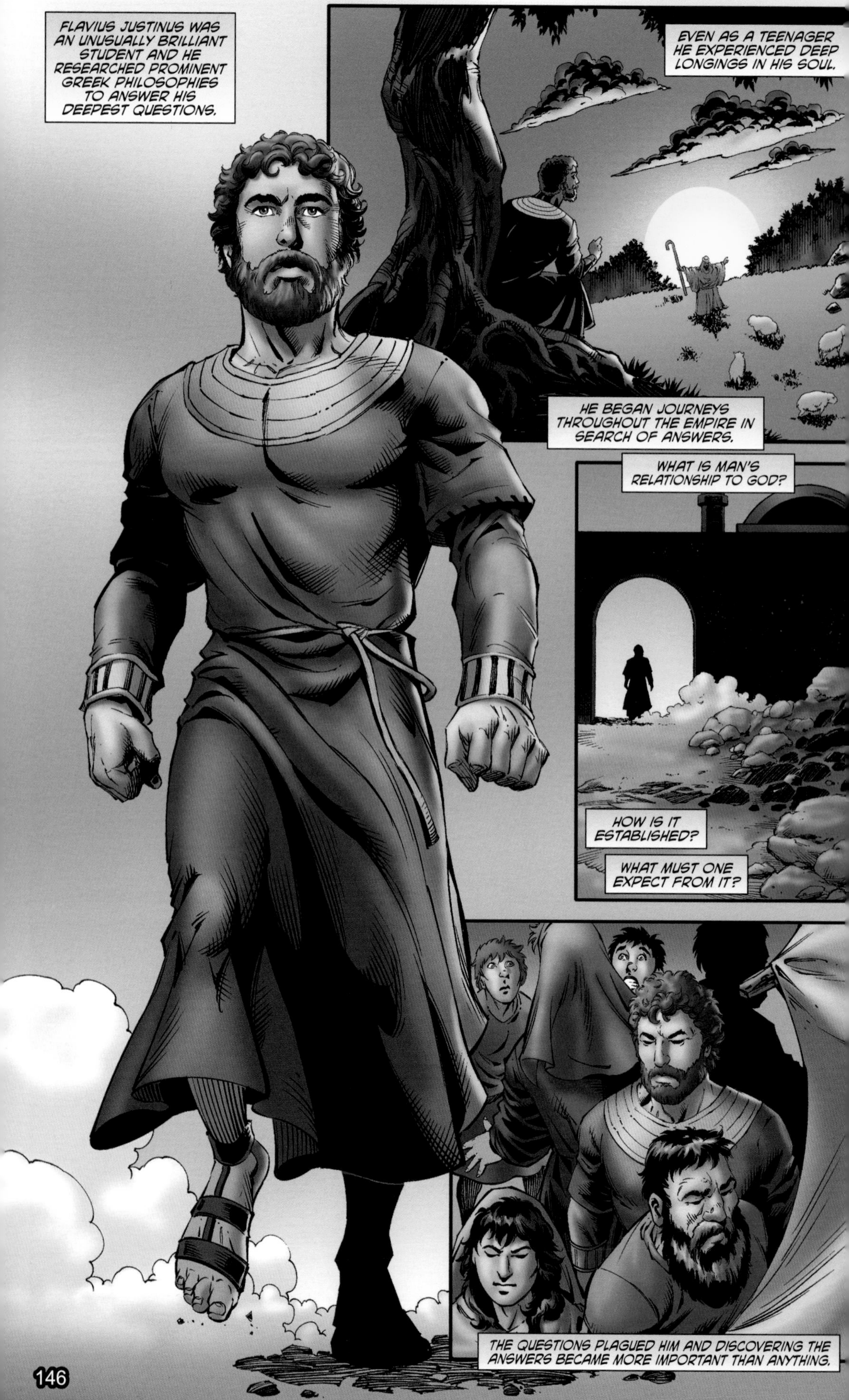
FLAVIUS JUSTINUS WAS AN UNUSUALLY BRILLIANT STUDENT AND HE RESEARCHED PROMINENT GREEK PHILOSOPHIES TO ANSWER HIS DEEPEST QUESTIONS.
EVEN AS A TEENAGER HE EXPERIENCED DEEP LONGINGS IN HIS SOUL.
HE BEGAN JOURNEYS THROUGHOUT THE EMPIRE IN SEARCH OF ANSWERS.
WHAT IS MAN'S RELATIONSHIP TO GOD?
HOW IS IT ESTABLISHED?
WHAT MUST ONE EXPECT FROM IT?
THE QUESTIONS PLAGUED HIM AND DISCOVERING THE ANSWERS BECAME MORE IMPORTANT THAN ANYTHING.

HE BEGAN WITH STOICISM.

EVERYTHING HAS ALREADY BEEN DETERMINED--BUT THROUGH THE DEVELOPMENT OF SELF-CONTROL AND FORTITUDE ONE CAN OVERCOME DESTRUCTIVE EMOTION.

TO LIVE A GOOD LIFE, ONE HAS TO UNDERSTAND THE RULES OF NATURAL ORDER AS EVERYTHING IS ROOTED IN NATURE.

THAT IS WHY THE EDUCATED AMONG US EMBRACE STOIC THOUGHT.

THIS SYSTEM OF BELIEF PROVIDES NO METAPHYSICAL INSPIRATION TO ME-- NOR DO YOU EXPLAIN GOD'S BEING.

THE PERIPATETIC SCHOOL OF PHILOSOPHY HAD BEEN STARTED BY ARISTOTLE.

SURELY SUCH A GREAT MIND WOULD FOSTER TRUTH.

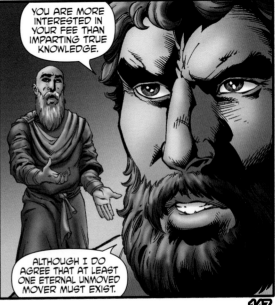

YOU ARE MORE INTERESTED IN YOUR FEE THAN IMPARTING TRUE KNOWLEDGE.

ALTHOUGH I DO AGREE THAT AT LEAST ONE ETERNAL UNMOVED MOVER MUST EXIST.

147

THE SCHOOL OF PYTHAGORAS.

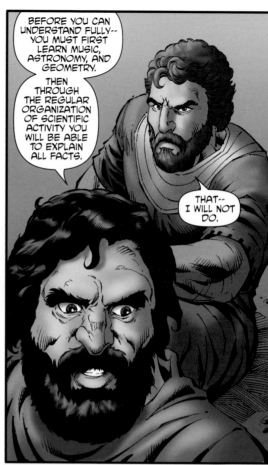

BEFORE YOU CAN UNDERSTAND FULLY-- YOU MUST FIRST LEARN MUSIC, ASTRONOMY, AND GEOMETRY.

THEN THROUGH THE REGULAR ORGANIZATION OF SCIENTIFIC ACTIVITY YOU WILL BE ABLE TO EXPLAIN ALL FACTS.

THAT-- I WILL NOT DO.

BUT IN THE TEACHING OF PLATO, FLAVIUS JUSTINUS FELT HE FOUND VESTIGES OF TRUTH.

HE WAS TO LATER SAY...

THE PERCEPTION OF IMMATERIAL THINGS QUITE OVER-POWERED ME, AND THE CONTEMPLATION OF IDEAS FURNISHED MY MIND WITH WINGS... I SUPPOSED THAT I HAD BECOME WISE; AND SUCH WAS MY STUPIDITY.

I EXPECTED FORTHWITH TO LOOK UPON GOD, FOR THIS IS THE END OF PLATO'S PHILOSOPHY.

NOW I CAN WITHDRAW FAR FROM THE TURMOIL OF THE WORLD--

--AND IN PERFECT SELF-COLLECTION GIVE MYSELF TO MY OWN CONTEMPLA-TIONS.

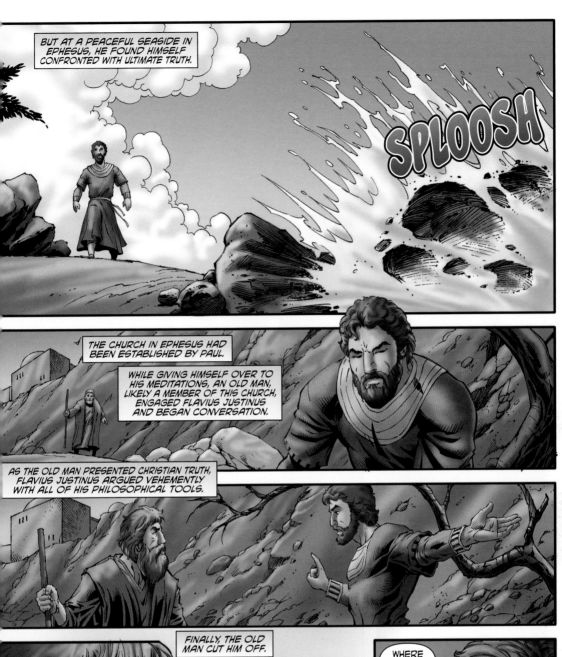

BUT AT A PEACEFUL SEASIDE IN EPHESUS, HE FOUND HIMSELF CONFRONTED WITH ULTIMATE TRUTH.

SPLOOSH

THE CHURCH IN EPHESUS HAD BEEN ESTABLISHED BY PAUL.

WHILE GIVING HIMSELF OVER TO HIS MEDITATIONS, AN OLD MAN, LIKELY A MEMBER OF THIS CHURCH, ENGAGED FLAVIUS JUSTINUS AND BEGAN CONVERSATION.

AS THE OLD MAN PRESENTED CHRISTIAN TRUTH, FLAVIUS JUSTINUS ARGUED VEHEMENTLY WITH ALL OF HIS PHILOSOPHICAL TOOLS.

FINALLY, THE OLD MAN CUT HIM OFF.

YOU ARE A MERE DEALER IN WORDS, BUT NO LOVER OF ACTION AND TRUTH.

YOUR AIM IS NOT TO BE A PRACTITIONER OF GOOD, BUT A CLEVER DISPUTANT, A CUNNING SOPHIST.

WHERE THEN CAN ONE FIND "TRUTH?"

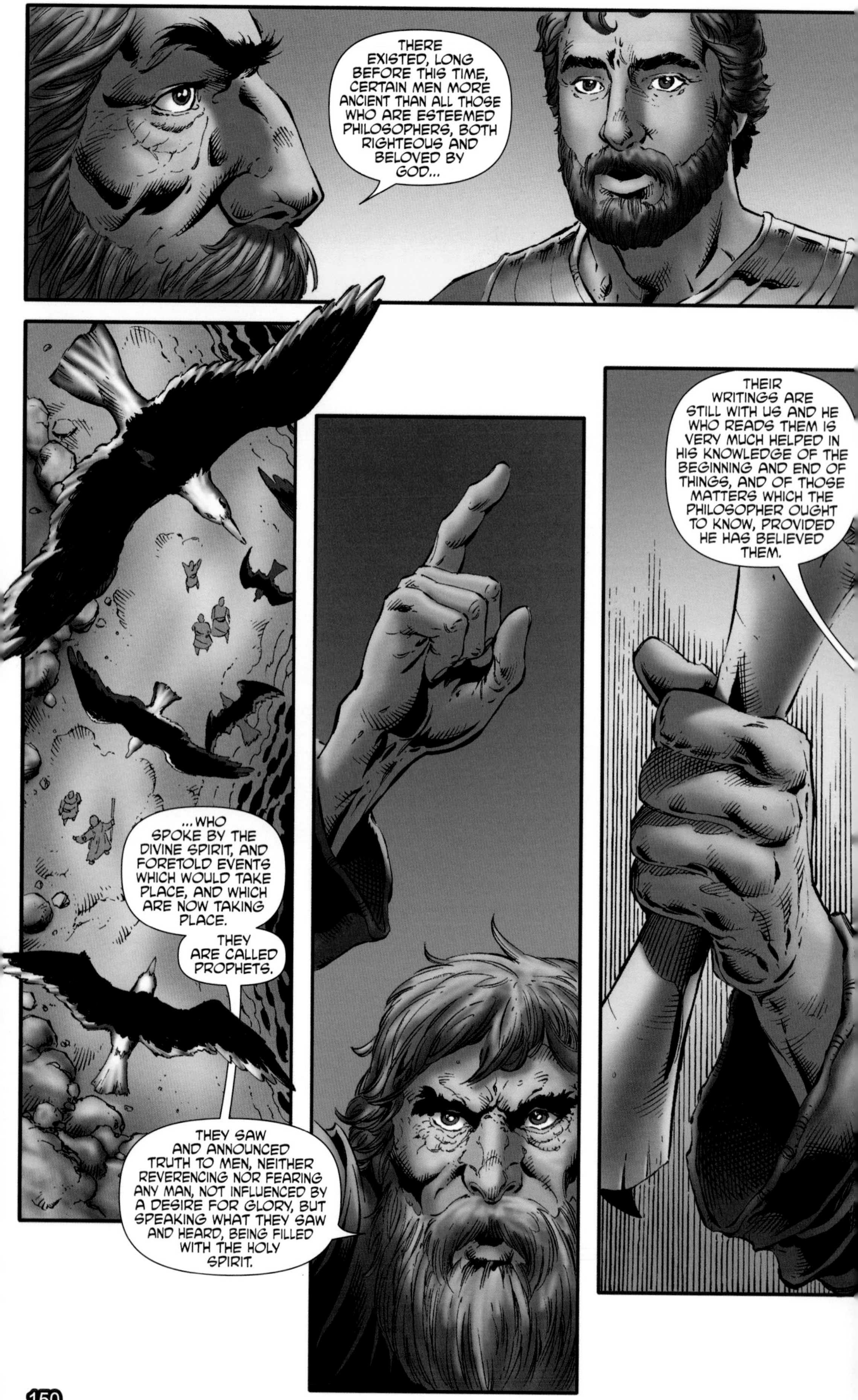
THERE EXISTED, LONG BEFORE THIS TIME, CERTAIN MEN MORE ANCIENT THAN ALL THOSE WHO ARE ESTEEMED PHILOSOPHERS, BOTH RIGHTEOUS AND BELOVED BY GOD...
...WHO SPOKE BY THE DIVINE SPIRIT, AND FORETOLD EVENTS WHICH WOULD TAKE PLACE, AND WHICH ARE NOW TAKING PLACE.
THEY ARE CALLED PROPHETS.
THEY SAW AND ANNOUNCED TRUTH TO MEN, NEITHER REVERENCING NOR FEARING ANY MAN, NOT INFLUENCED BY A DESIRE FOR GLORY, BUT SPEAKING WHAT THEY SAW AND HEARD, BEING FILLED WITH THE HOLY SPIRIT.
THEIR WRITINGS ARE STILL WITH US AND HE WHO READS THEM IS VERY MUCH HELPED IN HIS KNOWLEDGE OF THE BEGINNING AND END OF THINGS, AND OF THOSE MATTERS WHICH THE PHILOSOPHER OUGHT TO KNOW, PROVIDED HE HAS BELIEVED THEM.

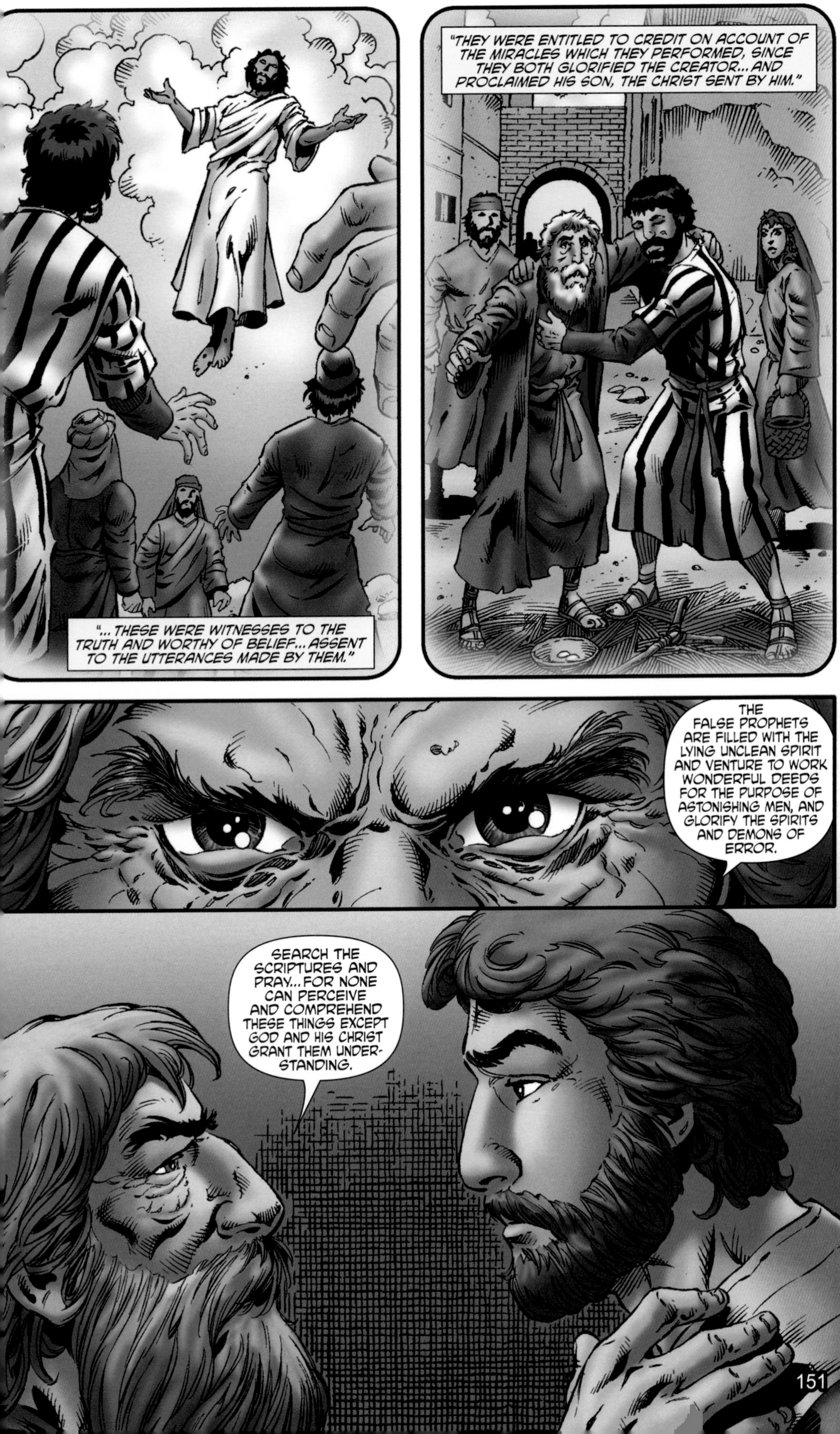
"...THESE WERE WITNESSES TO THE TRUTH AND WORTHY OF BELIEF... ASSENT TO THE UTTERANCES MADE BY THEM."
"THEY WERE ENTITLED TO CREDIT ON ACCOUNT OF THE MIRACLES WHICH THEY PERFORMED, SINCE THEY BOTH GLORIFIED THE CREATOR... AND PROCLAIMED HIS SON, THE CHRIST SENT BY HIM."
THE FALSE PROPHETS ARE FILLED WITH THE LYING UNCLEAN SPIRIT AND VENTURE TO WORK WONDERFUL DEEDS FOR THE PURPOSE OF ASTONISHING MEN, AND GLORIFY THE SPIRITS AND DEMONS OF ERROR.
SEARCH THE SCRIPTURES AND PRAY... FOR NONE CAN PERCEIVE AND COMPREHEND THESE THINGS EXCEPT GOD AND HIS CHRIST GRANT THEM UNDERSTANDING.

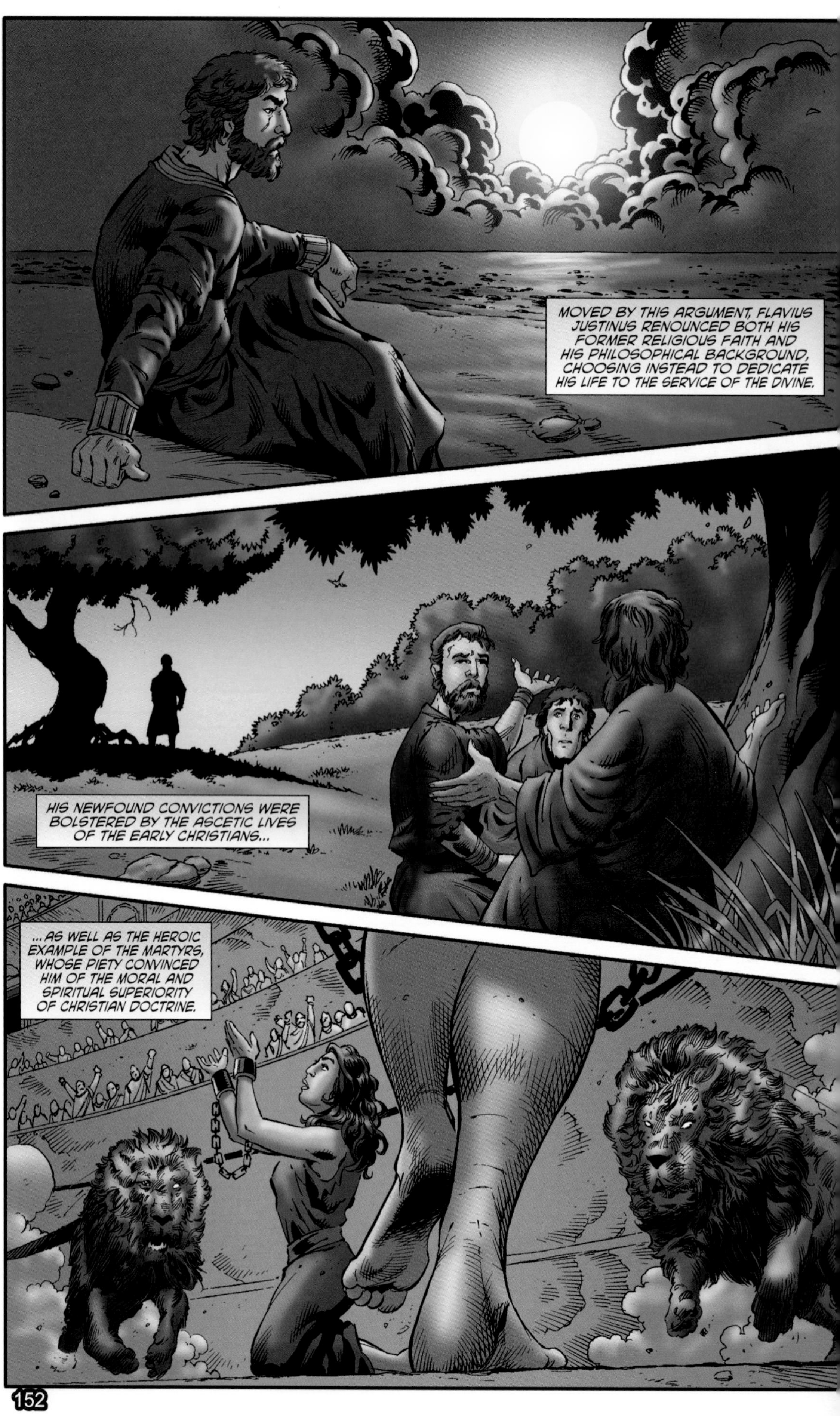
MOVED BY THIS ARGUMENT, FLAVIUS JUSTINUS RENOUNCED BOTH HIS FORMER RELIGIOUS FAITH AND HIS PHILOSOPHICAL BACKGROUND, CHOOSING INSTEAD TO DEDICATE HIS LIFE TO THE SERVICE OF THE DIVINE.
HIS NEWFOUND CONVICTIONS WERE BOLSTERED BY THE ASCETIC LIVES OF THE EARLY CHRISTIANS...
...AS WELL AS THE HEROIC EXAMPLE OF THE MARTYRS, WHOSE PIETY CONVINCED HIM OF THE MORAL AND SPIRITUAL SUPERIORITY OF CHRISTIAN DOCTRINE.

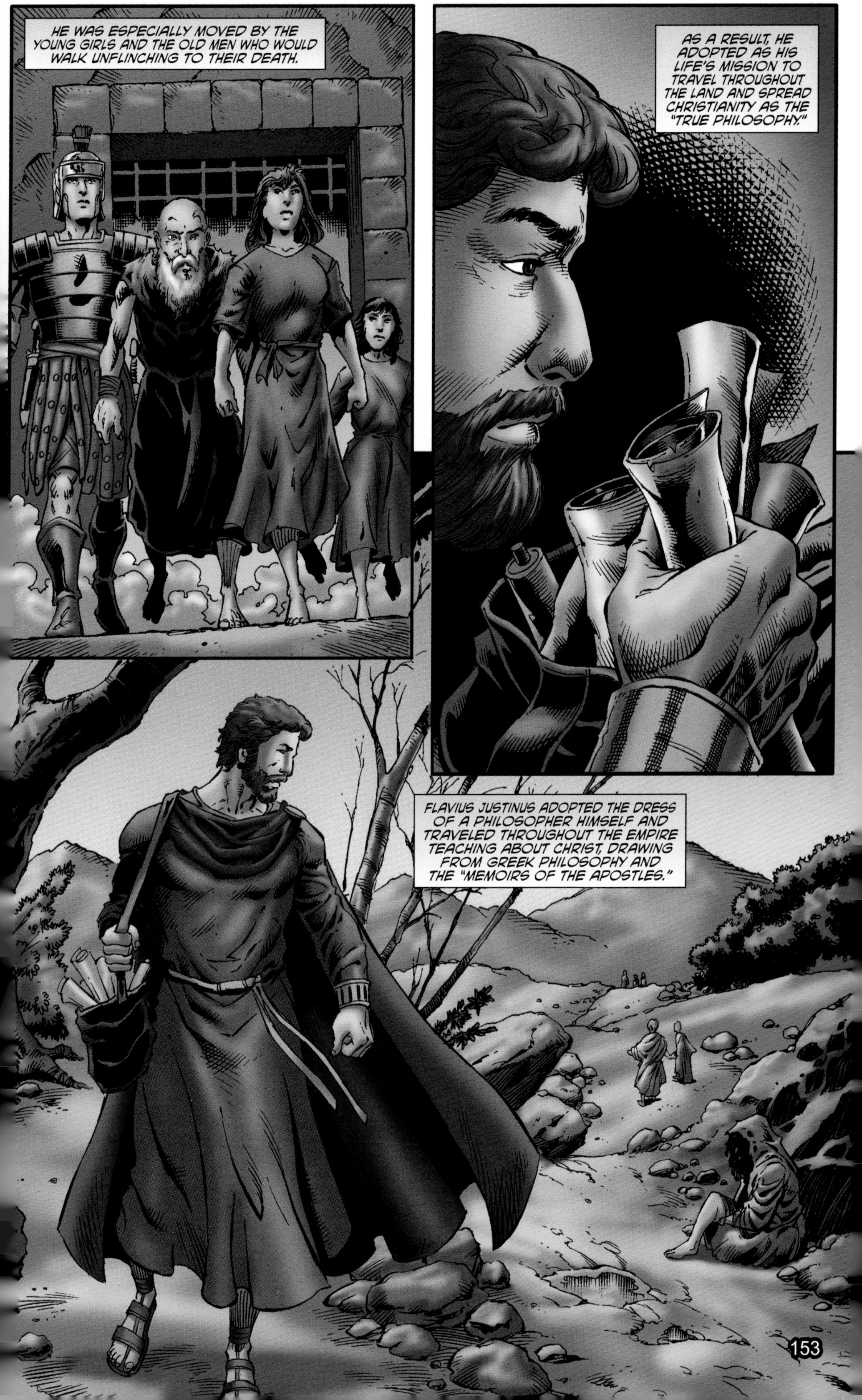
HE WAS ESPECIALLY MOVED BY THE YOUNG GIRLS AND THE OLD MEN WHO WOULD WALK UNFLINCHING TO THEIR DEATH.
AS A RESULT, HE ADOPTED AS HIS LIFE'S MISSION TO TRAVEL THROUGHOUT THE LAND AND SPREAD CHRISTIANITY AS THE "TRUE PHILOSOPHY."
FLAVIUS JUSTINUS ADOPTED THE DRESS OF A PHILOSOPHER HIMSELF AND TRAVELED THROUGHOUT THE EMPIRE TEACHING ABOUT CHRIST, DRAWING FROM GREEK PHILOSOPHY AND THE "MEMOIRS OF THE APOSTLES."

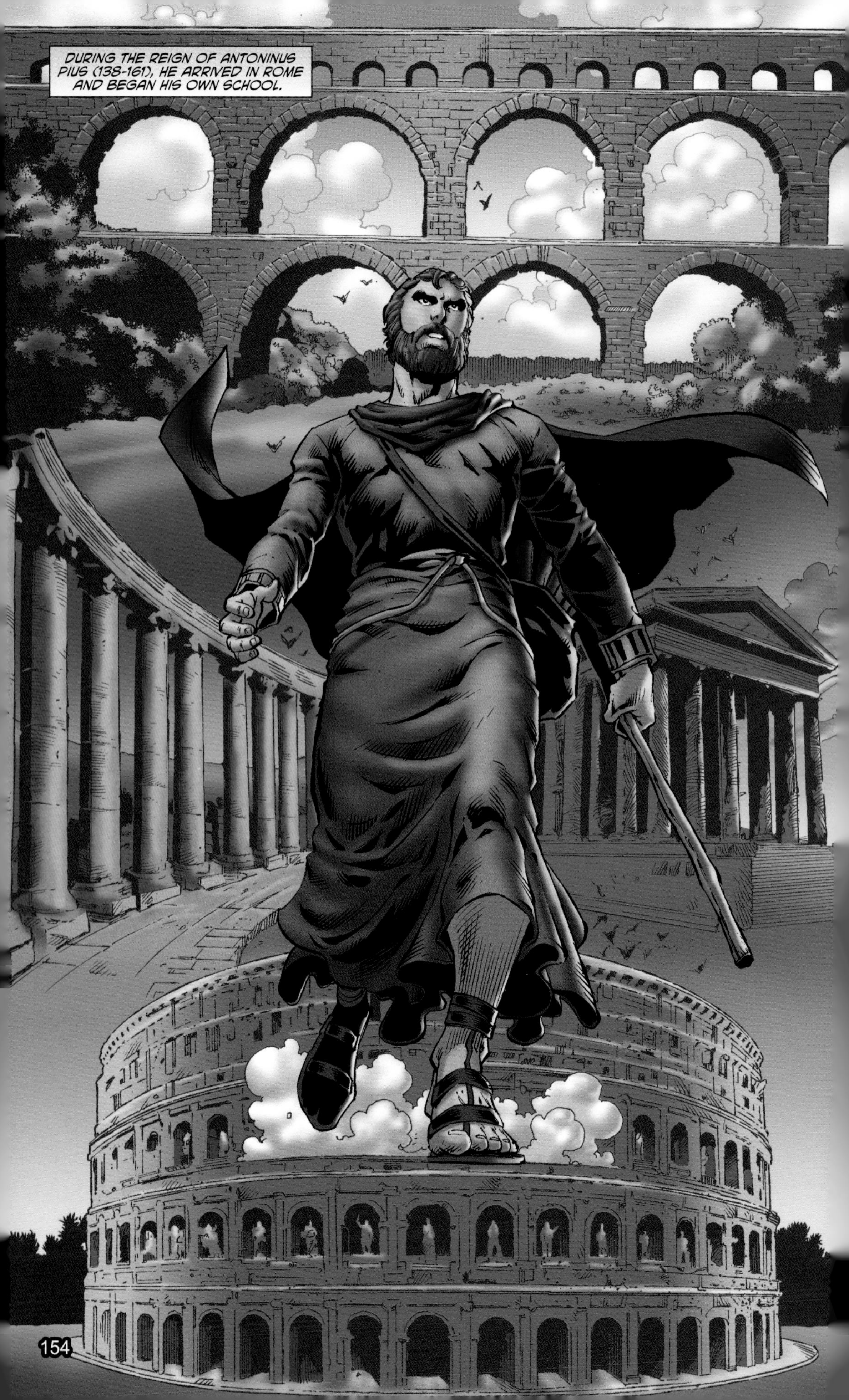
DURING THE REIGN OF ANTONINUS PIUS (138-161), HE ARRIVED IN ROME AND BEGAN HIS OWN SCHOOL.

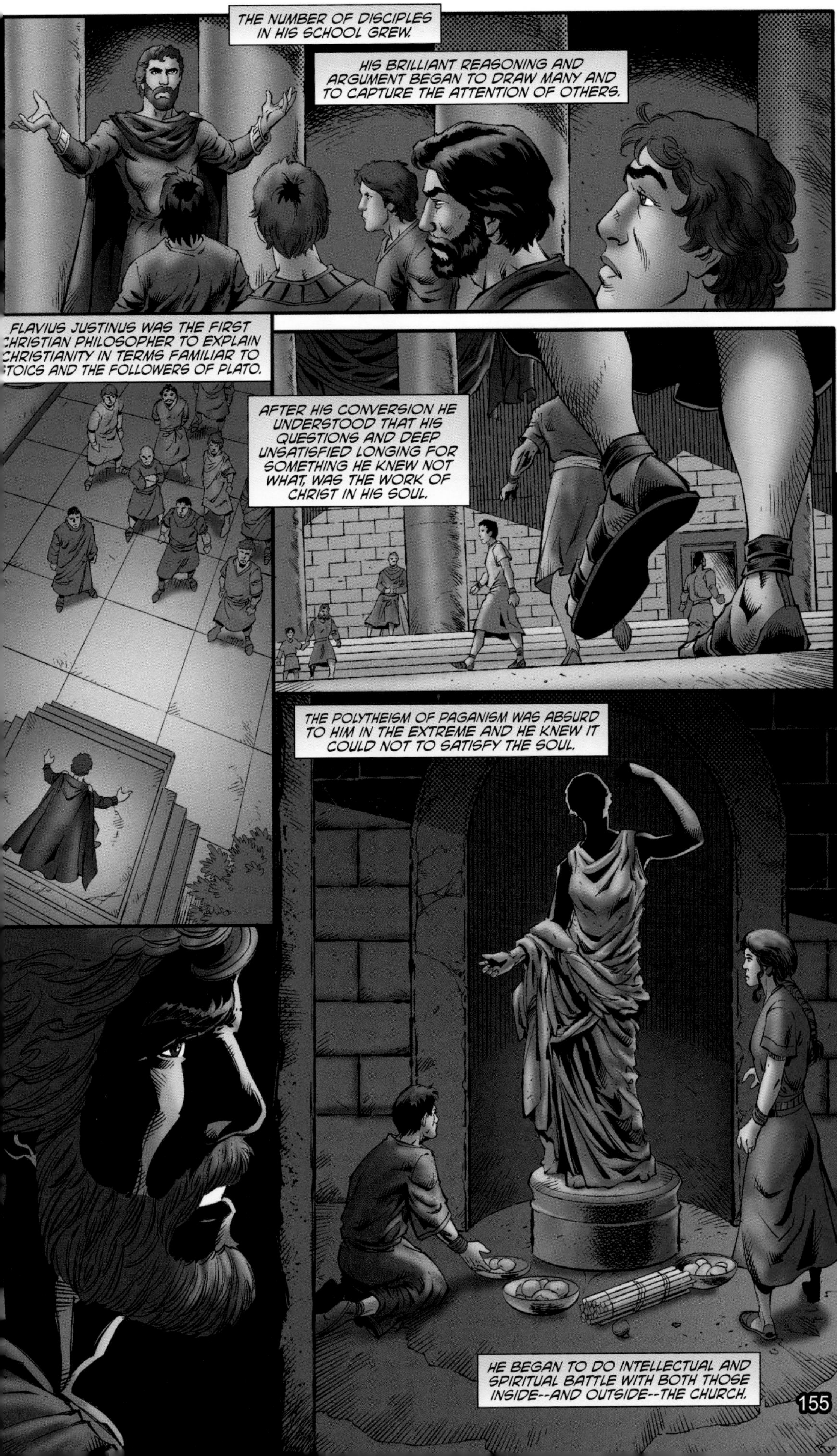
THE NUMBER OF DISCIPLES IN HIS SCHOOL GREW.
HIS BRILLIANT REASONING AND ARGUMENT BEGAN TO DRAW MANY AND TO CAPTURE THE ATTENTION OF OTHERS.
FLAVIUS JUSTINUS WAS THE FIRST CHRISTIAN PHILOSOPHER TO EXPLAIN CHRISTIANITY IN TERMS FAMILIAR TO STOICS AND THE FOLLOWERS OF PLATO.
AFTER HIS CONVERSION HE UNDERSTOOD THAT HIS QUESTIONS AND DEEP UNSATISFIED LONGING FOR SOMETHING HE KNEW NOT WHAT, WAS THE WORK OF CHRIST IN HIS SOUL.
THE POLYTHEISM OF PAGANISM WAS ABSURD TO HIM IN THE EXTREME AND HE KNEW IT COULD NOT TO SATISFY THE SOUL.
HE BEGAN TO DO INTELLECTUAL AND SPIRITUAL BATTLE WITH BOTH THOSE INSIDE--AND OUTSIDE--THE CHURCH.

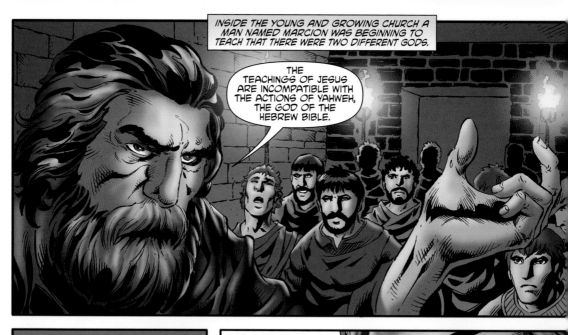

INSIDE THE YOUNG AND GROWING CHURCH A MAN NAMED MARCION WAS BEGINNING TO TEACH THAT THERE WERE TWO DIFFERENT GODS.

THE TEACHINGS OF JESUS ARE INCOMPATIBLE WITH THE ACTIONS OF YAHWEH, THE GOD OF THE HEBREW BIBLE.

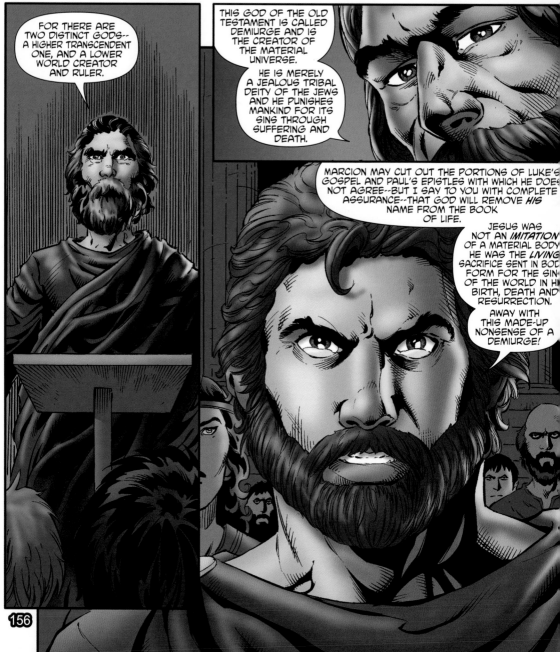

FOR THERE ARE TWO DISTINCT GODS-- A HIGHER TRANSCENDENT ONE, AND A LOWER WORLD CREATOR AND RULER.

THIS GOD OF THE OLD TESTAMENT IS CALLED DEMIURGE AND IS THE CREATOR OF THE MATERIAL UNIVERSE.

HE IS MERELY A JEALOUS TRIBAL DEITY OF THE JEWS AND HE PUNISHES MANKIND FOR ITS SINS THROUGH SUFFERING AND DEATH.

MARCION MAY CUT OUT THE PORTIONS OF LUKE'S GOSPEL AND PAUL'S EPISTLES WITH WHICH HE DOES NOT AGREE--BUT I SAY TO YOU WITH COMPLETE ASSURANCE--THAT GOD WILL REMOVE *HIS* NAME FROM THE BOOK OF LIFE.

JESUS WAS NOT AN *IMITATION* OF A MATERIAL BODY HE WAS THE *LIVING* SACRIFICE SENT IN BOD FORM FOR THE SIN OF THE WORLD IN H BIRTH, DEATH AND RESURRECTION.

AWAY WITH THIS MADE-UP NONSENSE OF A DEMIURGE!

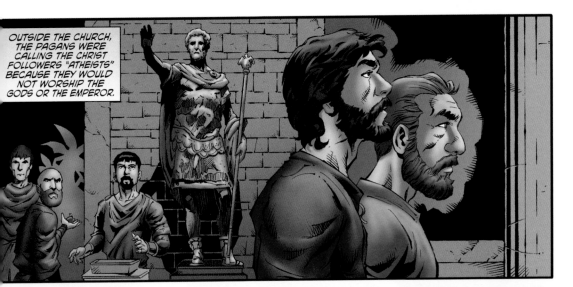

OUTSIDE THE CHURCH, THE PAGANS WERE CALLING THE CHRIST FOLLOWERS "ATHEISTS" BECAUSE THEY WOULD NOT WORSHIP THE GODS OR THE EMPEROR.

CHIEF IN THIS CHARGE AGAINST THE CHRISTIANS WAS THE CYNIC PHILOSOPHER CRESCENS.

THESE CHRISTIANS HAVE NO RIGHT TO LIVE AMONG US HERE IN ROME. THEY HONOR NEITHER OUR GODS NOR CAESAR.

BESIDES BEING A CYNIC, CRESCENS HAD A SORDID REPUTATION FOR SHAMELESS ACTS WITH YOUNG BOYS.

FLAVIUS JUSTINUS BROUGHT FORTH A SEARING MESSAGE UPON CRESCENS, HIS CYNIC PHILOSOPHICAL THOUGHT AND HIS SHAMELESSNESS.

IN RESPONSE TO CHARGES BY CRESCENS AND OTHERS, FLAVIUS JUSTINUS PENNED *THE FIRST APOLOGY* IN 155 A.D., ADDRESSED TO THE EMPEROR, ANTONINUS PIUS.

THE FIRST APOLOGY WAS PUBLISHED AROUND THE SAME TIME THAT POLYCARP WAS MARTYRED. MANY BELIEVE IT WAS WRITTEN IN RESPONSE TO THAT ACT.

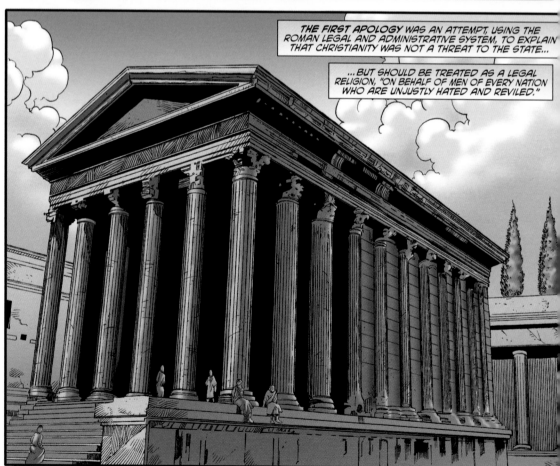

THE FIRST APOLOGY WAS AN ATTEMPT, USING THE ROMAN LEGAL AND ADMINISTRATIVE SYSTEM, TO EXPLAIN THAT CHRISTIANITY WAS NOT A THREAT TO THE STATE...

...BUT SHOULD BE TREATED AS A LEGAL RELIGION, "ON BEHALF OF MEN OF EVERY NATION WHO ARE UNJUSTLY HATED AND REVILED."

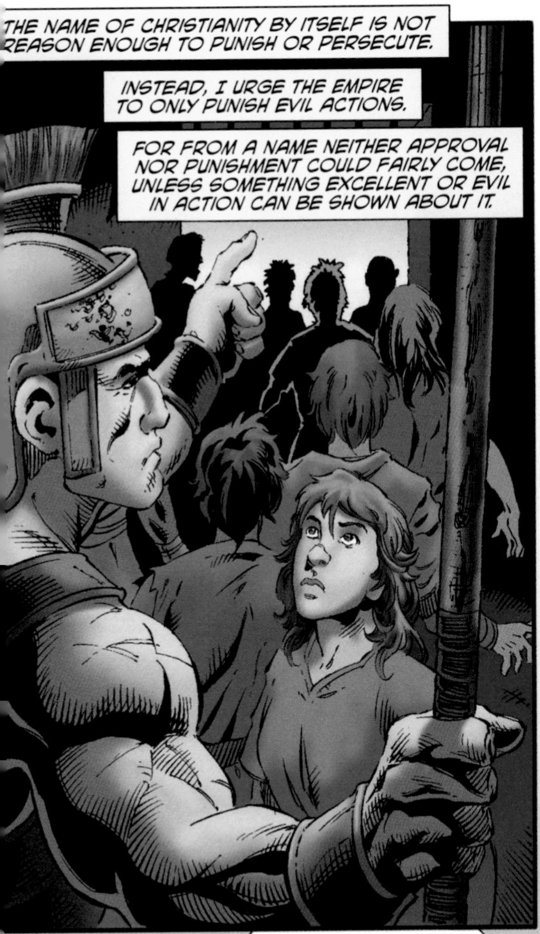
THE NAME OF CHRISTIANITY BY ITSELF IS NOT REASON ENOUGH TO PUNISH OR PERSECUTE.
INSTEAD, I URGE THE EMPIRE TO ONLY PUNISH EVIL ACTIONS.
FOR FROM A NAME NEITHER APPROVAL NOR PUNISHMENT COULD FAIRLY COME, UNLESS SOMETHING EXCELLENT OR EVIL IN ACTION CAN BE SHOWN ABOUT IT.

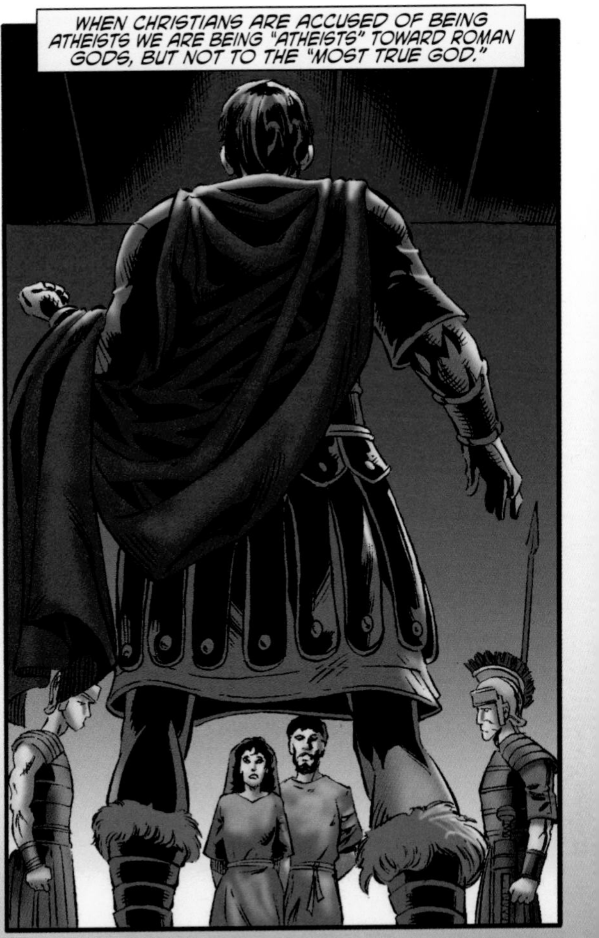
WHEN CHRISTIANS ARE ACCUSED OF BEING ATHEISTS WE ARE BEING "ATHEISTS" TOWARD ROMAN GODS, BUT NOT TO THE "MOST TRUE GOD."

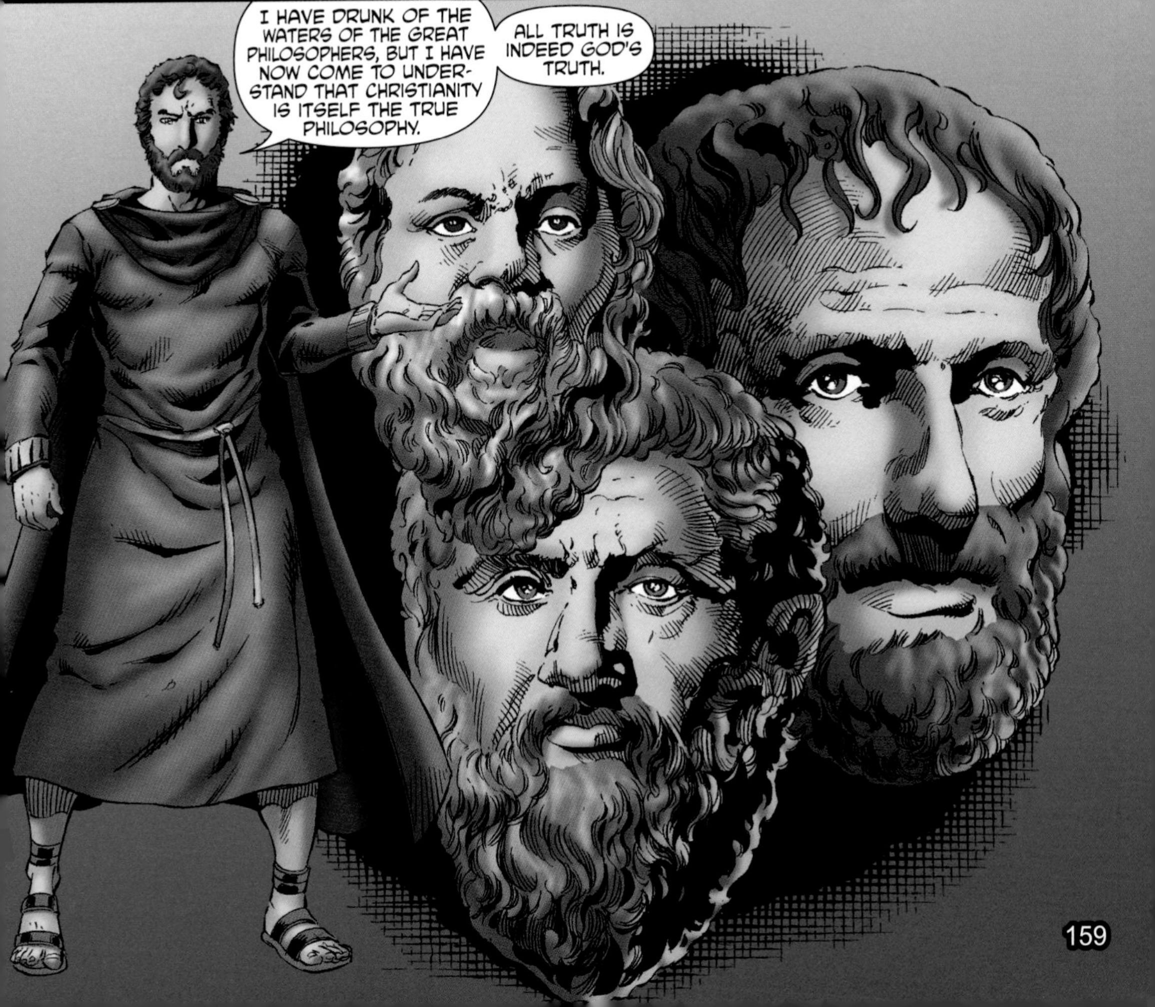
I HAVE DRUNK OF THE WATERS OF THE GREAT PHILOSOPHERS, BUT I HAVE NOW COME TO UNDERSTAND THAT CHRISTIANITY IS ITSELF THE TRUE PHILOSOPHY.
ALL TRUTH IS INDEED GOD'S TRUTH.

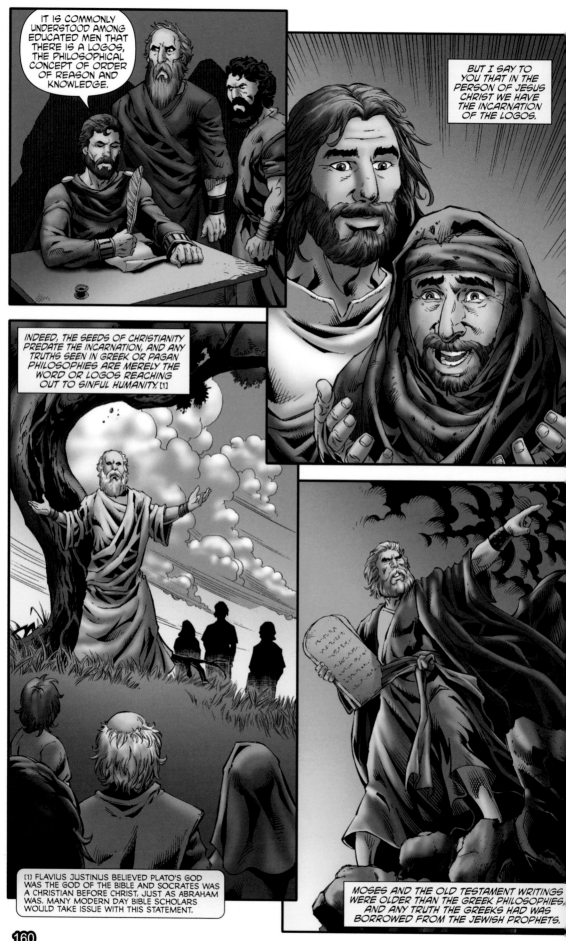

IT IS COMMONLY UNDERSTOOD AMONG EDUCATED MEN THAT THERE IS A LOGOS, THE PHILOSOPHICAL CONCEPT OF ORDER OF REASON AND KNOWLEDGE.

BUT I SAY TO YOU THAT IN THE PERSON OF JESUS CHRIST WE HAVE THE INCARNATION OF THE LOGOS.

INDEED, THE SEEDS OF CHRISTIANITY PREDATE THE INCARNATION, AND ANY TRUTHS SEEN IN GREEK OR PAGAN PHILOSOPHIES ARE MERELY THE WORD OR LOGOS REACHING OUT TO SINFUL HUMANITY. [1]

[1] FLAVIUS JUSTINUS BELIEVED PLATO'S GOD WAS THE GOD OF THE BIBLE AND SOCRATES WAS A CHRISTIAN BEFORE CHRIST, JUST AS ABRAHAM WAS. MANY MODERN DAY BIBLE SCHOLARS WOULD TAKE ISSUE WITH THIS STATEMENT.

MOSES AND THE OLD TESTAMENT WRITINGS WERE OLDER THAN THE GREEK PHILOSOPHIES, AND ANY TRUTH THE GREEKS HAD WAS BORROWED FROM THE JEWISH PROPHETS.

160

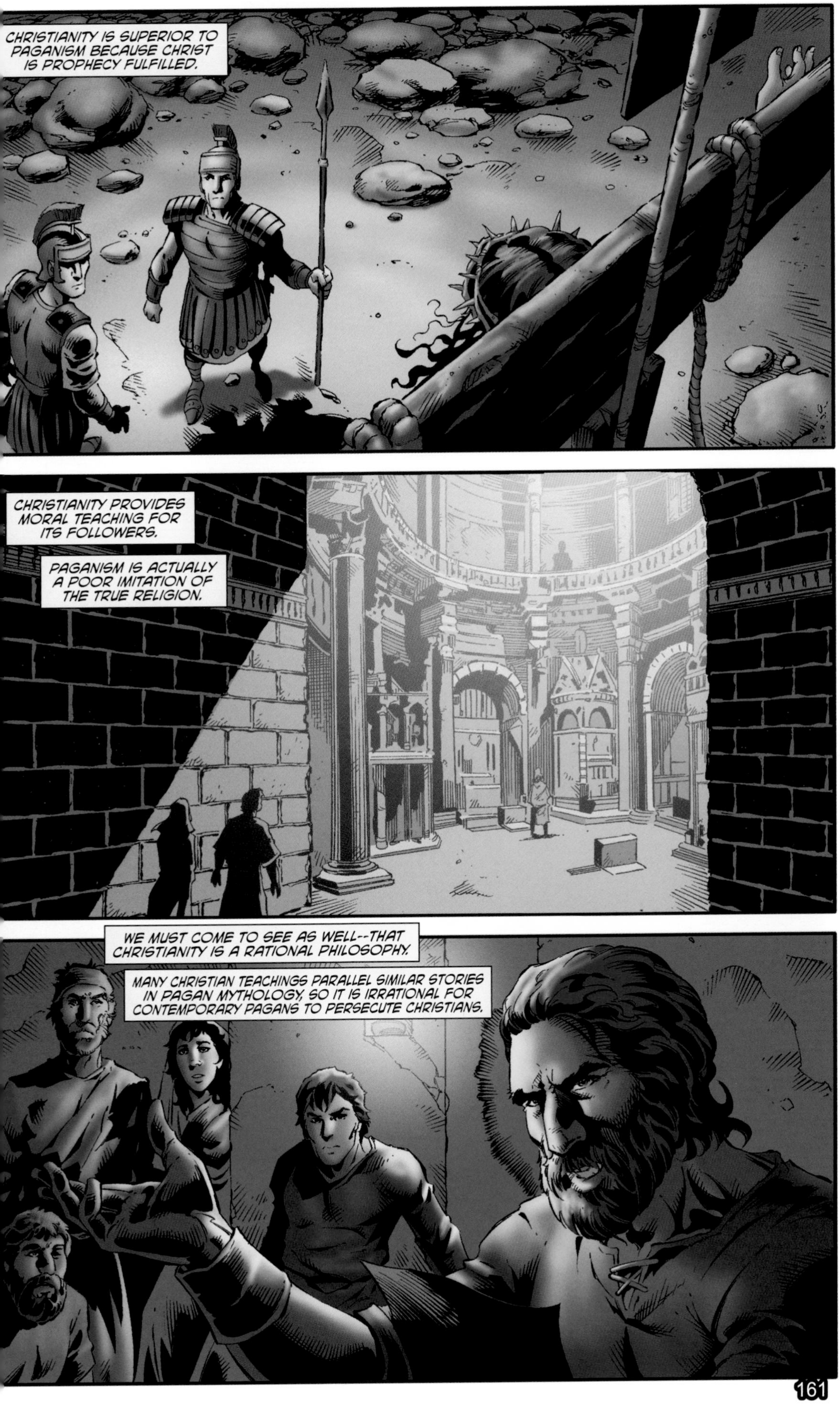
CHRISTIANITY IS SUPERIOR TO PAGANISM BECAUSE CHRIST IS PROPHECY FULFILLED.
CHRISTIANITY PROVIDES MORAL TEACHING FOR ITS FOLLOWERS.
PAGANISM IS ACTUALLY A POOR IMITATION OF THE TRUE RELIGION.
WE MUST COME TO SEE AS WELL--THAT CHRISTIANITY IS A RATIONAL PHILOSOPHY.
MANY CHRISTIAN TEACHINGS PARALLEL SIMILAR STORIES IN PAGAN MYTHOLOGY, SO IT IS IRRATIONAL FOR CONTEMPORARY PAGANS TO PERSECUTE CHRISTIANS.

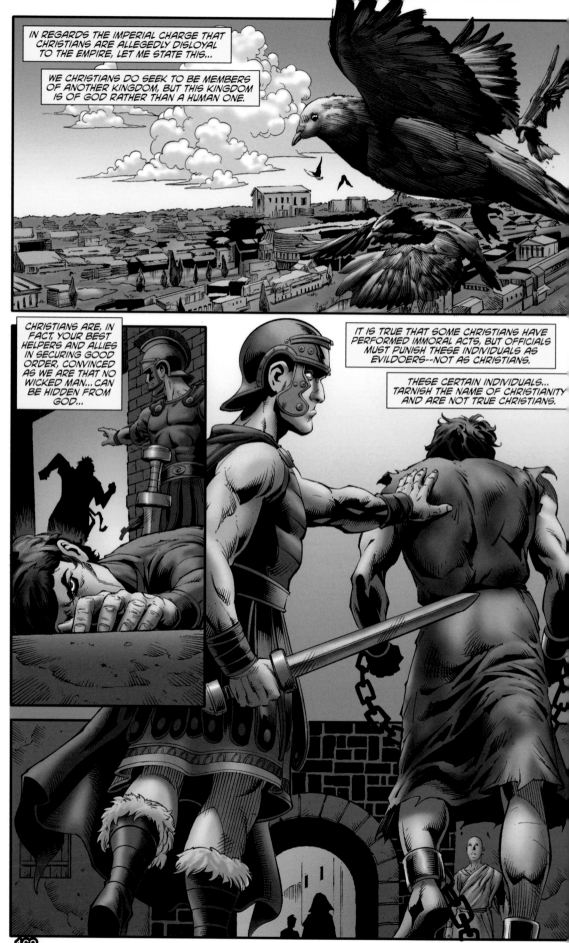

IN REGARDS THE IMPERIAL CHARGE THAT CHRISTIANS ARE ALLEGEDLY DISLOYAL TO THE EMPIRE, LET ME STATE THIS...

WE CHRISTIANS DO SEEK TO BE MEMBERS OF ANOTHER KINGDOM, BUT THIS KINGDOM IS OF GOD RATHER THAN A HUMAN ONE.

CHRISTIANS ARE, IN FACT, YOUR BEST HELPERS AND ALLIES IN SECURING GOOD ORDER, CONVINCED AS WE ARE THAT NO WICKED MAN... CAN BE HIDDEN FROM GOD...

IT IS TRUE THAT SOME CHRISTIANS HAVE PERFORMED IMMORAL ACTS, BUT OFFICIALS MUST PUNISH THESE INDIVIDUALS AS EVILDOERS--NOT AS CHRISTIANS.

THESE CERTAIN INDIVIDUALS... TARNISH THE NAME OF CHRISTIANITY AND ARE NOT TRUE CHRISTIANS.

FURTHER, THE CLAIMS OF CANNIBALISTIC RITUALS AND GROSS IMMORALITY ARE COMPLETELY WITHOUT BASIS.

WHAT YOU CONSIDER THE "EATING OF FLESH AND DRINKING OF BLOOD" IS A REGULAR REMINDER TO US OF THE SON OF GOD WHO GAVE HIS OWN FLESH AND BLOOD FOR THE SIN OF MANKIND.

WE CALL THIS THE EUCHARIST... NOT AS COMMON ELEMENTS DO WE RECEIVE THESE; BUT IN LIKE MANNER AS JESUS CHRIST OUR SAVIOR, HAVING BEEN MADE FLESH BY THE WORD OF GOD, HAD BOTH FLESH AND BLOOD FOR OUR SALVATION.

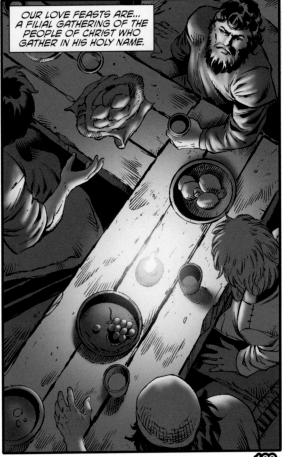

OUR LOVE FEASTS ARE... A FILIAL GATHERING OF THE PEOPLE OF CHRIST WHO GATHER IN HIS HOLY NAME.

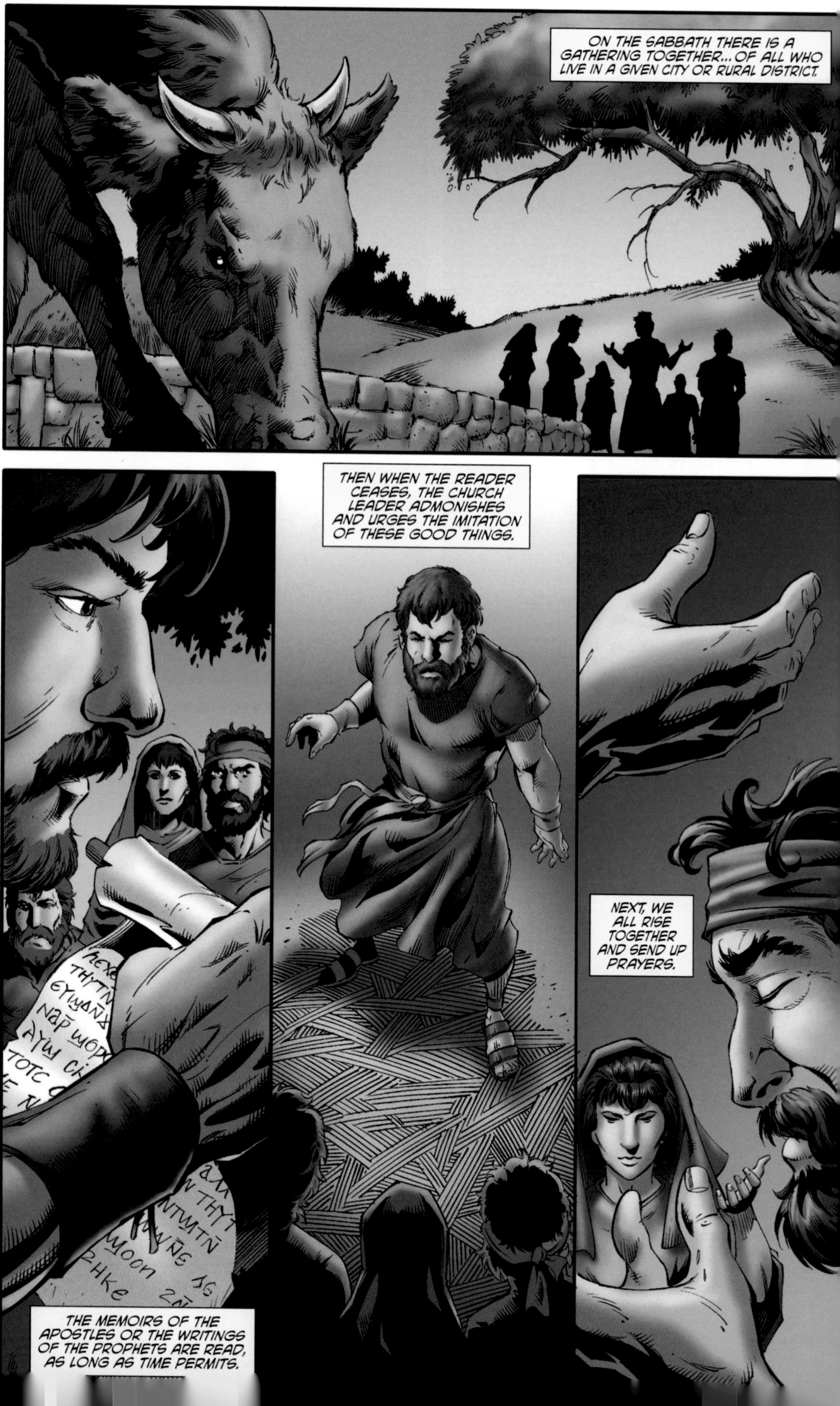
ON THE SABBATH THERE IS A GATHERING TOGETHER... OF ALL WHO LIVE IN A GIVEN CITY OR RURAL DISTRICT.
THE MEMOIRS OF THE APOSTLES OR THE WRITINGS OF THE PROPHETS ARE READ, AS LONG AS TIME PERMITS.
THEN WHEN THE READER CEASES, THE CHURCH LEADER ADMONISHES AND URGES THE IMITATION OF THESE GOOD THINGS.
NEXT, WE ALL RISE TOGETHER AND SEND UP PRAYERS.

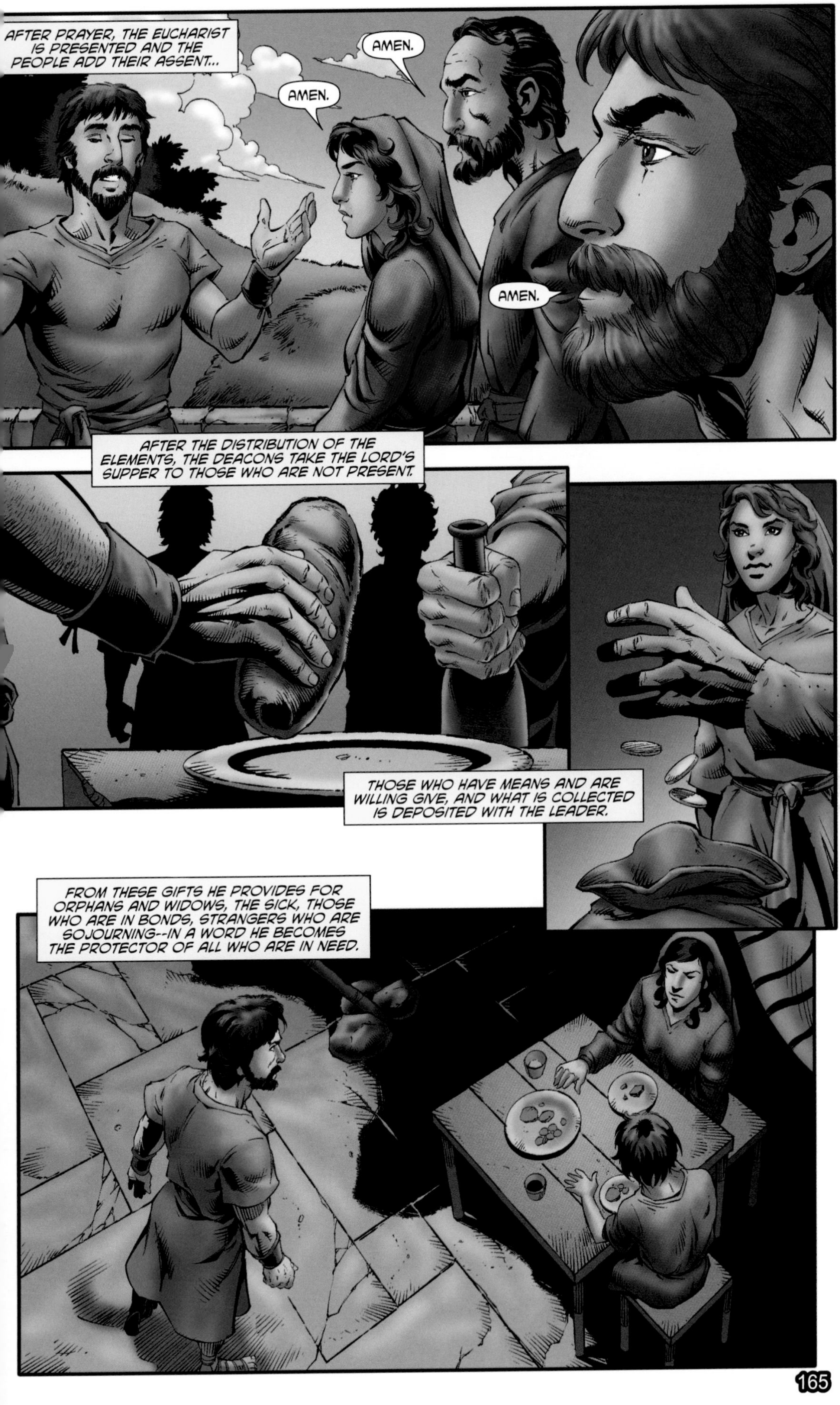
AFTER PRAYER, THE EUCHARIST IS PRESENTED AND THE PEOPLE ADD THEIR ASSENT...
AMEN.
AMEN.
AMEN.
AFTER THE DISTRIBUTION OF THE ELEMENTS, THE DEACONS TAKE THE LORD'S SUPPER TO THOSE WHO ARE NOT PRESENT.
THOSE WHO HAVE MEANS AND ARE WILLING GIVE, AND WHAT IS COLLECTED IS DEPOSITED WITH THE LEADER.
FROM THESE GIFTS HE PROVIDES FOR ORPHANS AND WIDOWS, THE SICK, THOSE WHO ARE IN BONDS, STRANGERS WHO ARE SOJOURNING--IN A WORD HE BECOMES THE PROTECTOR OF ALL WHO ARE IN NEED.

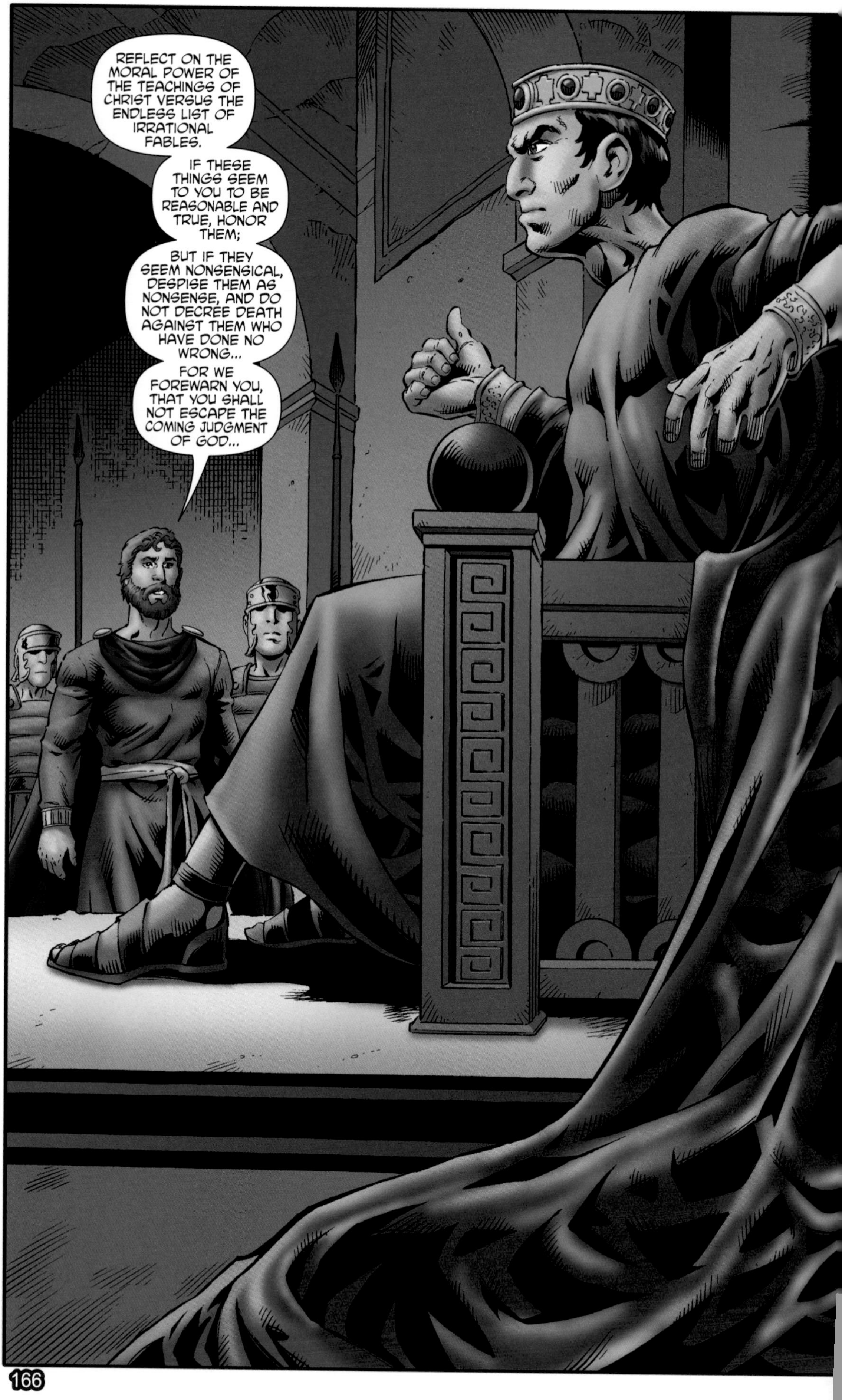
REFLECT ON THE MORAL POWER OF THE TEACHINGS OF CHRIST VERSUS THE ENDLESS LIST OF IRRATIONAL FABLES.
IF THESE THINGS SEEM TO YOU TO BE REASONABLE AND TRUE, HONOR THEM;
BUT IF THEY SEEM NONSENSICAL, DESPISE THEM AS NONSENSE, AND DO NOT DECREE DEATH AGAINST THEM WHO HAVE DONE NO WRONG...
FOR WE FOREWARN YOU, THAT YOU SHALL NOT ESCAPE THE COMING JUDGMENT OF GOD...

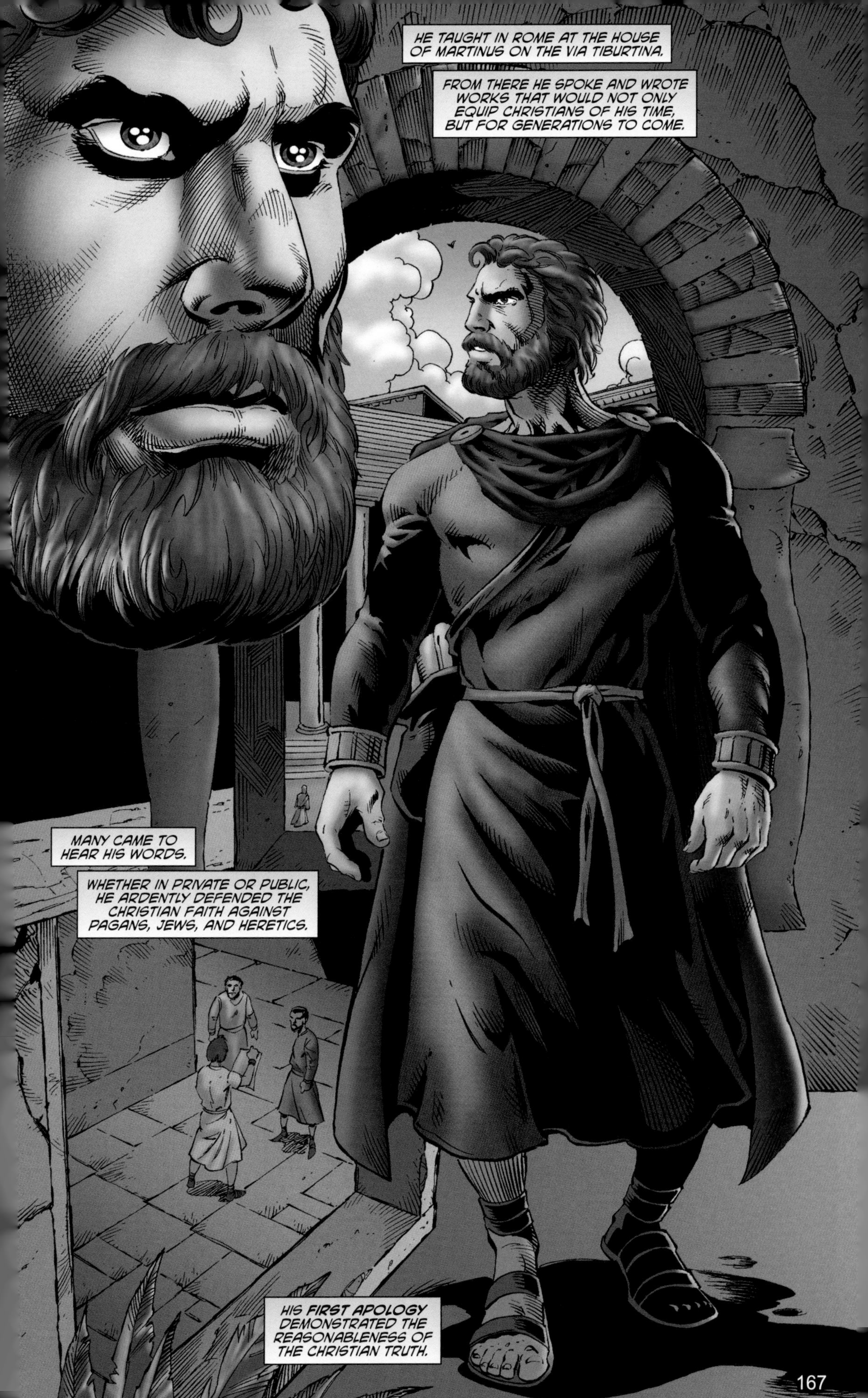
HE TAUGHT IN ROME AT THE HOUSE OF MARTINUS ON THE VIA TIBURTINA.
FROM THERE HE SPOKE AND WROTE WORKS THAT WOULD NOT ONLY EQUIP CHRISTIANS OF HIS TIME, BUT FOR GENERATIONS TO COME.
MANY CAME TO HEAR HIS WORDS.
WHETHER IN PRIVATE OR PUBLIC, HE ARDENTLY DEFENDED THE CHRISTIAN FAITH AGAINST PAGANS, JEWS, AND HERETICS.
HIS FIRST APOLOGY DEMONSTRATED THE REASONABLENESS OF THE CHRISTIAN TRUTH.

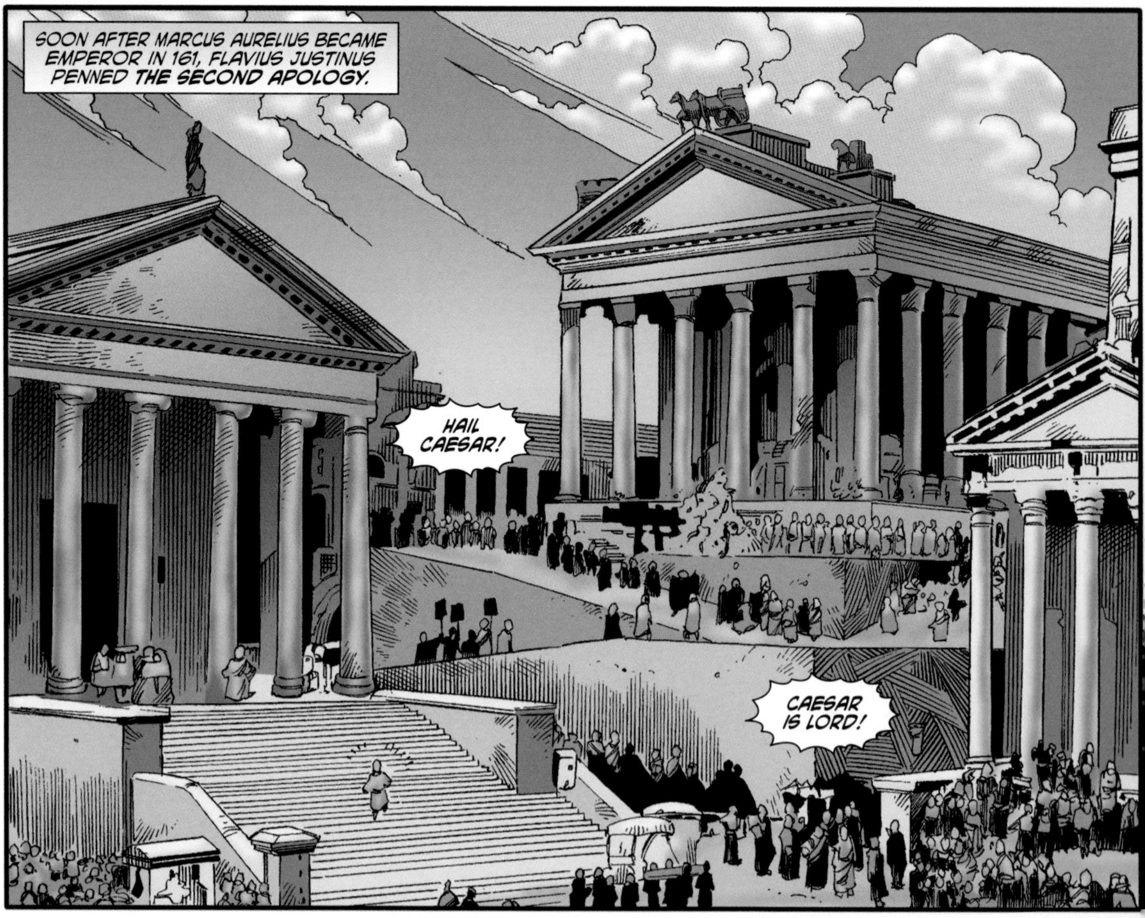
SOON AFTER MARCUS AURELIUS BECAME EMPEROR IN 161, FLAVIUS JUSTINUS PENNED THE SECOND APOLOGY.
HAIL CAESAR!
CAESAR IS LORD!

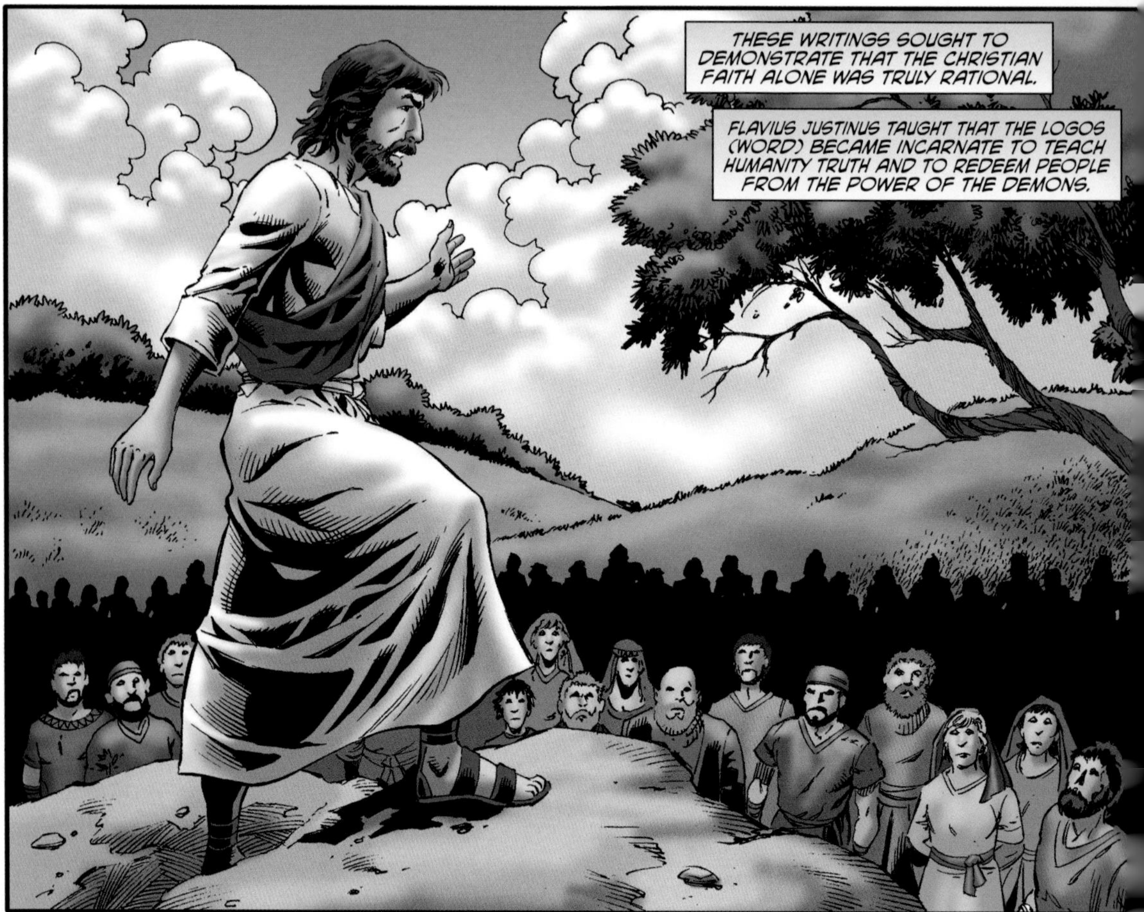
THESE WRITINGS SOUGHT TO DEMONSTRATE THAT THE CHRISTIAN FAITH ALONE WAS TRULY RATIONAL.
FLAVIUS JUSTINUS TAUGHT THAT THE LOGOS (WORD) BECAME INCARNATE TO TEACH HUMANITY TRUTH AND TO REDEEM PEOPLE FROM THE POWER OF THE DEMONS.

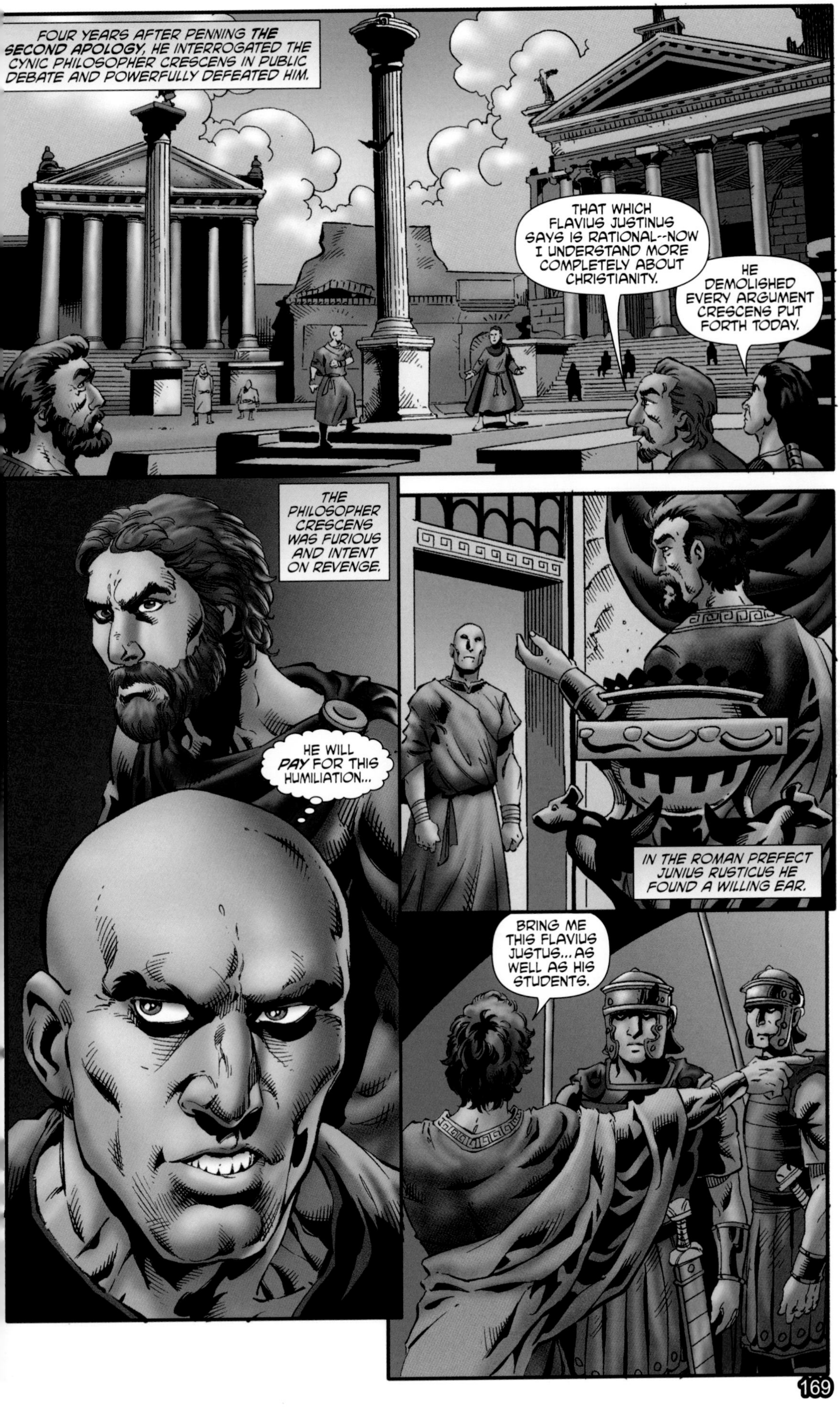
FOUR YEARS AFTER PENNING THE SECOND APOLOGY, HE INTERROGATED THE CYNIC PHILOSOPHER CRESCENS IN PUBLIC DEBATE AND POWERFULLY DEFEATED HIM.
THAT WHICH FLAVIUS JUSTINUS SAYS IS RATIONAL--NOW I UNDERSTAND MORE COMPLETELY ABOUT CHRISTIANITY.
HE DEMOLISHED EVERY ARGUMENT CRESCENS PUT FORTH TODAY.
THE PHILOSOPHER CRESCENS WAS FURIOUS AND INTENT ON REVENGE.
HE WILL PAY FOR THIS HUMILIATION...
IN THE ROMAN PREFECT JUNIUS RUSTICUS HE FOUND A WILLING EAR.
BRING ME THIS FLAVIUS JUSTUS... AS WELL AS HIS STUDENTS.

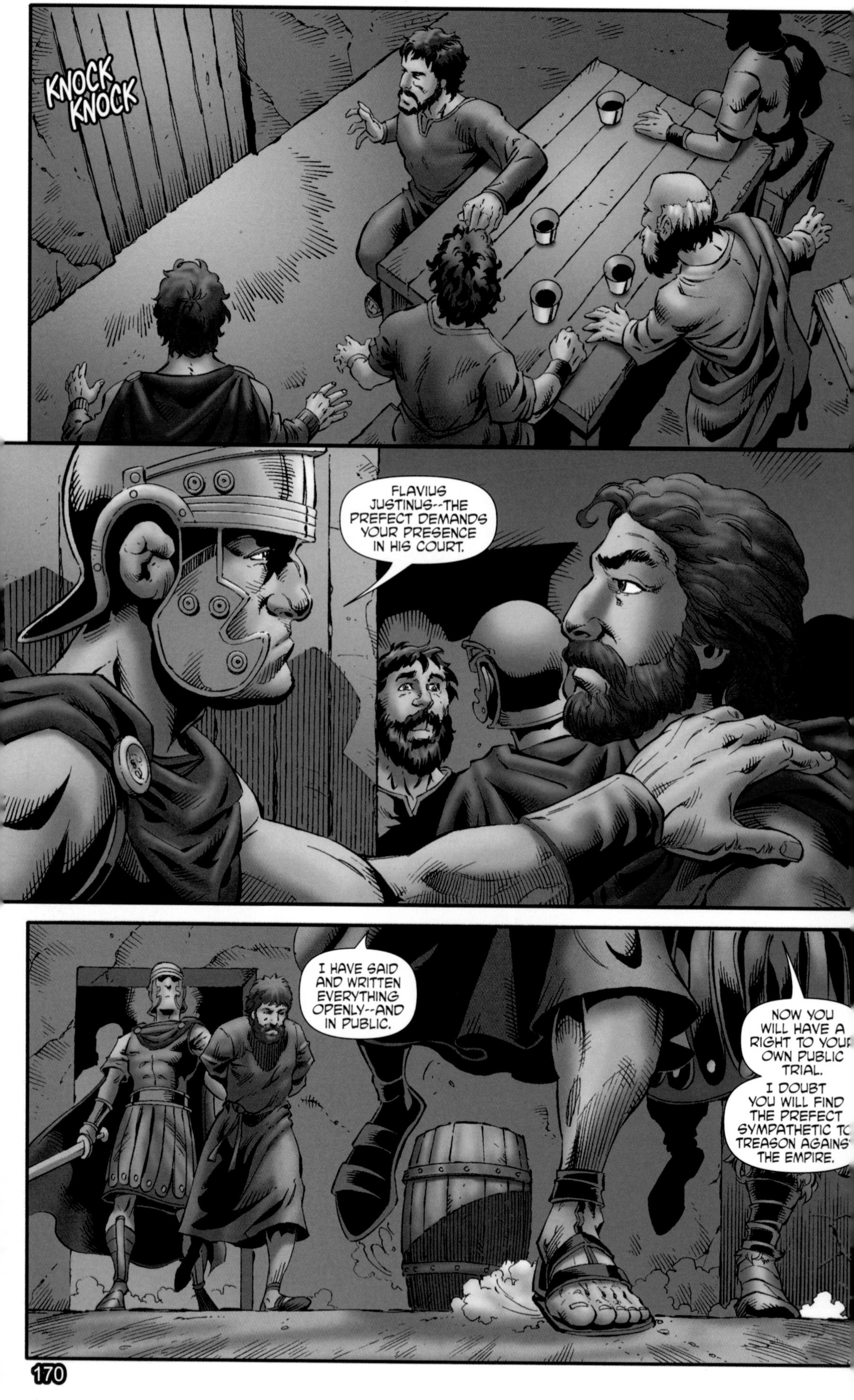
KNOCK KNOCK
FLAVIUS JUSTINUS--THE PREFECT DEMANDS YOUR PRESENCE IN HIS COURT.
I HAVE SAID AND WRITTEN EVERYTHING OPENLY--AND IN PUBLIC.
NOW YOU WILL HAVE A RIGHT TO YOUR OWN PUBLIC TRIAL.
I DOUBT YOU WILL FIND THE PREFECT SYMPATHETIC TO TREASON AGAINST THE EMPIRE.

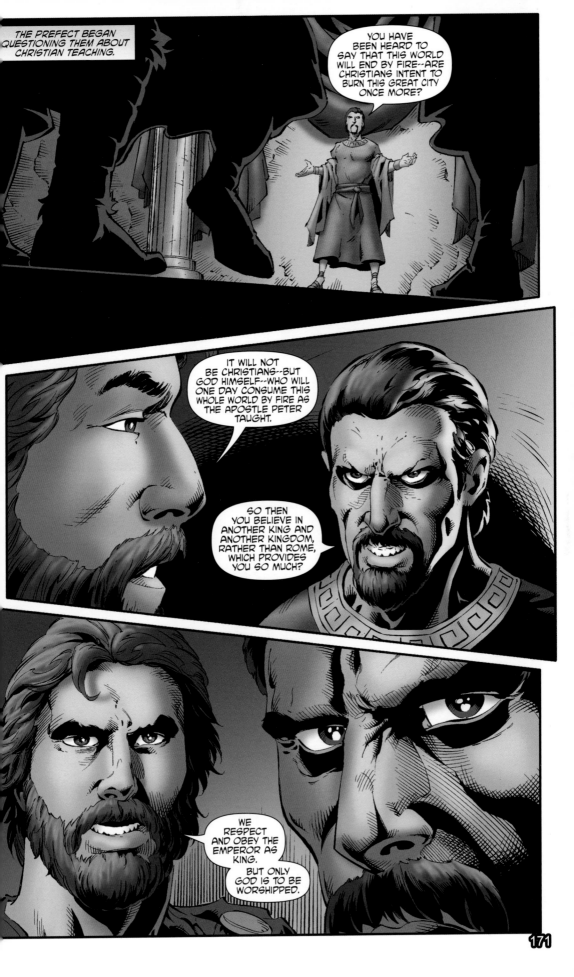

THE PREFECT BEGAN QUESTIONING THEM ABOUT CHRISTIAN TEACHING.

YOU HAVE BEEN HEARD TO SAY THAT THIS WORLD WILL END BY FIRE--ARE CHRISTIANS INTENT TO BURN THIS GREAT CITY ONCE MORE?

IT WILL NOT BE CHRISTIANS--BUT GOD HIMSELF--WHO WILL ONE DAY CONSUME THIS WHOLE WORLD BY FIRE AS THE APOSTLE PETER TAUGHT.

SO THEN YOU BELIEVE IN ANOTHER KING AND ANOTHER KINGDOM, RATHER THAN ROME, WHICH PROVIDES YOU SO MUCH?

WE RESPECT AND OBEY THE EMPEROR AS KING. BUT ONLY GOD IS TO BE WORSHIPPED.

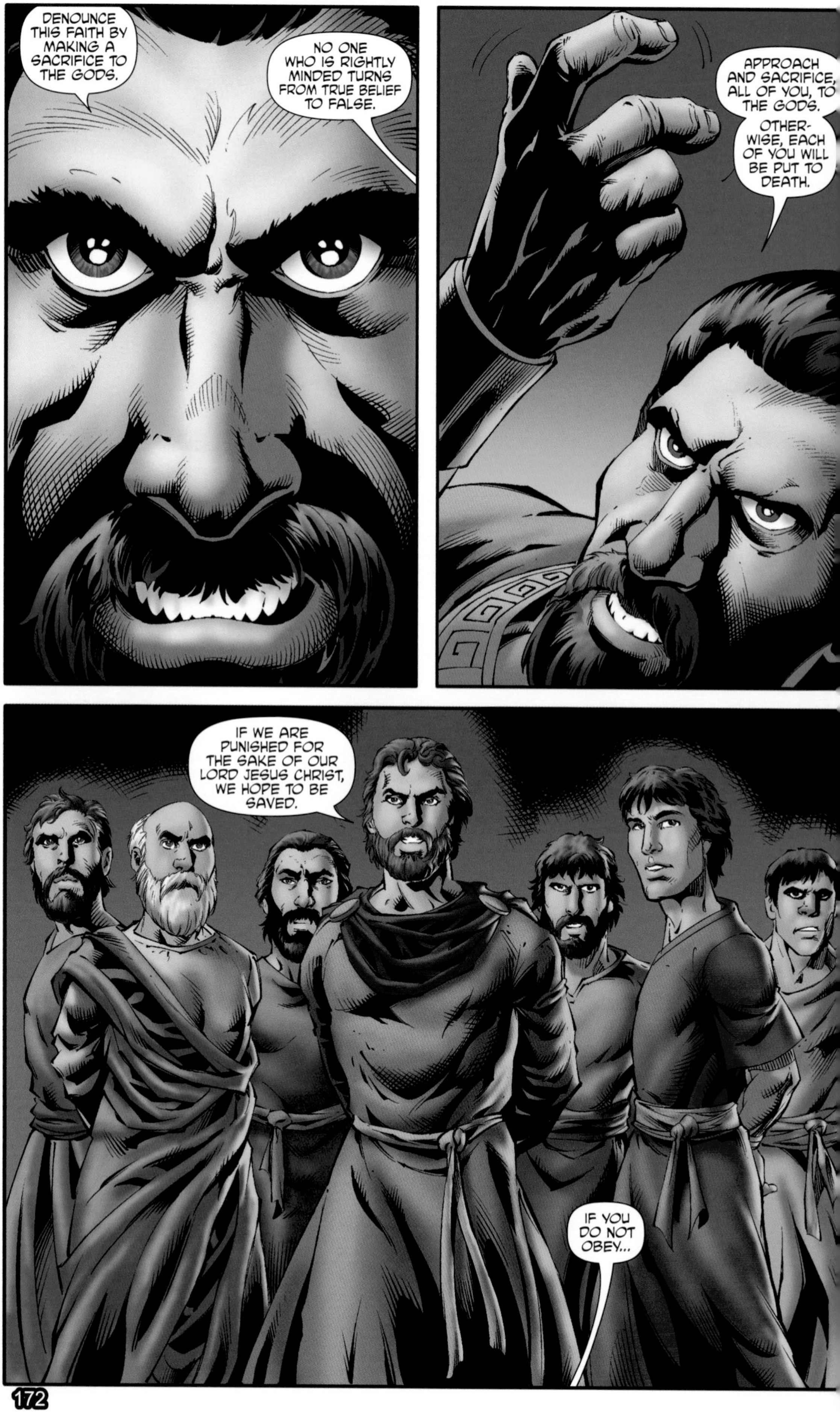

DENOUNCE THIS FAITH BY MAKING A SACRIFICE TO THE GODS.
NO ONE WHO IS RIGHTLY MINDED TURNS FROM TRUE BELIEF TO FALSE.
APPROACH AND SACRIFICE, ALL OF YOU, TO THE GODS.
OTHERWISE, EACH OF YOU WILL BE PUT TO DEATH.
IF WE ARE PUNISHED FOR THE SAKE OF OUR LORD JESUS CHRIST, WE HOPE TO BE SAVED.
IF YOU DO NOT OBEY...

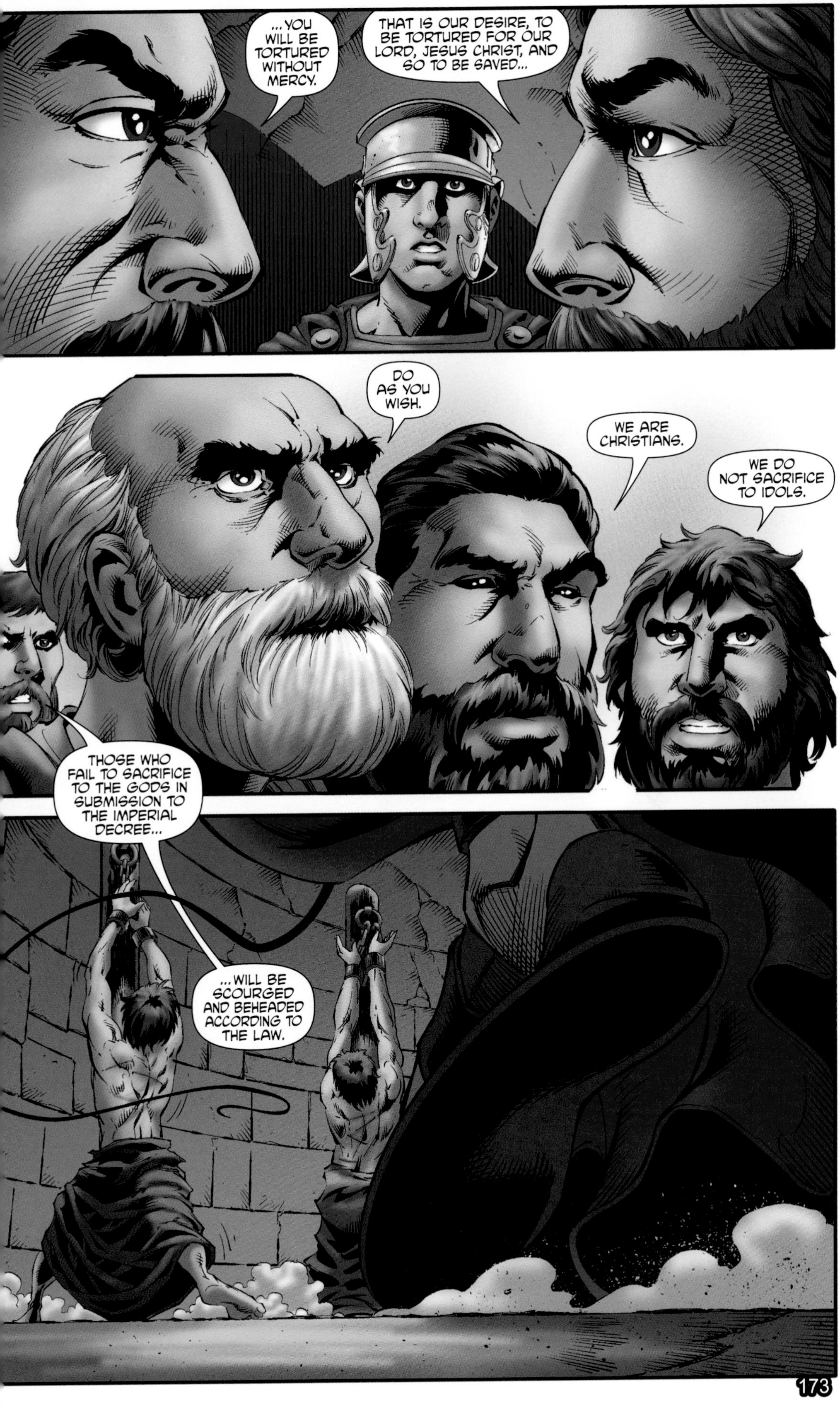

...YOU WILL BE TORTURED WITHOUT MERCY.
THAT IS OUR DESIRE, TO BE TORTURED FOR OUR LORD, JESUS CHRIST, AND SO TO BE SAVED...
DO AS YOU WISH.
WE ARE CHRISTIANS.
WE DO NOT SACRIFICE TO IDOLS.
THOSE WHO FAIL TO SACRIFICE TO THE GODS IN SUBMISSION TO THE IMPERIAL DECREE...
...WILL BE SCOURGED AND BEHEADED ACCORDING TO THE LAW.

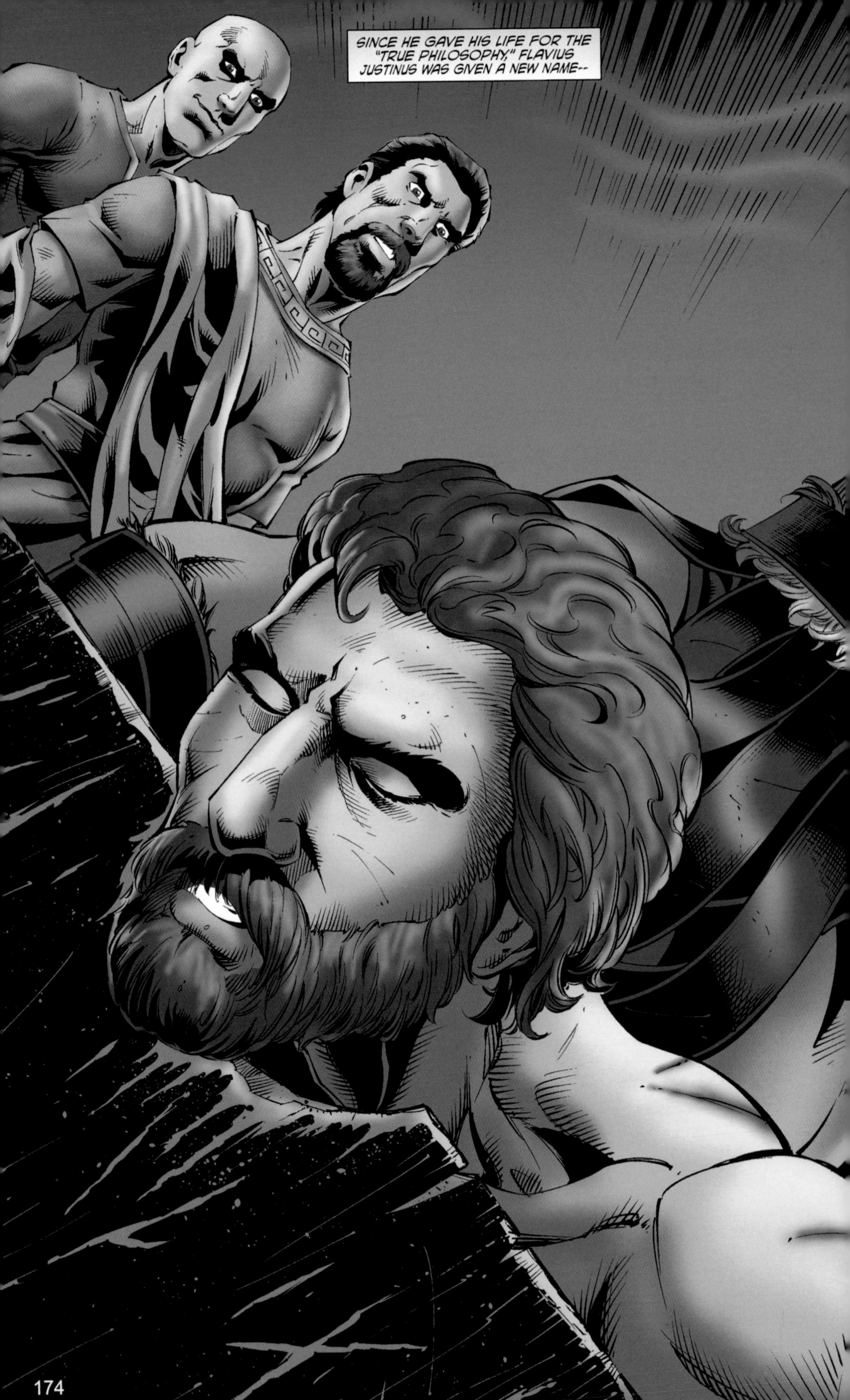
SINCE HE GAVE HIS LIFE FOR THE "TRUE PHILOSOPHY," FLAVIUS JUSTINUS WAS GIVEN A NEW NAME--

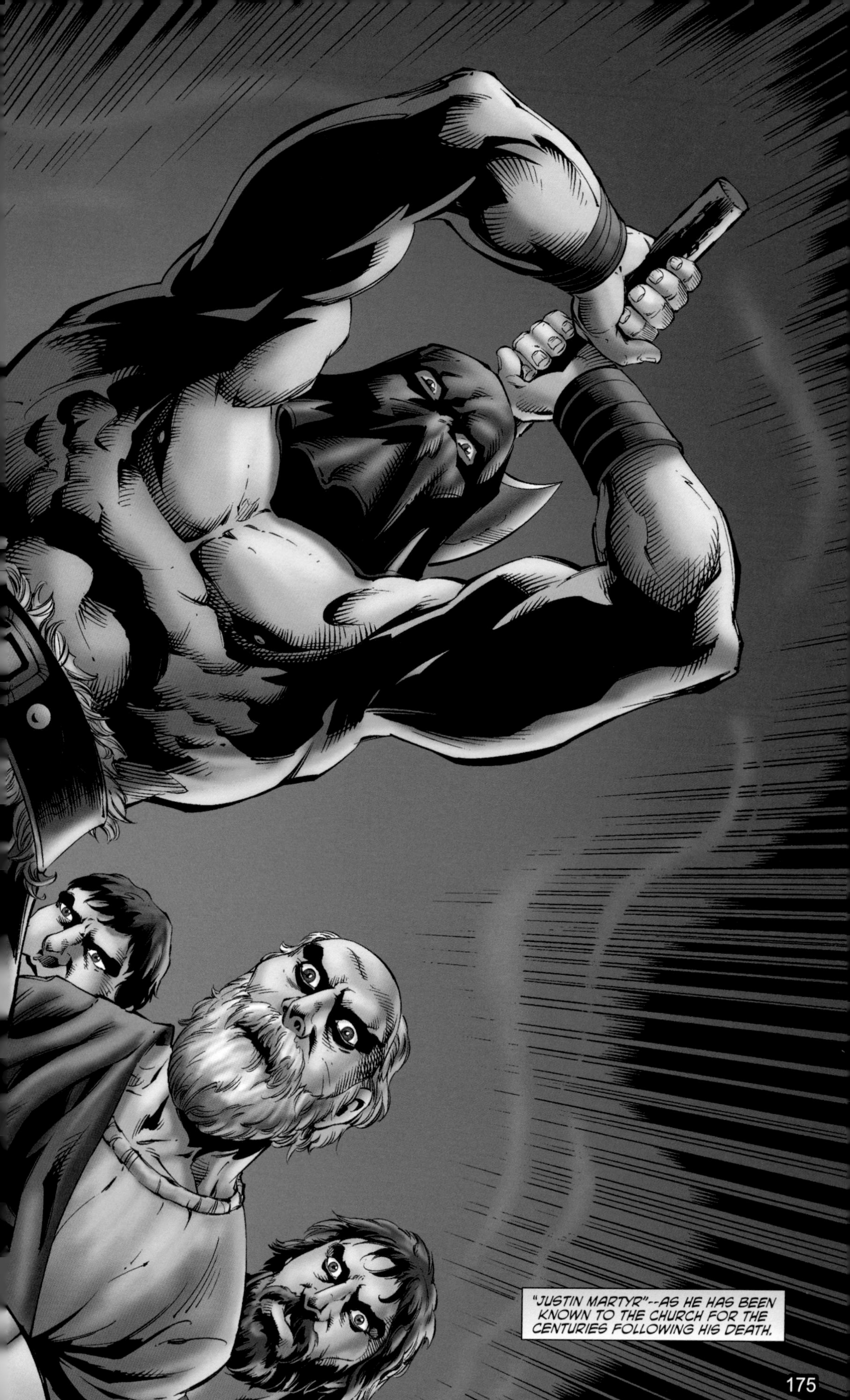
"JUSTIN MARTYR"--AS HE HAS BEEN KNOWN TO THE CHURCH FOR THE CENTURIES FOLLOWING HIS DEATH.

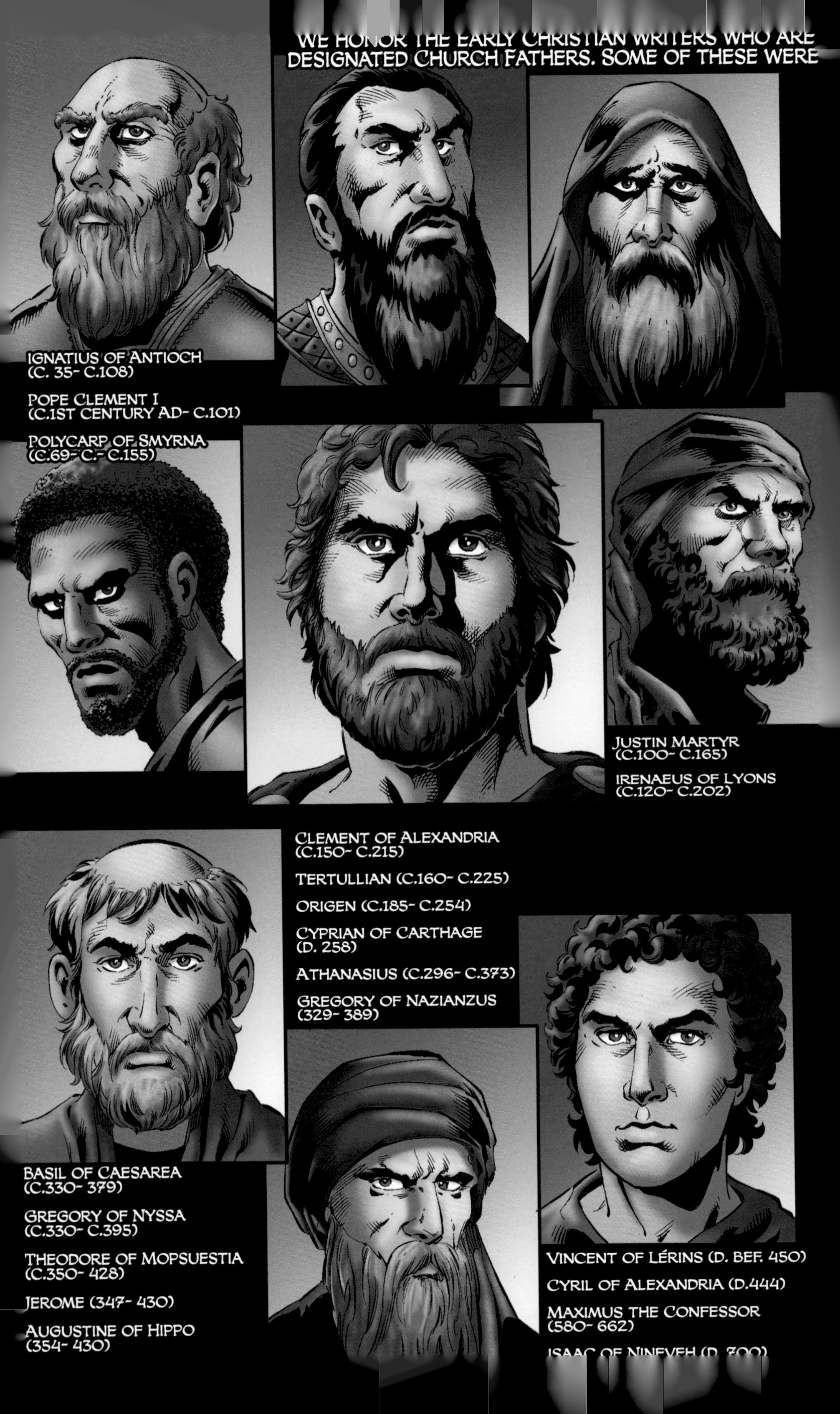
WE HONOR THE EARLY CHRISTIAN WRITERS WHO ARE DESIGNATED CHURCH FATHERS. SOME OF THESE WERE
IGNATIUS OF ANTIOCH (C. 35- C.108)
POPE CLEMENT I (C.1ST CENTURY AD- C.101)
POLYCARP OF SMYRNA (C.69- C.- C.155)
JUSTIN MARTYR (C.100- C.165)
IRENAEUS OF LYONS (C.120- C.202)
CLEMENT OF ALEXANDRIA (C.150- C.215)
TERTULLIAN (C.160- C.225)
ORIGEN (C.185- C.254)
CYPRIAN OF CARTHAGE (D. 258)
ATHANASIUS (C.296- C.373)
GREGORY OF NAZIANZUS (329- 389)
BASIL OF CAESAREA (C.330- 379)
GREGORY OF NYSSA (C.330- C.395)
THEODORE OF MOPSUESTIA (C.350- 428)
JEROME (347- 430)
AUGUSTINE OF HIPPO (354- 430)
VINCENT OF LÉRINS (D. BEF. 450)
CYRIL OF ALEXANDRIA (D.444)
MAXIMUS THE CONFESSOR (580- 662)
ISAAC OF NINEVEH (D. 700)

THE KINGSTONE

FIND FREE BIBLE LANGUAGE RESOURCES AT:
KINGSTONE.BIBLE

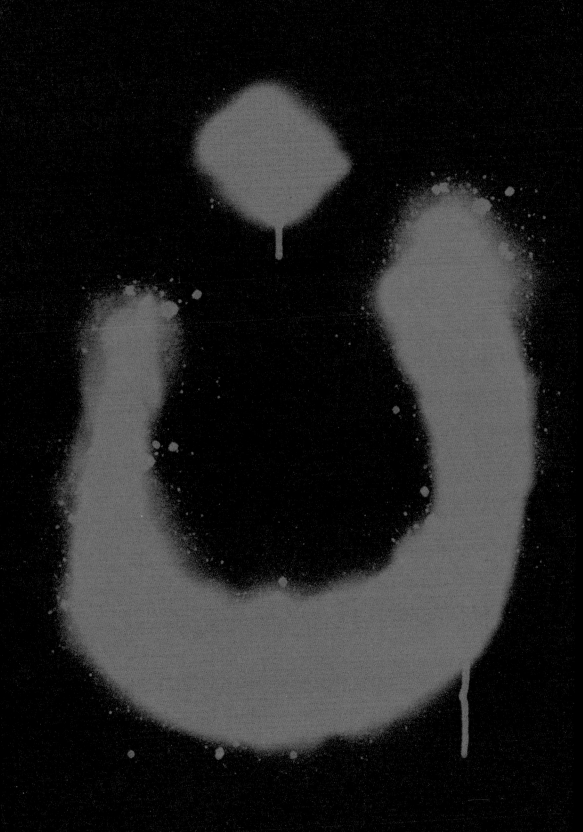

www.i-am-n.com

A New Symbol for Persecuted Christians

Within the first centuries following Jesus' death and resurrection, believers began to use several symbols to identify themselves as followers of Jesus Christ. One commonly used symbol was the "ichthus," from the Greek word meaning "fish."

The ichthus is thought to have been used by Christians in part as a secret symbol that wouldn't be recognized by persecutors. Today Christians are persecuted in more than 60 countries, including Muslim, communist and Hindu nations.

In Iraq, Islamic extremists are using a symbol of their own to identify Christians. In Mosul, the Islamists are using the Arabic "N" (pronounced nun) to label Christians' homes. The spray-painted "N" identifies property as belonging to "Nazarenes," or followers of Jesus of Nazareth. By marking their property, the extremists are laying claim to it.

In addition, Iraqi believers have been given an ultimatum: convert to Islam, pay an exorbitant tax, leave the area or be killed. Most Christians have chosen to flee, often with only the clothes on their backs.

We stand with our persecuted brothers and sisters, gladly identifying ourselves as "N" — followers of Jesus. We will not let them suffer alone.

عقارات الدولة الإسلامية
ن
ن

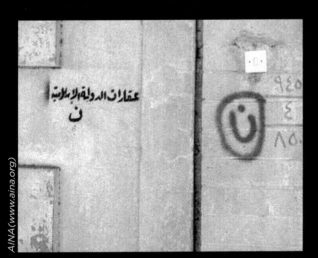

AINA (www.aina.org)

Are You "N"?

If you would like to know more about what it means for our Christian brothers and sisters to live in the presence of Islamic extremists and to know how you can stand with them, please visit www.i-am-n.com.

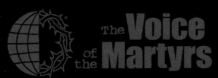

The Voice of the Martyrs

www.persecution.com

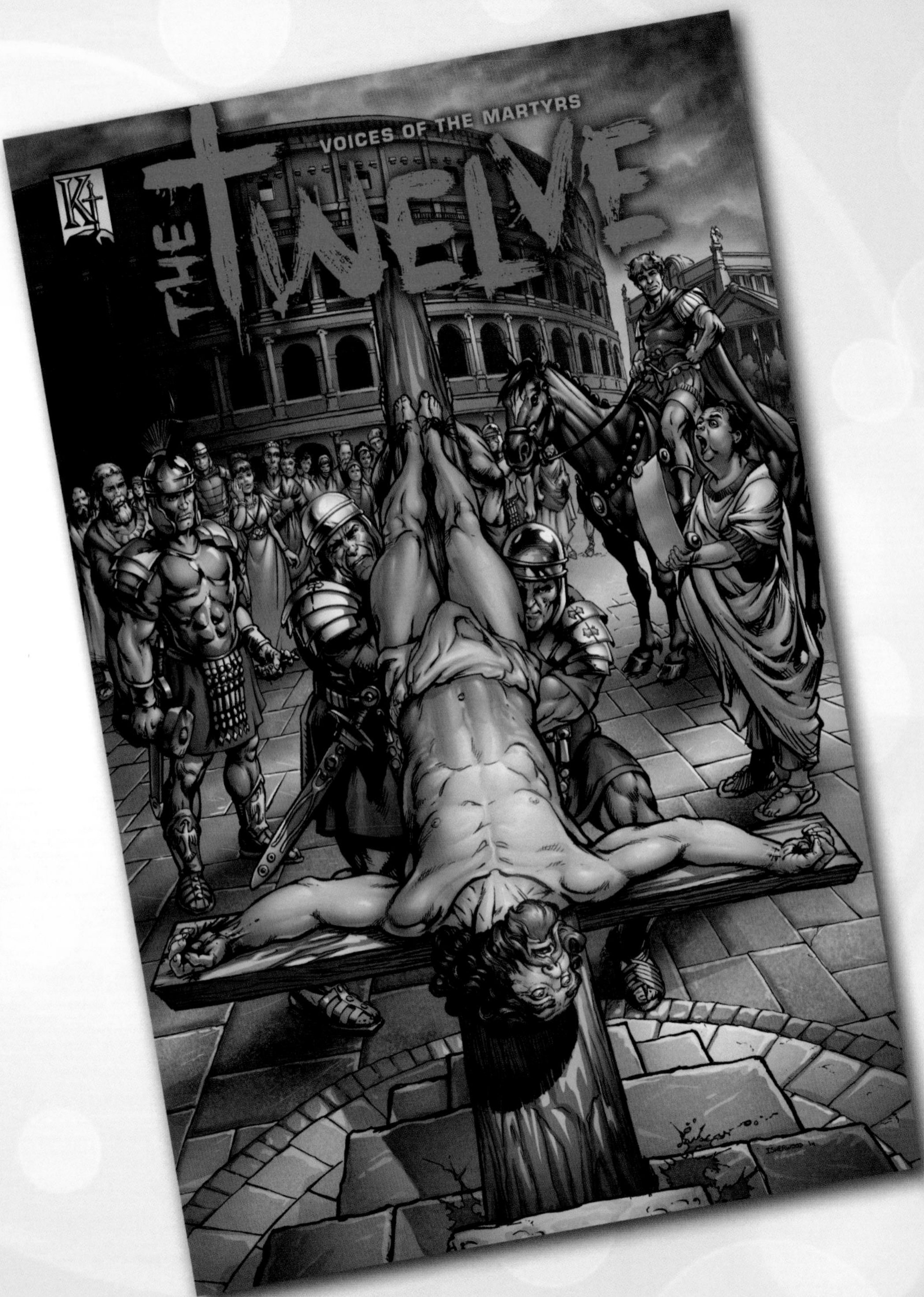
VOICES OF THE MARTYRS
THE TWELVE

FIND THEM NOW

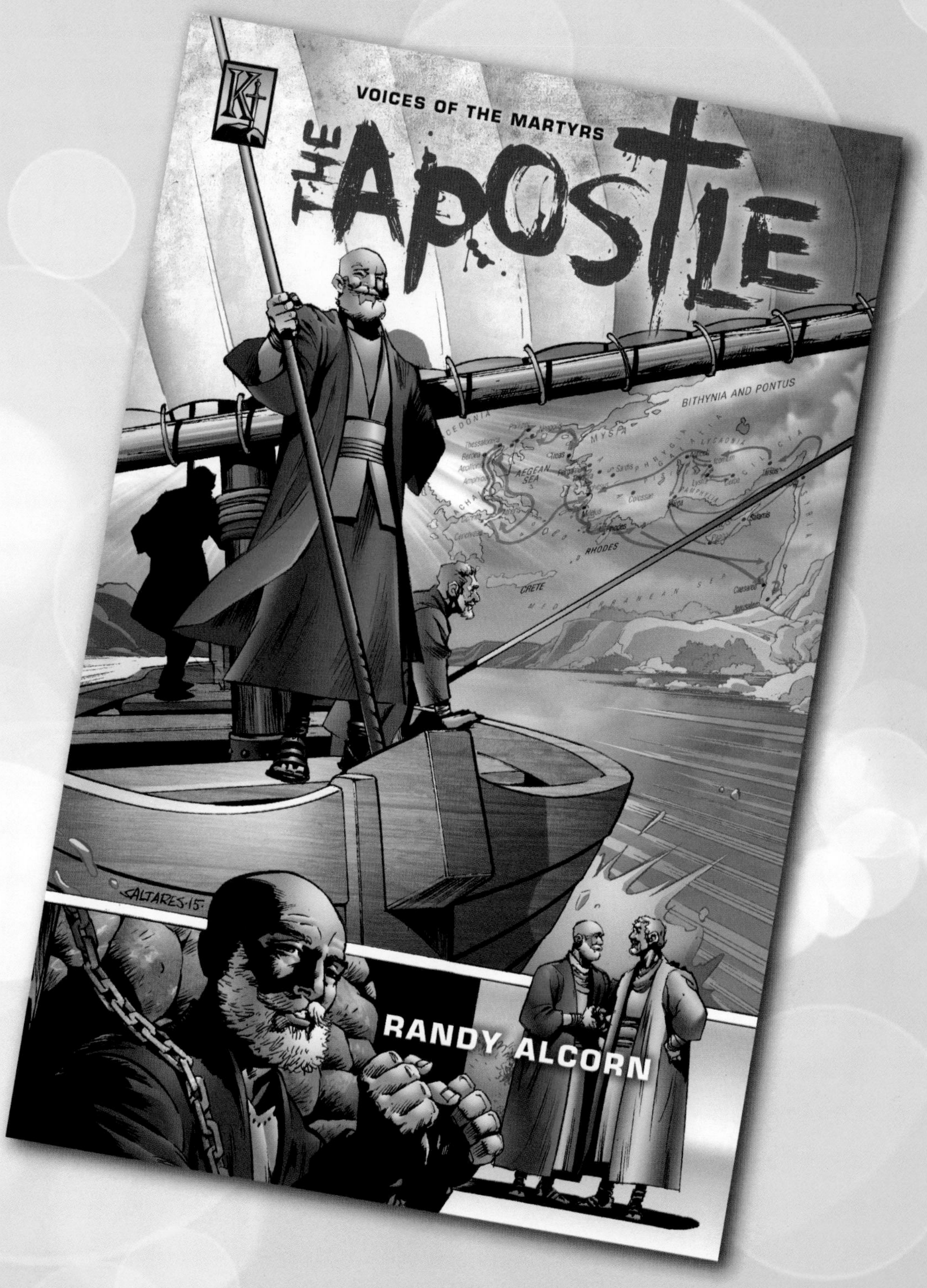

VOICES OF THE MARTYRS
THE APOSTLE
BITHYNIA AND PONTUS
AEGEAN SEA
RHODES
CRETE
RANDY ALCORN

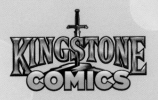

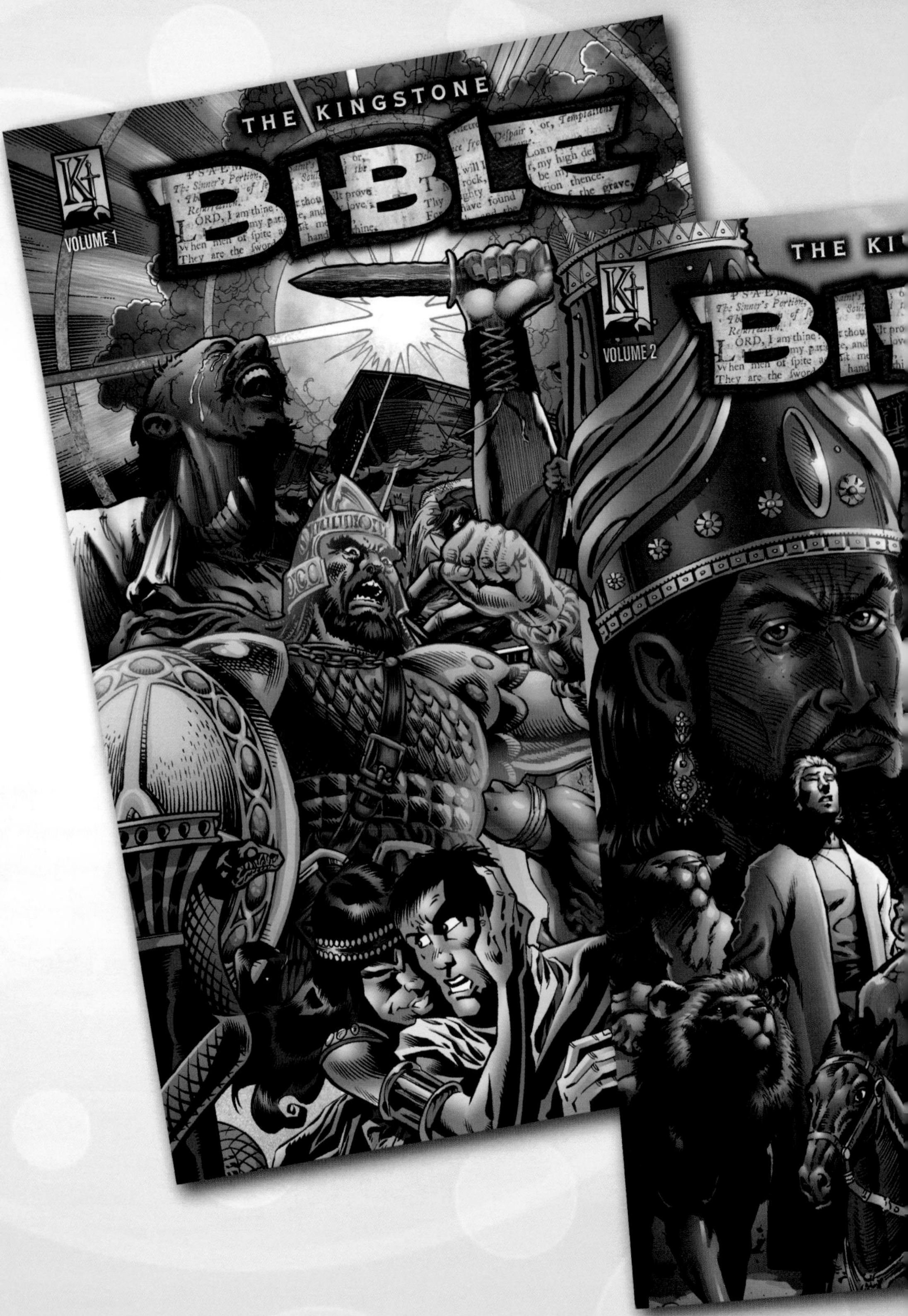
THE KINGSTONE
BIBLE
VOLUME 1
VOLUME 2

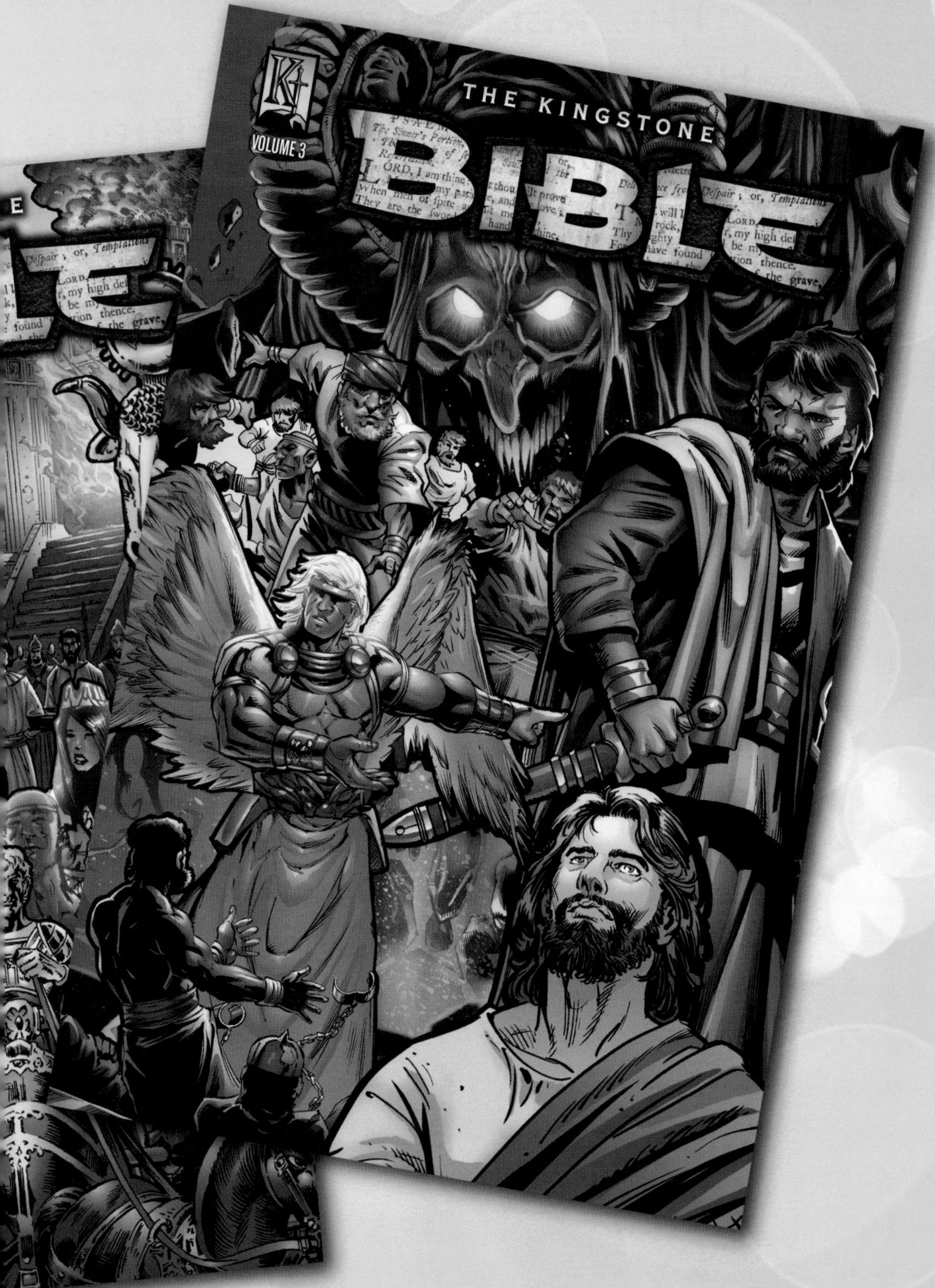
THE KINGSTONE
BIBLE
VOLUME 3

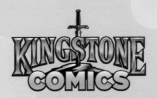

THE RELIABLE AND
HISTORICAL ACCOUNT
OF HOW GOD GAVE US THE BIBLE!

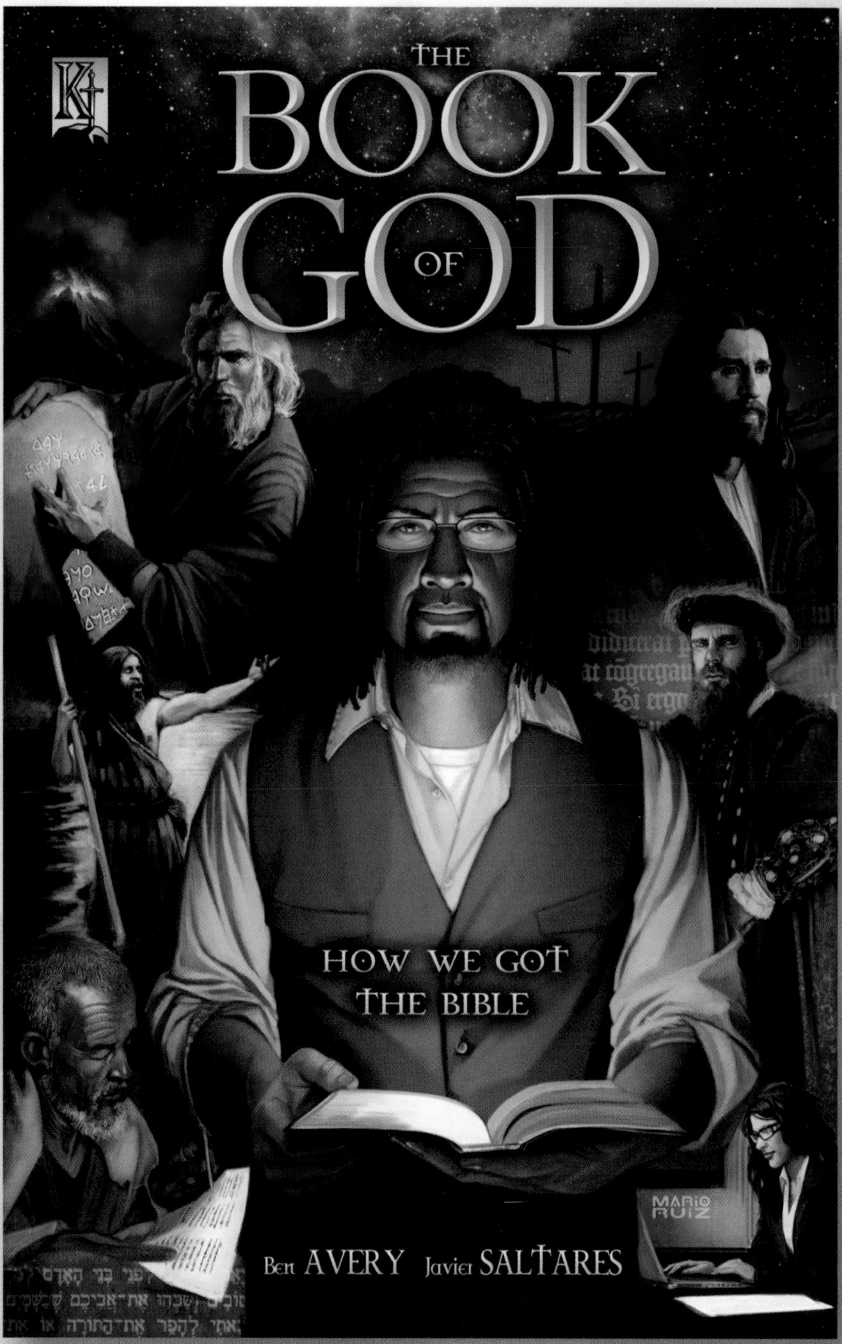
THE BOOK OF GOD
HOW WE GOT THE BIBLE
Bert AVERY Javier SALTARES
MARIO RUIZ

KINGSTONE COMICS

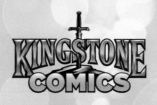